Criminology
Critical Canadian Perspectives

Kirsten Kramar
University of Winnipeg

D0792458

Pearson Canada
Toronto

Library and Archives Canada Cataloguing-in-Publication

Kramar, Kirsten Johnson

Criminology: Critical Canadian perspectives / Kirsten Kramar.
Includes index.

ISBN 978-0-13-175529-1

1. Criminology.   2. Criminology—Canada.   I. Title.

HV6025.K73 2010   364   C2010-905294-3

ISBN 978-0-13-175529-1

Vice-President, Editorial Director: Gary Bennett
Editor-in-Chief: Ky Pruesse
Editor, Humanities and Social Sciences: Joel Gladstone
Signing Representative: Duncan Mackinnon
Marketing Manager: Lisa Gillis
Developmental Editor: Rema Celio
Project Managers: Marissa Lok and Renata Butera (Central Publishing)
Copy Editor: Melanie Blake
Proofreader: Dheerandra Kumar Singh
Compositor: Aptara®, Inc.
Art Director: Julia Hall
Creative Art Director Central Design: Jayne Conte
Cover and Interior Designer: Anthony Leung
Cover Image: ShutterStockImages

For permission to reproduce copyrighted material, the publisher gratefully acknowledges the copyright holder Shutterstock.com listed on pages 2, 78, 116, and 190, which are considered an extension of this copyright page.

Statistics Canada information is used with the permission of Statistics Canada. Users are forbidden to copy the data and redisseminate them, in an original or modified form, for commercial purposes, without permission from Statistics Canada. Information on the availability of the wide range of data from Statistics Canada can be obtained from Statistics Canada's Regional Offices, its World Wide Web site at www.statcan.gc.ca, and its toll-free access number 1-800-263-1136.

2 2019

Printed and bound in the United States of America.

Brief Contents

PART 1   CRIMINOLOGY FOUNDATIONS 2

Chapter 1   Introduction to Criminology: What Is Crime? 3
Kirsten Kramar, *University of Winnipeg*

Chapter 2   Criminal Law and Criminal Responsibility 15
Diana Young, *Carleton University*

Chapter 3   Canadian Criminal Statistics: Knowledge, Governance
and Politics 33
Kevin D. Haggerty, *University of Alberta*

Chapter 4   A Specialized Criminal Justice System for Canadian Youth:
Critical Overview of Historical and Contemporary
Developments in Law and Procedures Governing Youth
Offending 57
Ruth M. Mann, *University of Windsor*

PART 2   THE RISE OF CRIMINOLOGICAL THOUGHT:
THE LEGACY OF THE 17TH, 18TH, 19TH
AND 20TH CENTURIES 78

Chapter 5   The Pathological Approach to Crime: Individually
Based Theories 79
Heidi Rimke, *University of Winnipeg*

Chapter 6   Sociological Theories of Crime and Criminality 93
Kirsten Kramar, *University of Winnipeg*

PART 3   CONTEMPORARY CONCEPTUAL TOOLS 116

Chapter 7   Feminist Contributions to Criminology 117
Kirsten Kramar, *University of Winnipeg*

Chapter 8   Critical Realist Criminology 145
Jon Frauley, *University of Ottawa*

Chapter 9   On Postcolonialism and Criminology 159
Renisa Mawani, *University of British Columbia*,
and David Sealy, *York University*

Chapter 10   Governmentality and Criminology   173
Randy Lippert, *University of Windsor,*
and Grace Park, *York University*

PART 4   CRITICAL PERSPECTIVES ON CURRENT
ISSUES   190

Chapter 11   Immigrant and Refugee Women and the Unintended
Consequences of Domestic Violence Policy   191
Rashmee Singh, *University of Toronto & American Bar
Foundation*

Chapter 12   Governing Security   205
Benoît Dupont, *Université de Montréal*

Chapter 13   "Speaking for the Dead": Forensic Science
and Wrongful Convictions   223
Kirsten Kramar, *University of Winnipeg*

Chapter 14   Talking Trash with the Supreme Court of Canada:
The Reasonable Expectation of Privacy under
the *Charter*   233
Richard Jochelson, *University of Winnipeg*

Index   243

Contents

PART 1   CRIMINOLOGY FOUNDATIONS   2

Chapter 1   Introduction to Criminology: What Is Crime?   3
Kirsten Kramar, *University of Winnipeg*
Representing Crime and Criminals   3
What Is Crime?   3
A History of Criminalization   5
What Is Criminology?   7
Criminological Discourse   10
The Value of Critical Criminological Analysis   12
References   12

Chapter 2   Criminal Law and Criminal Responsibility   15
Diana Young, *Carleton University*
Introduction   15
Civil Wrongs, Regulatory Offences and Criminal Offences   15
   Civil Wrongs   16
   Regulatory Offences   16
   Criminal Offences   16
The Definition of Criminal Offences   17
The Structure of the Criminal Justice System   18
   The Basis of Criminal Responsibility   18
   The Elements of an *Offence—Actus Reus* and *Mens Rea*   19
   Negligence and the Objective Standard of Culpability   21
The Mental Disorder Defence   23
   Procedural Matters   24
The Affirmative Defences   25
   Self-Defence   25
   Necessity and Duress   27
The Canadian Charter of Rights and Freedoms   27
   The Charter and the Police   28
   The Charter and the Prosecution of Criminal Cases   29
Reference   30
Government Documents   30

Legislation   30

Reported Cases   31

Chapter 3   Canadian Criminal Statistics: Knowledge, Governance and Politics   33
Kevin D. Haggerty, *University of Alberta*

Introduction   33

Statistics and Governance   33

Studying Crime and Deviance   36

   Official Crime Data   36

   Cautions about Crime Statistics   38

Victimization and Self-Report Studies   43

Politics and Statistics   47

Statistics and Identity   50

   Norms   51

   Identity   52

Conclusion   53

References   54

Chapter 4   A Specialized Criminal Justice System for Canadian Youth: Critical Overview of Historical and Contemporary Developments in Law and Procedures Governing Youth Offending   57
Ruth M. Mann, *University of Windsor*

Introduction   57

Youth Justice in Global Context   58

Child Saving—The Juvenile Delinquents Act   60

   Canadian Child Savers   60

   Juvenile Delinquents Act—Provisions   62

   Juvenile Delinquents Act—Outcomes   63

   The Young Offenders Act   63

   Young Offenders Act—Contradictory Provisions   64

   Alternative Measures—Encouraging What Works   65

   Young Offenders Act—Outcomes   65

   Managing Discontent   66

   The Youth Criminal Justice Act   67

   The Youth Criminal Justice Act—Philosophy and Provisions   68

   Youth Criminal Justice Act—Outcomes   70

Conclusion   72

References   74

Legislation   77

Cases Law   77

PART 2   THE RISE OF CRIMINOLOGICAL THOUGHT:
THE LEGACY OF THE 17TH, 18TH, 19TH
AND 20TH CENTURIES   78

Chapter 5   The Pathological Approach to Crime: Individually
Based Theories   79
Heidi Rimke, *University of Winnipeg*

Introduction   79

The Demonological Approach: Criminality as Sin   80

The Classical and Neoclassical Schools: Criminality as Hedonism   81

The Pathological Approach: Criminality as Sickness   82

Inventing Normal   85

Genetics and Criminality   86

Psychology and Criminality   86

Bio-Psychological Theories of Crime: The Influence
on Correctional Work   87

Psychology and Will: New Moral Discourses   89

Conclusion: Crime and the "Psy Sciences"   89

References   90

Chapter 6   Sociological Theories of Crime and Criminality   93
Kirsten Kramar, *University of Winnipeg*

Introduction   93

Early Sociological Positivism and the Emergence of Sociological
Criminology   93

German Sociological Positivism: Classical Marxism   95

Karl Marx (1818–1883)   96

French Sociological Positivism   97

Émile Durkheim (1858–1917)   97

Early American Sociological Positivism   100

History of Early Criminology in the United States (1895–1920)   100

Chicago School of Sociological Criminology   101

Robert E. Park and Ernest W. Burgess   101

Zone of Transition   102

Clifford Shaw and Henry McKay   102

Social Strain and Anomie   103

Robert Merton (1910–2003)   103

Differential Association and White-Collar Crime   105
Edwin H. Sutherland (1883–1950)   105
Mid-Century American Sociological Positivism   107
Howard Becker (1928–)   108
Neo-Marxism: New Left and Radical Criminology   109
New Left Criminology in Britain   111
French Postpositivism   113
Michel Foucault (1926–1984)   113
References   114

PART 3   CONTEMPORARY CONCEPTUAL TOOLS   116

Chapter 7   Feminist Contributions to Criminology   117
Kirsten Kramar, *University of Winnipeg*

Introduction   117
Feminist Criminology   118
Challenging Sexism within Criminological Theory   119
Feminist Critiques of Sexism in Early Theories of Women's
Criminality   120
Lombroso and Ferrero and the "Passive Female Criminal"   121
W. I. Thomas and the "Emancipation Hypothesis"   122
Feminist Critiques of Sexism in Post-World War II Theories of
Women's Criminality   123
Otto Pollak: Women's Deceitfulness and the "Chivalry
Hypothesis"   123
Cowie, Cowie and Slater: A Contemporary Degeneracy Theory
of Women's Criminality   125
The "Emancipation Hypothesis" Revisited   126
The Medicalization of Women's Deviance in Criminological
Theory   127
Early Psychocriminology of Women: Kleptomania, Nymphomania
and Infanticide   128
Challenging Criminal Law as a Medium of Patriarchy: Rape,
Spousal Assault, Abortion and Prostitution   130
The Law's Treatment of Women Victims of Male Violence   131
Reforming the Law of Rape   131
Spousal Assault: Demanding Action from the Police and the
Courts   132
Battered Woman Syndrome: The Thin Line between Survival
and Offence   135

Criminal Law Regulation of Women's Sexuality   136

    Contraception and Abortion: Our Bodies, Ourselves   137

    Prostitution: The Invisibility of Marginal Young Women   137

    Pornography's Challenge to Women's Equality   138

    R. v. Butler: A New Harms-Based Interpretation
of Obscenity   138

Challenging Punishment Practices in the Correctional Treatment
of Women   140

Women in Prison   141

References   142

Chapter 8   Critical Realist Criminology   145
Jon Frauley, *University of Ottawa*

Introduction   145

Critical Realism   145

Metatheory   146

Positivist and Conventionalist Metatheory   149

Critical Realist Metatheory   150

Ways of Theorizing: Induction, Deduction and Retroduction   153

Conclusion   157

References   157

Chapter 9   On Postcolonialism and Criminology   159
Renisa Mawani, *University of British Columbia,*
and David Sealy, *York University*

Introduction   159

Criminology and the Persistence of the Colonial in the "Culture
of Control"   160

Race and Incarceration   162

Colonial Knowledges and Aboriginal Crime   166

Criminology and the Possibilities of Postcolonial Critique   170

References   170

Chapter 10   Governmentality and Criminology   173
Randy Lippert, *University of Windsor,*
and Grace Park, *York University*

Introduction   173

What Is Governmentality?   173

Governmentality's Features and Concepts   174

Advanced Liberalism   177

Prisons and Empowerment   179

Crime Stoppers   181

CS Promotions and Partnerships   181

Governing and Deploying Anonymity   183

Rewards, Risk and Tipsters   184

Moral Categorization and Tipsters   184

Criticisms of Governmentality   185

Conclusion   187

References   187

PART 4   CRITICAL PERSPECTIVES ON CURRENT ISSUES   190

Chapter 11   Immigrant and Refugee Women and the Unintended Consequences of Domestic Violence Policy   191
Rashmee Singh, *University of Toronto & American Bar Foundation*

Introduction   191

The Early Years: Feminist Activism and Violence against Women   192

Societal and Criminal Justice Responses   192

Feminist Theorizations of Domestic Violence   194

Violence Against Women, the State and Feminist Praxis   194

"Just Like Any Other Crime": The Emergence of Mandatory Charging and Aggressive Prosecution Policies   196

Good Intentions and Misguided Assumptions: The Promises of Mandatory Charging and Prosecution   197

Forgotten Voices: The Experiences of Immigrant Victims of Domestic Violence   199

Immigration Status   199

Distrust and Fear of the Police   199

Isolation   200

Linguistic and Financial Dependence   200

Conclusion   201

References   203

Endnotes   204

Chapter 12   Governing Security   205
Benoît Dupont, *Université de Montréal*

Introduction   205

Governance Structures: State, Market and Networks   206

Actors and Levels of Governance   208

A Relational Typology of Governance   211

The Normative Implications of Security Governance:
Effectiveness and Accountability   215

References   217

Chapter 13   "Speaking for the Dead": Forensic Science
and Wrongful Convictions   223
Kirsten Kramar, *University of Winnipeg*

Wrongful Prosecution and Conviction in Cases Involving
Babies   224

What Can We Learn from These Cases?   226

Looking Beyond the Autopsy   226

Speaking for the Dead   227

Medical Expertise and Wrongful Conviction in England   228

Conclusion   229

References   229

Cases   231

Chapter 14   Talking Trash with the Supreme Court of Canada:
The Reasonable Expectation of Privacy under
the *Charter*   233
Richard Jochelson, *University of Winnipeg*

Introductions   239

Reviewing Some Basics   234

2004 and Beyond   235

Conclusion   239

References   239

Cases   240

Statutes   241

Index   243

Preface

The idea for this book began a number of years ago when many of us who graduated from programs in criminology began teaching criminology at various universities across Canada. While there are a number of very good textbooks on the market, they all have a similar format: They introduce students to core concepts in criminal law and criminology, present the range of historically significant criminological theories and examine a number of types of crime and criminal. For the contemporary teacher of introductory criminology courses, they exhibit a common problem in devoting inadequate space to current theoretical developments and contemporary issues which are of concern to critically focused criminologists. These books typically pay insufficient attention to feminist, neo-Foucaldian, postcolonial and critical research in law and criminology.

The purpose of this book is to fill the need for a well-rounded yet critically focused book on the theoretical and substantive debates in criminology. The book may be used to introduce students to the study of crime control in Canadian society and the theoretical and substantive debates among Canadian scholars. The contributions to this book provide a solid foundation of knowledge about theories of crime causation and measurement of crime, social control institutions and criminological research. Chapter 1 introduces students to the discipline of criminology by providing them with a brief intellectual history of its roots in European social and political thought and the application of some of those ideas in the United States and Canada. It locates the Canadian law and criminal justice system in a historical context, drawing necessary connections between Canadian law and British law. Chapter 2 provides students with some of the basic concepts they will need to understand the criminal law. Chapter 3 introduces students to the politics of counting crime to produce crime statistics. Chapter 4 introduces students to the specialized criminal justice system for youth, which is an area of considerable interest to students.

In Part Two, the legacy of historically significant criminological theories will be presented with clarity and brevity, focusing on the conditions in which each theory developed as well as their current academic significance. This section is sufficient to appeal to more traditional teachers steeped in these approaches and meets the needs of the younger generation of criminologists, who will wish their students to understand the development of their discipline in part because current theoretical work often emphasizes the historical significance of criminological theories in the development of criminal justice practices. This section is designed to be brief. Many textbooks require weeks of teaching outdated theoretical frameworks, leaving very little time to explore and learn contemporary conceptual tools such as feminist contributions to criminology, critical realist criminology, postcolonial contributions to criminology and governmentality. In Part Three, the most significant current theoretical developments are presented clearly and critically in a way that I hope appeals to the generation of professors who are coming to dominate the field. Part Four covers a range of contemporary substantive research topics, including immigrant and refugee women's experiences with Canadian domestic violence policies, security, the role of forensic authority in producing wrongful convictions and the relationship between you and your garbage as it relates to privacy and police powers. Each of these chapters represents a range of research engaged in by Canadian criminologists and sociolegal scholars. The chapters themselves provide instructors with a range of choice for teaching the final section of their courses in the sense that instructors can choose to focus on particular areas of substantive research depending on the number of weeks available in their respective courses.

CourseSmart for Instructors

CourseSmart goes beyond traditional expectations, providing instant, online access to the textbooks and course materials you need at a lower cost for students. And even as students save money, you can save time and hassle with a digital e-textbook that allows you to search for the most relevant content at the very moment you need it. Whether it's evaluating textbooks or creating lecture notes to help students with difficult concepts, CourseSmart can make life a little easier. See how when you visit www.coursesmart.com/instructors.

CourseSmart for Students

CourseSmart goes beyond traditional expectations, providing instant, online access to the textbooks and course materials you need at an average savings of 50%. With instant access from any computer and the ability to search your text, you'll find the content you need quickly, no matter where you are. And with online tools such as highlighting and note-taking, you can save time and study efficiently. See all the benefits at www.coursesmart.com/students.

Acknowledgements

I would like to thank each of the authors for their important contributions to this manuscript. I am grateful for the patience and generosity of Benoît Dupont, Jon Frauley, Kevin Haggerty, Richard Jochelson, Randy Lippert, Ruth Mann, Renisa Mawani, Grace Park, Heidi Rimke, David Sealy, Rashmee Singh and Diana Young.

Special thanks to those reviewers who agreed to be acknowledged: Jana Grekul, Oliver R. Stoetzer, Madonna Maidment, Aaron Doyle, Ann Parks, Amy Prevost, Frank T. Lavandier, Winston Barnwell, Tom Groulx, Ashley Carver, Dr. Wesley Crichlow and Carmela Murdocca, and to the remaining anonymous reviewers, I am grateful for the insights and comments each of you provided to make this a stronger manuscript.

Working with the people at Pearson was a wonderful experience. A very special thank you to Ky Pruesse, Editor-in-Chief, and Patti Altridge, Senior Developmental Editor, both of whom worked tirelessly to see this manuscript through the review process. Also to Laura Pratt, Acquisitions Editor; Joel Gladstone, Acquisitions Editor and Rema Celio, Developmental Editor, who picked up where Ky Pruesse and Patti Altridge left off and saw this manuscript through to completion, and to Peggy Brown, Production Manager; Andrea Falkenberg, Lead Production Manager; Melanie Blake, Copy Editor; Arthur Gee, Marketing Manager. I would also like to thank my research assistants, Melanie Murchison and Shayna Gersher, for their wonderful ability to create order out of my chaos.

I would like to thank my amazing children, Kindra, Mieka and Evie for enduring mommy's many hours in front of the computer and on the telephone which often resulted in late dinners and lost playtime. You give my life joy and meaning, and I am forever grateful for your love and patience. Finally, to my friend and mentor William Watson, a wee "thank you" is not near enough acknowledgement of your thoughtful guidance through the vagaries of academic life.

Criminology

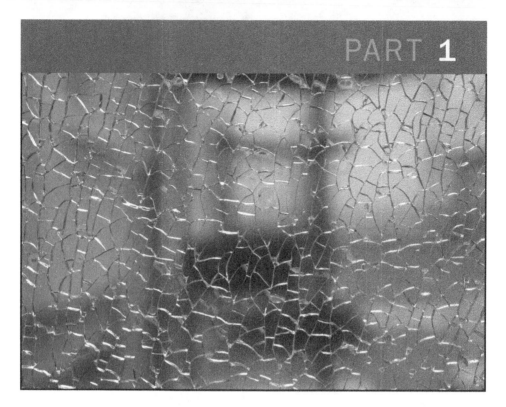

PART **1**

Criminology Foundations

Chapter 1   Introduction to Criminology: What Is Crime?
Kirsten Kramar, University of Winnipeg

Chapter 2   Criminal Law and Criminal Responsibility
Diana Young, Carleton University

Chapter 3   Canadian Criminal Statistics: Knowledge, Governance and Politics
Kevin D. Haggerty, University of Alberta

Chapter 4   A Specialized Criminal Justice System for Canadian Youth: Critical Overview
of Historical and Contemporary Developments in Law and Procedures
Governing Youth Offending
Ruth M. Mann, University of Windsor

CHAPTER 1

Introduction to Criminology

What Is Crime?

Kirsten Kramar, University of Winnipeg

REPRESENTING CRIME AND CRIMINALS

When Karla Homolka was released from the Joliette, Quebec, correctional facility in July 2005 after serving a full 12 years for manslaughter, the event was the lead story in most major Canadian newspapers. The Paul Bernardo–Karla Homolka sex killings provided sensational material for Canadian national newspapers such as *The Globe and Mail*, the *National Post* and provincial daily newspapers for many years. The story's details dominated the headlines, largely because it involved the rape and murder of young white women from a middle-class suburban neigbourhood in Southern Ontario. While the killings were certainly a dreadful event for those who were close to the murder victims, the news reports of the rape and murder of two white teenage girls in Southern Ontario by two white, blond-haired, middle-class newlyweds was much more widely reported than the cases of missing and murdered women in downtown Vancouver. It was only once political pressure was put on the Vancouver police and city officials by the friends and family of the Vancouver women who went missing that the bodies of the women were found and a suspect identified. Many of those women had been reported missing by friends and family and had also worked in the sex trade on the lower east side of downtown Vancouver. The suspect, Robert Pickton, was eventually charged in 2002 with 26 counts of first-degree murder in the deaths of as many women.

The Pickton case is the largest and most poorly handled serial killer investigation in Canadian history. Up until the time the case went to trial, the 26 missing and murdered women and girls had not attracted the same level of media attention as the three murders committed by Paul Bernardo and Karla Homolka. Dozens of women involved in the sex trade go missing, or are murdered, with little media coverage. Many believe that the Pickton killings were ignored because the murdered women and girls were involved in the sex trade and addicted to street drugs. Only when Pickton's trial began did the media begin to report the gory details of the crime scene investigation on Pickton's farm and how the discovery of multiple bodies and body parts required extensive DNA analysis. In 2007, Pickton was convicted by a jury in British Columbia of second-degree murder and sentenced to serve six life sentences following a trial that dealt with the first six victims. The charges and conviction established Robert Pickton as the worst killer in Canadian history.

WHAT IS CRIME?

Media coverage encourages us to think that crimes are simple facts, with the obvious moral connotations, that we know what are and should be crimes and how much fear and outrage are appropriate for any particular crime. Yet we have seen that the media plays a huge role in forming our responses to crime and criminals. Beyond the media, wider social forces are at work shaping our government's decisions about which behaviours will be defined as criminal. These forces also influence broadly how severe will be the penalties associated with crimes, police decisions about which crimes to investigate (or not investigate), prosecutors' decisions about which crimes to prosecute, judges' and juries' decisions about who is and is not guilty of crimes, judges' decisions about which particular crimes, and which particular criminals, deserve the most severe penalties and correctional staff decisions about what to do with different kinds of

3

criminals. We need to understand these processes, rather than assume crimes are simple, morally unambiguous social facts to which the criminal justice system responds in a pre-scribed manner. To begin at the beginning, we might ask: "What is crime?"

One can answer the question by examining the range of behaviours that are prohibited by the criminal law. This approach would give you a **formal** definition of crime: Crime is a culpable action or omission prohibited by law and punished by the state. An act or omis-sion is a crime because the law defines it that way. A very different definition, sometimes called a **normative** definition, views crime as conduct that violates cultural norms. When prevailing standards of conduct, or **norms**, are violated, the government responds with sanctions. When the norm violations are more serious, the government responds by pun-ishing those individuals found guilty of a crime. In this way, the normative approach to crime control and social regulation reacts to historical, political and economic variations; changing social conditions alter perceptions of what constitutes violation of cultural norms, and these alterations have an impact on criminal law and therefore the kinds of acts or omissions that are **criminalized** when they are prohibited by law. Take for example the criminalization of drunk driving. Beginning in the 1980s, social pressures placed on law enforcement officers resulted in tougher penalties for those caught driving over the legal blood alcohol limit of .08 gram of alcohol per 100 decilitres of blood. The penalties in-cluded loss of one's driving licence, stiff fines and even jail time for repeat offenders. Although Canada and some U.S. states adopted laws against drunk driving in the early 20th century, it was only after concerted public pressure from victims' rights groups such as Mothers Against Drunk Driving (MADD) that social attitudes and police responses to drunk driving began to change, resulting in the effective criminalization of drunk driving.

The concept of crime can therefore be defined from either a formal or normative per-spective. Even though these are very different definitions of crime, they ultimately become linked because social, political and economic goals alter cultural norms. These norms are then formalized through criminal laws and their enforcement. In the late 1960s, driving while intoxicated was criminalized by the *Criminal Law Amendment Act,* 1968–69 (S.C. 1968–69, c. 38) but poorly policed. Despite the formal law against drunk driving, its effec-tive policing came about only as a result of changes in cultural norms.

Understanding the development of criminal law from the normative perspective in-volves more than charting shifts in public sentiment or political programs because this in-vites us to identify and understand the social forces which shape these shifts. In particular, academic criminologists working in the normative tradition have been interested in the ways in which definitions of crime and its control through punishment reflect and repro-duce power relations within a given society. As Abell and Sheehy (2002, p. 22) put it, crim-inal law is "contingent on many factors, including the culture and values of the dominant society, the historical moment considered, the economic system and the nature of the state, and the relations of powers between various groups."

The established liberal philosophical ideal that crime and unwanted behaviour is that which causes **harm** assumes a societal consensus on the kinds of behaviour that cause harm. This liberal philosophical model implies that crime can be objectively measured and responded to in relation to the level of harm it causes both the individual and society as a whole. But this model requires an evaluation of harm and its causes and has been used to justify the creation of laws that promote certain kinds of social relations, particularly those that value individual freedom and private property. Harm, then, is anything that interferes with individual freedom, happiness and the ownership of private property. The state also justifies limits on our freedom to control what it views as a social nuisance, such as the drug trade and street prostitution. From this perspective, the state's role is to protect us from these kinds of harm through the enactment of criminal laws and punishment frameworks. Because of the risk of fatal injury to others associated with impaired driving, it is easy to see why driving ought to be criminalized. However, there is less societal consensus around the criminalization of various consensual sexual practices (such as, for example, sodomy, swinging, private prostitution, bondage and sadomasochism) that have historically been subject to criminal penalty. There has been considerable societal debate about whether these sexual practices ought to be criminalized when their practice is consensual, creates no social nuisance and causes no harm. Indeed, their criminalization has been linked to sexism, homophobia and the oppression of sexual minority groups by Christian religious zealots who seek to impose their own values as societal norms rather than provide legal frameworks that promote individual sexual freedom.

To a certain degree, both our criminal statues and cultural norms take the harms-based liberal philosophical approach to crime and punishment. Yet there remains considerable controversy over the range of harmful behaviours that ought to be criminalized. From this perspective, crime is seen not as the product of the behaviour of individual criminals who are evil or mad but as a strategy of organized ideas about and responses to human conduct that is *socially* established as "harmful," or "criminal."

In this sense, what we understand to be crime is rarely separate from a historical or political context. As Natalie Des Rosiers and Steven Bittle (2004) remind us,

> . . . for decades numerous legal, sociological, and criminological researchers have challenged the idea that crime and its control are objective phenomena. They have also challenged the belief that society unanimously agrees on the nature and extent of the social harm attributed to certain behaviour and that an official response is warranted. (p. xiii)

A HISTORY OF CRIMINALIZATION

In Canada, definitions of crime were imported into the first *Criminal Code* in 1892 when Parliament adopted the *English Draft Code* of 1879 (see Young, Chapter 2). However, there were also other provisions adopted into the body of criminal laws which were connected to Canada's history of colonization of Aboriginal peoples and use of immigrant labour to establish the infrastructure (roads, bridges, railways) of the country.

For example, the *Indian Act* criminalized Aboriginal practices in a way that facilitated colonization and the removal of Aboriginal peoples from their lands (see Mawani, Chapter 10). Until its amendment in 1951, the *Indian Act* facilitated colonization of Aboriginal peoples by criminalizing their cultural practices and by removing their children from parents and extended kin. An amendment to the *Indian Act* in 1884 outlawed the celebration of the Potlatch and Tamanawas dance ceremonies practiced by the Indians of the northwest Pacific coast. Later, in 1885, efforts were made to prevent dancing in the Prairie provinces by the Indians of the Blackfoot confederacy. Their cultural practices were subject to punishment by imprisonment for 2 to 6 months. Legal instruments such as these were created and used by whites to stamp out what they called "heathenism" and to transform Indigenous peoples into "civilized' Anglo-Canadian citizens (Titley, 1986). As Abell and Sheehy (2002) note, because these laws carried mandatory minimum sentences of imprisonment, they facilitated the imprisonment of Indigenous people in the newly established colonial jails such as the Stony Mountain Penitentiary built in Manitoba in 1877. Other examples include the imposition of the reserve system and mandatory Christian education for Aboriginal children in the 1880s through the establishment of residential schools; the prohibition preventing lawyers from representing Aboriginals (or a band) in legal actions against the Canadian government; and the requirement that Aboriginals give up their Indian status (along with their tax credit) in exchange for an allotment of land and the right to vote (Abell & Sheehy, 2002).

The *Indian Act of Canada* (1876) set aside reserve land for Indigenous peoples. In addition, the act established the Indian Register, which required that Indigenous peoples have their names recorded in order to be considered "Treaty Indians." The Indian Register provided only those with "Treaty" or "Indian" status the rights and benefits provided in exchange for Canadian territory under the *Indian Act*. There were a number of provisions within the act that discriminated among Indigenous peoples, particularly between Aboriginal men and women. Section 12(1)(b) of the *Indian Act* required Aboriginal women to give up all of their Treaty rights when they married non-Aboriginal men. However, the act did not make the same requirement of Aboriginal men who married non-Aboriginal women. This is an example of a sexist patriarchal law that created a framework for the denial of benefits which discriminated against Aboriginal women and their children. Sandra Lovelace eventually won her human rights complaint for sex discrimination against the Canadian government. In 1981, the United Nations Human Rights Committee ruled that section 12 (1)(b) contravened Canada's obligations under the United Nations Covenant on Civil and Political Rights. While sex discrimination and status requirements are not criminal offences, they did cause identifiable harms, creating different classes of persons with different access to resources and legal remedies. These laws have had strictly punitive effects and smoothed the way for the European colonization of Indigenous peoples.

Similar kinds of criminal laws enacted in the early 1900s later came to be known as the anti-Chinese laws. These laws were aimed at maintaining rigid racial boundaries by preventing persons of "Chinese" descent from employing "white" women. Various provincial acts made it an offence for Chinese businesses to employ white women in an effort to prevent miscegenation through interracial sexual relations so as to preserve racial purity. According to Constance Backhouse (1999):

> the 'White Women's Labour Law' was also a gendered construct. It was the horror of female sexual slavery that that act was meant to remedy. The protection of white women, and the symbolic emblem of the 'white race' became a crucial cornerstone in the attempt to establish and defend white racial superiority and white racism. White women were called into service in their reproductive capacity as the 'guardians of the race,' as symbol of the most valuable property known to white men, to be protected at all costs from the encroachment of other races. (p. 141)

In addition, by denying Chinese businesses access to less expensive female labour, the acts gave white-owned businesses an unfair economic advantage over Chinese-owned ones (Backhouse, 1999).

When we look back at these laws which singled out Indigenous peoples and Chinese Canadians, it is easy to see how the laws, including laws addressing what counted as a crime, were products of the power relations which marked Canadian society. Academic criminologists attempt to identify the same kinds of power relations underlying our current criminal law and its application, although these are often less obvious than those that operated in the past. While today's public sentiments and political programs may be just as much the product of social forces and power relations as those of a hundred years ago, we are all engaged in these power relations and in the thick of arguments about criminal law, making it difficult to look at the social processes affecting the law and its application with the detachment required.

WHAT IS CRIMINOLOGY?

As the laws affecting Indigenous peoples and Chinese immigrants were developing in Canada throughout the 19th and early 20th centuries, so too were early scientific ideas about crime and criminals. Modern criminology began to emerge at the end of the 19th century (Garland, 1985). It consisted of a ". . . framework of problems, concepts and styles of reasoning" and was "produced by the confluence of medical psychology, criminal anthropology, statistical inquiry, social reform and prison discipline" (Garland & Sparks 2000, p. 193). The emergence of modern criminology was very closely tied to the emergence of the prison within which the "techniques and data of the new discipline" could be applied (Garland, 1985). According to David Garland (2002), *criminology* is:

> a socially constructed and historically specific organization of knowledge and investigative procedures—a particular style of reasoning, representing and intervening—which is grounded in a particular set of institutions and forms of life. It is a 'discipline', a regime of truth with its own special rules for deciding between truth and falsity, rather than the epitome of right thought and correct knowledge. (p. 13)

There are two main branches of criminology. One is called **administrative criminology** (and sometimes **governmental criminology** or **correctionalism**) and the other **scientific or academic criminology**. Administrative criminology is that branch which seeks to inform the management and control of crime and criminals through policy-oriented research. It attempts to enhance the administration of criminal justice by providing governments with information on crime and by monitoring the practices of the police and prisons (Garland, 2002, p. 8). The aim of administrative criminology is to enhance the management of the overall population, largely in the interest of the economy, by providing knowledge of effective social control measures to police and other agents of the state. In this sense, it is also governmental criminology because it provides information on how to govern populations most effectively in order to achieve particular political aims. In Canada, administrative criminology is usually taught by police officers or legal professionals in criminal justice programs in community colleges and some small university campuses. These programs work hand in glove with the bureaucracy of the modern state where corrections officers, police and other agents of social control are employed and through which the law is enforced. Today, because of the growth of imprisonment as a social policy tool in most Western industrial nations, the modern state is sometimes referred to as a "prison-industrial complex." This is because of the shift in public spending on social welfare infrastructure to building and maintaining prisons and guarding inmates (Cayley, 1998).

Scientific or academic criminology began with the work of Italian positivists such as Cesare Lombroso (1835–1909) (discussed in Chapter 6). Through empirical research, academic criminology attempted to reveal the causes of crime. As we shall see in Chapters 5 and 6, the early theories of crime causation informed the criminal law reform efforts of the 18th and 19th centuries and established the "positivist" school of criminology. Later, especially after Word War II, academic criminology began to develop a more critical orientation, shifting from a sole focus on the causes of crime to the study of the expert knowledge and social practices that define and shape ideas about, and responses to, conduct deemed criminal. The discussion in the previous section "What Is Crime?" is largely informed by this critical aspect of contemporary academic criminology.

In Canada, academic criminology is typically taught by professors as a subspecialty in sociology and legal studies departments. Other academic disciplines such as anthropology, biology, history, law, philosophy, psychology and social work also offer courses in a sub-specialty related to crime and criminals. An increasing number of universities in Canada now offer undergraduate and graduate degrees in criminology. These programs provide students with specialized training in both the administrative and academic branches of criminology. Those who founded academic criminology in the middle decades of the 20th century had sought to inform governmental crime control policy through the development of criminological knowledge (Radzinowicz, 1999). They had their successes, for instance, in the promotion of rehabilitation programming as a core element correctional work. However, now in the early 21st century a "populist punitiveness" tends to drive criminal justice policy (Garland & Sparks, 2000, p. 192). Governments of the right and centre-left alike are apt to rely on heated **law and order rhetoric** rather than academic criminological knowledge in the formation of contemporary crime control policy. Today, this populist punitiveness drives the use of mandatory minimum sentences, yet it is at odds with the findings of criminological research on the deterrent value of imprisonment (Vold, Bernard, & Snipes, 2002). David Garland and Richard Sparks (2000) argue that popular culture tends to dominate the manner in which criminological issues are analyzed. Western culture is "saturated with images of crime and fear of crime," and sound criminological scholar-ship, which emphasizes economic investment in social welfare programs and policies, is seen as dull in comparison (Garland & Sparks, 2000, pp. 200–201).

Exaggerated law and order rhetoric is remarkably successful—both at currying favour with voters, and informing criminal justice policy—because we can all be conditioned by mass mediated popular culture. Certain kinds of images of crime and violence dominate our popular culture, often as forms of entertainment. Numerous television crime dramas such as *Law & Order*, *Law & Order: Special Victims Unit*, *CSI*, *CSI: Miami*, *CSI: New York* and true crime television shows such as *America's Most Wanted* and *Cops*, are devoted to the subject of investigating crime and catching violent criminals through meticulous law and order policing techniques.

Four decades ago, Kai Erikson suggested that representations of violence, crime and punishment are projections of deeper social and cultural concerns (Erikson 1966; Melossi, 2000, p. 150). Various representations of "criminal types" throughout history and geograph-ical location have drawn links between the criminal and the working class or those persons marginalized by "race." These representations of certain "types" of people as "criminal" have tended to represent the poor and the nonwhite as "outsiders," resulting in the creation of anxiety about those persons who do not conform to the popular representations of victims of crime who are predominantly white and middle class. Nowhere is the spectre of the vic-timization of whites more pronounced that with the popular representations of Muslims as potential terrorists in the wake of the successful terrorist attack on the World Trade Center in New York City and the Pentagon in Washington, DC, on September 11, 2001.

These representations of crime, its perpetrators and proposed solutions, are viewed on a daily basis and certainly have an impact on the politics of crime control and social regu-lation. The representations present a highly individualized account of crime which focuses on theft of personal property and interpersonal violence rather than the social contexts and causes of crime or corporate crimes committed by powerful individuals. Social harm caused in the pursuit of profit, such as environmental crimes, intentional workplace health and safety violations, corporate fraud, insider trading and fraudulent accounting practices of large corporations, have not been framed within the media or administrative criminology as crime but are seen instead as violations of government regulations. Nevertheless, sometimes corporate crimes do become news. For example, economic fraud concealed by high-ranking senior executives at Enron, a Houston, Texas-based energy trading company, was the largest securities fraud scandal in Western history. Enron was billions of dollars in debt by the beginning of the 21st century, yet this debt was concealed from shareholders and employees through the coordinated efforts of fraudulent accounting by the company's accounting firm Arthur Andersen and illegal loans from investment banking partners. Andrew Fastow, Enron's chief financial officer, was eventually charged with 78 counts of conspiracy, fraud and money laundering, but he pled guilty to only two conspiracy charges and agreed to testify against Enron's chief executive officer Kenneth Lay and top executive Jeffrey Skilling. Fastow was later sentenced to serve just 6 years in prison for his part in the multibillion- dollar securities fraud scandal. In May 2006, Enron's former chief executive Jeffrey Skilling and founder Kenneth Lay were both found guilty of conspiracy and fraud. However, in July 2006, Kenneth Lay died of heart disease while vacationing in Aspen, Colorado. Jeffrey Skilling, who sold $60 million of his stock in the company before Enron's debt became public, was sentenced to serve 24 years in a yet-to-be-determined federal penitentiary for his conviction on 19 counts of fraud, conspiracy and insider trading.

In general, however, criminal practices of the powerful economic classes have tended not to be seen as threats to the maintenance of social order, which leads to the misconception that corporate crime is less harmful to individuals and society as a whole than bank robbery or individual acts of interpersonal violence. In the Canadian context, Laureen Snider (1993, 2004, 2006) has conducted extensive research on corporate crime that demonstrates that corporate crimes have dramatically increased over the past decades. According to Snider (2006):

> The toll of lives lost, injuries sustained, species obliterated, watercourses decimated, savings and pensions destroyed, and life chances ruined by the various types of corporate crimes has dramatically increased with the advent of the global marketplace, the spread of capitalist workplaces and production to Third World countries, the new-found dominance of finance capital, and the decline in power of (most) nation-states. (p. 181)

However, the disappearance of corporate crime has been orchestrated by both provincial and federal governments, which consistently fail to police corporate crime, simply remove altogether the laws governing corporate crime from the books, or both. According to Snider (2006), the trend continues even in a post-Enron era:

> In the last two decades, the few laws and weak enforcement mechanisms enacted to control corporate crime—themselves the product of a century of struggle by employees, consumers, feminists, environmentalists, and others—have been systematically repealed and dismantled. In direct contrast to state law in every other jurisdiction, which has become ever more intrusive and increasingly punitive (with rates of incarceration spiralling for all traditional offences, despite falling crime rates) laws governing corporate crime have been negligently and inconsistently enforced, and many types of corporate crime have disappeared altogether from the books. (p. 180)

As such, it is argued that our perceptions of crime as a mainly individualized lower-class phenomenon is skewed both by the lack of enforcement of certain kinds of crime and by its representation as individual phenomena in popular and news culture. Unlike individual acts of violent crime which make up daily fodder for the front pages of Canadian newspapers, Jeffrey Skilling's sentence was reported on page 20 of the business section of *The Globe and Mail*. It is precisely because mass mediated popular culture conditions modern public sentiment that the sorts of "law and order" governmental crime control policies seen on television and in the print media may be more readily accepted by a fearful voting public. Governmental law and order policies that advocate increased police presence, longer prison sentences and less health and social spending chime with the popular narratives of the United States' television crime dramas. And, since there has been a dramatic rise in the number of successful television crime dramas, academic criminology may have become less relevant to criminal justice policy and crime control. This point is underscored by Garland and Sparks (2000), who argue that:

> Criminology is not just a creature of the academy. It is also located in other social and institutional settings and these other settings have shaped much of its development. To simplify a complex picture we could say that criminology is inscribed in three major social settings or matrices. It is located in (i) the world of the academy—of social science and scholarly discourse, (ii) the world of government—of crime control and criminal justice, and (iii) the world of culture—including mass mediated popular culture and political discourse. (p. 192)

Garland and Sparks (2000) tell us that criminological knowledge, only one expert voice amongst many, arose in specific circumstances which no longer hold:

> We need to view it instead as a specific kind of discourse inscribed in a particular set of institutions at a particular historical conjuncture. Modern criminology took shape as an element of the postwar welfare state. It developed as part of a governmental response to a specific problem of order, a certain collective experience and a definite set of class relations. It was a small part of the social solution to the problems of industrial society. Its fortunes have been tied up ever since with the fate of the social, the politics of welfare, and the dynamics of the criminal justice state. (p. 197)

Critical academic criminology, with its focus on understanding the connections amongst social inequalities and the rationalities informing the regulation and control of criminals and crime, has become a less influential source of knowledge about the causes and solutions for crime in the dominant **criminological discourse**.

CRIMINOLOGICAL DISCOURSE

In the 1970s, French philosopher Michel Foucault developed new concepts for understanding practices of punishment. In his book, *Discipline and Punish* (originally published in 1975 and translated in 1977), Foucault analyzed changing forms of surveillance in penal governance that made a significant theoretical contribution to criminology. This work was complemented by his work on sexuality and madness which highlighted various other forms of regulation by "experts" who created the knowledge that gave those in administrative positions of power the necessary "scientific authority" to justify the exercise of what he called "disciplinary power." Foucault's work is relevant to the discipline of criminology because he included in his discussion of experts those scientists of crime and criminals who produced the knowledge about crime we will study in this book. Foucault referred to the specialized knowledge produced by experts working in universities, prisons, hospitals, schools and various branches of government as *discourse*. For Foucault, these forms of specialized knowledge are not separate from the exercise of power. Discourses, in the form of "expert knowledges" or "expertise," are not composed of objective, "pure" scientific discoveries arising from disinterested study, but arise from the operations of powerful institutions of control and coercion such as the prison and the asylum and, in turn, authorize and mobilize governmental power. This is why Foucault used the convention **power/knowledge** to symbolize the interconnectedness of ideas and practices; of specialized and expert knowledge(s) and power.

Other nonstate structures of regulation also frame normal conduct by establishing certain kinds of behaviours to be "abnormal" or "unhealthy." In this context, scholars have developed the concept of **moral regulation** to study the effects of certain programs and public health campaigns in the areas of health and sexuality. Moral regulation refers to the process by which certain very specific kinds of morality are implicated in social regulation. Moral regulation also assumes an active agent who participates in her or his own self-regulation, which is partly achieved through the connection of health with virtue and morality. For example, dominant sexuality discourses produce sexual subjectivities that can either embrace or resist sexual norms of behaviour that are always tied to a particular idea about proper sexual practices and expression. For most of recent history, sexually explicit materials that depict homosexuality, including anal intercourse, have been deemed "obscene" and therefore criminalized. The basis upon which these materials are regulated is the moral value of heterosexuality dictated by a powerful Christian elite. Many of us actively self-regulate our own sexual desire and practices in order to conform to the morally established idea or ideal that heterosexuality is "healthy" and "normal." This example illustrates how certain moral values, underpinned by discourses of health and morality, are enforced using the criminal law.

The forms of human conduct to which formal legal responses are made are defined by law, police, courts, politicians, physicians, sociologists, psychologists, social workers, criminologists and other "experts" as unhealthy or harmful. The concept of criminalization directs our attention to the contingent nature of criminal law and other acts of Parliament that supplement the *Criminal Code*. This contingent nature of criminal law that defines crime and punishment draws our attention towards the historical context within which the content of criminal law and other statutory provisions governing social behaviour have developed. Foucault demonstrated that the forms of punishment used by the state to respond to crime are part of a range of ideas generated in the human sciences that shape how we understand ourselves and manage our own conduct.

Recently, academic criminologists have picked up on Foucault's later work on "governmentality," a concept used to understand how a variety of authorities govern beyond the state, in different sites and in relation to different objectives (Rose, O'Malley, & Valverde, 2006) which he introduced in the publications and lectures that followed the publication of *Discipline and Punish*. This later work transformed the language and theoretical tools used by academic criminologists to analyze political power, which had implications for analysing contemporary penal policy. Foucault's (1991, originally published 1977) investigation of political power through the concept of governmentality was organized around the theme of the art of government, or more precisely, "the government of others and the government of one's self" (Garland, 1997, p. 174). The concept contributed to the discipline of criminology by providing a new framework for understanding political power in relation to the governance of crime and criminals both within and beyond the state apparatus. This analytical framework allowed for empirical analysis of the various ways in which members of society *play an active role in their own self-governance* that works with and beyond the kinds of coercive and regulatory governing practices of the state (criminal law being but one example of coercive power exercised by the state). Foucault argued that "governmental practices are not restricted to the state and the state moreover has learnt or should have learnt the limits of what it can know and do . . . " (Dupont & Pearce, 2001, p. 125). According to Garland (1977), empirical analysis using the governmentality lens,

> . . . is focused upon the present, and particularly upon the shift from 'welfarist' to 'neoliberal' politics. It avoids reductionist or totalizing analyses, encouraging instead an open-ended, positive account of practices of governance in specific fields. It aims to anatomize contemporary practices, revealing the ways in which their modes of exercising power depend upon specific ways of thinking (rationalities) and specific ways of acting (technologies), as well as upon specific ways of 'subjectifying' individuals and governing populations. It also problematizes these practices by subjecting them to 'genealogical' analysis—a tracing of their historical lineages that aims to undermine their 'naturalness' and open up a space for alternative possibilities. (p. 174)

THE VALUE OF CRITICAL CRIMINOLOGICAL ANALYSIS

Despite Garland's admiration for Foucault's work, there remains a significant difference between their points of view, a difference which represents a core dilemma in contemporary academic criminology. For Foucault and those who follow him closely, the attempt to scientifically understand both the causes of crime and the operation of the criminal justice system is always implicated in the process of government; scientific or academic criminology is always suspect and is an adjunct to administrative criminology and a powerful element of the broader discourses of government, the "naturalness" of which must be undermined. (That some of the people engaged in this effort work within academic criminology programs is an irony that Foucault would doubtless have enjoyed!) For Garland, there exist within academic criminology critical possibilities associated with the analysis of social forces shaping the criminal law, the operation of the criminal justice system and wider processes of moral regulation which should be cherished. As we saw, Garland wishes that these critical strands of academic criminology had more impact on contemporary processes of government.

In this book, you will encounter a range of views and analyses. Each finds its own way through this contemporary dilemma, its own balance between the value of critical criminological analysis of the processes of government and the value of recognizing that all criminological discourse is prone to assimilation in these very processes of government.

References

Abell, J., & Sheehy, E. A. (2002). *Criminal law & procedure: Cases, context, critique*. Concord, Ontario: Captus Press. (Original work published 2000)

Backhouse, C. (1999). *Colour coded: A legal history of racism in Canada*. Toronto: Osgood Press.

Cayley, D. (1999). *The expanding prison: The crisis in crime and punishment and the search for alternatives*. Cleveland: The Pilgrim Press.

Criminal Law Amendment Act, 1968–69 (S.C. 1968–69, c. 38)

Criminal Code of Canada, R.S.C. 1985, c. C-46.

Des Rosiers, N., & Bittle, S. (2004). Introduction. *What is a crime? Defining crime in contemporary society*. Ottawa: Law Commission of Canada.

Dupont, D., & Pearce, F. (2001). Foucault contra Foucault. *Theoretical Criminology 5*(2), 123.

English Draft Code of 1879.

Erikson, K. (1966). *Wayward Puritans*. New York: John Wiley & Sons.

Foucault, M. (1977). *Discipline and Punish: The birth of the prison*. New York: Pantheon Books.

Foucault, M. (1991). Governmentality. In G. Burchell, C. Gordon & P. Miller (Eds.), *The Foucault effect: Studies in governmentality*. London: Harvester Wheatsheaf.

Garland, D. (2002). *The culture of control: Crime and social order in contemporary society*. Chicago: University Of Chicago Press.

Garland (1985). *Punishment and welfare: A history of penal strategies*. New York: Oxford University Press.

Garland (1997). Governmentality and the problem of crime: Foucault, criminology, sociology. *Theoretical Criminology 2,* 173.

Garland, D. & Sparks, R. (2000). *Criminology and social theory*. New York: Oxford University Press.

Indian Lands Agreement (1986) *Act* (1988, c. 39).

Mawani, R. (2003). Legal geographies of Aboriginal segregation in British Columbia: The making and unmaking of the Songhees Reserve. In Strange & Bashford (Eds.), *Isolation: Places and practices of exclusion*. London & New York: Routledge.

Melossi, D. (2000). Translating social control: Reflections on the comparison of Italian and North American cultures concerning social control, with a few consequences for "critical" criminology. *Social dynamics of crime and control: New theories for a world in transition*. Oxford: Hart Publishing.

Radzinowicz, L. (1999). *Adventures in criminology*. New York: Routledge.

Rose, N., O'Malley, P., & Valverde, M. (2006). Governmentality. *Annual Review of Law and Social Sciences 2*, 1–22.

Snider, L. (2006). *Bad business: Corporate crime in Canada*, Toronto: Nelson. (Originally published 1993)

Titley, B. E. (1986). *A narrow vision: Duncan Campbell Scott and the Administration of Indian Affairs in Canada*. Vancouver: University of British Columbia Press.

Vold, G., Bernard, T., & Snipes, J. (2002). *Theoretical criminology* (4th ed.). Chicago: Academic Internet Publishers.

CHAPTER 2

Criminal Law and Criminal Responsibility

Diana Young, Carleton University

INTRODUCTION

The focus of this chapter is on providing students of criminology with an overview of some of the basic concepts they will need to understand the criminal law. Students should always bear in mind, however, that there is a great deal more to the criminal justice system than the criminal law. The outcome of a criminal prosecution is not only the result of the operation of law. The prosecution process is the result of many "judgment calls"— discretionary decisions by a variety of officials connected to the criminal justice system who interact with the criminal law in complex ways. Policy makers, for example, will make decisions about where to focus policing resources, and this will have an effect on what kinds of crimes are detected, investigated and ultimately prosecuted. Police officers have to make decisions about whom to scrutinize, whether a complainant's account of events is credible enough to justify laying a charge and whether a charge, rather than a warning, is warranted. Many commentators suggest that the criminal justice system does not operate in an even-handed way but rather focuses on particular kinds of offences that result in selectivity about who is drawn into the system and who is not. Such critiques may give the lie to claims that legal rules effectively maintain the important principle of the rule of law.

And while the paradigm of the criminal justice system is often imagined to be the public trial before a jury of the accused's peers, in Canada, the vast majority of criminal charges are resolved through guilty pleas. Frequently, such pleas will come as the result of negotiations between a defence counsel and a Crown attorney in private discussions. These discussions will often result in an agreement as to what charges the Crown will

proceed with and what sentence the offender ought to receive. While in theory a judge has the power to reject a sentence recommendation arrived at through plea negotiations, the practice of plea agreements has given rise to concerns that a disturbing number of important decisions in criminal cases are being made outside of the public eye in a process that usurps the function of the judge.

In addition, the right to a trial by jury is limited to people who are accused of an offence carrying a maximum penalty of five years' imprisonment.[1] In Canada, the vast majority of criminal offences are quite minor in nature and are prosecuted by way of summary conviction in the provincial criminal courts. In this arena, trials take place before a judge alone—there is no jury. So the much-treasured image handed down to us from English legal tradition that an accused is found guilty only following trial before a jury of his peers is a reality in only a tiny percentage of all criminal prosecutions.

CIVIL WRONGS, REGULATORY OFFENCES AND CRIMINAL OFFENCES

Criminologists sometimes speak of their discipline as the study of deviance. The idea of deviance is of course itself controversial; can we speak of deviance as a moral failing attributable to individuals or as a socially constructed phenomenon?

While there are some connections to be drawn between the ways in which we conceive of criminal conduct and the ways in which we conceive immorality, the criminal law and morality are distinct from each other; many kinds of behaviour that are broadly seen as immoral are not recognized as wrongs that will bring about legal effects.

---

1 *Canadian Charter of Rights and Freedoms*, s. 11(f)

And not all legally recognized offences are criminal offences. Broadly speaking, we might divide legally recognized offences into three categories: civil wrongs, regulatory offences and criminal offences.

Civil Wrongs

Civil claims are associated with private law, as they are seen as disputes between individuals. Regulatory and criminal offences are seen to engage the public interest and therefore it is the state, through its representatives, that seeks redress. The most common private law disputes are torts and breach of contract. These constitute legally recognized breaches of private law and may result in a lawsuit, or action, for remedies. Such remedies are usually not punitive in nature but come in the form of monetary compensation; a successful private lawsuit will result in an award of damages sufficient to restore the plaintiff to the position she would have been in had the wrong never occurred. In rare cases, a civil action may also result in an additional award of punitive damages or an order for specific performance which requires the defendant to actually carry out a particular obligation, but generally the focus is on compensating the victim with a monetary award. Remedies for civil wrongs do not include such punitive measures as fines or imprisonment.

Regulatory Offences

Regulatory offences arise from breaches of legislation designed to protect the public interest, so generally they are prosecuted by the state through its agents. Regulatory schemes have become an increasingly important element of the idea of law as social control as the increased complexity of society has brought about a perceived need for state control over a wide variety of activities. They include the use of public roadways through the *Highway Traffic Act,* for example. There are also a wide variety of laws and regulations governing the conduct of various business enterprises. Public health authorities, for example, are charged with ensuring that food served in restaurants is prepared in accordance with basic standards of sanitation. There are also regulatory schemes designed to ensure a standard of safety in the workplace to prevent industrial accidents and to ensure that certain measures are taken to prevent harm to the environment. The list of regulatory schemes is long and diverse. But these schemes may include offences that will result in purely punitive sanctions, most often the imposition of fines but also in some cases imprisonment.

Criminal Offences

Criminal offences are similar to regulatory offences in that they are seen as offences against the state rather than disputes between private individuals and also focus primarily on punishment rather than on compensating victims. But there are a number of important differences; for example, we will see below in our discussion of *mens rea* that conviction for a criminal offence requires particular conditions be met. Trials in criminal matters take place either in the provincial criminal courts or in the superior courts of a province, while trials in regulatory matters often occur before specialized quasi-judicial tribunals, where there may be different rules governing such matters as procedure and the admissibility of evidence. Perhaps most important, there is a level of stigma associated with criminal offences that is not present with respect to either civil wrongs or regulatory offences.

Conviction for a criminal offence results in a criminal record which may have far-reaching effects on a person's life beyond the direct effects of punishment. A person with a criminal record may find that her opportunities for employment are restricted, she may be excluded from membership in some professional organizations and she may encounter difficulty crossing international borders, to name a few.

THE DEFINITION OF CRIMINAL OFFENCES

Perhaps because of the stigmatizing effect of a criminal conviction, it is important that the acts constituting a criminal offence be defined clearly. Therefore, unlike civil wrongs, many of which are defined by the common law, criminal offences are set out in federal legislation—the *Criminal Code* and related acts such as the *Controlled Drugs and Substances Act*. Here we have **formal** definitions of the kinds of acts or omissions that constitute criminal offences. Crimes are those behaviours **prohibited** and **sanctioned** by the *Criminal Code*. **Criminal law** can be found in the *Criminal Code*, but it also includes judicial decisions that interpret legislation known as **common law**. The general principles underpinning Canadian criminal law have been established by the Parliament of Canada, which amends the *Criminal Code* from time to time, and by judges in the course of deciding specific cases. The *Criminal Code* includes **substantive criminal law**, which defines the nature of criminal offences, as well as procedural law, which outlines the powers of criminal justice officials and provides specific procedures that must be followed in the prosecution of criminal cases.

Providing as clear a definition of an offence as possible is important for several reasons. The most important reason is that it allows people to make informed decisions before they act—we will see below that the basis for criminal responsibility lies largely in the assumption that individuals are free agents who are capable of choosing to break or comply with the law. If prohibited acts are not clearly defined, people will not know in advance what is permissible and what is not.[2] A vaguely worded criminal prohibition may be given more precise content through the process of judicial interpretation.[3] It is also worth noting that the creation of a vaguely defined criminal offence may result in an increase in the discretionary power invested in a number of nonjudicial officials, which can result in serious interference with people's lives. For example, police officers may arrest a person without a warrant where there are reasonable grounds to believe that the person has committed or will commit an indictable offence.[4] But if it is unclear exactly what actions constitute an offence, then the discretionary power to make an arrest will be very broad because the arresting officer will have to act in accordance with his own interpretation of the law. This kind of problem has also arisen with respect to the law concerning obscenity and the powers of customs officials to prevent the importation of visual and literary materials which have sexual content.[5]

---

2   See, for example, *R. v. Heywood*, [1994] 3 S.C.R. 761, 94 C.C.C. (3d) 481, 34 C.R. (4th) 133. In that case, the Supreme Court of Canada found that a *Criminal Code* provision prohibiting people convicted of sexual offences to be "found loitering in or near a school ground, playground, public park or bathing area" violated s. 7 of the Charter because the definition of prohibited conduct was too vague.

3   *Reference Re ss. 193 & 195 of the Criminal Code (Canada)* (1990), 56 C.C.C. (3d) 65 (S.C.C.); *R. v. Nova Scotia Pharmaceutical Society*, [1992] 2 S.C.R. 606, 74 C.C.C. (3d) 289, 15 C.R. (4th) 1.

4   *Criminal Code*, s. 495(1)(a).

5   *Little Sisters Book And Art Emporium v. Canada*, [2000] 2 S.C.R. 1120, 150 C.C.C. (3d) 1.

THE STRUCTURE OF THE CRIMINAL JUSTICE SYSTEM

Canada has a federal system of government. Legislative and executive powers are divided between the federal government and the provincial governments in accordance with sections 91 and 92 of the *Constitution Act* of 1982. Under the Constitution, the federal government has sole jurisdiction to pass legislation regarding the criminal law. The provincial governments have sole jurisdiction over the administration of justice. The result is that power over the criminal justice system is bifurcated; the federal government is responsible for writing laws that define offences, setting standards for the imposition of sentences, creating rules of evidence for criminal matters and the like. For example, the *Criminal Code* is federal legislation. The provincial governments are responsible for such matters as the organization of the court system, the hiring of Crown attorneys who prosecute *Criminal Code* offences and policies concerning the prosecution of *Criminal Code* offences.

In each province, the ultimate responsibility for Crown attorneys lies in the hands of the Ministry of the Attorney General. Attorneys general do not usually intervene directly in the prosecution of offences but may provide the Crown offices throughout the province with various policy directives. A separate ministry is responsible for the administration of police services.

At the federal level, Canada's Ministry of Justice is responsible for the federal Crown attorneys. Federal Crown attorneys are responsible for prosecuting offences under federal criminal legislation other than those offences defined in the *Criminal Code*, such as those contained in the *Controlled Drugs and Substances Act* or the *Customs and Excise Act*. Canada's Ministry of Public Safety is responsible for the Royal Canadian Mounted Police (RCMP), which is essentially Canada's national police force.

The prosecution of criminal offences may take place either before a provincial criminal court or a province's superior courts of justice. Summary conviction offences, which are usually fairly minor in nature and involve maximum penalties of less than 2 years, are dealt with by the provincial criminal courts. Indictable offences, which are more serious and involve heavier maximum penalties, are dealt with by the superior courts of justice.[6] Most *Criminal Code* offences are "hybrid" offences. When a person is charged with a hybrid offence, the Crown can elect to proceed either by way of summary conviction or by way of indictment. In most cases, the Crown elects to proceed by way of summary conviction, partly because procedures in summary conviction matters are far more streamlined. Because cases in the provincial criminal courts are heard before a judge sitting alone, there is no jury selection process to contend with, and summary matters do not require a preliminary hearing.

The Basis of Criminal Responsibility

We will see in the discussion below of *mens rea* and the defence of those who are not criminally responsible owing to mental disorder that the Canadian law's conception of criminal culpability is based very much on a classically liberal belief in free will. The core assumption that individuals are presumed to be freely choosing agents who can be held accountable for their intentional acts is deeply engrained in many areas of legal theory; however, it is an

---

6 However, in some cases an accused who wants to plead guilty to an indictable offence can agree to enter a plea and be sentenced by a provincial criminal court.

assumption that criminologists and people from other disciplines may take issue with. For one thing, psychology and psychiatry are heavily influenced by the Freudian belief that human behaviour is largely the result of impulses and perceptions rooted in the unconscious. These subconscious forces are largely responsible for making us who we are, but they are not necessarily rational or even explicable. Because they are rooted in the subconscious, they are not the result of anything like the processes of rational weighing of costs and benefits associated with the image of the rational choosing agent. In addition, sociologists may find explanations for criminality that do not lie in individual moral choice, but in social and cultural conditions that lead to deviance. People trained in these disciplines tend to focus not on the kinds of normative questions of blameworthiness or culpability that concern legal theorists but on the causes of deviance that arise from psychological or social factors.

Finally, many critical criminologists who are influenced by the work of Michel Foucault may find the conception of free will implied by legal theories of criminal responsibility to be deeply flawed and oversimplified. In Foucauldian social theory, there is no sense in which the individual can be understood as existing apart from broader social forces and therefore no way in which she can be seen as making choices that are entirely her own. Foucauldians also often argue that the definitions of legal culpability and broader notions of deviant behaviour are the result of complex social forces that have no inherent or objective value. For many such theorists, the interesting question for criminology is not what causes people to commit crimes at all, but what factors contribute to the construction and perception of the criminal.

The Elements of an Offence—*Actus Reus* and *Mens Rea*

The Crown has an initial onus of proving both the *actus reus* and *mens rea* of an offence beyond a reasonable doubt. Loosely translated from the Latin, *actus reus* means "guilty act" and *mens rea* means "guilty mind." So *actus reus* refers to a prohibited act bringing about certain consequences described in the *Criminal Code*. The *actus reus* of theft, for example, could be described as depriving another person of property to which that person had a legal right. So if a person walks into a store, puts an object for sale in her pocket and leaves without paying for it, she has committed the *actus reus* of theft.[7]

Mens rea refers to the state of mind a person has to have in order to be found guilty of a criminal offence. In most cases, *Criminal Code* offences require what is known as subjective *mens rea* in order to support a conviction. The idea of responsibility in criminal law turns on the notion of free will. The underlying assumption concerning the doctrine of *mens rea* is that people are guilty not only of bringing about a prohibited harm but also of choosing to do so. So in legal terms, the notion of a "guilty mind" focuses not on whether the accused is, in a general sense, a good person, or on what his motive may have been for committing a particular offence. The relevant question for the determination of *mens rea* for offences carrying the subjective standard is whether the accused intended to bring about the prohibited harm.[8] Therefore in the theft example above, in order to get a conviction

---

7   The physical act also has to be consciously controlled by the accused in order to constitute *actus reus*. So, for example, if someone while in the throes of a grand mal seizure strikes another person, he has not committed the *actus reus* of assault because he had no conscious control over the movements of his body.

8   *R. v. Theroux* [1993] 2 S.C.R. 5, 79 C.C.C. (3d) 449, 19 C.R. (4th) 194.

the Crown would have to show beyond a reasonable doubt not only that the accused had actually taken the item from the store without paying for it, but also that she had intended to do so. The accused might say in her defence, for example, that she had taken the item from the shelf intending to pay for it then simply forgot about it. If the adjudicator thought this explanation sufficiently credible to raise a reasonable doubt as to whether the accused had intended to steal the item, he would have to acquit her.

An interesting example of the narrow conception the law takes of the question of *mens rea* and a guilty mind can be found in the well-known case of *R. v. Latimer*.[9] Robert Latimer was charged with murder after he killed his severely disabled daughter, Tracy. There was no doubt that he had intentionally brought about her death; however, the circumstances of the case caused a great deal of controversy because Latimer's act was widely seen as a mercy killing. Latimer claimed—and his account was accepted by the trial court—that he had killed Tracy because she was in severe pain and that he had taken the only means available to put an end to her suffering. The motive, in other words, was compassion for his daughter's suffering. Nonetheless, he was charged and ultimately convicted of second-degree murder, an offence carrying a mandatory minimum sentence of life imprisonment with no chance of parole for 10 years. The Supreme Court of Canada upheld the conviction and the sentence.

A mistake of fact can be a defence to a criminal charge because it can vitiate *mens rea*, but a mistake of law cannot. Students will probably have heard the expression "ignorance of the law is no excuse," and it is true that the law distinguishes between ignorance of fact and ignorance of law. For example, if a person is found to be in possession of a substance that she believed to be baking powder but that was in fact heroin, she has a good defence to a charge of possession of narcotics.[10] She committed the *actus reus* of narcotics possession, but because of her mistake as to the nature of the substance she was carrying, she could not be said to have intended to commit the offence and therefore lacked the element of *mens rea*. On the other hand, an accused who is found to be in possession of a substance that she knew to be heroin but who did not realize that heroin was an illegal substance is in a different position. She has made a mistake not about the salient facts but about the law itself and has no defence to the charge of possession of narcotics.[11]

There are some subjective *mens rea* offences that punish people for unintentional harms; these are situations where a person deliberately commits an offence and, as a result, brings about a certain result. For example, it is a criminal offence to drive while impaired.[12] The maximum penalty if the accused is charged by way of summary conviction is six months' imprisonment.[13] However, if a death resulted from the impaired driving, the maximum penalty is imprisonment for life.[14] The intent of the driver in both cases is the same, but the law imposes harsher punishments where the result is death because of the serious nature of the harm.

---

9 [2001] 1 S.C.R. 3, 150 C.C.C. (3d) 129, 39 C.R. (5th) 1.

10 *R. v. Beaver*, [1957] S.C.R. 531, 188 C.C.C. 129, 26 C.R. 193, 118 C.C.C. 129, 26 C.R. 193.

11 *R. v. Molis* [1980], 2 S.C.R. 356, 55 C.C.C. (2d) 558, 116 D.L.R. (3d) 291.

12 *Criminal Code* s. 253

13 *Ibid.*, s. 255(1)(c). A number of offences stipulate minimum and maximum penalties; however, it is very rare for an offender to receive the maximum.

14 *Ibid.*, s. 255(3)

Negligence and the Objective Standard of Culpability

So far we have discussed subjective *mens rea* offences, where Crown must prove the accused actually intended to bring about a prohibited result or actually knew that his actions would bring about the prohibited result in order to sustain a conviction. Most *Criminal Code* offences are subjective *mens rea* offences. But there are some offences that carry what is called an objective standard of fault. In these cases, a person may be convicted not for a harm brought about intentionally, but for a harm brought about negligently. In these kinds of cases, the courts apply the standard of the "reasonable person." The reasonable person is an image that recurs often in both civil and criminal cases. It is difficult to define with any certainty; however, generally we could say that it represents the standard of care we could expect from an ordinary person who has ordinary levels of intelligence, perception and foresight. So while in a subjective *mens rea* offence we might ask whether the accused actually foresaw the consequences of his actions; in an objective *mens rea* offence we would ask whether a reasonable person would have foreseen the consequences of those actions. While in civil negligence cases any departure from the reasonable person standard can give rise to liability; in criminal cases courts require that the conduct of the accused show a "marked departure" from what would be expected from the reasonable person.[15]

In effect, the subjective standard requires the adjudicator to look at the events from the point of view of the accused and determine what he actually knew or intended at the time he committed the *actus reus* of the offence. In making this determination, the adjudicator may take into account evidence showing that the accused, perhaps owing to limited education or experience or even absentmindedness, was unusually prone to making mistakes of fact or to failing to foresee the likely consequences of his actions. On the other hand, the objective standard is so called because it is not concerned with the particularities of the individual and what effect they might have had on his ability to foresee a risk of harm.[16] The objective standard sets a basic standard of conduct that everyone has to meet regardless of his or her individual circumstances.

For example, a person who brings about the death of another person by means of an unlawful act is liable to be convicted of manslaughter.[17] It is not any unlawful act that gives rise to a conviction, however. The act must be one which a reasonable person could foresee might cause bodily harm that is neither trivial nor transitory. For example, in *R. v. Creighton*[18] the accused had injected a woman with a quantity of cocaine, with her consent. As a result, she overdosed and died. Although he had not intended to cause the victim's death, Creighton was convicted of manslaughter because he had committed the predicate offence of trafficking, and a reasonable person would have foreseen that this offence carried a risk of bodily harm.

---

15 *R v. Hundal,* [1993] 1 S.C.R. 867, 79 C.C.C. (3d) 97, 19 C.R. (4th) 169; *R. v. Creighton,* [1993] 3 S.C.R. 3, 83 C.C.C. (3d) 346, 23 C.R. (4th) 289; *R. v. Tutton* [1989] 1 S.C.R. 1392, 48 C.C.C. (3d) 129, 69 C.R. (3d) 289.

16 In a group of cases decided in the 1990s, the Supreme Court of Canada found that personal characteristics of the accused should not be taken into account in determining whether he ought to have known the relevant facts or perceived the risk involved in his actions, unless those factors had a bearing on his capacity. See *R. v. Creighton, ibid., R. v. Naglik,* [1993] 3 S.C.R. 122, 83 C.C.C. (3d) 526, 23 C.R. (4th) 335; *R. v. Gosset,* [1993] 3 S.C.R 76, 83 C.C.C. (3d) 494, 23 C.R. (4th) 280.

17 *Criminal Code* s. 222(5) (a).

18 *Supra,* note 15.

Critics of the objective standard of liability often suggest that it is unfair to hold everyone to the same standard of conduct. People may have different levels of intelligence, education and experience, all of which might affect their abilities to avoid causing harm. In addition, such aspects as language barriers and cultural differences may have an effect on the ability of a person to perceive a risk. For example, we might say that a reasonable person would heed a clearly marked warning sign. But would it be fair to demand the same from someone who did not read English or who was illiterate?

Other offences carrying the objective standard of liability include manslaughter by criminal negligence,[19] criminal negligence causing bodily harm,[20] dangerous operation of a motor vehicle[21] and failure to provide the necessaries of life.[22]

A fairly recent amendment to the *Criminal Code* changed the offence of sexual assault from a subjective *mens rea* offence to a mixed standard including both objective and subjective elements. Traditionally, mistaken belief in consent was a defence to a charge of sexual assault.[23] Because sexual assault was a subjective *mens rea* offence, there was no requirement that the mistaken belief be reasonable. In sexual assault cases the defence would often argue that the accused believed that the complainant had consented, and this would be a good defence regardless of whether there were any reasonable grounds for that belief. One of the criticisms made by feminists of the subjective standard with respect to sexual assault is that sometimes mistakes as to consent can be the result of discriminatory attitudes about women. For example, a person who lacks respect for women's sexual autonomy might simply not turn his mind to the question of whether a particular woman was consenting to sexual contact. Or a person who assumed that any sexually active woman was sexually available might assume that he had consent even if, objectively speaking, there were clear indications to the contrary. However, in 1992 the *Criminal Code* was amended to include section 272.2(b), which reads as follows:

> It is not a defence to a charge under section 271, 272, or 273 that the accused believed that the complainant consented to the activity that forms the subject-matter of the charge, where, b) the accused did not take reasonable steps, in the circumstances known to the accused at the time, to ascertain that the complainant was consenting.

The use of the word "reasonable" in this section shows that it imposes an objective standard with respect to the question of whether the accused took appropriate measures to ensure that the complainant was consenting. But a subjective element to the test is included in the words "in the circumstances known to the accused at the time." The adjudicator has to consider whether a reasonable person who understood the facts of which the accused was *actually* aware would have taken additional steps to ensure that he had consent. This approach to the issue of mistake of fact in sexual assault cases is also unique in that it imposes a duty on the accused to show an active concern with respect to the question of consent.

---

19 *Criminal Code* ss. 220, 222(5)(b).

20 *Ibid.*, s. 221.

21 *Ibid.*, s. 249; *R. v. Hundal*, [1993] 1 S.C.R. 867, 79 C.C.C. (3d) 97, 19 C.R. (4th) 169.

22 *Criminal Code*, s. 215.

23 *R. v. Pappajohn* [1980], 2 S.C.R. 120, 52 C.C.C. (2d) 481, 14 C.R. (3d) 243.

THE MENTAL DISORDER DEFENCE

In Canada, as in most common law jurisdictions, everyone over the age of 12 years is presumed to have the mental capacity to be held accountable for criminal offences.[24] There are cases where a person suffering from a mental disorder will not be held accountable. The nature of the defence of mental disorder is outlined in section 16(1) of the *Criminal Code* as follows:

> No person is criminally responsible for an act committed or an omission made while suffering from a mental disorder that rendered the person incapable of appreciating the nature and quality of the act or omission or of knowing that it was wrong.

This is sometimes referred to as a cognitive test of criminal responsibility. To succeed in a plea under section 16, a person must produce psychiatric evidence to show not only that he was suffering from a medically recognized mental illness but also that the illness destroyed his ability to understand that his act was wrong according to the moral standards of society or to appreciate the physical consequences of his act.[25] So, for example, a person shoots someone while under the delusion that the victim was immortal would have a defence under section 16, because he could not appreciate the consequences of his action. But a person who, suffering from a manic disorder, commits a crime believing that he has superhuman powers and will never be caught is still regarded as a criminally responsible because he has the cognitive ability to understand that what he is doing constitutes a violation of the law.[26] Similarly, people who are affected by an antisocial personality disorder will ordinarily be held criminally responsible.[27] People with such disorders are incapable of feeling empathy or remorse; however, they do have the cognitive ability to appreciate the consequences of their actions and that what they are doing is in violation of social norms. Similarly, a disorder that affects impulse control—for example, fits of rage that lead to acts of violence or a sexual attraction to children—is not by itself sufficient for a section 16 defence.[28]

We can see in this approach to criminal responsibility the view of individuals as rationally choosing agents that underlies the conception criminal culpability discussed above with reference to the subjective *mens rea* offences. Criminal responsibility is not a function of the severity of a particular mental illness but of its effect on an accused's abilities to make rational choices—to appreciate the nature of what he is doing and to know that it violated a norm of conduct. Many people suffering from very severe mental illnesses will not be able to avail themselves of the "not criminally responsible on account of mental disorder" (NCR) defence.

There are a number of critiques of the law's approach to questions of criminal responsibility, however. For one thing, many people suggest that the law's approach to issues of mental illness and criminality is at odds with psychiatric practice. While the legal analysis

---

24 *Criminal Code* s. 13. Children between the ages of 12 and 17 who commit criminal offences are, however, prosecuted in accordance with the provisions of the *Youth Criminal Justice Act.*

25 *R. v. Chaulk,* [1990] 3 S.C.R. 1303, 62 C.C.C. (3d) 193, 2 C.R. (4th) 1.

26 *R. v. Abbey* [1982], 2 S.C.R. 24, 68 C.C.C. (2d) 394, 29 C.R. (3d) 193.

27 *R. v. Simpson* (1977), 35 C.C.C. (2d) 337, 77 D.L.R. (3d) 507 (Ont. C.A.); *R. v. Kjeldson,* [1981] 2 S.C.R. 617, 64 C.C.C. (2d) 161, 24 C.R. (3d) 289.

28 *R. v. Wolfson* [1965], 3 C.C.C. 304, 46 C.R. 8 (Alta. S.C. App. Div.).

is predicated on the assumption that responsibility arises from the individual's ability to rationally choose, many psychiatric professionals maintain that it is not possible to divide the human psyche into rational processes and affective responses as distinct compartments.

The disciplines of law and psychiatry seek to achieve very different things. Legal theory is an attempt to provide a normative framework through which we can analyze questions of blameworthiness and criminal culpability for certain specific kinds of behaviour. Psychiatry is an attempt to understand the roots of behaviour and address them. Courts depend on information produced by medical experts in order to make factual determinations concerning the NCR defence; in such cases, we see two very different disciplines interacting in complex ways to produce a particular result.

On a deeper level, many Foucaultian theorists would challenge the claim that categories of illness recognized by psychiatric professionals represent objectively verifiable scientific fact. Foucault (1965) suggested that categories of mental disorders were developed not through a set of objective criteria and objective scientific observation, but through a variety of social processes that classify people with certain characteristics as mentally ill.

Procedural Matters

It is not only defence lawyers who can raise the section 16 issue. The Crown can apply for an assessment order to determine the issue, even against the wishes of the accused, if it satisfies the court that there are reasonable grounds to believe that the accused was not criminally responsible at the time of the offence.[29] It may seem odd that the Crown would want to raise a defence to a charge that the accused himself has chosen not to rely on; however, it is not the Crown's function to convict as many accused as possible. The Crown, as a minister of justice, also must act in the public interest and in the interests of justice. Neither interest is served by the conviction of a person who cannot legally be held responsible for his actions.

The power of the Crown to raise the mental disorder defence has raised some concerns, however. Raising the issue of the mental health of the accused during a trial might prejudice the jury against him; jurors might convict because they think that if the accused is mentally ill, then he must be the "type of person" to commit the crime. Also, in raising such a defence the Crown may be taking control of the defence away from the accused, interfering with the strategy of the defence and distracting the adjudicator's attention from the question of actual guilt. This problem has been resolved by a procedural rule prohibiting the Crown from raising the mental disorder defence until after the trial as to actual guilt has been completed and a guilty verdict on the charge returned.[30] There is an exception to this rule, however: If the accused puts his capacity for criminal responsibility in issue, the Crown may raise the mental disorder defence in rebuttal.

Unlike other defences, which must only raise a reasonable doubt in the mind of the adjudicator in order to succeed, the mental disorder defence must be proven on a balance of probabilities. This is the standard of proof that is ordinarily associated with civil cases, and it requires evidence that shows it is more likely than not that the accused suffered from a mental disorder that would relieve her of criminal responsibility within the meaning of section 16 of the *Criminal Code*.

---

29 *Criminal Code* s. 672.12(3)(b).

30 *R. v. Swain* [1991], 1 S.C.R. 933, 63 C.C.C. (3d) 481, 5 C.R. (4th) 253.

A successful section 16 defence does not result in an outright acquittal, but in a verdict of NCR.[31] A person found not criminally responsible is not free to walk away from the courtroom; instead, he may be subject to continued detention in a psychiatric hospital or have other limits placed on his freedom. When an NCR verdict is returned, the court may make a disposition[32] or, if it does not do so, the individual appears before a provincial review board for a determination of the measures that ought to be taken.[33] If the review board determines that the accused does not pose a significant danger to the public, it must grant an absolute discharge. Otherwise, it can either discharge the accused with certain conditions, or it can direct that the accused be detained in a hospital.[34] The disposition must be "the least onerous and least restrictive to the accused" as possible, having regard to the "need to protect the public from dangerous persons, the mental condition of the accused, the reintegration of the accused into society and the other needs of the accused." If the accused is detained or released with conditions, the review board has to hold a hearing every year,[35] or at the request of the person in charge of the facility that the accused attends[36] to determine whether detention, the conditions imposed on the accused, or both continue to be warranted. The Supreme Court of Canada has found that the ongoing supervision of a person found not criminally responsible is consistent with sections 7 and 15 of *The Charter of Rights and Freedoms*.[37] There are provisions in the *Criminal Code*, not yet proclaimed in force, that would impose a "cap" on the length of time a person found not criminally responsible can be subject to detention or conditions, according to the seriousness of the offence with which he was initially charged. At present, however, a person can theoretically be detained or subject to conditions indefinitely even if he committed a fairly minor offence.

THE AFFIRMATIVE DEFENCES

We saw above that the Crown has to prove both the *actus reus* and the *mens rea* of an offence in order to obtain a conviction. The defence of mistake of fact, if successful, leads to an acquittal because it vitiates *mens rea*—the actor did not intend to commit the offence. On the other hand, the affirmative defences of self-defence, necessity and duress arise in cases where the *actus reus* and the *mens rea* of an offence have been proven. In these cases the image of the reasonable person also comes into play.

Self-Defence

Under certain circumstances a person can use force—even deadly force—to repel an assault. Section 34 of the *Criminal Code* reads:

1. Every one who is unlawfully assaulted without having provoked the assault is justified in repelling force by force if the force he uses is not intended to cause death or grievous bodily harm and is no more than is necessary to enable him to defend himself.

---

31 *Criminal Code*, s. 672.34.

32 *Criminal Code* s. 672.45.

33 *Ibid.*, s. 672.47.

34 *Ibid.*, s. 672.54.

35 *Ibid.*, s. 672.81(1).

36 *Ibid.*, s. 672.81(2).

37 *Winko v. British Columbia (Forensic Psychiatric Institute)* (1999), 135 C.C.C. (3d) 129 (S.C.C.).

    2. Every one who is unlawfully assaulted and who causes death or grievous bodily harm in repelling the assault is justified if

        a. he causes it under reasonable apprehension of death or grievous bodily harm from the violence with which the assault was originally made or with which the assailant pursues his purposes; and

        b. he believes, on reasonable grounds, that he cannot otherwise preserve himself from death or grievous bodily harm.

Section 34(1) deals with situations where a person who uses force that is not intended to cause grievous bodily harm. Subsection (2) provides that a person can use force that is intended to cause death or grievous bodily harm only if he reasonably believes his assailant will cause him death or grievous bodily harm and reasonably believes that he cannot otherwise protect himself.

    The use of the word "reasonable" in this section tells us that an objective standard is used in this defence. An accused can succeed on a plea of self-defence only if, in the circumstances, a reasonable person would perceive the threat and, in the case of section 34(2), a reasonable person would see no alternative to the use of force. We saw that in the negligence cases that there are concerns about the fairness of the use of the reasonableness standard, where courts decline to take the personal characteristics of the accused into account when determining the reasonableness of her actions. Is it just to hold everyone to the same standard of care when there are differences in people's abilities to foresee the risk of harm? Similar concerns arise with respect to the use of the objective standard in self-defence cases. However, in self-defence, as in all the affirmative defences, the adjudicator can take certain individualized factors into account. This standard is called the modified objective standard. The modified objective standard allows the adjudicator some leeway to consider the individual circumstances and characteristics of the accused when determining whether her actions were reasonable.

    The use of the modified objective standard can be demonstrated by the well-known case of *R. v. Lavallee*.[38] It had been settled, judge-made law until *Lavallee* that one could use self-defence only if the threat was imminent. The rationale for this was that generally if a threat was not imminent there would be alternatives to the use of violence—the threatened party could call the police, for example. Many feminist legal scholars argued that this was sometimes unfair to battered women who killed their spouses. Often in such cases the threat was not imminent, or might not appear to be so to a third party; nonetheless, the women's violence might have been a reasonably necessary act of self-defence. Lavallee had been subjected to severe abuse by her common-law spouse. One night, after a violent altercation, the spouse handed Lavallee a gun and told her that if she didn't kill him he would kill her at the end of the evening. Lavallee shot him as he was leaving the room. The Supreme Court of Canada found that evidence from an expert on battered wife syndrome was admissible to provide the jury with information concerning the context of the shooting. Although it is commonly referred to as the "battered wife defence," in fact no such defence exists in Canada. Nor is the expert evidence in such cases designed to show that the accused was deprived of her ability to act rationally or to restrain herself. Instead, the trier of fact can take the abusive relationship into account in making a determination of whether the accused's violence was the result of a reasonable apprehension of death or grievous bodily harm and whether the accused reasonably believed she had no other avenue of escape.

---

38 [1990] 1 S.C.R. 852, 55 C.C.C. (3d) 97, 76 C.R. (3d) 329.

In *R. v. Lavallee* the Supreme Court appears to be recognizing that sometimes individualized factors are necessary to put the accused's actions in context. It appears, as well, that the approach taken in *R. v. Lavallee* is not limited to situations where the accused was a battered spouse. In *R. v. McConnell*[39] the accused, who was an inmate at a federal penitentiary, killed another inmate. The victim was a member of a powerful group of inmates who had threatened McConnell with violence. McConnell, having prepared to fend off an attack, saw the victim and several of his friends near McConnell's cell. McConnell and another inmate attacked the group, killing one of them. McConnell pleaded self-defence, but the Crown argued that since at the time of the offence the assault on McConnell was not imminent self-defence was not available. The Supreme Court of Canada adopted the reasoning of the dissenting judgment of the Alberta Court of Appeal, ruling that just as evidence of abuse was admissible in *Lavallee,* expert evidence concerning prison conditions was admissible in these circumstances to show that the killing was a reasonable act of self-defence.

Necessity and Duress

The defences of necessity and duress are related to self-defence in that they arise where the Crown has proven both the elements of *actus reus* and *mens rea*. They also implicate the image of the reasonable person. The defence of duress can be used where an accused commits a crime in response to a threat from another person. For example, if an accused committed theft because someone was forcing him to do so at gunpoint, he would be able to rely on the defence of duress. Necessity arises where there is an emergency other than a threat by a third party and the accused commits a crime in order to avoid some serious harm. In necessity, the accused must show that there was an imminent danger, and in duress he must show that there was a threat of death or bodily harm to himself or to another person. In both doctrines, there must have been no legal way to escape the danger and the harm cause by committing the offence must have been proportionate to the harm so avoided.[40] As in the doctrine of self-defence, the image of the reasonable person is implicated in necessity and duress. The situation faced by the accused must be one where a reasonable person would perceive a threat or a danger, and a reasonable person would not see any reasonable avenue of escape. The courts employ a modified objective standard in necessity and duress so that some of the accused's personal circumstances may be taken into account.

THE CANADIAN CHARTER OF RIGHTS AND FREEDOMS

Charter arguments often arise in criminal cases. *The Canadian Charter of Rights and Freedoms* governs the legislature's lawmaking function, but it also governs the actions and policies of state agents, including police officers and Crown attorneys. Under section 24 of the *Charter,* courts are accorded wide discretion to fashion remedies for breaches of the *Charter,* including striking down laws that infringe the *Charter* and excluding from trial

---

39 [1996], 1 S.C.R. 1075, 48 C.R. (4th) 199, affirming the dissenting judgment of Conrad, J.A., 97 W.A.C. 321, 169 A.R. 321, 32 Alta. L.R. (3d) 1 (C.A.).

40 *Perka v. R,* [1984] 2 S.C.R. 232, 14 C.C.C. (3d) 385, 42 C.R. (3d) 113; *R. v. Latimer,* [2001] 1 S.C.R. 3, 150 C.C.C. (3d) 129; *R. v. Ruzic,* [2001] 1 S.C.R. 687, 153 C.C.C. (3d); *R. v. Hibbert,* [1995] 2 S.C.R. 973, 99 C.C.C. (3d) 193, 40 C.R. (4th) 141.

evidence obtained in a manner that infringes the rights of an accused. Students may be aware that in the United States any evidence that is obtained by the police in violation of an accused's constitutional rights is inadmissible at trial against him. In Canada, the law is not so cut-and-dried. Evidence obtained in a manner that infringed the *Charter* rights of the accused is excluded only if admitting it could bring the administration of justice into disrepute in the eyes of a reasonable person, dispassionate and fully apprised of the circumstances of the case.[41] In some cases, courts may rule that *excluding* evidence obtained in a manner contrary to the *Charter* would bring the administration of justice into disrepute. The decision to exclude evidence will depend on a number of factors, including whether the breach would affect the fairness of the trial, whether the police acted in good faith, whether the breach of the *Charter* right was trivial in nature, the availability of other techniques of investigation and the seriousness of the offence.

In addition, even where a law or a policy infringes a right guaranteed under the *Charter*, it may be saved under section 1, which reads:

> The Canadian Charter of Rights and Freedoms guarantees the rights and freedoms set out in it subject only to such reasonable limits prescribed by law as can be demonstrably justified in a free and democratic society.

In criminal cases, the onus is on the accused to prove that one of her rights under the *Charter* has been breached. If the Crown wishes to avail itself of the saving provision of section 1, it has the onus of showing that the objective of the impugned law or state action relates to concerns that are pressing and substantial in a free and democratic society, that the law or action is designed to achieve the objective, that it is rationally connected to the objective, that it limits the *Charter* right as little as possible and that the objective is proportionate to the harm caused by the limits placed on the *Charter* right.[42]

Although there is a public perception that the *Charter* has allowed many guilty people to escape punishment, it is worth noting that, as mentioned above, most criminal charges result in guilty pleas; if a case never goes to trial then a *Charter* argument is never even made. In addition, since the *Charter* came into force a quarter century ago, the number of people convicted of criminal offences and the number of people serving time in prison has grown at a rate far greater than the growth of the general population.

The following are some examples of *Charter* rights that may be implicated in the criminal justice system.

The Charter and the Police

Many of the *Charter* rights have a bearing on the investigation of a crime.

For example, section 8 of the *Charter* provides that "[e]veryone has the right to be secure against unreasonable search or seizure." This section protects the individual from arbitrary or unnecessary intrusions into areas wherein a person would have a reasonable expectation of privacy. In order to be reasonable, a search must be authorized by law, the law itself must be reasonable and the search must be carried out in a reasonable manner.[43] Usually, the police have to obtain a warrant[44] in order to undertake a search of areas that

---

41 *R. v. Collins*, [1987] 1 S.C.R. 265, 33 C.C.C. (3d) 1, 56 C.R. (3d) 193.
42 *R. v. Oakes* (1986), 24 C.C.C. (3d) 321, [1986] 1 S.C.R. 103, 50 C.R. (3d) 1.
43 *R. v. Collins*, [1987] 1 S.C.R. 265, 33 C.C.C. (3d) 1, 56 C.R. (3d) 193.
44 *Criminal Code* s. 487.

are usually regarded as private—the most obvious of these is a person's home. An exception arises where there is a risk that someone will be injured or that evidence will be destroyed if the search is not undertaken immediately. Police are also permitted to conduct a search "incident to arrest;" the arrest itself must not be unlawful, the search must be for some legitimate objective of the criminal justice system (such as the discovery of an object that poses a threat to police or the public, or which would facilitate an escape, or the discovery of evidence) and must not be conducted in an abusive manner.[45] The purpose of the search has to be connected to the reason for the arrest.[46]

Section 9 of the *Charter* protects people from arbitrary detention and imprisonment. This means, among other things, that the police cannot stop someone and question him without some reasonable suspicion that he has been involved in a crime. The rule against arbitrary detention limits the powers of the police, but this rule is sometimes seen as particularly important in view of the evidence that certain minorities may be disproportionately targeted for questioning and surveillance by the police.[47] Certain exceptions have been made to the rule, however. It is permissible for police to randomly stop motorists for Breathalyzer tests—commonly referred to as RIDE programs—even though there are no objective reasons for suspecting the individual motorists of impaired driving. In these cases, the Supreme Court found that being subjected to random stops and Breathalyzer tests did, in fact, infringe on the motorists' section 9 rights. However, the practice was saved under section 1 of the *Charter* because it was a reasonable measure designed to achieve the important goal of traffic safety.[48] A person who has been unlawfully detained can seek release through an application for habeas corpus.[49]

Section 10(b) of the *Charter* provides that on arrest or detention everybody has a right "to retain and instruct counsel without delay and to be informed of that right." If a detained person requests counsel, the police must provide her with access to a telephone[50] and cannot continue to question her. A detained person can waive the right to counsel as long as the waiver is voluntary.

The Charter and the Prosecution of Criminal Cases

Section 7 of the *Charter* provides that "everyone has the right to life, liberty and security of the person and the right not to be deprived thererof except in accordance with the principles of fundamental justice." Any time a person faces a criminal charge that person's right to liberty is engaged, of course, because in these cases the person may be subject to a penalty of imprisonment if convicted. Under section 7, a person can be deprived of the right to life, liberty and security of the person as long as it is in accordance with the principles of

---

45 *Cloutier v. Langlois*, [1990] 1 S.C.R. 158, 46 C.R.R. 37; *R. v. Stillman*, [1997] 1 S.C.R. 607, 113 C.C.C. (3d) 481, 5 C.R. (5th) 1.

46 *R. v. Belnavis* (1996), 107 C.C.C. (3d) 195, at p. 213 (Ont. C.A.).

47 *Report of the Manitoba Aboriginal Justice Inquiry* (Winnipeg: Queen's Printer, 1991); *Report of the Commission on Systemic Racism in the Ontario Criminal Justice System* (Toronto: Queen's Printer, 1995); Ontario Human Rights Commission, *Paying the Price: The Human Cost of Racial Profiling* (Toronto: Ontario Human Rights Commission, 2004).

48 *R. v. Hufsky*, [1988] 1 S.C.R. 621, 40 C.C.C. (3d) 398, 64 C.R. (3d) 14; *R. v. Ladouceur*, [1990] 1 S.C.R. 1257, 56 C.C.C. (3d) 27, 77 C.R. (3d) 27.

49 *Canadian Charter of Rights and Freedoms*, s. 10(c).

50 *R. v. Manninen*, [1987] 1 S.C.R. 1233, 34 C.C.C. (3d) 385, 58 C.R. (3d) 97.

fundamental justice. The principle of fundamental justice is a difficult one which has been interpreted fairly broadly; however, its requirements include a degree of procedural fairness that must be observed in criminal trials. This includes the right of the accused to make a full answer and defence to the charge she is facing. For example, the Crown has an obligation to disclose all the evidence—both inculpatory and exculpatory—it has to the defence prior to trial.[51] Failure to disclose may result in a successful appeal from conviction and a new trial, or in some cases a stay of proceedings.

The accused also has a right to trial within a reasonable time under section 11(b) of the *Charter*. The remedy for failure to bring an accused to trial within a reasonable time is usually a stay of proceedings.[52] Generally, once a charge has been laid a trial should take place within 8 to 10 months, although there is no absolute time limit and longer delays may be acceptable under some circumstances.[53]

In some cases accused have raised defences claiming that certain sections of the *Criminal Code* are contrary to *Charter* guarantees. For example, section 2(b) provides that everyone has freedom of thought, belief, opinion and expression. There are, however, some provisions of the criminal law limit freedom of expression. For example, section 163 of the *Criminal Code* prohibits making and distributing obscene materials. In *R. v. Butler*,[54] the Supreme Court found that section 163 constituted a violation of the right to freedom of expression; however, as there might be a reasoned apprehension of harm from some kinds of pornography, the provision was a reasonable limit under section 1 as long as it was interpreted not to criminalize sexually explicit material that is not violent and that is not "degrading and dehumanizing."

References

Foucault, M. (1965). *Madness and civilization: A history of insanity in the Age of Reason*. New York: Vintage.

Government Documents

Manitoba. (1991). *Report of the Manitoba Aboriginal justice inquiry*. Winnipeg: Queen's Printer.

Ontario. (1995). *Report of the commission on systemic racism in the Ontario criminal justice system*. Toronto: Queen's Printer.

Ontario Human Rights Commission. (2004). *Paying the price: The human cost of racial profiling*. Toronto: Ontario Human Rights Commission.

Legislation

Canadian Charter of Rights and Freedoms. Enacted as Schedule B to the Canada Act 1982, (U.K.) 1982, c. 11, which came into force on April 17, 1982.

Criminal Code. In *Revised Statues of Canada*. (1985, c. C-46).

---

51 *R. v. Stinchcombe* (1991), 68 C.C.C. (3d) 1.

52 *R. v. Askov* (1990), 59 C.C.C. (3d) 449 (S.C.C.).

53 In some circumstances, for example, a delay might be caused by the defence, in which case no stay will be allowed.

54 [1991] 1 S.C.R. 452, (1992), 70 C.C.C. (3d) 129 (S.C.C.), 11 C.R. (4th) 137.

Reported Cases

Cloutier v. Langlois [1990] 1 S.C.R. 158, 46 C.R.R. 37.

Little Sisters Book And Art Emporium v. Canada [2000] 2 S.C.R. 1120, 150 C.C.C. (3d) 1.

Perka v. R [1984] 2 S.C.R. 232, 14 C.C.C. (3d) 385, 42 C.R. (3d) 113.

R. v. Abbey [1982], 2 S.C.R. 24, 68 C.C.C. (2d) 394, 29 C.R. (3d) 193.

R. v. Askov (1990), 59 C.C.C. (3d) 449 (S.C.C.).

R. v. Beaver [1957] S.C.R. 531, 188 C.C.C. 129, 26 C.R. 193, 118 C.C.C. 129, 26 C.R. 193.

R. v. Belnavis (1996), 107 C.C.C. (3d) 195, at p. 213 (Ont. C.A.).

R. v. Butler [1991] 1 S.C.R. 452, (1992), 70 C.C.C. (3d) 129 (S.C.C.), 11 C.R. (4th) 137.

R. v. Chaulk [1990] 3 S.C.R. 1303, 62 C.C.C. (3d) 193, 2 C.R. (4th) 1.

R. v. Collins [1987] 1 S.C.R. 265, 33 C.C.C. (3d) 1, 56 C.R. (3d) 193.

R. v. Creighton [1993] 3 S.C.R. 3, 83 C.C.C. (3d) 346, 23 C.R. (4th) 289.

R. v. Gosset [1993] 3 S.C.R 76, 83 C.C.C. (3d) 494, 23 C.R. (4th) 280.

R. v. Heywood [1994] 3 S.C.R. 761, 94 C.C.C. (3d) 481, 34 C.R. (4th) 133.

R. v. Hibbert [1995] 2 S.C.R. 973, 99 C.C.C. (3d) 193, 40 C.R. (4th) 141.

R. v. Hufsky [1988] 1 S.C.R. 621, 40 C.C.C. (3d) 398, 64 C.R. (3d) 14.

R. v. Hundal [1993] 1 S.C.R. 867, 79 C.C.C. (3d) 97, 19 C.R. (4th) 169.

R. v. Kjeldson [1981] 2 S.C.R. 617, 64 C.C.C. (2d) 161, 24 C.R. (3d) 289.

R. v. Ladouceur [1990] 1 S.C.R. 1257, 56 C.C.C. (3d) 27, 77 C.R. (3d) 27.

R. v. Latimer [2001] 1 S.C.R. 3, 150 C.C.C. (3d) 129, 39 C.R. (5th) 1.

R. v. Lavallee [1990] 1 S.C.R. 852, 55 C.C.C. (3d) 97, 76 C.R. (3d) 329.

R. v. Manninen [1987] 1 S.C.R. 1233, 34 C.C.C. (3d) 385, 58 C.R. (3d) 97.

R. v. McConnell [1996], 1 S.C.R. 1075, 48 C.R. (4th) 199, affirming the dissenting judgment of Conrad, J.A., 97 W.A.C. 321, 169 A.R. 321, 32 Alta. L.R. (3d) 1 (C.A.).

R. v. Molis [1980], 2 S.C.R. 356, 55 C.C.C. (2d) 558, 116 D.L.R. (3d) 291.

R. v. Naglik [1993] 3 S.C.R. 122, 83 C.C.C. (3d) 526, 23 C.R. (4th).

R. v. Nova Scotia Pharmaceutical Society [1992] 2 S.C.R. 606, 74 C.C.C. (3d) 289, 15 C.R. (4th) 1.

R. v. Oakes (1986), 24 C.C.C. (3d) 321, [1986] 1 S.C.R. 103, 50 C.R. (3d) 1.

R. v. Pappajohn [1980], 2 S.C.R. 120, 52 C.C.C. (2d) 481, 14 C.R. (3d) 243.

R. v. Ruzic, [2001] 1 S.C.R. 687, 153 C.C.C. (3d).

R. v. Simpson (1977), 35 C.C.C. (2d) 337, 77 D.L.R. (3d) 507 (Ont. C.A.).

R. v. Stillman [1997] 1 S.C.R. 607, 113 C.C.C. (3d) 481, 5 C.R. (5th) 1.

R. v. Stinchcombe (1991), 68 C.C.C. (3d) 1.

R. v. Swain [1991], 1 S.C.R. 933, 63 C.C.C. (3d) 481, 5 C.R. (4th) 253.

R. v. Theroux [1993] 2 S.C.R. 5, 79 C.C.C. (3d) 449, 19 C.R. (4th) 194.

R. v. Tutton [1989] 1 S.C.R. 1392, 48 C.C.C. (3d) 129, 69 C.R. (3d) 289.

R. v. Wolfson [1965], 3 C.C.C. 304, 46 C.R. 8 (Alta. S.C. App. Div.).

Winko v. British Columbia (Forensic Psychiatric Institute) (1999), 135 C.C.C. (3d) 129 (S.C.C.).

CHAPTER 3

Canadian Criminal Statistics

Knowledge, Governance and Politics

Kevin D. Haggerty, University of Alberta

INTRODUCTION

University students often postpone fulfilling their statistics course requirements until the last possible moment, and many students would skip them entirely if they could figure out how to do so and still graduate. It is an understandable relationship to a topic that is usually taught as a form of pure technique; that is, statistics are routinely approached as a skill to be painstakingly mastered, akin to memorizing the multiplication tables, so that one can move on to more stimulating matters.

Now imagine that you have been asked to write a textbook chapter about crime statistics and have been encouraged to make the chapter "sexy." It is a tall order; few things appear to be less seductive than statistics. Nonetheless, it is something that I hope to accomplish in the following pages, perhaps not attaining the lofty heights of making statistics sexy, but making them more interesting and perhaps even controversial than is typically the case. To do so I resist the temptation to blind the reader with science, to needlessly present formulas, calculations and long lists of numbers. Instead, the focus here is on three central factors pertaining to statistics about deviance. The first concentrates on "the facts," outlining some of the more consistent and interesting things that statistics have revealed about the dynamics of crime. This includes a prominent emphasis on the methodological limitations of crime statistics. The second focus is on the broad politics of statistics. While it might appear peculiar to suggest that statistics are political, we explore several attributes of statistical processes that can have a political dimension. Third, I conclude by briefly noting how statistics can inform our sense of who we are. Combined, this three-part orientation provide readers with insights into some of the main statistical facts pertaining to crime and deviance and with an appreciation for how statistics can be studied as social phenomena in their own right.

At the end of the chapter, students will be able to identify some of the more prominent statistics relating to crime and victimization. Readers will be aware of the different sources of statistical knowledge about crime and recognize prominent limitations of each method. Students will develop a greater appreciation for how statistics can be manipulated and why such manipulations have become a familiar component of public politics. Finally, readers will be exposed to some of the broader social implications of statistics.

These topics are significant because of the centrality of statistics in contemporary society. Statistics are both a form of knowledge and a form of power. Hence, all citizens should be attuned to how social numbers are produced, what their inherent limitations are, and how they can be shaped by dominant interests. Even people who loudly proclaim that they "hate statistics" will one day find that they (perhaps unfortunately) need to become familiar with a set of statistical indicators.

STATISTICS AND GOVERNANCE

Historically, the state was the main institution capable of collecting statistics; it was something they originally did to enhance taxation. Today, most businesses, community groups and voluntary organizations collect numbers on different phenomena. Such numbers are used to direct organizational practices but also to manage different groups.

Statistics are a prominent component of governance, where "governance" simply refers to efforts to direct individuals or groups of individuals (populations) to behave in certain ways. Governance in

Western societies is now almost unthinkable without statistics. This is because to govern something (a population, person or organization) requires knowledge of that phenomenon, and statistics provide a unique and powerful way to understand social processes by situating individuals in the context of a larger population. In the process, statistics have come to shape how we think about the practice of governance, informing the day-to-day techniques of governing, and they are used to assess if governance is being done effectively and efficiently.

The first efforts to count the population were also an early step on a road that has culminated in the rise of our contemporary surveillance society (Lyon, 2001; Haggerty & Ericson, 2006). While surveillance often brings to mind hidden cameras and microphones, sociologists understand surveillance more broadly to refer to all efforts to monitor or scrutinize different phenomena. Today, the collection of numerical information on population groups—often called dataveillance—is a key attribute of surveillance. We have progressed from the earliest censuses that simply sought to determine the number of people living in a geographical territory to sophisticated studies such as Statistics Canada's National Longitudinal Survey of Children and Youth. This survey follows more than 22,000 youths until they are 25, collecting data at 2-year intervals on such a diverse array of topics as the child's education, behaviour, motor and social development, social activities, smoking and drug use. Each child's teachers and parents are also surveyed, and parents are asked to provide information on education, social support, family functioning, income and dwelling. Such comprehensive statistical scrutiny can produce remarkably rich data. At the same time, for the people being monitored, it can be a laborious and somewhat invasive form of bureaucratic scrutiny.

The historical emergence of statistical knowledges introduced new ways to think about the aims and effectiveness of governmental efforts. That is because statistics allow us to contemplate such things as the overall criminal victimization rate or the total prison population. The ultimate aims of governance, whether these are to increase the total volume of wealth, health or security of the population, quickly became oriented toward attempts to modify such statistical indicators in a desired direction. So, for example, rather than a politician simply saying that she wants to improve the financial situation of Canadian children, you are now more likely to hear her announce that she aims to decrease the child poverty rate by 14%. Such ambitions, and the efforts to bring them into effect, are examples of statistical governance, a form of governance that is understood and evaluated in predominantly statistical terms.

An inherent tension in public discussions of statistical facts involves the distinction between the individual and the aggregate. Statistics deal with aggregate phenomena; that is, they are concerned with the total volume of something, such as crime, infant mortality or unemployment. While we might have personal experience of crime or be aware of a child who has died, only by examining statistics on such events can we personally experience them as aggregate phenomena. This distinction between individualized and aggregate knowledges can be confusing and controversial. So, for example, if a professor reports that the rate of car thefts has decreased (meaning that fewer cars are being stolen now than in the past), individual citizens will occasionally claim that the findings are obviously flawed because the numbers do not mesh with their personal experiences. If you have had your car stolen three times in the past year—a very high personal experience of crime—you might be suspicious of these statistics since they do not accord with your personal experience of car theft. What gets confused in such situations is that individual experience and aggregate phenomena are different forms of knowledge. This might appear to be fairly obvious point, but people regularly dismiss statistical data because they do not correspond with their personal experiences.

Perhaps more importantly, the difference between aggregate and individual experiences is important to remember in public culture more generally. Politicians and advertisers now market products, political policies and assorted social agendas using personal testimonials—inviting individual citizens to talk (or complain) about their personal experience of such things as crime or hospital waiting times. Audiences are tacitly encouraged to assume that these personal experiences accurately represent the experiences of a much larger group of people. In fact, the statistical trends might be the exact opposite of this person's experiences. Hence, while the following pages provide several reasons to be wary of the political manipulation of statistics, one should also be suspicious of personal testimonials, many of which have no relationship to broader aggregate tendencies.

The power of an agency such as Statistics Canada derives from its ability to create fundamentally new phenomena. Statistical organizations effectively produce such things as "the suicide rate," and "public opinion" which do not exist otherwise. This might seem like a peculiar suggestion, but it is an important point to grasp. While it might appear that such things are out there in the world simply waiting to be accurately recorded on a survey, in reality it is the act of collecting the numbers which effectively calls these entities into being. So, for example, there is no such thing as a "rate of mental illness" that exists independently of the efforts to collect information about such maladies. Once that data is collected and publicized, however, it is often treated as if it this rate existed independently of human and institutional routines. The same is true for public opinion. While individuals have always held views on assorted social issues, it was only after public opinion organizations established their infrastructure of polls, analysis and publications that we could meaningfully talk about "public opinion" or see it as something to which politicians should be responsive (Osborne & Rose, 1999). Hence, one of the curious attributes of statistics is that the measurement rules, standardized definitions and official categories that they use to measure the world also effectively create the phenomena they are measuring. If you change the rules for how to count something like crime victimization, then the victimization rate changes, sometimes dramatically. Moreover, if you stop collecting data, the phenomenon disappears entirely. That is not to say that victimization disappears if you stop collecting data, but that the victimization rate itself disappears as a form of knowledge and as a social fact.

While the remainder of this chapter concentrates on efforts by government officials and academic researchers to compile statistics on crime and deviance, it is worth noting at the outset that those practices now exist alongside the statistical monitoring conducted by private corporations. Major corporations constantly analyze data on their customers. They acquire such information from a person's recorded purchases, but they also increasingly access and integrate statistical datasets which were originally produced by other institutions. An entire industry now amasses and scrutinizes the assorted informational traces that people record in their day-to-day lives. This includes not only their name, age, address and telephone numbers but also marital status, estimated income, home value, value of car, occupation, religion and ethnicity. Some privately owned data collection systems record people's medical condition, what they read, what they order over the telephone and on-line and where they go on vacation. Once these data are integrated with other datasets, they are subjected to sophisticated statistical analysis to produce revealing profiles about a person's lifestyle and consumption patterns which are then used for marketing purposes (Gandy, 1993; Turow, 1997).

Such market-based statistical scrutiny is relevant to contemporary dynamics of deviance because it is increasingly part of efforts to detect suspicious or deviant behaviour. Major companies have responded to concerns about identity theft by routinely analyzing all customer purchasing patterns for signs of suspicious transactions. So, if a customer makes a distinctive pattern of purchases (buying in a specific order, in a certain timeframe and in a way that does not accord with that person's historical consumption patterns) and if this resembles the purchasing patterns of identity thieves—say buying a cellular telephone, gasoline and an electric guitar in quick succession—the credit card might be automatically suspended. Such strategies are an interesting development in how society responds to deviance because here deviant behaviour is not detected through personal observation of a human being or situation, but through the computerized scrutiny of statistical patterns. As the amount of data about the public increases and as computing power continues to grow, we can expect to see efforts to use such data to predict deviance based on a person's statistical profile.

STUDYING CRIME AND DEVIANCE

Almost every social scientific discipline contributes to our understanding of deviance. The methodologies used to study this topic are extremely diverse, and include such things as historical archival methods, laboratory experiments and legal analysis. This chapter is primarily concerned with statistical analyses of crime and deviance. While every discipline uses statistics there are several unique methodological considerations to keep in mind when using statistics to study crime and deviance (see generally, Mosher, Miethe & Phillips, 2002; Maguire, 2002).

Official Crime Data

Canadian criminologists often analyze data produced by the Canadian Centre for Justice Statistics (CCJS), which is the unit within Statistics Canada responsible for national data on crime, courts and corrections (Haggerty, 2001). The CCJS's most prominent publication is the *Juristat*, a convenient series of reports suitable for both students and experts who want concise information on statistical trends pertaining to crime-related topics. The most popular dataset produced by the CCJS is the Uniform Crime Reports (UCR), which provides standardized measures of recorded crimes in Canada. When a journalist or academic talks about crime trends she is typically referring to the numbers derived from the UCR. The UCR have several advantages: the data are readily available and they use standardized definitions, which allows for national comparisons. The data have been collected since 1962, meaning that historical patterns in criminal behaviour can be studied. Finally, the fact that the United States also has a form of UCR means that we can compare crime trends between the two countries with some degree of accuracy.

Official crime data have revealed important regularities in criminal behaviour. One of the most consistent findings is that crime, with some notable exceptions, is disproportionately committed by young people. In 2003, for example, persons aged 15 to 24 represented only 14% of the total Canadian population, but they accounted for fully 45% of those accused of property crimes and 32% of those accused of violent crime (Wallace, 2004). Moreover, it is predominantly young men who are involved in criminal

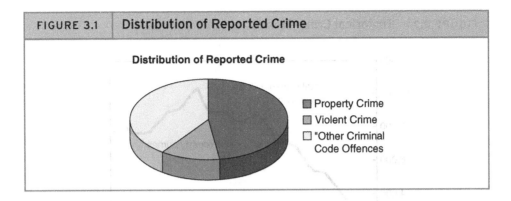

FIGURE 3.1 | **Distribution of Reported Crime**

Distribution of Reported Crime

- Property Crime
- Violent Crime
- "Other Criminal Code Offences

behaviour. Indeed, in all societies young males are consistently more criminal than other social groups.

We also know that the vast majority of crime is not violent. Of all the crimes reported to the police in Canada in 2005, only 12% were violent offences. The remainder were property crimes (48%) and "other *Criminal Code* offences" (40%), a category which includes crimes such as mischief, disturbing the peace and bail violation (Gannon, 2006), see Figure 3.1 (Distribution of Reported Crime). Looking more closely at those crimes officially categorized as "violent" (see Figure 3.2, we see that the vast majority of violent

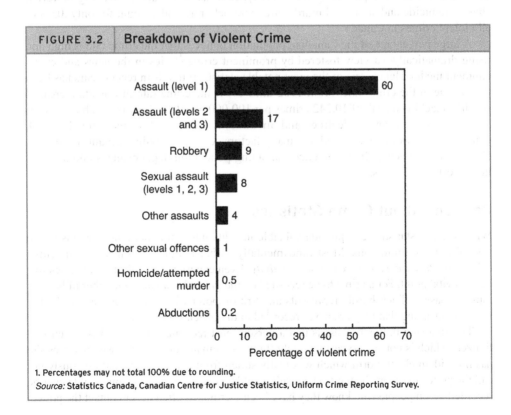

FIGURE 3.2 | **Breakdown of Violent Crime**

Assault (level 1) — 60
Assault (levels 2 and 3) — 17
Robbery — 9
Sexual assault (levels 1, 2, 3) — 8
Other assaults — 4
Other sexual offences — 1
Homicide/attempted murder — 0.5
Abductions — 0.2

Percentage of violent crime

1. Percentages may not total 100% due to rounding.

Source: Statistics Canada, Canadian Centre for Justice Statistics, Uniform Crime Reporting Survey.

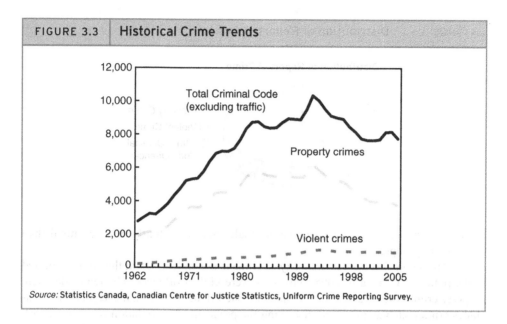

FIGURE 3.3 | Historical Crime Trends

Source: Statistics Canada, Canadian Centre for Justice Statistics, Uniform Crime Reporting Survey.

crimes (60%) consist of "Level 1 Assaults," which are the least serious forms of assault. These can include comparatively low-level types of assaults such as shoving or verbal abuse. Homicide and attempted murder are extremely rare and account for only .05% of all violent crimes in Canada.

A large percentage of the Canadian population believes that the crime rate is high and rising dramatically—a view fostered by prominent crime stories in the news and entertainment media. Hence, one of the most notable statistical trends in recent years has been the decline in the crime rate. From 1962 until 1991, the crime rate in Canada increased steadily, reaching a peak of 10,342 crimes per 100,000 people in 1991 (see Table 2). After 1991 the rate began to decline, and in 2005 it was 7,761 crimes per 100,000. Criminologist have hypothesized that many factors could potentially account for this decline, including new policing practices, an aging population, legal changes and new police reporting practices.

Cautions about Crime Statistics

While official statistics can provide valuable insights into crime patterns, they also have several notable limitations. Most fundamentally, rather than being a measure of crime, *crime statistics are a measure of police activity.* Even experienced analysts sometimes forget this vital point. For a crime to be recorded on the official statistics, a number of hurdles must be passed. Each hurdle represents an attrition point where some crimes fall by the wayside, meaning that they are never recorded in the official statistics.

The first step in this process is that a person must recognize that they have been victimized, which is not as easy as one might think. A woman, for example, who believes she has mislaid an electric drill which was really stolen from her garage would obviously not call the police to report the theft. The result would be that her victimization would never be recorded. Even people who know they have been victimized often never contact the police.

There are many reasons for this nonreporting, including a belief that the event was too triv-ial to report, a sense that the police cannot do anything to rectify the situation, a distrust of the police in certain cultural communities or a sense that calling the police might make things worse (as can be the case with reporting sexual assault). The cumulative effect of such nonreporting is that the official crime statistics can severely underestimate the vol-ume of crime—a topic we return to in the next section.

Even reporting a crime does not guarantee that it will be recorded on the official statis-tics. A police officer might decide that a citizen's complaint is not a criminal matter and not take a report. At other times the police might refer citizens to another social service organ-ization (Meehan, 2000). Alternatively, an officer might conclude that there is no prospect of making an arrest and therefore not bother to do the paperwork necessary to ensure that the event is officially recorded. For example, a study conducted in 2000 found that in one-third of instances where an identity theft victim contacted the police, the victim could not convince an officer to complete an official report (Sullivan, 2004, p. 146).

These processes highlight the sociological distinction between social reality and doc-umentary reality which needs to be borne in mind when examining any statistics or offi-cial reports. Social reality refers to the world as it is, what *really* happened. In contrast, documentary reality refers to how real world events and processes have been recorded on official reports and statistical categories. There can be profound differences between so-cial reality and the documentary reality produced to describe an event or person (Smith, 1974). A major part of these differences is attributable to the role played by assorted "street-level enumerators" in recording documentary reality. These are the officials re-sponsible for writing the official reports which serve as the basis for assorted statistics. The police are among the most prominent street-level enumerators, and the details they record on their reports serve as the basis of official crime statistics. While the media fos-ters an image of policing as an action-packed profession, the vast majority of an officer's time is consumed by paperwork. For example, processing a traffic accident that involves personal injuries and an impaired driver can involve completing 16 separate forms, a process that can consume several hours of an officer's shift (Ericson & Haggerty, 1997, p. 23). How completely or accurately officers complete these reports is an ongoing con-cern. For assorted personal or institutional reasons, what gets recorded on the official police reports (documentary reality) might have little relationship to what really tran-spired (social reality).

In a study of the production of gang statistics in a large city in the United States, Meehan (2000) provides several examples of considerable leeway in police statistics. He was interested in the process by which an event came to be officially classified as a "gang incident." What he found was that the dispatchers who answer the police telephones and assign officers to incidents play a major role in this process. When a citizen telephones the police, a dispatcher must quickly try and determine what type of crime she is dealing with. Dispatchers then classify the crime as belonging to one of a host of official police cate-gories such as break and enter, disturbing the peace or gang incident and then assign the call to a police officer or police cruiser. Many of these early classifications "stick" in that they remain the official categorization used by the police agency to report the type of crime they dealt with. Meehan examined the 911 telephone transcriptions for calls that the offi-cial police statistics classified as "gang incidents" and demonstrated that many of these incidents do not conform to popular understandings of gangs. So, for example, both of the following calls to the police were officially recorded as a "gang incident" in the official statistics. In the first example it appears that the simple use of the term "gang" by the caller is enough to classify a group of teenagers as a criminal "gang":

Police: Bigcity police three eight five.

Caller: In Corktown?

Police: Yes.

Caller: In front of ninety eight Bedford Street there's a gang of teenagers playing tag football under these new lights. Can you get them out of here please?

Police: Yes ma'am.

The second example dramatically reveals the latitude in what types of youths can be officially classified as involved in a gang incident:

Caller: Hi **I'd like to report some boys** right now there on Masters Street, somebody has to call the cops right?

Police: Alright, what number Masters?

Caller: It's right down from the . . . one twenty nine Bastille Way.

Police: What number are you at now?

Caller: One twenty nine.

Police: You're at one twenty nine Bastille Way?

Caller: Yes.

Police: And the gang is out there?

Caller: The gang is out there yeah they gotta go home and go to bed.

Police: All right we'll be down.

While such youths were obviously annoying this caller, they hardly seem to conform to the gang stereotype of the Crips and Bloods. Nonetheless, their behavior was reported as a "gang incident" in the official statistics.

Medical examiners can also serve as street-level enumerators with implications for crime statistics by virtue of their role in determining the cause of death in instances of suspicious death. While medical examiners typically operate in a sound and fair fashion—in that they follow the rules, employ the best available science and show little evidence of outright bias or corruption—there are lingering questions about whether the documentary reality they record about a 'cause of death' accurately records the social or biological reality of what caused a person to die. Television shows such as *CSI: Miami* have fostered an expectation that medical examiners will almost inevitable arrive at accurate determinations. In reality, questions often remain about, for example, whether a single car accident might have been a suicide. It can be difficult or even impossible to accurately determine whether the death of an infant was an instance of crib death or shaken baby syndrome, something that is particularly germane to crime statistics as a child who dies from being shaken is a victim of homicide.

Cause of death determinations can also be complicated by scientific limitations. Some poisons, for example, are almost impossible to detect on a body that has been immersed in water for a long time. Medical examiners also employ questionable shorthand rules to arrive at their decisions. For example, Timmermans (2006) reports that medical examiners routinely assign "coronary artery disease" as the cause of death for individuals who have 75% of their coronary arteries occluded and who demonstrate no other evidence of contributing factors. This informal working rule helps them make sense of otherwise ambiguous cases, but it also sits uncomfortably with the fact that it is not unheard of for people to live with up to 95% of their arteries occluded.

Such studies accentuate the major disjuncture that can exist between social reality and how that reality is recorded on official documents. In the process, they highlight the importance of understanding the actual routines and protocols whereby crime statistics are produced.

As cases proceed through the criminal justice system, a certain percentage are filtered out at every stage in the process. Criminologists refer to this as the **crime funnel**. At the top of the funnel are the very large number of events that could potentially be recorded as crimes. At each step in the funnel, more and more cases fall by the wayside. So, for most recorded crimes the police never make an arrest. For many arrests a charge is never laid. Even when the police lay a charge most of these cases never appear in court but instead are resolved through a plea arrangement negotiated between the defence and the prosecution. Finally, most individuals convicted of a crime spend no time in prison, but instead receive some form of alternative punishment such as probation or community service. Figure 3.4 (Crime Funnel) provides a sense of how the crime funnel operates. A key thing to therefore keep in mind when analyzing official crime statistics is that they only deal with a proportion of crimes that occur in society. The volume of crime that is unknown and unmeasured is referred to as the "dark figure of crime."

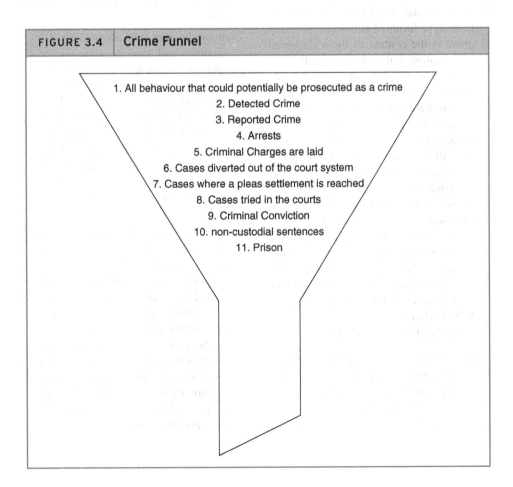

FIGURE 3.4   Crime Funnel

1. All behaviour that could potentially be prosecuted as a crime
2. Detected Crime
3. Reported Crime
4. Arrests
5. Criminal Charges are laid
6. Cases diverted out of the court system
7. Cases where a pleas settlement is reached
8. Cases tried in the courts
9. Criminal Conviction
10. non-custodial sentences
11. Prison

DEBATE

Race and Crime Statistics

One of the most contentious and recurrent data-related issues in Canadian criminal justice concerns whether the police or Statistics Canada should collect information on the racial or ethnic status of offenders (Haggerty, 2001). Historically, Canadian crime statistics routinely included information on occupation, education and religion, along with place of birth and a crude measure of ethnicity. Criminologists used this information to discuss group differences in criminal behaviour. Ethnic differences in crime and delinquency were expected, and sociologists used the data to analyze forms of culture conflict that arose in the context of the widespread immigration that took place earlier last century—a form of conflict that some thought could account for certain types of criminal behaviour (Sellin, 1938).

Today, however, some fear that crime statistics based on race or ethnicity will be used to promote hatred and discrimination. Evidence for this can occasionally be seen in sensationalist stories about "Asian gangs," "Jamaican criminals" or the "Russian Mafia." Such stories typically ignore how the vast majority of any racial or ethnic group are law abiding. Consequently, there has been debate about whether such data should be collected or published. Below are some of the arguments against collecting this data.

1. Official crime rates are a function of police behaviour. Hence, differences in ethnic or racial crime rates might be a result of police paying over-attention to the behaviours of certain groups more than such individuals being unduly criminal.

2. Some ethnic differences in crime can be attributed to the crimes we chose to examine. For example, white-collar crimes are under-reported compared to arrests for street-level drug sales. Individuals from the predominately white Canadian establishment commit more of the former and recent immigrants more of the latter. This fosters an inaccurate picture of the relationship between ethnicity and crime.

3. It can be very difficult to achieve a rigorous and accurate definition of race and ethnicity (Roberts, 1994). Lack of agreement on the traits that distinguish ethnic groups leads to difficulties in unambiguously classifying many individuals into distinct ethnic and racial groups. Also, increasing intermarriage means that ever-fewer Canadians can claim that their ancestors came from only one group.

4. Finally, even if the crime rates for those individuals who can demonstrate only one racial or ethnic background were collected (which would leave out many Canadians), it would be important to examine the rates of these groups in their homelands, as immigrants to other lands besides Canada, and over time, to see if similar rates occurred. If they did not, then something besides ethnicity and race must account for their criminal behaviour.

Taken together, these measurement difficulties and the political controversy surrounding this issue has lead Statistics Canada to not collect such data. This decision has also produced its own problems. For example, we know that some Canadian ethnic groups, most particularly Aboriginal peoples, are over-represented in terms of their arrest and incarceration rates. Without statistics identifying the ethic identity of offenders, it is difficult or impossible to learn about the extent to which they and other groups are over-represented or to develop and evaluate programs that might help rectify this situation.

VICTIMIZATION AND SELF-REPORT STUDIES

Over the past two decades criminology has seen a rapid growth in the subfield of "victimology," which is the study of criminal victimization patterns and the experiences of victims. Victimization surveys have emerged as one of the most important sources of knowledge on victimization because they have been able to demonstrate how victimization patterns vary according to assorted demographic characteristics and lifestyle patterns.

The methodology for victimization surveys, such as Statistics Canada's General Social Survey (GSS), involves telephoning individuals to ask them whether and how they might have been victimized in the past 12 months. The GSS has been conducted at 5-year intervals since 1988, and the latest imputation of the study was conducted in 2004 when 24,000 individuals over the age of 15 were interviewed about their experiences of crime. The following discussion draws predominantly from the findings of the most recent GSS (see Gannon, 2006).

Rather than identify the exact crime that each person might have experienced, the GSS groups crimes into three main categories:

1. **Violent Victimization**
   a. *Sexual assault:* Including forced sexual activity, attempts, unwanted sexual touching, grabbing, kissing or fondling.
   b. *Robbery:* Theft or attempted theft where the perpetrator had a weapon or there was violence or the threat of violence against the victim.
   c. *Physical assault:* Personal attack (victim was hit, slapped, grabbed or beaten), a face-to-face threat of physical harm or an incident involving a weapon.

2. **Theft of Personal Property**
   Theft or attempted theft of personal property (unlike robbery, the perpetrator does not confront the victim).

3. **Household Victimization**
   a. *Break and enter:* Illegal entry or attempted entry into a residence or other building on the victim's property.
   b. *Motor vehicle/parts theft:* Theft or attempted theft of a vehicle or part of a motor vehicle.
   c. *Theft of household property:* Theft or attempted theft of household property.
   d. *Vandalism:* Wilful damage of personal or household property.

TABLE 3-1	Victimization Incidents Reported to the Police, 2004[1]						
	Total no. of incidents	Incidents reported to the police[2]		Incidents not reported to the police		Don't know/ not stated	
	(000s)	(000s)	%	(000s)	%	(000s)	%
Total	7,723	2,613	34	4,962	64	148	2
Total violent	2,109	687	33	1,381	66	41^E	1^E
Sexual assault	512	42^E	8^E	448	88	F	F
Robbery	274	127	46	144	53	F	F
Physical assault	1,323	519	39	789	60	16^E	1^E
Total household	3,206	1,188	37	1,958	61	59	2
Break and enter	505	275	54	223	44	7	1
Motor vehicle/parts theft	571	281	49	285	50	5	1
Theft household property	1,136	330	29	786	69	20	2
Vandalism	993	303	31	664	67	26	3
Theft personal property	2,408	738	31	1,623	67	47^E	2^E

Note: Figures may not add to total due to rounding.
E use with caution
F too unreliable to be published
1. Excludes all incidents of spousal sexual and physical assault.
2. Includes incidents reported by the victim or by someone else.

Source: Statistics Canada, General Social Survey, 2004.

One of the most important findings of victimization studies concerns the volume of crime that is *not* reported to the police. While we noted previously that criminologists have long been concerned about the dark figure of crime, victimization studies have provided evidence of the volume and profile of unreported crimes. As Table 3.1 (Victimization incidents reported to the police) (Ganon & Mihorean, 2005) suggests, only 34% of violent criminal incidents are ever reported to the police. Moreover, some crimes are reported to the police more routinely than others, with only 8% of sexual assaults being reported as compared to 49% of motor vehicle thefts. Some of the reasons why individuals indicated that they did not report their household victimization are reported in Figure 3.5 (Reasons for not reporting household victimization). Such findings accentuate how the official crime statistics can severely underestimate the volume of certain types of crimes.

Victimization is also more pervasive among particular sociodemographic groups. We noted previously that young people commit a disproportionate number of criminal acts. Youths are also more likely to be the victims of crime. In 2004, Canadians aged 15 to 24 had a violent victimization rate that was 1.5 to 19 times the rate of other age groups. The general pattern is that as individuals age their risk of victimization goes down significantly. Hence, people aged 25 to 34 had a violent victimization rate of 157 per 1,000 while those aged 65 and older had a rate of only 12 violent incidents per 1,000.

FIGURE 3.5	Reasons for not Reporting Household Victimization

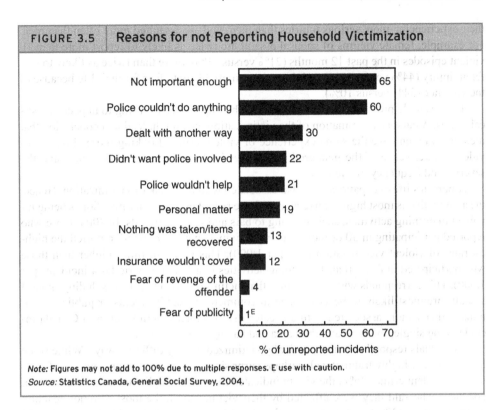

Note: Figures may not add to 100% due to multiple responses. E use with caution.

Source: Statistics Canada, General Social Survey, 2004.

The data also reveals that Canadian Aboriginals are at high risk of being victims of violent crime.[1] In fact, they experience the highest rates of violent victimization in Canada as compared to both the total non-Aboriginal population and to other minority groups. Those who identified themselves as Aboriginals were three times more likely than the non-Aboriginal population to be the victim of a violent crime (319 people per 1,000 versus 101 per 1,000). This pattern is particularly acute for Aboriginal women, whose violent victimization rates are 3.5 times higher than those reported from non-Aboriginal women.

One of the more surprising findings of the GSS is that men and women experience comparable rates of violent crime (102 per 1,000 women and 111 per 1,000 men) and similar rates of spousal violence. Closer examination of the numbers, however, reveals very important differences in the gender dynamics of these crimes. So, for example, there are differences in the types of criminal violence experienced by men and women. Men's rates of victimization by violent assault (91 per 1,000) and robbery (13 per 1,000) are considerably higher than those of women. However, women have a rate of sexual assault victimization that is five times higher than that for men (35 per 1,000 women versus 7 per 1,000 men). Important differences are also apparent in the dynamics of spousal assault. While men and women have a comparable rate of spousal assault (7% of women and 6% of men), women who are assaulted by a spouse tend to be assaulted more violently (as evidence by

---

1 Note that while the official crime statistics do not collect data on a person's race or ethnicity, victimization surveys ask individuals to identify their ethnic heritage.

their experiencing more serious injuries than men) and are assaulted more often than men. For example, female victims of spousal assault are twice as likely to report more than 10 violent episodes in the past 12 months (21% versus 11%), more than twice as likely to suffer an injury (44% versus 18%) and three times more likely to fear for their life because of the violence (34% versus 10%).

This example provides a valuable lesson in the importance of trying to unpack statistical trends. A cursory examination of the victimization data might lead to a conclusion that men and women have the same experience of violent crime. Looking more closely provides a better sense of the gendered differences in the forms of such violence and the severity and frequency of such acts.

A person's lifestyle patterns are also associated with their risk of victimization. Hence, the activity that is most highly correlated with the risk of criminal victimization is being involved in evening activities, such as going to bars and visiting friends. In 2004, those who reported participating in 30 or more evening activities in a given month reported the highest rates of violent victimization (174 per 1,000). This was four times higher than those who participated in fewer than 10 evening activities in a 1-month period (44 incidents per 1,000). This corresponds with the findings that victims of violent crime (excluding spousal assault) are most likely to be victimized in commercial establishments or public institutions. Other factors associated with a greater risk of violent victimization in Canada include being single, living in an urban area and having a low income.

Individuals respond to being criminally victimized in very different ways. While some individuals are highly traumatized, perhaps surprisingly, in more than one quarter of incidents of violent crime (26%) the victim indicated that the event did not affect them much. For those who said they were affected by their victimization, the most common reaction was to be angry (32%), to be upset, confused and frustrated (20%) and to be more fearful (18%). And while we might anticipate that being the victim of a violent crime would be the most traumatic form of victimization (which is true for many individuals) being victimized by the nonviolent crime of break and enter appears to be the most consistently upsetting. Forty-one percent of victims of break and enters reported feeling the strongest emotions (anger) as a result of their victimization as opposed to 32% of victims of violent crime.

Another methodology that is worth briefly noting is self-report studies, as these have also provided valuable insights into criminal behaviour. Like victimization studies, self-report studies ask individuals about their personal experience of crime, but here they are asked to identify the crimes that *they have personally committed* over the previous year. Again, an advantage of this approach is that it can measure crimes that are never recorded on the official statistics. Such studies, however, do not have the same public profile as the UCR or the GSS. There are no official state-sponsored self-report studies, and those studies which are conducted are therefore undertaken by academics working alone or in small teams. Nonetheless, Canadian self-report studies have helped demonstrate that crime is not a rare phenomenon attributable to a few notorious individuals. Instead, crimes of various stripes are very common; in the words of criminologist Thomas Gabor (1994), "Everybody Does It." Certainly, not everyone commits heinous forms of violent crime, but many individuals engage in more prosaic behaviours for which they could be prosecuted if they were caught, including tax evasion, impaired driving, over billing, copyright infringement, theft (often from the workplace), illegal drug use, purchasing stocks on the basis of an insider tip, simple assault (which can include shoving or verbally berating someone) and so on.

While victimization surveys and self-report studies provide important alternatives to official crime data, they too have their limitations. Like all survey research, they study only a sample of the population, which means that a sufficient number of people must be contacted to ensure statistically significant findings. Some crimes are also unreported because individuals might be unaware that they were victimized or that they had engaged in a criminal act. Victimization studies also omit crimes with no obvious victim, such as prostitution, drug dealing or impaired driving, and do not study people under the age of 15—an important limitation if one wants to study child abuse victims. These problems are compounded by the fact that participants often forget prior victimization or cannot remember exactly when a crime occurred—one reason why they are only asked about crimes committed in the past twelve months. A particularly acute difficulty for studying crime is that people will lie about their criminal behaviour. So, some respondents exaggerate the extent to which they are involved in crime. More commonly, individuals can be reluctant to admit to having committed serious crimes, even when they are assured that research findings will remain anonymous and confidential.

POLITICS AND STATISTICS

When I call for statistics about the rate of infant mortality, what I want is proof that fewer babies died when I was Prime Minister than when anyone else was Prime Minister. That is a political statistic.

Sir Winston Churchill

To suggest that statistics are political is *not* to claim that they are necessarily fraudulent. As we will see, outright misrepresentation sometimes occurs, but the politics of statistics includes a broader series of processes concerning questions about what should be studied, how to measure those phenomena, how concepts are to be defined and when findings should be released. Each of these decisions is political in that it can help or hurt the interests of different social groups. Such groups therefore occasionally lobby statistical agencies to establish statistical practices that are best suited to their specific political interests.

Official statistics are produced by the state, which means that the studies conducted by agencies such as Statistics Canada are linked to the state's interests in generating certain forms of knowledge which, it is hoped, will be useful in governing. It can also mean that the studies which different social organizations would like to see conducted are not undertaken because the government is not interested in the same issues and sometimes fears that such studies might be politically embarrassing. The cumulative result of this situation is that the statistical needs of socially marginal or oppositional groups are often neglected, leaving activists to work with numbers derived from studies that were not designed with their interests in mind. It can therefore be a small victory for political activists when the state includes variables they are interested in on an existing study, or, ideally, if they can convince the state to conduct a survey explicitly on their issue. So, for example, allowing individuals to identify their same-sex partner as their "spouse" on a governmental survey both acknowledges the existence of such relationships and is a small symbolic victory for gay rights activists as it helps officially recognize such relationships.

Statistical agencies produce thousands of reports. While most are publicly available, only a small subset of findings ever receives serious or sustained publicity. Again, which numbers the public becomes aware of can also be shaped by powerful interests. Findings favourable to the government's agenda are apt to be highly publicized, whereas those that are more embarrassing often receive less attention. Sometimes, the release of reports containing statistical "bad news" stories has been consciously timed to ensure that they receive little publicity, as when findings are released on the Friday before a long weekend or immediately before Christmas vacation (Tant, 1995).

One of the most routine ways that political considerations can inform the production of statistics involves the practice of classification, more formally known as "operational definition" (Bowker & Star, 1999). Once politicians or bureaucrats decide to conduct a survey of, say, homelessness, public transit usage or drug use, statisticians must determine how to count these phenomena. Although an outsider might think this is a relatively straightforward process, deciding what to include and exclude within these definitions can be an extremely complicated process and one that is sometimes shaped by political factors. Consider the following questions: Should bisexuals be counted among the gay population?; Are Métis Aboriginals?; Is alcohol a drug?; Is a person who has stopped searching for work unemployed?; Should raising your own child be counted as work? How a specific study answers these questions will shape the final statistical results. Consequently, there have been high-level political battles where different political constituencies advocated for the official embrace of their preferred definition.

As noted previously, organizations occasionally fixate on one particular statistical indictor as the key measure of their institutional success. This is the process we deemed "statistical governance." For example, police organizations routinely judge their success or failure based on their ability to reduce the crime *rate*. This emphasis on changing assorted statistical rates makes perfect sense in an increasingly quantified world, but it can also lead to a single-minded fixation on altering statistical indicators that is open to manipulation and misrepresentation. So, for example, if the police want to reduce the violent crime rate they can try to arrest more violent criminals and develop policies that help rectify the underlying causes of such behaviour. However, making more arrests can preset the police with a public relations dilemma. This is because more arrests are likely to *increase* the crime rate because more criminal behaviours will be recorded on the official statistics than in previous years. Hence, at the end of the year, precisely because the police have been so proactive in making arrests, they are likely to be criticized because the crime rate has increased. Alternatively, officers can also reduce crime rates by engaging in a series of recording practices that will alter the statistics without necessarily modifying the amount of crime. So, for example, when faced with intense pressures to reduce violent crime, police officials have been known to stop arresting certain categories of violent offenders, or charging them with a crime that is not officially deemed to be "violent." Such actions can reduce the violent crime rate without necessarily changing anything about criminal behaviour. So, to take a different example, if a highly cynical police agency wanted to reduce the rate of impaired driving, the easiest thing that it could do would be to simply stop its holiday-season traffic stops. Its statistics on impaired driving would decrease dramatically, because the agency would be arresting fewer people, but the number of drunken people driving cars would undoubtedly remain the same, and might increase.

To appreciate the wider political dynamics of statistics one must also contemplate the public politics of social problems. At any given moment a host of social organizations want the government to change different policies and social practices. Social activists might want to eliminate child abuse, increase recycling, reduce impaired driving and so on. Advocates for such issues quickly discover that if they expect to receive funding or craft new policies they must do more than simply point out that such situations are troublesome. To be effective they must enlist a wider public constituency in their cause; something that is done almost exclusively through the media. However, the media and the public can only pay attention to a fairly limited set of issues at any given moment (Hilgartner & Bosk, 1988). Hence, advocates for public causes find themselves in a battle for public attention, competing with other social organizations for media coverage.

It is in this context that statistics become a central dynamic of public politics. Some of the most familiar ways to attract public attention to an issue is to claim that a social problem is particularly large, that it affects many people, and is growing rapidly. Statistics are routinely employed (and manipulated) to make such claims as they provide activists with an ostensibly neutral and scientific way to demonstrate the size and importance of a problem.

When activists start a campaign to rectify a public problem—say hate crimes—they immediately face questions from politicians and the media about whether this is a "big" problem and if so, exactly how big is it? The logic is that large and escalating problems deserve more public attention and resources. When activists are dealing with a comparatively new social issue such numbers are typically not available. Only after a social problem has been recognized as important will that a government or funding agency dedicate the resources to study the phenomena. When numbers are lacking, activists have occasionally simply invented large "shocking" numbers to demonstrate the magnitude of a problem. So when a leading activist for the homeless was asked for the source of his claim that there were two or three million homeless persons in America, he explained: "Everybody demanded it. Everybody said we want a number . . . . We got on the phone, we made a lot of calls, we talked to a lot of people, and we said 'Okay, here are some numbers.' They have no meaning or value" (Best, 2001, p. 34).

Simply inventing numbers, however, remains comparatively rare. It is more common for individuals to make highly selective presentations or manipulations of data to demonstrate the large size of a problem. There are several ways that this has can be done. The controversy over the number of missing children in the United States is a telling example of how some groups will use an extremely broad definition of a problem in order to produce and publicize a "big" number. In the 1980s, the issue of missing children surged onto the political agenda in North America. Provoked by the claim that 50,000 American children were missing, various state and private agencies swung into action. Missing children's bureaus and police databases were established. Cautionary public service announcements were aired and the faces of missing children started to appear on milk cartons. Authorities urged parents and children to be constantly vigilant against potential abduction. In such an emotionally charged context, the typical image of a "missing child" that was conveyed in media accounts was that of a vulnerable youth who had been abducted by a stranger for a comparatively long period and often ended up being assaulted or murdered. Such were the individualized horror stories that typically accompanied the media accounts about the missing children problem.

It soon became apparent, however, that there was considerable latitude in what was being counted as an instance of a missing child. Suspicious journalists investigated how advocates had arrived at the claim of 50,000 missing children and discovered that different data sources used dramatically different definitions of both "missing" and "child." Some studies used very broad definitions, such that any or all of the following would be included in the numbers on missing children: youths who were momentarily out of their parents' sight, missing teenagers, teenagers who slept over at a friend's house, youths living with a noncustodial parent or grandparent and a significant number of runaways. Depending on what definitions and data source a person used, the count of missing children in America could be as high as 50,000 or as low as 67 (Best, 1989). Not surprisingly, activists who wanted to foster public concern about this issue routinely employed the largest and most alarming numbers.

Another way to produce large numbers about the scope of a social problem is to extrapolate from an unrepresentative study. An example of this occurred in relation to the often-repeated claim that there are 1 million abused elderly people in America. Again, however, when suspicious journalists investigated this issue they found serious problems with how researchers had arrived at this number. The claim about 1 million abused elderly people was an estimate based on a survey of 433 elderly residents of Washington, DC. Only 73 of these individuals responded, giving the study a response rate of only 16%, which is far too low to allow researchers to generalize the findings to the wider population. Nonetheless, when the study found that three of the 73 respondents indicated that they had experienced some form of psychological, physical or material abuse, the authors extrapolated this number to the entire population of elderly people in the United States, arriving at the shocking figure of 1 million abused elderly people. Hence, a front-page story about 1 million abused elderly people was created from only three incidents (Gilbert, 1997).

The exaggerated claims about missing children and abuse of the elderly are examples of manipulating statistics to persuade a wider public audience about the relative importance of a particular phenomenon. At various times the numbers about homelessness, crime, poverty and disease have all been manipulated; something that can be done in many ways including selectively using broad or narrow definitions of the problem, extrapolating from a nonrepresentative study, ignoring or downplaying contrary evidence, manipulating graphs so that statistically insignificant fluctuations appear to be dramatic increases, changing operational definitions or making highly selective comparisons with different years, groups and jurisdictions (see generally Gilbert, 1997; Orcutt & Turner, 1993; Best, 2001). While we might be dismayed by such actions, the activists or politicians who communicate such numbers are typically convinced that their cause is important, although they are perhaps uncertain of its exact scope. They produce and reproduce shocking numbers as a way to simply proclaim: "This is an important social issue that we should try and rectify." It has become a condition of modern society that such claims must now be presented statistically.

STATISTICS AND IDENTITY

To this point we have examined the intimate relationship between statistics and governance, outlined some of the main findings of statistical studies of crime and accentuated some of the political dynamics of statistics. In the concluding two subsections we turn our attention to the relationship between statistics and personal identity.

Statistics tend to objectify people—treating individuals as objects to be counted, rather than as individuals with unique personalities and histories. Concerns about this process are captured in the expression "I'm not a statistic," which is a populist reaction to the alienation fostered by modern administrative processes. And while statistics do gloss over our unique identities, statistics can also inform our deepest sense of ourselves and our relationships with others. This is apparent in dynamics pertaining to the production of statistical norms and of the creation of official identity categories.

Norms

There is an intimate relationship between statistics and norms. There are, however, two different sociological understandings of norms. The first approach is purely statistical, where "norm" refers to a central tendency in a group of numbers: the mean, median or mode. So, for example, the norm for the height of high school boys might be 155 cm. This is a purely descriptive understanding that does not judge whether the norm is desirable—it simply is. In contrast, the second understanding of norms is concerned explicitly with evaluation and judgment. In this latter version, "norm" refers to socially approved behaviour. So, urinating in public violates a norm in the sense that it is socially unacceptable. Here, the terms *normal* and *abnormal* are often synonymous with "good" and "bad." This is the prescriptive understanding of norms in that it is concerned with demarcating prescribed behaviour. Discussions about prescriptive norms are often deeply emotional as contrasted with the dispassionate language used to discuss statistical norms.

In practice, there can be a complicated relationship between statistical and prescriptive norms. This is particularly the case when measuring human behaviour, as in this context statistical norms can become imbued with judgments about what is right and wrong. We have come to equate behaviours that are statistically average with what is socially normative; that is, with what is desirable. People who find that some aspect of their behaviour falls outside of a statistical norm will often try and alter that behaviour to bring it more into line with that norm. This process is a powerful and subtle way that statistics can shape how we understand and relate to ourselves.

One of the easiest ways to understand this tendency is to think about statistical indicators on human sexuality. Since the famous Kinsey reports in the 1950s where behavioural scientists first asked the public about their sex lives, sociologists have amassed volumes of data on such things as number of sexual partners, age at first sexual encounter, same-sex encounters, frequency of masturbation, number of sexual liaisons per month and so on. For social scientists these numbers are purely descriptive; they outline the total volume and regularity of such behaviours in the population and can be used to produce statistical profiles for such acts, including mid-range statistical averages. A peculiar thing about statistical norms on human behaviour, however, is that individuals tend to evaluate their own life in light of those norms. As human beings we are continually scrutinizing and altering our actions in light of how others behave. Statistics present a way to learn about the behaviour of large groups of people, and in the process they inadvertently encourage people to contemplate where they might fall within that distribution. So, for example, if people learn that they have fewer sexual encounters per month than is the statistical average for someone their age, they might wonder if perhaps they are mildly sexually repressed. Alternatively, people who discover that they are dramatically above this average might become anxious about whether they are compulsive about sex, that perhaps they are a "sex addict." The point is that statistical indicators that are morally neutral can quickly become transformed into a standard for judging our behaviour and that of others, becoming a factor that encourages us to shape our behaviour in a particular direction. While this is not inevitable, for many individuals it appears that simply publicizing statistical norms can encourage them to alter their behaviour to correspond more closely to statistical averages.

Identity

A comparable process of personal transformation can occur in relation to the official identity categories used by statistical agencies. To count the population one must first divide it into a series of discreet categories such as age, employment status, professional group, health status, criminal history, country of origin or groups who are "at risk" of any number of untoward eventualities. However, assigning people to a category is different from classifying animals or rocks because humans are conscious of the categories to which they are assigned. Unlike animals, people can embrace or reject these categories. Occasionally we embrace the terms that official agencies use to count us as part of how we understand ourselves, a process that Ian Hacking (1986) refers to as "making up people." This process has been identified in how people relate to the official categories for social class, occupation, and illness, but the most unambiguous examples come from efforts to officially categorize race.

As noted previously, many nations measure the racial composition of their population. In racist regimes, such as South Africa under apartheid, such practices have been used to entrench racial forms of exclusion (Bowker & Star, 1999). In liberal democracies, racialized forms of counting are justified as a way to help eliminate racial inequities. Such practices are complicated by the fact that social scientists now recognize that racial groupings do not refer to discrete biological groupings but are social conventions that rely upon a series of often contentious classifications that have varied over time and space (Jenkins, 1997). Racial classifications that were once dominant have disappeared and new ones have emerged. The United States census, for example, in addition to classifying people as white and black, formerly employed the categories of mulatto, quadroon and octoroon to refer to people with varying degrees of "mixed blood." Not long ago it would have been common for a subset of American citizens to refer to and understand themselves as a "quadroon," but today such terminology is well outside of the mainstream (Goldberg, 1997).

The often fluid nature of racial identity is connected to statistical processed by virtue of the fact that statistical institutions have helped to establish and reproduce identity categories for the purpose of counting the population, and these categories have in turn helped to fashion people's sense of themselves. Censuses and surveys authorize sets of categories that can influence how we understand ourselves and our wider community. Benedict Anderson (1991), for example, recounts how the colonial census of Southeast Asia originally imposed a series of racial designations on the population that were entirely alien to the locals. Over time, however, these new categories became part of the colonial administrative structure and were used in schools, hospitals and other governmental institutions. The locals eventually came to identify themselves and others in terms of these originally foreign terms. An almost identical process occurred in Canada when the British colonial administration introduced the legal and bureaucratic category of "Indian" as shorthand to classify and manage North America's First Nations peoples. That category bore no relationship to how the existing people identified themselves or understood their history, or their relationships with other groups (Francis, 1992). Today, however, the term "Indian" is a familiar, if often contested, term that people use to identify themselves.

Contrary to the slogan "I'm not a statistic," we can, in fact, be statistics, in the sense that our understanding of ourselves and others can be informed by the authorized identity categories established by statistical agencies.

Conclusion

Statistics are now one of the dominant tools that we use to understand our world. While statistics might not be sexy, it should be apparent by now that they are not just something that we use to study society but are themselves an intimate part of the social world. Producing numbers also produces rippling effects that extend in diverse and unpredictable directions.

Numbers have become central to commerce and state functioning. Since the 19th century, crime and deviance have been among the most central topics of official statistical scrutiny. The cumulative result of these efforts is the assorted statistical tools we now have to analyze deviance, including official statistics, victimization surveys and self-report studies. These now allow us to know more about the trends in crime and victimization than at any point in the past. However, no tool is perfect, and the statistical methods used to study deviance have their limitations. The role played by police officers in recording official statistics, for example, can present some of the most extreme instances of the disjuncture between social reality and documentary reality. Moreover, all statistical methods have difficulty in unearthing the true scope of the dark figure of crime.

Nonetheless, scrutinizing these different data sources has produced important insights into criminal behaviour in Canada. Prominently, this includes the somewhat surprising decline in crime over the past decade. Statistical revelations about differences in how arrest and victimization patterns can vary according to assorted factors such as a person's age, gender, physical location and ethnicity provide government officials with opportunities and insights into how to address crime-related problems.

One consequence of the increasing quantification of criminal justice has been the ascendance of increasingly statistical forms of governance, as the aims of the police or politicians, for example, are expressed in statistical terms, with their successes or failures also being evaluated statistically. This greater centrality of statistics to politics has produced pressures on social activists to provide "big numbers" on social problems in order to capture public attention and justify dedicating greater resources to such issues. A predicable downside of this development has been the public manipulation of numbers to achieve political gains. And while such instances can be disheartening, resulting in the public sentiment that "you can prove anything with statistics," this is only true when individuals are ill informed about statistics and statistical methodology. The only antidote to ever more statistical manipulation is a citizenry what has achieved a degree of statistical literacy—or "numeracy" (Paulos, 1988).

As the public becomes more familiar with the routines and protocols of statistical practices, it is inevitable that such practices will shape them as human beings. Learning about statistical averages for human behaviours, for example, can serve as a subtle encouragement for individuals to shape their own behaviour in certain directions. Likewise, greater familiarity with the identity categories used to classify individuals on official surveys or censuses can also modify how people think of themselves and their wider community.

References

Anderson, B. (1991). Census, map, museum. In *Imagined communities*. London: Verso.

Best, J. (1989). Dark figures and child victims: Statistical claims about missing children. In *Images of issues: Typifying contemporary social problems*. New York: Aldine de Gruyter.

———. (2001). *Damned lies and statistics: Untangling numbers from the media, politicians and activists*. Berkeley: University of California Press.

Bowker, G. C., & Star, S. L. (1999). *Sorting things out: Classification and its consequences*. Cambridge, MA: MIT.

———. (1999). The case of racial classification and reclassification under apartheid. In *Sorting things out: Classification and its consequences*. Cambridge, MA: MIT.

Ericson, R. V., & Haggerty, K. D. (1997). *Policing the risk society*. Toronto: University of Toronto Press, and Oxford: Oxford University Press.

Francis, D. (1992). *The imaginary Indian: The image of the Indian in Canadian culture*. Vancouver: Arsenal Pulp Press.

Gabor, T. (1994). *Everybody does it! Crime by the public*. Toronto: University of Toronto Press.

Gandy, O., Jr. (1993). *The panoptic sort: A political economy of personal information*. Boulder, CO: Westview.

Gannon, M. (2006). *Crime statistics in Canada, 2005*. Ottawa: Statistics Canada.

Ganon, M., & Mihorean, K. (2005). *Criminal victimization in Canada, 2004*. Ottawa: Statistics Canada.

Gilbert, N. (1997). Advocacy research and social policy. *Crime and Justice, 22,* 101–148.

Goldberg, D. T. (1997). Taking stock: Counting by race. In *Racial subjects: Writing on race in America*. New York: Routledge.

Hacking, I. (1986). Making up people. In T. Heller, M. Sosna, & D. Wellbery (Eds.), *Reconstructing individualism: Autonomy, individuality and the self in Western thought*. Stanford: Stanford University Press.

Haggerty, K. D. (2001). Counting race: The politics of a contentious classification. In *Making crime count*. Toronto: University of Toronto Press.

———. (2001). *Making crime count*. Toronto: University of Toronto Press.

Haggerty, K. D., & Ericson, R. V., eds. (2006). *The new politics of surveillance and visibility*. Toronto: University of Toronto Press.

Hilgartner, S., & Bosk, C. L. (1988). The rise and fall of social problems: A public arenas model. *American Journal of Sociology, 94*(1), 53–78.

Jenkins, R. (1997). Ideologies of identification. In *Rethinking ethnicity: Arguments and explorations*. London: Sage.

Lyon, D. (2001). *Surveillance society: Monitoring everyday life*. London: Open University Press.

Maguire, M. (2002). Crime statistics: The "data explosion" and its implications. In M. Maguire, R. Morgan, & R. Reiner (Eds.), *The Oxford handbook of criminology*. Oxford: Oxford University Press.

Meehan, A. J. (2000). The organizational career of gang statistics: The politics of policing gangs. *The Sociological Quarterly, 41* (3): 337–370.

Mosher, C. J., Miethe, T. D., & Phillips, D. M. (2002). *The mismeasure of crime*. London: Sage.

Orcutt, James D., & Turner, J. B. (1993). Shocking numbers and graphic accounts: Quantified images of drug problems in the print media. *Social Problems, 40,* 190–206.

Osborne, T., & Rose, N. (1999). Do the social sciences create phenomena? The example of public opinion research. *British Journal of Sociology, 50*(3), 367–96.

Paulos, J. A. (1988). *Innumeracy: Mathematical illiteracy and its consequences*. New York: Hill and Wang.

Roberts, J. (1994). Crime and race statistics: Toward a Canadian solution. *Canadian Journal of Criminology, 36*, 175–185.

Sellin, T. (1938). *Culture conflict and crime*. New York: Social Science Research Council.

Smith, D. (1974). The social construction of documentary reality. *Sociological Inquiry, 44*(4), 257–268.

Tant, A. P. (1995). The politics of official statistics: A case study. *Government and Opposition, 30*, 254–266.

Timmermans, S. (2006). *Postmortem: How medical examiners explain suspicious deaths*. Chicago: University of Chicago Press.

Turow, J. (1997). *Breaking up America: Advertisers and the new media order*. Chicago: University of Chicago Press.

Wallace, M. (2004). Crime statistics in Canada, 2003. In *Juristat*. Ottawa: Canadian Centre for Justice Statistics.

CHAPTER 4

A Specialized Criminal Justice System for Canadian Youth:

Critical Overview of Historical and Contemporary Developments in Law and Procedures Governing Youth Offending

Ruth M. Mann, University of Windsor

INTRODUCTION

This chapter reviews and critically examines legislative efforts to establish and implement specialized youth justice procedures in Canada from the late 19th century to the present. Specifically, it examines the rationale, influences, practices and outcomes of each of three legislative acts. The first act focused efforts of governments and community agencies on promoting social welfare by saving children from criminal influences under the 1908 *Juvenile Delinquents Act*. The second act sought to balance the protection of society against youths' legal rights and special needs under the 1984 *Young Offenders Act*. The current *Youth Criminal Justice Act*, which came into effect on April 1, 2003, seeks to activate a "**preventative partnerships**" (Garland, 2000, p. 348) strategy that situates responsibility for preventing and responding to youth offending and reoffending onto society at large. This "advanced liberal" (Muncie, 2005, p. 37) governmental initiative involves reallocating social and economic responsibilities for crime control across various levels of government, voluntary organizations, professional bodies, citizen groups, victims, families, and youth themselves, a development in evidence across Western jurisdictions (Department of Justice Canada, 2000; see also, for example, Bazemore, 2005; Burnett & Appleton, 2004; Edwards & Huges, 2005; Garland, 1996; Jurik, Blumenthal, Smith, & Portillos, 2000; Leonard, Rosario, Scott, & Bressan, 2005; Mann, Senn, Girard, & Ackbar, 2007; Ohlin, 1998; Stenson, 2005).

There is considerable debate on where this preventative partnerships strategy is taking youth justice. Some argue that the *Youth Criminal Justice Act* and similar new millennium legislation in other Western jurisdictions take youth justice in an increasingly reactionary and punitive or exclusionary direction, driven by globalization and the fears, divisions and inequalities that globalization, and neoconservative responses to globalization, foster. Others view the *Youth Criminal Justice Act* as a hopeful, progressive, inclusive turn away from **punishment**, an example of what a U.K. commentator on new youth justice in Britain calls a "resurgence of welfarism in the face of policy changes to replace it" (Burnett & Appleton, 2004, p. 50; see also Crawford & Newburn, 2003; Doob & Sprott, 2006; Reid & Zuker, 2005). Most, however, including those cited above who are most and least critical, see both exclusionary and inclusionary potential in the volatile and contradictory mix of preventions and sanctions that the *Youth Criminal Justice Act* and similar youth justice legislation authorize (Bala, 2005a, 2005b; Barnhorst, 2004; Bazemore, 2005; Denov, 2005; Hillian, Reitsma-Street, & Hackler, 2004; Leonard et al., 2005; Mann et al., 2007; Muncie, 2005; Ohlin, 1998; O'Malley, 1999; Roberts, 2003, 2004; Trépanier, 2004).

The chapter addresses this debate on preventative partnerships youth justice strategies in three ways. First, it briefly situates Canadian youth justice in a global context, directing attention to how re-emergent rehabilitative and preventative strategies fit with "right" versus "left" political agendas and the public sentiments and social interests that drive these agendas within and across jurisdictions. Next, it situates the legislative development, provisions and implementation outcomes of each of Canada's three youth justice acts, directing attention to the ways competing political parties, lobbies and justice professionals shaped these practices. Third, it addresses political and practical challenges inherent to the current and future success of the *Youth Criminal Justice Act*. As four Ontario justices commenting on this new legislation state (Harris, Weagant, Cole, & Weinper, 2004, p. 386) write, our collective response to these challenges "will determine the type of society we convey to future generations."

YOUTH JUSTICE IN GLOBAL CONTEXT

In Canada, the United States, Britain, Australia and Europe, youth justice has followed a common trajectory, propelled by shifts in social and structural conditions, and as importantly, by discursive shifts on the cause of crime and the perceived need for and purpose of a specialized youth justice system (Muncie, 2005). The first phase or wave was a reaction against preindustrial crime control strategies which aimed to deter crime through public whippings, public executions, transportation to the New World and, as the latter grew increasingly infeasible, penal **incarceration**—sanctions imposed upon children as young as 7, though under English common law it was recognized that a child may not be legally culpable until age 14 (Carrigan, 1998). During this first phase the aim was to prevent crime by saving children from social influences that foster delinquency and adult criminality, perceived to include the immoral milieu of urban poverty, bad parenting and the spread of criminal influences in penal institutions where children and adults were cohoused (Beattie, 1977; Crawford & Newburn, 2003; Moak & Wallace, 2003; Moon, Sundt, Cullen, & Wright, 2000; Platt, 1969; Trépanier, 1991). To counter these influences, children's courts and a host of paid and volunteer court workers were authorized to supervise and **rehabilitate** delinquent and predelinquent children in their own families and communities, or when necessary in foster homes, reformatories and training schools. This child welfare juvenile justice strategy was founded on the "progressive" (Garland, 2000, p. 466) belief that social conditions cause children to enter into criminal pathways and that it is the responsibility of society to prevent crime through interventions that advance children's best interests. This agenda entailed the downplaying of **punishment** and **deterrence** (Butts & Mears, 2001), or in the case of Canada, the formal repudiation of punishment and deterrence as youth justice goals (Bullen, 1991; Carrigan, 1998; Chunn, 1992; Havemann, 1986; Tanner, 2001).

The second phase in juvenile justice emerged in the 1960s and 1970s as concern with causality and rehabilitation gave way to a discourse of **children's rights** and consequently youth accountability, influenced by the growing prominence of human rights codes and the prioritization of legal rights within these codes at international and national levels (Bala, 2005a; Butts & Mears, 2001; Denov, 2005; Giles & Jackson, 2003; Garland, 2000, 2006; Hartnagel, 2004; Havemann, 1986; Reid & Zuker, 2005). This coincided with dramatic increases in official rates of youth and adult crime and violence and a media-disseminated "nothing works" critique of rehabilitation (Cavender, 2004, p. 335; see also Butts & Mears, 2001; Garland, 1996; Maurutto & Hannah-Moffat, 2006; Raynor, 2002). These concurrent developments gave rise to juvenile justice reforms that subordinated child saving and child welfare to crime control, especially in Anglo-American jurisdictions where calls for a get-tough return to deterrence and punishment coincided with the rise of neoliberal economic strategies and neoconservative politics (Giles & Jackson, 2003; Hogeveen, 2005; Knight, 1998; Muncie, 2005; Newburn, 2002; O'Malley, 1999; Pratt, 2002; Schehr, 2005; Stenson, 2005). In the United States particularly, but also in Canada, a re-embrace of youth accountability legitimated juvenile justice reforms that facilitated or mandated the transfer of youths charged with a range of "serious" offences to adult courts, where they face adult sentences including, in the United States, the death penalty (Butts & Mears, 2001; Moak & Wallace, 2003; Roberts, 2004; Ruddell, Mays, & Giever, 1998). However, in more left-leaning or social democratic jurisdictions, including Canada, a latent or persistent focus on **treatment** and rehabilitation facilitated the development of innovative diversion, rehabilitation and **prevention** programs that lead to a global re-embracing of "what works" discourse and policy (Bala, 2005b; Burnett & Appleton, 2004; Crawford & Newburn, 2003; Farrington, 2002; Hillian et al., 2004; Huges & Gilling, 2004; Leonard et al., 2005; Maurutto & Hannah-Moffat, 2006; Muncie, 2005; Newburn, 2002; Ohlin, 1998; O'Malley, 1999; Reid & Zuker, 2005; Raynor, 2002; Surgeon General, 2001; Welsh & Farrington, 2005).

The third or current phase in juvenile justice is marked by this rediscovery that prevention and rehabilitation work to prevent offending and reoffending, especially when targeted toward appropriately assessed risks (Maurutto & Hannah-Moffat, 2006) and when delivered through restorative or "quasi restorative" (Bazemore, 2005, p. 138) community justice initiatives. Equally important, it is influenced by robust findings that incarceration is broadly ineffective both in deterring youth offending and in fostering youth accountability, especially in the case of minor offenders (Raynor, 2002; Reid & Zuker, 2005; Welsh & Farrington, 2005). These rediscoveries coincided with unanimous acceptance and near unanimous ratification (with the exception of the United States and Somalia)[1] of the 1989 United Nations (U.N.) Convention on the Rights of the Child (see also Giles & Jackson, 2003; Muncie, 2005; Reid & Zuker, 2005). This international rights instrument requires states that are party to the convention to recognize

> [T]he right of every child alleged as, accused of, or recognized as having infringed the penal law to be treated in a manner consistent with the promotion of the child's sense of dignity and worth, which reinforces the child's respect for the human rights and fundamental freedoms of others and which takes into account the child's age and the desirability of promoting the child's reintegration and the child's assuming a constructive role in society. (Article 40)

This set of developments coincided with the discovery that publics support prevention and rehabilitation as well as punishment, not only in Canada (Doob & Sprott, 2006; Hartnagel, 2004) but also in the United States (Matthews, 2005; Moon et al., 2000). All of the above contributed to and coincided with the global "mainstreaming" (Leonard et al., 2005, p. 235) of pragmatic and some argue cynical (e.g., Hogeveen, 2005; Jurik et al., 2000) preventative partnerships strategies, which as noted above shift responsibility for crime control and prevention to society at large.

In each of these phases, juvenile justice policy has responded to shifting social, cultural and structural conditions through policy innovations and policy transfers, attesting to the globalized nature of juvenile justice (Edwards & Huges, 2005; Estrada, 2004; Garland, 2006; Newburn, 2002; O'Malley, 1999; Reid & Zuker, 2005; Stenson, 2005). However, the specifics of youth justice are shaped by the "political agency" (Huges & Gilling, 2004, p. 145) of social reformers, politicians, justice stakeholders and members of the general public who develop and implement youth justice legislation and intervention programs at national, subnational and local levels (Edwards & Huges, 2005; Huges & Gilling, 2004;

---

1. The 1989 *U.N. Convention on the Rights of the Child* is the most widely endorsed of all U.N. conventions (Denov, 2005). This landmark instrument, accords children not only legal, social and political rights but also economic rights. Canada ratified the convention in 1991.

Mann et al., 2007; Muncie, 2005; O'Malley, 1999). In Canada, a constitutional division of powers complicates this process, as the Constitution assigns the federal government the authority to legislate and the provinces and territories the authority to administer justice policy (*Constitution Act,* 1867, s. 91, s. 92). Consequently, as this chapter outlines, from the *Juvenile Delinquents Act* forward the Government of Canada has forged legislative compromises that mediate the demands of politicians and their presumed constituencies at federal, provincial-territorial and local levels (Bala, 2005a; Campbell et al., 2001; Hartnagel, 2004; Roberts, 2003, 2004; Trépanier, 1991, 2004). These compromises necessarily bear the influence of democratically elected right-leaning and left-leaning politicians, who pander to their various bases or constituencies. Just as important, they bear the influence of the multiple, ideologically divided justice and social service stakeholder groups and other representatives of the public who participate in legislative consultations and hearings and who implement and bear the consequences of legislative choices.

CHILD SAVING—*THE JUVENILE DELINQUENTS ACT*

Juvenile justice in Canada was established through the activities of Canadian participants in child saving, a social movement that emerged in the United States through the actions of middle-class social reformers "dedicated to rescuing the less fortunately placed in the social order" (Platt, 1969, p. 3). Child saving, which was part of this larger reform agenda, drew upon the so-called discovery of childhood and the spread in the 19th century of notions that children have the right to a childhood free of exploitation, cruelty, neglect, onerous labour and immoral influences; and that society, and therefore the criminal justice system, has a responsibility to guide those "in a condition of delinquency" (*Juvenile Delinquents Act*, s. 3(2)) towards responsible and productive citizenship (Bala, 2005a; Crawford & Newburn, 2003; Denov, 2005; Moak & Wallace, 2003; Reid & Zuker, 2005; Tanner, 2001; Trépanier, 1991).

Canadian Child Savers

Three prominent Canadians led efforts to establish a justice response founded upon these child saving principles in Canada. The first was *Toronto Globe* reporter George Brown, whose 1846 article on the brutal and sadistic treatment of children and other prisoners at Ontario's Kingston Penitentiary fostered moral outrage (Beattie, 1977). The 1849 commission on penal reform that Brown subsequently headed documented two cases of 11-year-old boys who were "flogged" for such "trifling offences as talking, idling, and laughing," the first boy 38 times with rawhide and six times with a cat-o'-nine-tails during a 3-year sentence; the second boy 57 times during an eight-and-a-half month sentence (Beattie, 1977, pp. 26–27). Brown, who saw crime as a moral disease suffered by "a class of men . . . who were the products of drunken and neglectful parents, idleness [and] ignorance . . . that they would pass on to others until in time the whole working population would be infected" (Beattie, 1977, p. 34), recommended separate detention facilities for delinquent children, where they would not be exposed to adult criminal influences, and where they would receive moral guidance and education.

The first Canadian youth reformatory opened little more than a decade later, following passage of an 1857 act that conferred special legal status on children through age 14 charged with minor offences in Upper and Lower Canada, now Ontario and Quebec (Carrigan, 1998). Two decades later, in the 1880s, training schools were established to provide minor delinquents and homeless children moral and industrial training to prepare them for productive citizenship (Carrigan, 1998). These legislative actions were not adequate, however, to address the growing numbers of destitute children who roamed the streets of Toronto, Montreal and other cities on both sides of the Atlantic in the late 19th century. Britain reportedly shipped 73,000 street children to Canada between 1869 and 1911, where they served as unpaid labourers on farms, officially as adoptees (Trépanier, 1991).

The second prominent Canadian child saver was J. J. Kelso, another *Toronto Globe* reporter and founder of the Toronto Children's Aid Society (Bullen, 1991), who brought the plight of Toronto's street children to the attention of the public in an 1887 news article. This article chronicled his unsuccessful attempt to find an institution that would lodge two children he found begging after nightfall, who told him they would be "beaten by their drunken father if they returned home empty handed" (Bullen, 1991, p. 135). Largely in response to Kelso's lobbying, Ontario passed an 1888 act that empowered judges to commit any child under age fourteen who lacked a "proper moral environment . . . due to parental neglect, crime, drunkenness or other vices" and any child under age 16 "found in the company of thieves or prostitutes" to an industrial school, refuge or charitable institution (Bullen, 1991, pp. 138–39). Kelso continued lobbying, however, determined to convince justice professionals and politicians to abandon punishment and direct full attention "to the better care and protection of children as the real preventive of crime in adult years" (Bullen, 1991, p. 140; see also Trépanier, 1991).

In 1893, the Ontario legislature passed what became known as the *Children's Act.* Borrowing heavily from Australia's *Children's Protection Act* of 1872 and England's *Protection Act* of 1889, this legislation imposed fines and imprisonment on anyone who "abandoned, mistreated, or neglected a child in their care," defined as any boy under age 14 and any girl under age 16, as well as "anyone found guilty of procuring a child to beg, perform, or sell goods in public" (Bullen, 1991, p. 143). At the same time, it facilitated the organization of child protection agencies or Children's Aid Societies (CAS) across the province though the creation of a Superintendent of Neglected and Dependent Children, a position that Kelso held for 40 years. Moreover, it empowered this province-wide organization to "apprehend without warrant" any child who "lacked a proper home environment or was found destitute in a public place or in the company of thieves, drunkards, vagrants, or prostitutes" (Bullen, 1991, pp. 143–4). Apprehended children were to be housed in municipally financed shelters until they could be placed in CAS supervised foster homes, ideally with families in the countryside rather than in reformatories or industrial schools, which Kelso argued were "nurseries of vice and hotbeds of crime" (Carrigan, 1998, pp. 47–8).

The third child saver was William L. Scott, who was chairman of the Ottawa Children's Aid Society, son of a federal senator and author of the *Juvenile Delinquents Act*, which addresses juvenile justice and child protection as necessarily mutual endeavours (Trépanier, 1991; Carrigan, 1998). Senator Scott, William Scott's father, introduced the bill that would become the *Juvenile Delinquents Act* in 1907, where it met considerable resistance (Trépanier, 1991). Some parliamentarians objected that the bill was unconstitutional since child protection is a provincial not a federal responsibility. Others argued that the bill infringed on the civil liberties and natural rights of parents. Still others argued that it was simply a bad idea to abandon punishment. However, Scott persuaded a requisite majority that the legislation was warranted given the root causes of delinquency and crime, which he identified as "the morally reprehensible milieu of urban poverty, the negative impact of unfit family environments, and the housing of delinquent children in adult penal facilities" (Trépanier, 1991, p. 212). As important, a requisite majority agreed that it was reasonable and necessary to extend child protection into juvenile justice through the institution of probation, an American innovation designed to prevent future delinquency through CAS or other court-authorized probation officer supervision and surveillance of delinquent children in their own homes or in foster homes (see also Chunn, 1992; Tanner, 2001).

Juvenile Delinquents Act—Provisions

The *Juvenile Delinquents Act* came into effect in 1908 and remained in force for over 70 years (1908–1984), subject to minor modifications through 1970.[2] The act provided a specialized justice response for "any child who violates any provision of the *Criminal Code* or . . . or who is guilty of sexual immorality . . . or vice . . . or who is liable for any other reason to be committed to an industrial school" (section 2(1)). It defined a child as any male or female "actually or apparently" between the ages of 7 and 16, 17 or 18, depending on the province (section 2(1)(2)). The purpose, as reiterated throughout the act (e.g., sections 3(3), 9(1), 39) and as emphasized in section 38, is to save the juvenile delinquent from adult criminality by treating him or her "not as a criminal, but as a misguided and misdirected child, and one needing aid, encouragement, help and assistance," to be provided through "care, custody and discipline" that was to "approximate as nearly as may be that which should be given by his [*sic*] parents."

During the 70 years the *Juvenile Delinquents Act* was in effect, trials were informal and held "separately and apart" from the trials of adults, "without publicity" (section 12(1)), including explicitly publicity through "newspapers and other publications published anywhere in Canada" (section 12(4)). If the court adjudged a child to be in "a condition of delinquency" (section 3(2)), it could suspend or adjourn the case or impose a fine (section 20(1)(a)(b)(c)), or it could "commit the child to the care of custody of a probation officer" (section 20(1)(d)); "allow the child to remain in its home subject to visitation of a probation officer" (section 20(1)(e)); "cause the child to be placed in a suitable family" (section 20(1)(f)); "commit the child to the charge of any children's aid society" (section 20(1)(h)); and as a last resort, "commit the child to an industrial school" (section 20(1)(i)) [defined to include refuges and reformatories (section 1(2))]. Regardless of how a child was dealt with, once adjudged a delinquent a child could be summoned to a hearing and brought before the court at any time and could, at the court's discretion and without a right to appeal (section 5(1)(a)), be placed or committed in any of the ways provided under the act until he or she reached the age of 21 (section 20(3)).

The *Juvenile Delinquents Act* contained two provisions that proscribe or imply punishment, one aimed at parents, the other at delinquents who committed indictable, which is to say serious, offences. First, the act made parental abuse and neglect, and indeed any act by a parent or guardian adjudged to be "producing, promoting, or contributing" to a child's delinquency, a criminal offence punishable by fine or imprisonment (section 33(1)(2)). This provision had particular salience since as outlined above a delinquent child, and therefore the home and parents of a delinquent child, were subject to court surveillance until the child reached the age of 21(see also Chunn, 1992; Bala, 2005b; Tanner, 2001). Second, though this course of action was rare (Roberts, 2004), and was "in no case" to be followed unless the court was "of the opinion that the good of the child and the interest of the community demand it" (section 9(1)), a child age 14 or older who committed an indictable offence could be transferred to an ordinary or adult court. When this occurred, protections from the

---

2. Bala (2005a, footnote #1) notes, the *Juvenile Delinquents Act* was enacted in 1908 as S.C. 1908, c. 40. This act was finalized with minor modifications in 1970.

harms of publicity no longer applied (section 3(4)), nor did protections from the harms of adult criminal influences in custodial institutions (section 13(3)).

Juvenile Delinquents Act—Outcomes

As is well documented, the *Juvenile Delinquents Act* often failed in its benevolent mission to rescue children in need of protection and thereby prevent crime (Tanner, 2001). When the *Juvenile Delinquents Act* was replaced by the far less paternalistic *Young Offenders Act* in 1984, two out of three training school wards were emerging as adult offenders (Leschied & Jaffe, 1991), many of whom were presumably committed not for criminal offences but because they were children of poor and troubled families (Bullen, 1991; Carrigan, 1998; Chunn, 1992; Havemann, 1986; Trépanier, 1991). However, community-based supervision through probation, not committal, was the preferred option; indeed, custodial placement or committal was officially and practically a last resort. Moreover, especially from the 1960s forward, police cautioning of children and youths was a common first response, followed by informal police diversions to community-based programs (Bala, 2005b; Hillian et al., 2004; Raynor, 2002; Tanner, 2001; Trépanier, 2004). These diversion programs emerged in Canada, the United States, Britain and other jurisdictions (Butts & Mears, 2001; Newburn, 2002; Ohlin, 1998) in part because they were cost effective, in part because they seemed to work and also because key stakeholders, judges included, became increasingly uncomfortable with the arbitrary, paternalistic and intrusive infringements of children's and parents' rights that the *Juvenile Delinquents Act* and similar legislation authorized. This emergent sensitivity to rights coincided, however, in Canada (Carrigan, 1998) as in other jurisdictions (Butts & Mears, 2001; Garland, 2000; Newburn, 2002), with mounting public concern over escalating drug use, sexual permissiveness and other forms of youth rebellion. The result was insistent calls from the 1960s forward for youth justice reforms to institute due process protections for youth who come into contact with the law, on the one hand, and to get tough with those who engage in serious and persistent offending, on the other (Bala, 2005a; Havemann, 1986; Tanner, 2001).

The *Young Offenders Act*

The *Young Offenders Act* developed over a 20-year period and was amended three times during the 17 years it was in force, first in 1986 to introduce technical amendments relating to custodial placements, then in 1992 and especially in 1995 to "bifurcate" (Campbell et al., 2001, p. 280) or divide youth offenders and responses to youth offending into two distinct categories, minor and serious (see also Hartnagel, 2004; Hogeveen, 2005).[3] The act and its amendments bear the influence of three competing voices or lobbies: **law and order**, children's rights and treatment or prevention (Bala, 2005a; Campbell et al., 2001; Hartnagel, 2004; Havemann, 1986; Tanner, 2001). The most vocal and arguably the most influential was law and order, a voice represented by law enforcement professionals, authoritarian minded members of the general public, and some Progressive Conservative politicians, who demanded tougher penalties and the prioritization of public safety, rather than youths' assumed

---

3. Similar to the *Juvenile Delinquents Act,* the *Young Offenders Act* authorized a "hierarchy of dispositions" (Rosen, 2000). These ranged from an absolute discharge to committal to an open or closed youth custody facility (s. 20(a-k)). Additionally, the courts could make a conditional supervision order, accompanied by "any reasonable and ancillary conditions as it deemed advisable and in the best interest of the young person and the public" (s. 20(1)(l)).

needs. Complementing this media disseminated call for law and order (Cavender, 2004) was a children's rights lobby represented by child advocates, legal professionals and civil libertarians. This lobby called for the extension of due process rights to children and youths, an end to indeterminate sentencing and generally less state surveillance and intrusion into the lives of poor and troubled families. Less influential and temporarily out of repute were treatment advocates, a modern version of child saves, who faced criticism from both the right and the left (Tanner, 2001). This lobby drew upon the expertise of child welfare workers, psychologists, psychiatrists and other helping professionals in efforts to retain a treatment-based system dedicated to meeting the needs of offending youths and their families.

Young Offenders Act—Contradictory Provisions

In response to law and order demands, the *Young Offenders Act* "recognized and declared" that young persons who commit offences must be held accountable and that society must be afforded necessary protection from their illegal behaviour—a law and order principle prioritized as the first two of eight contradictory (Rosen, 2000) or indeed "inscrutable" (Roberts, 2003, p. 419) goals in the act's Declaration of Principle (section 3(1)(a)(b)). To ensure this accountability, trials were open to the public, including the press, though the personal identity of youths and their families could not be disclosed (sections 17, 38). The act authorized the transfer of any young person age 14 or older who was charged with an indictable offence to an adult court (section 16), as had the *Juvenile Delinquents Act*. However, instead of legislative direction to prioritize the best interests of the youth, the new act instituted a detailed set of criteria to be considered in making a transfer, which both facilitated and discouraged this option (Bala, 2005a; Roberts, 2004). In 1992, these provisions were toughened to stipulate "the protection of society must be paramount" (section 16(1.1)(b)), and in 1995, adult transfer provisions were amended again to institute a presumptive transfer, subject to transfer criteria, of any youth age 16 or older charged with murder, attempted murder or aggravated sexual assault (section 16(1.01)).

Second, the *Young Offenders Act* responds to due process or children's rights concerns, as does the *Canadian Charter of Rights and Freedoms*, which Parliament adopted in 1982, the same year as it passed the *Young Offenders Act* (Bala, 2005a). It accorded young persons full legal rights and also special guarantees of these rights, outlined in three of eight subsections of the *Declaration of Principle*, which cites both the *Canadian Charter of Rights and Freedoms* and the *Canadian Bill of Rights* (section 3(1)(e)(f)(g)). These include a right to the least possible interference with personal freedom consistent with public safety, the right to be heard and participate in sentencing and other justice-related decisions, the right to counsel and the right when in custody to be kept separate and apart from adults (see also section 11). Importantly, the act identified as offences only activities proscribed by federal, provincial or municipal law (section 2), set determinate limits for all custodial and noncustodial dispositions (sections 20, 20.1, 28–32) and prohibited custodial placement to meet child protection, medical or other social needs (section 24(1.1)(a)). Further, it accorded young persons the right to consent to and thereby to refuse medical or psychological treatment (section 20). Moreover, it accorded to youth the right to choose pretrial detention in a youth custody facility rather than accept detention conditions or placement in a group home or with a person designated by the court, including the youth's own parent or parents (section 7). It also accorded youth the right to refuse to participate in any alternatives to judicial proceedings that might be offered (section 4(1)(d)).

Last, interspersed with this mix of accountability and due process measures, the *Young Offenders Act* addressed treatment concerns through provisions that recognize, declare and accommodate young persons' special needs and society's responsibility to address the underlying causes of their offending. As enacted in 1982, and through amendments in 1992 and 1995, it identified rehabilitation and crime prevention as essential to the long-term protection of society (section 3(1)(a–c)). In 1995, clauses were added to the *Declaration of Principle* that authorized multidisciplinary approaches as an effective component of prevention and rehabilitation (section 3(1)(a)(c.1)). Most important, however, from 1982 forward the act included as a guiding principle the principle that "where it is not inconsistent with the protection of society, taking no measures or taking measures other than judicial proceedings under this Act should be considered for dealing with young persons who have committed offences" (section 3(1)(d)). It therefore authorized alternatives measures (section 4). In 1995, Parliament inserted the requirement that youth courts consider these alternatives, specifying that custody "shall only be imposed when all available alternatives to custody that are reasonable in the circumstances have been considered" (section 24(1)(c); see also Bala, 2005a; Roberts, 2004; Rosen, 2000).

Alternative Measures—Encouraging What Works

The *Young Offender Act's* take "no measures" or take alternative measures provisions draw upon an internationally disseminated research literature on "radical non-intervention" (Reid & Zuker, 2005, p. 94) that emerged in evaluations of *Juvenile Delinquents Act*-era diversion programs (Bala, 2005b; Ohlin, 1998; Newburn, 2002; Raynor, 2002; Tanner, 2001). This research supports the contention that "doing less may be just as effective as doing more" (Lundman, 2001, p. 141). Recognizing this, the authors of the *Young Offenders Act* sought to encourage the use of diversions as a way to discourage court processing and custody. However, it laid out two preconditions that simultaneously encouraged their use and undermined this intent. First, an alternative measures program had to be authorized by a province or territory, and second, a young person alleged to have committed an offence had to accept moral (though not legal) responsibility and consent to participate (section 4(3)). If a young person refused to admit he or she had done wrong or failed to comply with the alternative measure imposed, he or she could be formally charged and if found guilty incarcerated (see also Rosen, 2000). Consequently, diversions no longer operated informally at the discretion of police and the communities they served. Rather, especially in Ontario, which imposed the most stringent conditions of any province (Bala, 2005a; Marinelli, 2004), diversions from formal justice functioned more as a justice alternative than as an alternative to justice.[4]

Young Offenders Act—Outcomes

With the exception of Quebec, which adopted a unique, integrated, diversion-based approach to implementing the *Young Offenders Act* (Trépanier, 2004), official youth offending rates climbed across Canada both through increased use of alternative measures (Ontario

---

4. Ontario initially resisted setting up alternative measures programs and then required, as no other province did, that a police charge be laid before an alternative measure was offered. These practices largely account for Ontario's disproportionately high youth charge and incarceration rate throughout the *Young Offenders Act* era (Marinelli, 2004; see also Bala, 2005a).

required that a charge be laid) and through increases in formal police charging (Marinelli, 2004). Except in Quebec, this development coincided with provincial-territorial policy changes that transferred authority for youth corrections from social service ministries to justice ministries (Bala, 2005b). At the same time, youth judges interpreted the *Young Offenders Act* as a call for harsher sentencing (Bala & Kirvan, 1991). The result was dramatic increases in short custodial sentences, or short shocks, often imposed not for a criminal offence but for failure to comply with the terms of a noncustodial sentence or detention condition (Roberts, 2004; Tanner, 2001). Thus, while innovative restorative justice and other community-based programs emerged as a core component of the intervention tool kit of Canadian youth corrections, treatment and rehabilitation receded as youth justice goals (Giles & Jackson, 2003; Hillian et al., 2004; Hogeveen, 2005; Reid & Zuker, 2005). With the exception of Quebec, alternative measures contributed to "net widening" (Bala, 2005b, p. 179) as more offences entered into official youth crime statistics. At the same time, Canada gained international notoriety for having the highest, or one of the highest, youth incarceration rates in the Western world (Bala, 2005a; Calverley, 2006; Hogeveen, 2005; Muncie, 2005; Roberts, 2004; see also Department of Justice Canada, 1998, 2006a).

These developments fuelled mounting public concern that youth were increasingly out of control (Bala, 2005a; Carrigan, 1998; Hogeveen, 2005; Tanner, 2001), concern spurred by media coverage of sensational youth violence trials and alleged lenient sentencing of youth found guilty, and a late 1980s "epidemic" (Surgeon General, 2001) of gang-related youth homicides in the United States. In Canada, there was no increase in this most serious form of youth crime (Dauvergne & Li, 2006). However, between 1984, when the *Young Offenders Act* came into force and 1995, when youth violence rates peaked, official youth violence rates increased dramatically. Most of this increase was for minor acts of violence, leading many criminologists to attribute rate increases to zero-tolerance violence policies in schools and related arenas (e.g., Doob & Sprott, 1998; Tanner, 2001). Polled citizens, however (Cesaroni & Doob, 2003; Hartnagel, 2004; Roberts 2003, 2004; Rosen, 2000), and a vocal contingent of teachers, enforcement professionals, victim advocates and conservative politicians blamed the *Young Offenders Act* and its alleged leniency (Bala, 2005a; Campbell et al., 2001; Carrigan, 1998; Hartnagel, 2004; Hogeveen, 2005).[5]

Managing Discontent

The federal government's initial response was to amend the *Young Offenders Act*, both to toughen measures for serious offenders and to encourage greater use of rehabilitative alternatives to formal justice, as discussed above (Bala, 2005a; Campbell et al., 2001; Hartnagel, 2004; Hogeveen, 2005; Trépanier, 2004). Law and order politicians and advocacy groups, from Alberta and Ontario especially, reacted with furious demands for stronger get-tough measures. In contrast, Quebec politicians and treatment or rehabilitation advocates from across the provinces and territories objected to what they regarded as a progressive weakening of the *Young Offenders Act*'s rehabilitative and prevention potential (see also Bala, 2005b; Denov, 2005; Rosen, 2000). In 1996, the federal and provincial-territorial governments established a task force to consider further reforms, which captured intense polarization along law

---

5. Conservative politicians and polled citizens have persistently blamed crime on the youth justice system and its alleged leniency, often inaccurately claiming or believing that crime rates are high or increasing (Bala, 2005a; Campbell et al., 2001; Cesaroni & Doob, 2003; Clark, 2007; Hartnagel, 2004; Hurst, 2003; Roberts, 2003, 2004).

and order and treatment camps (Bala, 2005a; Hartnagel, 2004; Hogeveen, 2005). To better assess a full breadth of opinion and ideas, Prime Minister Jean Chrétien's Liberal government held parliamentary committee hearings in communities across Canada in 1997 (see review in Bala, 2005a). This committee produced a majority report and two minority reports that document the extent and nature of the polarization, which led the Chrétien Liberals to abandon hope of forging a consensus over how to reform the *Young Offenders Act*. The majority report and the government's subsequent plan for an entirely new youth justice initiative attest to the Chrétien government's embrace of the bifurcated strategy that it introduced through the 1992 and 1995 amendments. More important, they attest to its embrace of preventative partnerships, a strategy that shifts responsibility for crime control and prevention to society at large.

The Youth Criminal Justice Act

The *Youth Criminal Justice Act* is the "cornerstone" (Department of Justice Canada, 2003) of a larger effort to take youth justice in a new direction. The Liberal government introduced its plan for achieving this in 1998 through the Youth Justice Renewal Initiative, a broad-based strategy that situates multiple levels of government, community-based agencies, citizen groups, victims, families and youth as partners who share responsibility for youth crime and its prevention (Department of Justice, 2000, 2006a). The Chrétien government launched this preventative partnerships strategy with a $32 million commitment to combat the root causes of crime and delinquency at the community level, funding that it subsequently expanded to $950 million (Department of Justice Canada, 1998, 2003). This investment, to be spent over a 5-year period ending in 2004–2005, followed upon significant cutbacks in federal transfers for youth justice throughout the *Young Offenders Act* era (Bala, 2005a). These cutbacks fostered, or arguably necessitated, provincial policies of retrenchment that seriously undermined the capacity of community agencies to meet social needs and *Young Offenders Act* goals (Hillian et al., 2004; Giles & Jackson, 2003). The negative impacts of this disinvestment were especially evident in Ontario under the Progressive Conservative government of Mike Harris and his successor Ernie Eves (1995–2003). This government's "draconian" (Chunn & Gavigan, 2004, p. 228) cutbacks to social welfare and social programs coincided with zero-tolerance policies in schools and on the streets backed by the assertion that "crime is caused by criminals, not by social conditions" (Ontario, 1998, as cited in Parnaby, 2003, p. 298; see also Bala, 2005a; Gaetz, 2004; Hogeveen, 2005; Knight, 1998; Mann et al., 2007; O'Malley, 1999).

The Chrétien government's Youth Justice Renewal Initiative promised to restore community capacity to address conditions that foster crime not through direct funding of programs, but rather through activation of partnerships and innovation. This initiative aimed to elicit participation across a broad range of social partners, including child protection, children's mental health, education and recreation (Department of Justice Canada, 2000; see also Mann et al., 2007). To achieve this, the federal government channelled funding to collaborative efforts that depended upon provincial-territorial and local support. Part of this funding was distributed through a community-partnerships fund that promoted, as an "overriding goal," development of pilot projects that funders believed held promise of promoting "fair and just outcomes for criminal justice system youth who are socially excluded or marginalized" (Department of Justice Canada, 2003).[6]

---

6. The text *Youth Justice Renewal Fund Community Partnerships Criteria 2003–04* (Department of Justice, 2003) is unfortunately no longer posted on the Youth Justice Renewal website.

The *Youth Criminal Justice Act* went through three drafts. All three elicited heated political rhetoric and polarized opinion, expressed as is typical in Canada in parliamentary hearings and briefs (Bala, 2005a; Campbell et al., 2001; Hartnagel, 2004). Members of the Progressive Conservative and Reform parties (since united into the Conservative Party), denounced the bill as yet more Liberal leniency. They and other law and order critics decried the federal government's refusal to lower the age of youth accountability to age 10, its refusal to enshrine deterrence and denunciation as youth justice goals and generally its persistent "mollycoddling" (Hartnagel, 2004, p. 361) of youth offenders. The Mike Harris Ontario government proposed over 100 amendments to "finally get tough on youth crime" (Ontario, 2001, as cited in Bala, 2005a, p. 49). In contrast, Quebec lobbied to retain the *Young Offenders Act* (Trépanier, 2004). Indeed, Quebec and a chorus of "left voices" (Doob & Sprott, 2006, p. 230) from across Canada called for the elimination of punitive language and provisions that emphasize justice, accountability, proportionality, consequences and sanctions; the abolition of presumptive adult sentences; and the prioritization of rehabilitation and prevention as the principle aims of youth justice (e.g., Denov, 2005; Giles & Jackson, 2003; Hogeveen, 2005).

The *Youth Criminal Justice Act*—Philosophy and Provisions

The final draft of the *Youth Criminal Justice Act* (C-7) received royal assent on February 19, 2003, and entered into force April 1, 2003 (Department of Justice Canada, 2006a). Inevitably a legislative compromise, it endeavours to satisfy and "hold the line" (Roberts, 2003, p. 416) against penal forces by shifting responsibility for preventing crime and sanctioning minor offenders to society as a whole, while reserving custody for persistent, non-compliant and seriously violent youth offenders (Department of Justice Canada, 2006a). It is a complex, lengthy, highly directive, and, despite the polarized forces that shaped it, remarkably "adaptive" (Garland, 1996, p. 445) to what-works evidence, reviewed above.[7]

The preamble sets out the *Youth Criminal Justice Act*'s philosophical underpinnings in five points. First, members of society share a responsibility to address the needs of young people. Second, society should "take reasonable steps to prevent youth crime" by providing guidance and support to youth at risk. Third, information about youth crime, the youth justice system and the effectiveness of measures to address youth crime should be publicly available. Forth, young people have rights and special safeguards to these rights under international and Canadian law (children's rights), namely the *U.N. Convention on the Rights of the Child*, the *Canadian Charter of Rights and Freedoms* and the *Canadian Bill of Rights*. Finally, "Canadian society should have a youth criminal justice system that commands respect, takes into account the interests of victims, fosters responsibility and ensures accountability through meaningful consequences and effective rehabilitation and reintegration, and that reserves its most serious intervention for the most serious crimes and reduces the over-reliance on incarceration for non-violent young persons."

These "lofty objectives" (Barnhorst, 2004, p. 244) are reiterated in the *Declaration of Principle* in s. 3(1)(a):

> The youth criminal justice system is intended to (i) prevent crime by addressing the circumstances underlying a young person's offending behaviour, (ii) rehabilitate young persons who commit offences and reintegrate them into society, and (iii) ensure that a young person is subject

---

7. David Garland (1996, p. 445–446) contrasts "adaptive strategies" which accommodate "what works" evidence, with "strategies of denial," which deny, ignore or challenge this body of evidence.

to meaningful consequences for his or her offence in order to promote the long-term protection of the public (s. 3(1)(a)(i)(ii)(iii)).

At the same time, within the limits of fair and proportionate accountability, the *Declaration of Principle* states that youth justice measures should reinforce respect for societal values; encourage repair of harm to victims and the community; be meaningful given the young person's needs and level of development; involve, where appropriate, parents, family members, the community and social or other agencies; and finally, respect gender, ethnic, cultural and linguistic differences and respond to the needs of youth with special requirements, including specifically Aboriginal youth (section 3(1)(c)(i)(ii)(iii)(iv)).

On the level of practice, the act's major and overriding purpose is to reduce overreliance on the courts and custody, not simply through a cynical bifurcation of youths and offences into minor and serious categories, but through a series of graduated extrajudicial and judicial, noncustodial and custodial sanctioning options that are designed to address the needs of all youth.[8] No matter how serious an offence, the *Youth Criminal Justice Act* requires the courts to consider all available sanctions other than custody, apply the least restrictive sentence that is consistent with this aim and choose a sentence that is "most likely to rehabilitate the young person and reintegrate him or her into society, and promote a sense of responsibility in the young person" (section 38(2)(ii)(iii)). The purpose of youth sentences is expressly not to deter, denounce, or punish (Roberts, 2004). It is to "responsibilize" (Mann et al., 2007, p. 43) and support youth in their struggle toward citizenship.

To achieve this inclusive aim the *Youth Criminal Justice Act* institutes a highly structured series of discretionary mechanisms (Barnhorst, 2004). First, the act directs police to consider the extrajudicial measure police have always had of taking no action (see Harris et al., 2004, p. 376). Next, police are directed to consider and use warnings, cautions and referrals to community agencies (sections 6–9), measures that are "presumed to be adequate" (s. 4(c)) to hold first-time nonviolent youth offenders accountable. In the event police decide to go beyond a warning, caution or referral, the act provides extrajudicial sanctions (section 10). This course of action is taken at the discretion of the Crown and is intended for youths who admit moral guilt and agree to participate in an extrajudicial sanctions process that may or may not include a conference (sections 2(1), 18(2)(e), 19) or other restorative justice intervention (see Harris et al., 2004; Hillian et al., 2004). A case is to go before a youth court only in the event an extrajudicial sanction is deemed inadequate or is rejected by the youth. For cases that do go before the court, custody is "restricted" to youth found guilty of violence, youth who have failed more than twice to comply with a noncustodial sentence, youth found guilty of an indictable offence for which an adult would receive a sentence of incarceration longer than 2 years and exceptional cases where aggravating circumstances make a noncustodial sentence inconsistent with the goals of sentencing (section 39(1)(a)(b)(c)(d)).

To further minimize the use of custody, the act provides for a range of intense sentencing options that incorporate community-based supervision and sanctioning for even the most serious youth offenders. These include, with varying conditions to be set by the court (s. 42(1)(c)), orders to attend an intensive support and supervision program (section 42(2)(l)), orders to attend a nonresidential program (section 42(2)(m)) and deferred custody

---

8. Butts & Mears (2001) and Matthews (2005) are among those who regard the construct bifurcation as inadequate to capture the range and complexity of sentencing options instituted in third phase juvenile justice. Those who find this construct useful include Campbell et al., 2001; Hartnagel, 2004; Hogeveen, 2005; Hughes & Gilling, 2004; Newburn, 2002; Pratt, 2002.

and supervision orders (section 42(2)(p)). As important, with rare exception the last third of a youth custody sentence must be served in the community under conditions that include intensive supervision and support under the direction of a youth worker, who is to work with the youth to ensure his or her reintegration and desistance from future offending (sections 2(1), 42(2)(n), 90). At the same time, the *Youth Criminal Justice Act* places restrictions on the use of pretrial detention (ss. 28–29), and prohibits the use of either pretrial or posttrial custody to meet child protection, child welfare or child mental health needs (section 39(4)).

This range of options for court processed youth is complemented by the act's most controversial set of provisions, those which authorize a presumptive adult sentence and public disclosure of the identity of any young person age 14 or older found guilty of an expanded range of a serious violent offences, namely murder, attempted murder, aggravated sexual assault, and the commission of a third "serious violent offence" (sections 61–73, see also ss. 2(1), 42(9)). Consistent with the spirit of the act as a whole, this option, which replaces transfers to adult courts, is to be imposed subject to a "test" that curtails its overuse. Specifically, the youth court must consider "the seriousness and circumstances of the offence, and the age, maturity, character, background and previous record of the young person and any other factors that the court considers relevant," and most importantly, it must "be of the opinion" that a youth sentence, imposed in accordance with the purpose and principles of sentencing as laid out in sections 3 and 38, would not be of sufficient length to achieve these goals (section 72(1)). As the act repeatedly makes clear, whether the court is imposing a youth sentence or an adult length sentence, it is required to apply the least restrictive sentence that is consistent with promoting a sense of responsibility in the young person while fostering his or her rehabilitation and reintegration. Deterrence, denunciation and punishment are explicitly not youth justice goals even when an adult-length sentence is imposed (Roberts, 2004).

Youth Criminal Justice Act—Outcomes

The first outcome of the *Youth Criminal Justice Act* came in the form of a legal challenge. On March 31, 2003, the day before the *Youth Criminal Justice Act* came into force, Quebec's highest court ruled s. 72(2) a violation of the *Canadian Charter of Rights and Freedoms* (*Quebec v. Canada*). In particular, the Quebec Court of Appeal ruled that placing the onus on a youth to demonstrate why they should not receive an adult sentence and why their identity should not be disclosed in the event they do violates principles of fundamental justice guaranteed under section 7 of the *Charter*. In March 2006, the Ontario Court of Appeal similarly ruled that sections 62 and 63, subsections 64(1) and (5), section 70, subsections 72(1) and (2) and subsection 73(1) violate the *Charter* (*R. v. D.B.*). In contrast, also in March 2006, British Columbia's highest court ruled that given the test in section 72(1), the full set of presumptive adult sentence provisions are reasonable, and consistent with the aims of justice (*R. v. K.D.T.*). These contradictory actions speak to the unsettled status of the *Youth Criminal Justice Act*, and the possibility, or perhaps likelihood, of a Supreme Court challenge to the act's most serious sanctioning provisions. In short, one outcome of the *Youth Criminal Justice Act* is continuing controversy and polarization on how to address the problem of serious youth offending (Bala, 2005a; Doob & Sprott, 2006; Roberts, 2004; Trépanier, 2004).

A second set of outcomes are more hopeful. It appears that the courts and police are interpreting sections of the act that aim to reduce overuse of the courts and custody as Parliament intended (Bala, 2005a; Barnhorst, 2004; Doob & Sprott, 2006). Since the act came into effect, youth crime and youth *incarceration* rates have both declined significantly.

Three facts stand out. First, there has been a significant increase in police reported incidents "cleared otherwise" than through the laying of a charge, up from 43% of all police recorded incidents in 2002–2003 to 57% in 2004–2005 (Gannon, 2006, p. 21). This proportional increase in police discretion attests to at least the surface success of the act's extrajudicial measures provisions (Harris et al., 2004). Second, over this period the youth crime rate, calculated to include both apprehended and charged youth, has also declined. This decline is part of a 15-year de-escalation in both youth and adult crime, including violent crime (Gannon, 2006).[9] Importantly, this is evident not only in official statistics but also in victimization survey findings, which are generally considered to be a better or more accurate measure of the true incidence of crime (Bala, 2005a; Cesaroni & Doob, 2003; Hurst, 2003). Finally, since the coming into force of the *Youth Criminal Justice Act* the youth incarceration rate has declined 33% (Calverley, 2007, p. 9; see also Cooke & Finlay, 2007). This decline also participates in a longer trend. Indeed, since the final set of *Young Offender Act* amendments in 1995, which instituted both presumptive transfers to adult courts and restrictions on the use of custody for nonviolent offences, Canadian youth custody rates have dropped a full 57% (Calverley, 2007, p. 9). This incarceration decline is a result of decreasing use of both sentenced custody and pretrial detention. It is therefore no longer, at the time of this writing (April 22, 2007), feasible to assert that Canada participates in an increasingly punitive response to youth offending or that Canada has the highest youth incarceration rate in the Western world (see Doob & Sprott, 2006).

The third outcome is the issue of how the system is dealing with youth for whom youth courts and custody are reserved. Since the *Youth Criminal Justice Act* came into force, cases that come before the youth courts have become on average far more serious, complex and lengthier (Thomas, 2005). This is to say, the act's bifurcated or graduated strategy is effectively capturing and targeting smaller numbers of persistent, noncompliant and seriously violent youth offenders for intensive intervention. As has been the case from the *Juvenile Delinquents Act* forward, these youth are overwhelmingly from economically and socially marginalized families and communities (Bala, 2005b; Bala & Kirvan, 1991; Gaetz, 2004; Havemann, 1986). Most dramatically overrepresented among serious youth offenders are Aboriginal youth (Roberts & Melchers, 2003), who in 2003–2004 were seven times more likely to be victims and 10 times more likely to be perpetrators of homicide than non-Aboriginal youth (Brzozowski, Taylor-Butts, & Johnson, 2006, p. 8). Indeed, Aboriginal youth comprised 5% of the youth population in 2004–2005 but accounted for one in four youth in sentenced custody and one in five youth in pretrial detention (Calverley, 2007, p. 6).

Whether they are Aboriginal or non-Aboriginal, research confirms that impoverished youth and their families face more than economic disadvantage and deprivation, they face disproportionately high rates of expected and actual violence (Brzozowski et al., 2006; Eisler & Schissel, 2004). Unlike youth in the broad mainstream, whose minor, episodic and sometimes serious altercations and misadventures bring them into occasional conflict with the law (Tanner, 2001); these youth command repeated and intensive criminal justice attention. Importantly, their problems and hardships have often been exacerbated by intrusive and ineffective child protection interventions, interventions that Ontario youth identify as a

---

9. Numbers of Canadian youth homicides vary from year to year, at a persistently low level. Highs of 65–68 youth homicides are recorded for 1975, 1995 and 2005. In contrast, in 2001 there were 32 youth homicides, fewer than any year since 1969. Similar low numbers (36 or lower) are recorded for 1984, 1987 and 1993 (Dauvergne & Li, 2006).

gateway into the youth justice system (Cooke & Finlay, 2007).[10] It will take years to determine whether the adaptive mix of custodial and community-based support and supervision measures authorized under the Youth Criminal Justice System work, or not, to reduce the rates at which these youth enter into adult criminal pathways. Emergent research on Canadian corrections gives reason to hope that they will (Cooke & Finlay, 2007; Farrington, 2002; Maurutto & Hannah-Moffat, 2006; Raynor, 2002; Welsh & Farrington, 2005).

Conclusion

The *Youth Criminal Justice Act* is the culmination of a century and a half development. From the establishment of reformatories in the 1850s, through the 76-year long *Juvenile Delinquent Act*, the far shorter-lived *Young Offenders Act*, and into our "new age" (Harris et al., 2004, 368) *Youth Criminal Justice Act*, federal and provincial-territorial governments and community partners have struggled to institute policies that balance societal protection, just and appropriate sanctions, and rehabilitation and reintegration of youth offenders. As stated in the preamble and numerous Department of Justice Canada texts (e.g., 1998, 2000, 2003a, 2003b, 2006a), the new act exists to promote the long-term protection of the public through activation of community-based prevention, sanctioning, and rehabilitation efforts that require the support and involvement of all levels of government and all Canadians. It exists to reduce overuse of the courts and custody by reserving this option for violent and persistent youth offenders, for whom intensive custodial and community-based interventions and in rare instances adult-length sentences are retained. Most important, it exists to restore public confidence in the youth justice system.

Youth Justice Renewal texts emphasize that the first goal, the long term protection of the public, is beyond the justice system to deliver (Department of Justice Canada, 2006a; see also 1998a, 1998b, 2000, 2005). At the same time, these texts recognize that the federal government must assume a capacity building role. The federal government's initial $950 million investment is now spent, however, and to date there has been no new funding announcement. Rather, nongovernmental organizations and Aboriginal organizations interested in youth justice issues may apply for grants "to test innovative features" of the act; "broaden the range and nature of community groups involvement;" develop "informational tools to increase public understanding, participation, confidence and trust in the justice system;" and in the case of Aboriginal communities, "develop capacity to participate in and/or deliver community-based youth justice options" (Department of Justice Canada, 2006b). Unfortunately, none of these funding goals addresses the root or underlying causes that lead youth to enter into a life of crime, though this is a stated aim of Youth Justice Renewal (Department of Justice Canada, 1998, 2000, 2005, 2006a). As researchers from across Western jurisdictions emphasize, the long-term protection of society requires no less (e.g., Bazemore, 2005; Hughes & Gilling, 2004; Garland, 1996, 2000; Hillian et al., 2004; Hogeveen, 2005; Jurik et al., 2000; Mann et al., 2007; Ohlin, 1998; Pratt, 2002).

The second goal, to reduce overuse of the courts and custody, is within the capacity of the youth justice system, and as reviewed above, appears on the surface to have occurred.

---

10. A survey of all Ontario youth custody facilities found that a third of youth in custody had been in the care of the child welfare system, and half had child welfare involvement (Cooke & Finlay, 2007, p. 18). The survey was conducted by the Office of the Child and Family Services.

However, as other commentators note, community justice or preventative partnerships strategies carry dangers of net-widening, and as importantly overreach and rights infringements. Police referrals can serve as off the record coercion into treatment (Barnhorst, 2004); conferences can negotiate harsher sanctions than a court would impose (Harris et al., 2004); and community supervision with conditions can foster breaches, leading to charges, leading to more breaches and ultimately to incarceration even when an initial offence does not warrant custody (Harris et al., 2004; Roberts, 2004).

The *Youth Criminal Justice Act* clearly aims to avoid these dangers or pitfalls (Bala, 2005b; Doob & Sprott, 2006; Reid & Zuker, 2005).[11] A change in the political climate, however, could foster or indeed encourage net-widening and attendant exacerbation of marginalization and exclusion. Specifically, a shift in a volatile and ambivalent left versus right political balance could produce a majority for the Conservative Party of Canada, whose platform outlines a plan to amend the *Youth Criminal Justice Act* to provide effective punishment and deterrence for all youth offenders, and adult trials, not just adult-length sentences, for youth who engage in violent and serious repeat offending:

> A Conservative Government will introduce measures to hold young lawbreakers accountable to their victims and the larger community. A Conservative Government will introduce measures to ensure that violent or serious repeat offenders 14 and over are tried as adults. . . . The justice system for young people will provide effective punishment that deters criminal behaviour and instils a sense of responsibility in young offenders for their behaviour; and gives young people better opportunities for rehabilitation. (Conservative Party Platform, M 83(i)(ii))[12]

The politics of youth justice is at the heart of last challenge facing the *Youth Criminal Justice Act*. This is the challenge to effectively meet the needs of serious youth offenders through measures that promote confidence in the youth justice system. Ultimately, though, youth justice is not likely a decisive issue for a majority of voters, it is up to Canadians to choose between the relatively coherent evidence-based prevention, rehabilitation and reintegration strategy authorized under the current *Youth Criminal Justice Act,* or the more explicitly exclusionary mix of deterrence, punishment and "opportunities for rehabilitation" proposed by the Conservatives. Compromises and contradictions notwithstanding, Canada has resisted punishment and deterrence as formal aims of youth justice for a century. It remains to be seen whether, despite evidence, despite the *U.N. Convention on the Rights of the Child*, and despite the *Charter*, Canada chooses them now. It also remains to be seen how Canada's progressive youth justice stakeholders would implement this choice, how the courts would respond and how practices would vary across the provinces and territories. These contingencies are among those that will shape the type of society that Canada conveys to future generations.

---

11. Net-widening, overreach potentials and rights infringements are widely noted dangers of restorative justice and other community justice strategies (Bazemore, 2005; Burnett & Appleton, 2004; Campbell, 2005; Crawford & Newburn, 2003; Muncie, 2005; Pratt, 2002).

12. At the time of this writing (May 1, 2007), Prime Minister Stephen Harper leads an instable minority government. Polled Canadians' support for the Conservative Party and its Liberal Party, New Democratic Party, Bloc and Green Party opponents is in constant flux, a reflection of collective ambivalence over how best to address four key challenges: the environment, Afghanistan, health care and economic globalization. Despite the Conservative Party's efforts to mobilize law and order sentiments, crime is not shaping up as a pre-election concern, arguably because crime rates are at a 15-year low (Clark, 2007; see also Dauvergne & Li, 2006; Gannon, 2006).

References

Bala, N. (2005a). The development of Canada's youth justice law. In K. Campbell (Ed.), *Understanding youth justice in Canada* (pp. 41–63). Toronto: Pearson.

Bala, N. (2005b). Community-based responses to youth crime: Cautioning, conferencing, and extra-judicial measures. In K. Campbell (Ed.), *Understanding youth justice in Canada* (pp. 176–197). Toronto: Pearson.

Barnhorst, R. (2004). The *Youth Criminal Justice Act:* New directions and implementation issues. *Canadian Journal of Criminology and Criminal Justice, 46,* 231–250.

Bazemore, G. (2005). Whom and how do we reintegrate? Finding community in restorative justice. *Criminology and Public Policy, 4,* 131–148.

Brzozowski, J-A., Taylor-Butts, A., & Johnson, S. (2006). Victimization and offending among the Aboriginal population in Canada. *Juristat, 26,* 1–29.

Bullen, J. (1991). J. J. Kelso and the "new" child-savers: The genesis of the children's aid movement in Ontario. In R. Smandych, G. Dodds, & A. Esau (Eds.), *Dimensions of childhood: Essays on the history of children and youth in Canada* (pp. 135–158). Winnipeg: Legal Research Institute of the University of Manitoba.

Burnett, R., & Appleton, C. (2004). Joined-up services to tackle youth crime: A case study in England. *British Journal of Criminology, 44,* 34–54.

Butts, J. A., & Mears, D. P. (2001). Reviving juvenile justice in a get-tough era. *Youth & Society, 33,* 169–198.

Calverley, D. (2007). Youth custody and community service in Canada, 2004/2005. *Juristat, 27,* 1–18.

Campbell, K., Dufresne, M., & Maclure, R. (2001). Amending youth justice policy in Canada: Discourse, mediation and ambiguity. *Howard Journal of Criminal Justice, 40,* 272–284.

Carrigan, D. O. (1998). *Juvenile delinquency in Canada: A history.* Toronto: Stoddart Publishing.

Cavender, G. (2004). Media and crime policy: A reconsideration of David Garland's The culture of control. *Punishment & Society, 6,* 335–348.

Cesaroni, C., & Doob, A. N. (2003). The decline in support for penal welfarism: Evidence of support among the elite for punitive segregation. *British Journal of Criminology, 43,* 434–441.

Chunn, D. E., & Gavigan, S. A. M. (2004). Welfare law, welfare fraud, and the moral regulation of the "never deserving" poor. *Social and Legal Studies, 13,* 219–243.

Chunn, D. E. (1992). *From punishment to doing good: Family courts and socialized justice in Ontario, 1880–1940.* Toronto: University of Toronto Press.

Clark, C. (2007, April 30). Does Harper's message match the statistics? Recent figures seem to contradict PM's assertions about high rates and trend toward serious offences. *Globe and Mail,* p. A4.

Conservative Party of Canada (2006). *Conservative party platform.* Retrieved on March 28, 2007, from http://www.conservative.ca/EN/2692/41655

Cooke, D., & Finlay, J. (2007). Review of open detention and open custody. *Office of Child and Family Service Advocacy.* Retrieved on March 28, 2007, from http://www.children.gov.on.ca/advocacy/documents/en/Open%20Custody-OpenDetention%20Review.pdf

Crawford, A., & Newburn, T. (2003). *Youth offending and restorative justice: Implementing reform in youth justice.* Devon, UK: Willan.

Dauvergne, M., & Li, G. (2006). Homicide in Canada, 2005. *Juristat, 26,* 1–25.

Department of Justice Canada (2006a). *The Youth Criminal Justice Act: Summary and background.* Retrieved on March 28, 2007, from http://www.justice.gc.ca/en/ps/yj/ycja/explan.html

Department of Justice Canada (2006b). *Funding youth justice*. Retrieved online March 28, 2007, at http://www.justice.gc.ca/en/ps/yj/funding/funding.html

Department of Justice Canada (2005). *A strategy for the renewal of youth justice: A need for balance.* Retrieved on March 28, 2007, from http://www.justice.gc.ca/en/ps/yj/aboutus/yoas4.html

Department of Justice Canada (2003). *Youth Justice Renewal Fund community partnerships criteria 2003–04.* Retrieved on August 28, 2005 from http://canada.justice.gc.ca/en/ps/yj/initiat/criteria.html

Department of Justice Canada (2000). *Community partnerships symposium on youth justice renewal.* Retrieved on March 28, 2007, from http://www.justice.gc.ca/en/ps/yj/partnership/sympo.html

Department of Justice Canada (1998). *Youth justice strategy*. Retrieved on March 29, 2007, from http://canada.justice.gc.ca/en/news/nr/1998/yoasum.html

Denov, M. S. (2005). Children's rights, juvenile justice, and the U.N. Convention on the Rights of the Child: Implications for Canada. In K. Campbell (Ed.), *Understanding youth justice in Canada* (pp. 65–86). Toronto: Pearson.

Doob, A. N., & Sprott, J. B. (2006). Punishing youth crime in Canada: The blind men and the elephant. *Punishment & Society, 8*, 223–233.

Doob, A. N., & Sprott, J. B. (1998). Is the "quality" of youth violence becoming more serious? *Canadian Journal of Criminology, 40*, 185–194.

Eisler, L., & Schissel, B. (2004). Privatization and vulnerability to victimization for Canadian Youth. *Youth Violence and Juvenile Justice, 2*, 359–373.

Estrada, F. (2004). The transformation of the politics of crime in high crime societies. *European Journal of Criminology, 1*, 419–443.

Farrington, D. P. (2002). Developmental criminology and risk-focused prevention. In M. Maguire, R. Morgan, & R. Reiner (Eds.), *The Oxford handbook of criminology* (3rd ed.), (pp. 657–701). Oxford: Oxford University Press.

Gaetz, S. (2004). Safe streets for whom? Homeless youth, social exclusion, and criminal victimization. *Canadian Journal of Criminology and Criminal Justice, 46*, 423–455.

Gannon, M. (2006). Crime statistics in Canada, 2005. *Juristat, 26*, 1–22.

Garland, D. (2006). Concepts of culture in the sociology of punishment. *Theoretical Criminology, 10*, 419–447.

Garland, D. (2000). The culture of high crime societies: Some preconditions of recent "law and order" policies. *British Journal of Criminology, 40*, 347–375.

Garland, D. (1996). The limits of the sovereign state: Strategies of crime control in contemporary society. *British Journal of Criminology, 36*, 445–471.

Giles, C. & Jackson, M. (2003). Bill C-7: The new *Youth Criminal Justice Act:* A darker *Young Offenders Act? International Journal of Comparative and Applied Criminal Justice, 27*, 19–38.

Harris, P., Weagant, B., Cole, D., & Weinper, F. (2004). Working "in the trenches" with the YCJA. *Canadian Journal of Criminology and Criminal Justice, 46*, 367–389.

Hartnagel, T. F. (2004). The rhetoric of youth justice in Canada. *Criminal Justice, 4*, 355–374.

Havemann, P. (1986). From child saving to child blaming: The political economy of the *Young Offenders Act* 1908–1984. In E. Comack & S. Brickey (Eds.), *The social basis of law* (pp. 225–241). Halifax: Garamond Press.

Hillian, D., Reitsma-Street, M., & Hackler, J. (2004). Conferencing in the *Youth Criminal Justice Act* of Canada: Policy developments in British Columbia. *Canadian Journal of Criminology and Criminal Justice, 46*, 343–366.

Hogeveen, B. R. (2005). "If we are tough on crime, if we punish crime, then people get the message": Constructing and governing the punishable young offender in Canada during the late 1990s. *Punishment & Society, 7*, 73–89.

Hughes, G. & Gilling, D. (2004). Mission impossible?: The habitus of the community safety manager and the new expertise in the local partnership governance of crime and safety. *Criminal Justice, 4*, 129–149.

Hurst, L. (2003, July 26). Why fear remains high as crime rates fall. *The Toronto Star*, pp. A1–A17.

Jurik, N. C., Blumenthal, J., Smith, B., & Portillos, E. L. (2000). Organizational cooptation or social change? A critical perspective on community-criminal justice partnerships. *Journal of Contemporary Criminal Justice, 16*, 293–320.

Knight, G. (1998). Hegemony, the media, and new right politics: Ontario in the late 1990s. *Critical Sociology, 24*, 105–129.

Leonard, L., Rosario, G., Scott, C., & Bressan, J. (2005). Building safer communities: Lessons learned from Canada's national strategy. *Canadian Journal of Criminology and Criminal Justice, 47*, 233–250.

Lundman, R. J. (2001). *Prevention and control of juvenile delinquency*. New York: Oxford University Press.

Mann, R. M., Senn, C. Y., Girard, A., & Ackbar, S. (2007). Community-based interventions for at-risk youth in Ontario under Canada's *Youth Criminal Justice Act:* A case study of a "runaway" girl. *Canadian Journal of Criminology and Criminal Justice, 49*, 37–73.

Matthews, R. (2005). The myth of punitiveness. *Theoretical Criminology, 9*, 175–201.

Maurutto, P. & Hannah-Moffat, K. (2006). Assembling risk and the restructuring of penal control. *British Journal of Criminology, 46*, 438–454.

Moak, S. C. & Wallace, L. H. (2003). Legal changes in juvenile justice: Then and now. *Youth Violence and Juvenile Justice, 1*, 289–299.

Moon, M. M., Sundt, J. L., Cullen, F. T., & Wright, J. P. (2000). Is child saving dead? Public support for juvenile rehabilitation. *Crime and Delinquency, 46*, 38–60.

Muncie, J. (2005). The globalization of crime control—The case of youth and juvenile justice. *Theoretical Criminology, 9*, 35–64.

Newburn, T. (2002). Young people, crime, and youth justice. In M. Maguire, R. Morgan, & R. Reiner (Eds.), *The Oxford handbook of criminology* (3rd ed.) (pp. 531–578). Oxford: Oxford University Press.

O'Malley, P. (1999). Volatile and contradictory punishment. *Theoretical Criminology, 3*, 175–196.

Parnaby, P. (2003). Disaster through dirty windshields: Law, order and Toronto's squeegee kids. *Canadian Journal of Sociology, 28*, 281–307.

Pratt, J. (2002). Critical criminology and the punitive society: Some new "visions of social control." In K. Carrington & R. Hogg (Eds.), *Critical criminology: Issues, debates, challenges* (pp. 168–184). Devon, UK: Willan.

Raynor, P. (2002). Community penalties: Probation, punishment, and "what works." In M. Maguire, R. Morgan, & R. Reiner (Eds.), *The Oxford handbook of criminology* (3rd ed.) (pp. 1168–1205). Oxford: Oxford University Press.

Reid, S. A., & Zuker, M. A. (2005). Conceptual frameworks for understanding youth justice in Canada: From the *Juvenile Delinquents Act* to the *Youth Criminal Justice Act*. In K. Campbell (Ed.), *Understanding youth justice in Canada* (pp. 89–113). Toronto: Pearson.

Roberts, J. V. (2004). Harmonizing the sentencing of young and adult offenders: A comparison of the *Youth Criminal Justice Act* and Part XXIII of the *Criminal Code. Canadian Journal of Criminology and Criminal Justice, 46,* 301–326.

Roberts, J. V. (2003). Sentencing juvenile offenders in Canada: An analysis of recent reform legislation. *Journal of Contemporary Criminal Justice, 4,* 413–434.

Roberts, J. V., & Melchers, R. (2003). The incarceration of Aboriginal offenders: Trends from 1978–2001. *Canadian Journal of Criminology and Criminal Justice, 45,* 211–242.

Rosen, P. (2000). *The Young Offenders Act.* Government of Canada. Retrieved on March 28, 2007, from http://dsp-psd.communication.gc.ca/Pilot/LoPBdP/CIR/8613-e.htm

Ruddell, R., Mays, G. L., & Giever, D. M. (1998). Transferring juveniles to adult courts: Recent trends and issues in Canada and the United States. *Juvenile and Family Court Journal, 49,* 1–15.

Schehr, R. C. (2005). Conventional risk discourse and the proliferation of fear. *Criminal Justice Policy Review, 16,* 38–58.

Stenson, K. (2005). Sovereignty, biopolitics and the local government of crime in Britain. *Theoretical Criminology, 9,* 265–287.

Surgeon General (2001). *Youth violence: A report of the surgeon general.* Surgeon General. Retrieved on March 28, 2007, from http://www.surgeongeneral.gov/library/youthviolence/

Tanner, J. (2001). *Teenage troubles: Youth and deviance in Canada* (2nd ed.). Toronto: Nelson Thomson Learning.

Thomas, J. (2005). Youth Court Statistics, 2003–04. *Juristat, 25,* 1–18.

Trépanier, J. (2004). What did Quebec not want? Opposition to the adoption of the *Youth Criminal Justice Act* in Quebec. *Canadian Journal of Criminology and Criminal Justice, 46,* 273–299.

Trépanier, J. (1991). The origins of the *Juvenile Delinquent Act* of 1908: Controlling delinquency through seeking its causes and through youth protection. In R. Smandych, G. Dodds, & A. Esau (Eds.), *Dimensions of childhood: Essays on the history of children and youth in Canada* (pp. 205–232). Winnipeg: Legal Research Institute of the University of Manitoba.

Welsh, B. C., & Farrington, D. P. (2005). Evidence-based crime prevention: Conclusions and directions for a safer society. *Canadian Journal of Criminology and Criminal Justice, 47,* 337–354.

Legislation

Criminal Code, R.S.C. 1985, c. C-46.

Canadian Charter of Rights and Freedoms, Schedule B, *Constitution Act, 1982.*

Canadian Bill of Rights (1960, c. 44).

Constitution Act, 1867 (British North American Act).

United Nations Convention on the Rights of the Child (CRC), 1989.

Juvenile Delinquents Act, R.S.C. 1970, c. J-3.

Youth Criminal Justice Act, S.C. 2002, c.1.

Young Offenders Act, R.S.C. 1985, c.Y-1.

Case Law

R. v. K.D.T. *(Youth Criminal Justice Act)* 2006 BCCA60.

R. v. D.B. (A Young Offender) OCA 20060324 C42719 C42923.

Québec (Minister of Justice) v. Canada (Minister of Justice) (2003), 175 C.C.C. (3d) 321.

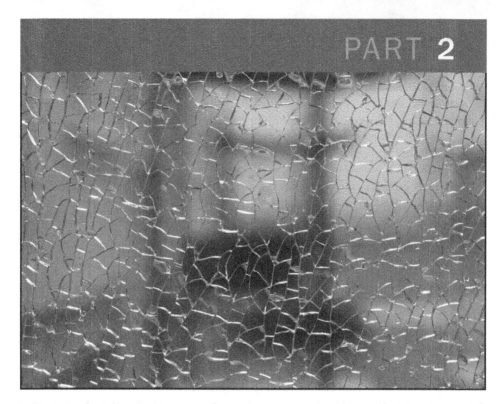

The Rise of Criminological Thought: The Legacy of the 17th, 18th, 19th and 20th Centuries

Chapter 5   The Pathological Approach to Crime: Individually Based Theories
Heidi Rimke, *University of Winnipeg*

Chapter 6   Sociological Theories of Crime and Criminality
Kirsten Kramar, *University of Winnipeg*

The Pathological Approach to Crime
Individually Based Theories
Heidi Rimke, University of Winnipeg

INTRODUCTION

The notions of the criminal as "sick," or, specifically, "psychopathic" are prevalent in North American society, finding regular expression in academic writings, in everyday life and in popular media and culture alike. Persons suspected or convicted of crimes are commonly represented as inherently bad or defective individuals suffering from a **pathology**, or abnormal condition. One need only think of Oliver Stone's 1994 movie *Natural Born Killers* and its sensationalistic storyline that documents the random, senseless murder spree of two young lovers who themselves insist they were "born bad." Paul Bernardo, convicted in 1995 of raping and murdering two teenage girls, is also commonly presented in the media as a sociopathic/psychopathic/antisocial personality suffering from a clinical pathology. More recent is the case of Vince Weiguang Li, who stood trial for the 2008 stabbing, beheading and cannibalization of 22-year-old Tim McLean. Li was found not criminally responsible on account of a mental disorder (NCRMD), sparking public demands for reinstating the death penalty and abolishing human rights for the mentally ill. In a culture obsessed with consuming crime, the spectacle and horrors of these cases often overshadow serious academic examination, thus perpetuating various problematic assumptions about the nature of criminality.

The idea that some people are criminal by nature and commit crimes due to their essential makeup as human beings is a powerfully alluring idea, but one that poses serious questions and challenges. This chapter provides an overview of the historical development of nonsociological theories that focus on criminal conduct and criminality as pathology. In order to understand individually based theories of criminality, it is necessary to examine their history and social contexts of emergence. Understanding the history of the development of pathological approaches is important in this context because 21st-century criminological theory is the product of theories developed in previous centuries. While most of these theories did not originate in Canada, they have influenced Canadian criminal justice policies and university based research, not to mention popular representations and misconceptions about crime and criminality in contemporary society. As will be seen, individually based theories of criminality are distinct from the sociological theories presented in Chapter 6, and they are based on a different set of assumptions and goals.

Individually based theories generally rely on the pathological perspective rooted in the tradition of Western human sciences whereby criminality is akin to a sickness or illness. Central to the pathological approach is the idea that criminality is inherent in the individual (e.g., in the mind, hormones, personality, brain, neurotransmitters or genetic makeup) and that it can be explained by isolating biological differences, psychological differences, or both in individuals. Another basic feature of the pathological approach is that it is positivist. The scientific approach or **positivism** in criminology assumes that the methods of the natural sciences should be applied to the objective (value-free) study of criminality. The basis of knowledge (epistemology) is dispassionate data collection and analysis based on observation, experimentation and measurement and is thus quantitative rather than qualitative in its approach. The emergence of positivistic criminology in the late 19th century was part of broader movement whereby all social problems were increasingly viewed through the widening lens of science. Biogenic and psychogenic theories are a hallmark of the pathological approach to crime and criminal conduct. In order to explain criminal behaviour, biological and/or psychological factors and attributes are isolated and measured. The body and/or mind/psyche are taken as flawed and at the root of criminal activity. Positivists assumed that human conduct was determined by biological, psychological or psychiatric factors. The new perspective argued that criminality had natural causes beyond individual control; thus, with the proper application of the positivist method, social progress would be achieved and social ills such as crime (and vice) would be eliminated.

Constructing a science of criminality has proven problematic and elusive, yet millions of dollars are spent researching it and millions of viewers tune in to watch enormously popular crime shows based on these ideas. Biological explanations have historically been among the most popular and influential of all theories of crime. Today they are again proliferating in academia, recast in terms of evolutionary psychology, biochemistry, neuropsychology, behavioural genetics and so on.

While popular conceptions of the criminal as "psychopath," or in some other way biologically constituted have become taken for granted in everyday discourses, sociological approaches have long rejected this hypothesis on theoretical, empirical and ethical grounds (Taylor, Walton, & Young, 1971). However, the resurgence of biological theories—in academia and popular culture alike—makes it imperative to address the serious implications of the concept of individual criminality whether defined in biological, psychological or psychiatric terms.

The crusade to establish bio- and psycho-scientific theories of crime and criminality has a long, erratic and tragic history. Before the 18th century, ideas about evil and human nature were essentially derived from a religious framework developed by church authorities. Supernatural theories of criminality were eventually rejected and replaced by philosophical explanations developed by the classical school in the 18th century, postulating that crime was the result of calculated choices made by rational human agents rather than the result of mystical forces circulating the cosmos. With the birth of positive philosophy during the Enlightenment, scientific theories of crime and criminality emerged and replaced the speculative philosophy of the classical theories. The positivist criminology of the late 19th and early 20th centuries hypothesized that criminality was the result of biological, physiological or psychological factors, or all three. Such new explanations were the product and effects of the growing scientific rationality of society. Theories shifted towards individual explanations that searched for "endogenous" (or internal) causes rooted in the body and mind of the individual.

We will look at each of these approaches in turn.

THE DEMONOLOGICAL APPROACH: CRIMINALITY AS SIN

The oldest known explanation for criminality is the demonological perspective or spiritualism characteristic of prescientific Europe during the Middle Ages (1300–1700 AD) (Pfohl, 1985). The demonological approach derives its basis from religious authority and viewed crime as a sin and the criminal as a sinner. This framework sees crime and criminality as the product of supernatural or "otherworldly" forces operating on mortal beings in a spiritual battle between good and evil. Two main explanations for transgression dominate this viewpoint: temptation and demonic possession. The cause of criminal conduct is thus supernatural or preternatural; that is, it stems from otherworldly forces external to and coercive of the individual neatly summed up by the phrase "the devil made me do it."

Although the chapter is organized around historical developments and paradigm shifts, it is imperative to understand that hard and fast breaks between perspectives are more fictitious than factual. For example, it is both naïve and incorrect to assume that the religious perspective is simply a relic of the past rather than an influential force on modern discourses operating in contemporary society. The doctrine of moral insanity, the precursor to "antisocial personality disorder," or psychopathy, is an example of the hybridization of religious views and scientific discourses: Psychiatric discourses about "moral insanity" were the product of both Christian moralism and scientific theories. Thus what was viewed as a sin or sinfulness became renamed spiritualism still impacts the operation of law; the mandates that politicians mobilize during election campaigns when they frequently call for punishments to be based on retribution; in corrections, where various kinds of chaplaincy remain important; and in treatment, for instance, in any one of the number of available "twelve-step" programs based on the work of Alcoholics Anonymous and the idea of a "higher power."

THE CLASSICAL AND NEOCLASSICAL SCHOOLS: CRIMINALITY AS HEDONISM

The Enlightenment, emerging in the late 17th century and dominating the 18th, produced the first formal academic theories about criminality. These theories, dating from the 18th century, sought to establish the criminal as a calculating individual exercising rationality and free will. They rejected the perspective that had dominated for many centuries which viewed transgression as a sin committed against God owing to human weakness in the face of exogenous or external forces such as demons or evil spirits that compelled particular behaviours. The cruel and arbitrary punishment characteristic of earlier centuries, organized around ideas of revenge and retribution, was increasingly criticized as barbaric, inhumane and ineffective. For example, the English penal code was referred to as the "bloody code" because over 250 offences were punishable by death. In 1878, a 7-year-old girl was sentenced to death by the Canadian State for stealing a petticoat.

In the global North and West, social and political upheavals such as the French and American revolutions overthrew the feudal system of monarchical power, resulting in governmental reform and major political gains for the middle classes. One of the principal operations of this emergent Enlightenment positivism was the provision of a scientifically constructed framework deployed to oversee the "health" of disruptive and otherwise "abnormal" individuals. The law was essential in ensuring the new social order could be policed. The campaign for property-owner rights and demands for enlightened legal rationality, as seen in the writings of classical liberal utilitarian philosophers such as Jeremy Bentham and John Stuart Mill, occurred alongside the development of industrial capitalism. As Newburn (2007, p. 115) writes: "Property needed to be protected, systems of production maintained, workers disciplined and urban centres given a degree of order."

Influenced by the ideas emerging from British utilitarianism and Enlightenment thought more generally, Cesare Beccaria (1738–1794) and the classical school rejected religious authority in law and criminal matters. For the utilitarians, punishment could be justified only if it served the greatest good for the greatest number. This philosophical approach set out to provide a rational theory of crime and criminality. At the heart of the classical conception is the view of the criminal as a rational actor endowed with free will and reason. According to the classical school, crime is committed based upon a cost-benefit calculation. This approach viewed the individual as hedonistic, guided by a pleasure–pain principle used to calculate the risks and rewards involved in one's choice to act. The pleasure–pain principle, or **felicity calculus**, states that human beings conduct themselves in such ways as to maximize pleasure and minimize pain. The theory argued that the severity of the punishment had to override the pleasure derived from committing the crime to deter criminality. This provided the rationale to devise a graduated system of punishment. In order to be effective, the goal of punishment was deterrence—the prevention of criminal activity—by making a lasting impression on the minds of offenders and others, with the least necessary torment to the body of the offender. The foundation of modern criminal justice systems was built on the classical tenet that the punishment must fit the crime; excessive punishment was not effective. Previously, punishment had been both harsh and very public (Foucault, 1977) but the classical theorists pointed out this had failed to reduce criminal conduct. This school of thought resulted in a reduction of barbarity and helped establish "modern" criminal justice systems.

The classical approach, in treating individuals as rational agents, overlooked problems of incapacity and impairment as well as other important differences based on age. This gave birth to what is referred to as neoclassical thought where mitigating factors and other allowances are made to accommodate issues of age, mental illness and learning difficulties, for example. The neoclassical line of thought can be seen in most modern criminal justice legislation. The *Youth Criminal Justice Act* is a good example illustrating this influence on Canadian criminal justice policy.

THE PATHOLOGICAL APPROACH: CRIMINALITY AS SICKNESS

The classical approach to crime and criminality dominated for approximately 100 years until criminological positivism emerged in the last half of the 19th century, giving rise to scientific criminology. An "enlightened" modern science determined that criminality was chiefly a state due to a disordered psyche, mind or body. As Foucault (1987, p. 1988) has shown, "the psychiatrization of the criminal" in the 19th century involved creating a new social group and scientific identity to fear and govern. The positivist school emerged as a loose network of experts from diverse disciplines and fields that took the individual criminal as its object of concern and is best understood as an aspect of the development of what are broadly understood as **the human sciences**. The disciplinary composition thus moves beyond what is typically thought of as the social sciences to include medical knowledges and other disciplines such as social work, sexology, kinesiology and so forth. It is important to bear in mind that the theories surveyed in this section of the chapter provide a general historical and intellectual mapping of the most influential developments that impacted the rise of pathological theories of individual criminality rather than a comprehensive account of the "human sciences." Drawing strict boundaries between the disciplines—criminology, psychology, sociology, medicine, anthropology, biology and psychiatry—is particularly difficult due to the great overlap between 19th-century subfields and research within the human sciences.

The pathological approach to crime occurred alongside several other important and interrelated 19th- and 20th-century developments: the rise of the professions, the emergence of the middle classes, secularization, urbanization, compulsory schooling and governmental reform. The rise of "the expert"—psychiatrists, academic researchers, teachers, social hygiene reformers, psychologists, health workers and social workers—marked the development of professional knowledges that relied upon a scientific rationality to understand, explain and control human conduct. Positivist techniques were thus increasingly sought in projects aimed at identifying and improving individuals deemed biologically unfit, degenerate and inferior. This process involved the shift from focusing on the act (crime) to one that redefined the identity of the person (criminal) in scientifically positive terms. This served to regulate the population through a regime of medical discourses and expert truths that eventually almost entirely replaced the barbarous examples of bloody spectacle of punishment of previous eras, which had been declining under the influence of the classical school (Foucault, 1979).

The emergence of the Age of Reason had marked a shift in thinking about the individual and society. A modern, progressive, "civilized" society thus rested upon the new ideals of science, reason and progress. Human problems were increasingly viewed as scientific problems that could be studied, known, categorized, regulated, treated and cured. Under late 19th-century positivism, explanations of crime could specifically be found in the differences among individuals, whether in terms of "character" or circumstance. The optimistic conviction was that crime and criminality could be understood and cured by the proper application of science. Scholars started positing that perhaps a set of underlying forces propelled individuals to conduct themselves in particular ways. Just as the scientific theory of gravity could explain falling apples, positivist approaches set out to identify the underlying forces causing criminality in the human being. While the classical school emphasized the free will of individuals, the new positivist approaches were interested in determining the "natural laws" predisposing an individual to criminal conduct. Rather than provide a speculative and therefore subjective view, the positivists insisted that through systematic observation, human behaviour could be explained in the same objective manner as the hard sciences explained the natural world.

In the wake of the French Revolution, as industrialization and urbanization were expanding both in Western Europe and North America, the traditional social bonds based upon religious convictions and moral duties to the monarchy and the church were being challenged, criticized and overthrown, creating massive social, economic and political unrest. Positive criminology suggested social disorder could be remedied without specific reference to discredited spiritual explanations. As a result of the positivist movement, any kind of conduct viewed negatively could be classified and calcified as "scientifically sick." Not only was criminality seen as a social problem to be combated for the general health of the social body, it was at the social body's very foundations owing to physiology, biology, ancestry and place of birth—all factors indisputably beyond the control of the individual.

Yet popular religious and spiritual discourses were also important in the development of nonsociological positivism. Johann Kaspar Lavater (1741–1801) argued that there was a direct relationship between facial features and character. His 1789 text on physiognomy provided a means of performing "character diagnosis" on the basis of facial characteristics which, although written by a clergyman and famous spiritual consultant, made an enormous impact on psychiatric medicine and helped to push characterology to the popular fore in both medicine and the wider literate middle classes. This resulted in the influential psychological discourse of the nineteenth century: phrenology, which would eventually branch off into the physiognomic sciences. Between 1810 and 1819, Franz Joseph Gall (1758–1828) and Johann Caspar Spurzheim published five volumes on the anatomy and functions of the brain, arguing that all mental differences among human beings were due to character differences localized in the brain and connected to the shape of the skull. Gall claimed to have identified a "murder organ" in murderers and a "theft organ" in convicted thieves. **Phrenology** was considered a scientific practice that studied the shape of the head to determine anatomical correlates of human behaviour. The theory posited that the divisions of the brain could be compartmentalized into separate and distinct organs, each responsible for a particular mental faculty and its normal functioning, thus reducing the individual to a healthy or deviant skull. **Physiognomy** also posited a direct relationship between external bodily structure and quality of the soul but encompassed the entire body in its analysis of the individual. Phrenology and physiognomy were key 19th-century developments in the positivist effort to quantify and measure the soul or psyche of human subjects.

Prichard's doctrine of moral insanity was the first attempt in the West to provide a systematic scientific theory for the commission of immoral acts, the precursor to the now popular "anti-social personality disorder" (Rimke & Hunt, 2002; Rimke, 2003). Proponents of the doctrine set out to prove that human character and immoral conduct had biological roots and represented a dangerous degeneration of the evolutionary process, threatening the health of "civilized, white society." The invention of moral insanity gave 19th-century scientists a unique claim to expertise in the topical issues of morality and health in an age of disruptive modernization. Industrialization, political revolutions and resistance, urbanization, secularization and capitalist expansionism altered the social landscape, giving rise to a human science which could account for these effects as individual problems or psychopathologies. Thereafter, a host of experts in a variety of fields including biology, medical psychology, physiognomy, phrenology, evolutionism, criminal anthropology, psychology, mental and moral hygiene, eugenics and genetics joined the search for the causes of crime (Garland, 1994; Pick, 1989; Rimke & Hunt, 2002; Rafter, 2005). The disciplinary discourses offered "scientific" means to explain, identify, regulate and combat degeneration in all its dangerous forms and guises. Psychiatrists established their expertise and demanded wider public recognition based on the general argument that society required a remedy for its ills and only medical experts possessed the scientific knowledge to achieve such ends. The attempts to make human qualities a tangible substance or give them a materialist foundation for the classification of criminality can be seen most strikingly in the work of Cesare Lombroso (1835–1909), an Italian professor of legal psychiatry. Usually considered the founder of positive criminology, Lombroso more than any other thinker popularized the pathological approach by his criminal anthropological studies on prisoners' bodies, living and dead.

The emergence of the pathological perspective was thus influenced by many scientific developments: the spiritual characterology of Lavater's and Gall and Spurzheim's phrenology and physiognomy, Darwin's theories of evolution and Prichard's doctrine of moral insanity. These theories and studies influenced Lombroso and his key text, *Criminal Man*. Drawing upon the doctrine of moral insanity, a product of Christian morality, anthropology and evolutionary perspectives, he devised a "criminal anthropology" where humans were thought to fit into a typology based on biological, racial and moral differences. Using prisoners as laboratory subjects, he photographed, catalogued and studied physical differences of virtually every body part to determine a material, physical cause for crime. Based on the measurement of these bodily differences, Lombroso claimed that the "born criminal" was a regression in the natural process of human evolution. For Lombroso, the criminal or atavist was an "evolutionary throwback" suffering from arrested development rooted in a degenerate ancestry displayed by visible bodily characteristics and expressions. **Atavism**, Lombroso argued, could be identified by a number of measurable physical stigmata, which included anomalies of the cranium, left-handedness, outstretched ears, drooping eyes, a protruding jaw, heavy forehead and asymmetries of the face.

Widespread circulation of medical knowledge had been accomplished through mass publication and reproductions made available to interested experts on both sides of the Atlantic. Lombroso's work was accepted as part of this dissemination. One of the main "solutions" to the dilemma of crime was the application of biological and other scientific theories of human difference. The dangerous classes were thus categorized as naturally criminal owing to physical factors. The argument that criminality was physiological advanced the idea that material, objective criteria could scientifically differentiate human groups. However, it also justified a moral apartheid and even elimination of those dangerous classes that threatened the health and safety of the nation. This was linked to the social Darwinist perspective that claimed that social hierarchies, including racial classes and gender distinctions, were the biological product of evolutionary forces rooted in "natural" selection. The scientific theory of progressive degeneration was mobilized as a "principle of causation." The misappropriation of evolutionary approaches in the human sciences is notable and also made a particularly strong mark Lombroso's research and theories.

The influence of Lombroso's "positive criminology" remains in the many bio- and psycho-scientific approaches. Whatever the specific approach, individual differences are measured and classified according to culturally defined standards of normality that are assumed to be universal rather than historically and socially defined and produced. Focus is placed on the nature of the individual in biological terms, psychological terms or both. Emphasis is placed on personal characteristics or traits, individual deficiencies and innate predispositions. Personal deficits are accentuated and explained as the by-product of any one, or a combination of, heredity, environment and so forth. The goals of this approach are the diagnosis, classification and treatment or cure of offenders by trained experts.

INVENTING NORMAL

Measurement and quantification became hallmarks of the positivist approach in the human sciences. In the 1840s, the Franco-Belgian statistician Adolphe Quetelet (1796–1894) created the notion of *l'homme moyen*, which translates to "the average man" or "the normal man," as a way to measure traits in the human population. Through the collection of statistical data on social characteristics, Quetelet sought to establish the basis of the average or normal man by employing statistical techniques to find patterns and regularities in the population. The "normal man" was a mathematical abstraction which brought together the diversity of human characteristics and conduct in the form of "the mean." Using the noncriminality of the average man, Quetelet juxtaposed the criminality of vagabonds, vagrants, primitives, gypsies, the "inferior classes," certain ethnic groups of "inferior moral stock" and "persons of low moral character" (Bierne, 1987, p. 1159). Quetelet's invention helped to institutionalize the notion of "the normal" as scientific, but "normal" is always already socially defined because it is based upon social judgments and prescriptions of desirability and respectability, thus defying the possibility of universal objectivity and neutrality. The practical outcome of conceiving the average person as a mathematical mean was the justification for defining those who deviated from it as criminal types or otherwise abnormal. Criminality could therefore be defined not just as a cluster of signs signifying personal weakness or evil but also as an example of pathological variance from a norm (Hacking, 1990). Pathological theories thus set out to demonstrate that criminality could be identified and verified by discrete, measurable physical traits.

GENETICS AND CRIMINALITY

Studies of supposedly biological normality and deviance were linked to heredity. The notion that humanity can and should be improved—if not, perfected—by selective breeding and the elimination of certain individuals and groups deemed undesirable is called **eugenics**. Eugenicists claimed they could scientifically identify heritable inferior traits so that the human population could be improved by preventing inferior individuals from passing on their inferiorities through programs of incarceration, sterilization and even extermination. The goal of eugenics was to improve the stock of the human race. Not only were eugenicists willing to strip those whom they regarded as inferior stock of their most basic rights, the movement had distinctly racist—and murderous—aspects.

Genetic approaches to studying crime and criminality examine the heritability of criminal conduct. As for other individualist theories, there are many competing frameworks within this school of thought. Although research approaches differ greatly in aim and methodology, they share the basic assumption that genetics play a determining role in the mental, moral and behavioural differences among individuals. Such approaches seek to differentiate genetic from environmental effects in order to determine predispositions to criminal behaviour due to inherited factors (Wasserman & Wachroit, 2001). A great deal of research is conducted searching for evidence of a genetic component of criminality. Key methodologies have been family studies, twin and adoption studies, molecular genetics research that search for markers of aggression and violence, neurobiological approaches that examine neural pathways to study impulsivity, aggression and so forth. Despite a lack of evidence of causal genetic mechanisms and the absence of any conclusive research that genetic transmission accounts for criminality, the idea that genes predispose to crime is still widely held today. Further, it appears that a resurgence of biocriminology and neoevolutionism in recent years has occurred.

The long held tenet that "crime runs in families" dates back to the mid-19th-century doctrine of moral insanity and now infamous studies of a small number of supposedly criminal families: the Kallikaks, the Chesters and the Jukes (Rimke & Hunt, 2002). The idea that individual inherited differences account for criminality has been a consistent trend since Lombroso.

New public health programs of crime control seek to identify, classify, treat and cure individuals predisposed to aggressive or impulsive conduct. The search for biological dispositions has also played an increased role in preventive detention, treatment as a condition of a noncustodial sentence, genetic screening in risk assessments and other preemptive interventions in the name of security, protection and public safety in the early 21st century (Rose, 2000; Taylor, 2001; Rafter, 2004, 2006, 2007).

PSYCHOLOGY AND CRIMINALITY

Psychological explanations reduce the causation of criminal activity to specific qualities of the mind or psyche of the offender, identifying various internal factors or determinants: low intelligence, abnormal personality types and traits, aggression, impulsivity, childhood trauma, failures of psychosocial development, stress or cognitive dysfunction, for example. Cognitive psychologists see crimes as resulting from criminals' deficits in cognitive processing, while psychoanalytic theorists have suggested crimes are the result of unconscious psychodynamics.

Psychologically based explanations grew out of human scientific knowledge, from observation of prisoners, animal studies and academic research. Broadly speaking, the major difference between biological and psychological explanations is that the former views criminality as inborn or innate, while the latter approaches it as an effect of psychological processes or external factor(s) influencing the mind or psyche. Still, psychological theorists view crimes are the direct product of some internal flaw or defect, whatever its cause. As a result, psychological and biological approaches are not mutually exclusive; in fact, an increasing number of studies are examining the interrelationship between the two, where the growing focus appears to be on nurture and nature rather than one or the other.

BIO-PSYCHOLOGICAL THEORIES OF CRIME: THE INFLUENCE ON CORRECTIONAL WORK

The pathological approach to crime relies upon the medical model by characterizing the offender as "abnormal" or "sick" and in need of a cure or treatment. Because criminality is understood as determined by a scientifically identifiable cause, this approach is described as deterministic. This can be seen in the psychical determinism of psychoanalytic or personality theory or the genetic or neurochemical determinism found in biological approaches. The issue of legal responsibility in criminal law is based on a conception of the free will of the individual, not the determinism that defines the positivist approach. The scientific determinism of the pathological approach is thus at odds with the legal practice of holding the individual responsible.

The debate on criminality and responsibility dates back 200 years. The insanity defence is best known as the M'Naghten Rules due to the highly publicized 1843 trial of Daniel M'Naghten, who shot and killed Edward Drummond, the secretary to Conservative English prime minister Robert Peel. M'Naghten's lawyers argued that he was not guilty of murder by reason of insanity. He was experiencing paranoia and delusions and did not rationally understand the nature of his act, and even if he did, M'Naghten had no understanding that it was wrong. He believed that Peel was organizing a conspiracy against him and that he was acting in self-defence. The case gave rise to the most thorough debate on criminal responsibility and the legal test of insanity largely because the verdict roused a great deal of opposition. This stemmed in large part from accusations that the doctrine condoned criminal behaviour through a determinist model of disease which contradicted the widely endorsed doctrine of the free will and moral responsibility. The practical consequences of using the insanity plea based on a medical condition undermined the long-held belief in the necessity of punishing the dangerous with "a just measure of pain." Psychiatrists exclaimed that it was unjust and inhumane to punish, legally or otherwise, an individual for a biological condition. Objections to the doctrine involved charges that it subverted the doctrine of free will and by extension the cherished classical liberal discourses of moral responsibility, accountability, rationality and calculability—in short, the free agency of the subject. Another clear challenge was the difficulty of distinguishing criminality from sin and the problem of drawing a clear conceptual boundary between willful vice and disease (Valverde, 1998; Rimke, 2003).

The rise of positivist science not only signaled, as Foucault (1978) has pointed out, the modern transformation of the criminal into the mad; it thereby transformed the ungovernable sinner into a morally mad degenerate who needed medical attention by scientific experts above all else (Rimke & Hunt, 2002). Modern science would begin to address the old social evils and ills in new ways.

Psychocentrism, or the reduction of human problems and life to psychological discourses, should be understood as the cultural corollary of neoliberalism. The rise of psychocentrism has had the effect of recuperating, nullifying or both all forms of human challenges, differences and difficulties as pathology. As an enduring characteristic of Western societies, psychocentrism can be seen as the compulsory ontology of pathology. Culturally, we are expected to view human existence through the lens of the psy complex rather than alternative frameworks for understanding and acting. To date, there exists no theory of criminality that explains all criminal conduct. Psychiatric theories are flawed because not all convicted persons are mentally ill, and few individuals diagnosed as mentally ill have criminal records. Similarly, not all convicted offenders are "psychopathic" or "sociopathic," related diagnoses most directly associated with criminality, so psychiatric theories of crime also are inadequate. Yet psychiatric and bio-psychological approaches to corrections remain immensely influential. Individualism is a key aspect of these approaches because the focus is on the individual offender. The punishment came to be designed to suit the criminal, not the crime. This emphasis on the supposed characteristics of the criminal is seen in probation, parole, indeterminate sentencing, dangerous offender legislation and community sentences. Individualization is further entrenched by the discretionary powers exercised by expert authorities using a therapeutic model.

Variants of psychology influencing correctional work include:

1. *Psychoanalytic theory, developed initially by Sigmund Freud.* Psychoanalytic theory basically assumes that criminal conduct stems from unresolved unconscious conflicts in the psyche or structure of the personality. Disturbances or malfunction in the ego (reality-based) and superego (conscience) allow the id (primitive instincts) to satisfy its urges regardless of laws and the consequences of violating legal rules. For example, criminal behaviour is viewed as the result of an inability to delay gratification due to an underdeveloped superego that cannot regulate the desires of the id. Other psychoanalysts have claimed that individuals with an overdeveloped superego experience excessive guilt and anxiety and thus unconsciously seek punishment in efforts to restore psychical balance. In other words, individuals commit crimes because they have an unconscious and compulsive need to experience punishment. In the psychoanalytical framework, unconscious motivations and internal conflict, often related to parental attachment issues, are taken as the driving forces of criminal behaviour.

2. *Personality theory.* Personality can be defined as a complex set of emotional, mental and behavioral attributes that generally remain stable (persist over a long period of time) and constant (in different situations).

3. *Psychiatry.* Psychiatrists require medical and specialized training and legally prescribe medication and other forms of medical intervention (lobotomy, electro-convulsive shock therapy, etc.).

4. *Social psychology.* Focus is placed on personal cognitive development through childhood experiences. Explanations for criminality include, poor parenting, lack of supervision and emotional, physical and sexual abuse.

PSYCHOLOGY AND WILL: NEW MORAL DISCOURSES

If one examines concepts such as "lack of willpower," one can see how both the religious and philosophical still operate in the academic biogenic and psychogenic explanations. Hirschi and Gottfriedson's (1990) control theory reduces criminal activity to impulsivity, self-centeredness, the inability to delay gratification, the propensity for risk-taking and low threshold for stress. The inability to resist a sinful temptation and the metaphysical notion of "will" are retained within this contemporary approach.

The partly deterministic individualism of this approach can be criticized for avoiding the consideration of broader structural factors which might help explain crimes. For example, Marc Lépine, who gunned down 13 women engineering students at Montreal's École Polytechnique on December 6, 1989, is often described in mainstream media as suffering from antisocial personality disorder (psychopathy, sociopathy, dyssocial disorder) or from having a bad relationship with his mother. Feminists and critical thinkers have provided social and political explanations claiming that his act of violence was an extreme expression of the general and systematic physical, sexual, emotional and economic violence against women that occurs regularly in a patriarchal society. Asocial explanations chose to ignore that fact that Lépine wrote in his suicide letter that he "hated all feminists" and that "women were the reason he failed at life." A social perspective would explain that the murder of explicitly females is an occurrence is an explicit act of misogyny, the hatred of females. An individualist explanation would argue his crime was the result of an innate pathology or perhaps blame his mother (itself considered a misogynist and otherwise problematic theory; why not blame the absent father, for example?), whereas a socially based theory would point to the social factors that influence and shape behaviour itself.

Conclusion: Crime and the "Psy Sciences"

Positivists rejected the claim that criminality was the result of demonic possession or to the calculated decision to do evil. This was a key transformation in the history of explanations for criminal conduct. The respectability of science rested upon objective and testable theories of criminality rather than upon superstition and subjective claims characteristic of the demonological framework that dominated for many centuries. With the rise of positivism, previous definitions of sinful conduct (crime) became reconfigured as abnormal conditions which required attention by human scientific experts, not theologians or philosophers. Rather than attribute the cause of criminality to an exogenous demon, the new and modern sciences insisted that crime must be an effect of an internal disordered state, initially identified by Lombroso and others as a purely biological or physiological. Criminality, like other human pathologies, was thus taken to be caused by organic or endogenous factors rooted in the body itself. As such, the soul—eventually the psyche, mind or personality—became the object to study, know, regulate, reform, treat and cure. At first, these mental phenomena were seen as purely effects of the disordered or abnormal body, although later psychological theories also emphasized the traumatic or deficit-producing effects of a dysfunctional biography. The paradigm shift produced by positive criminology introduced a medical model of crime where criminality became seen as a mental or biological pathology.

The history of individualist theories of crime and criminality demonstrates that a unilinear or progressivist analysis of the progress of science so characteristic of scientists' understanding of their own places in history is insufficient to account for the multiple and often contradictory claims advanced within expert domains of knowledge. The heterogeneous and often inconsistent or contradictory expert claims and the reigning ambiguity and claims about the scientific discourses can be seen in the problematic theoretical distinctions between disease/depravity, responsibility/nonculpability, freedom/determinism and normal/pathological, not to mention the mind-body relationship.

Forensic psychologists and psychiatrists, now qualified specialists, today dominate the most recent developments in the field. Forensic psychology and psychiatry can be defined as pathological approaches in service to the criminal justice system. That is, the field of "psy forensics" works explicitly for the system in clinical and administrative capacities rather than engaging in the pursuit of empirical knowledge or the improvement of social conditions, for example. Many roles are played by forensic psy experts: predicting and classifying risk (of reoffending), interpreting offender culpability, providing presentence reports, acting in the capacity of expert witnesses, providing expert testimony and implementing treatment programs. Crime prevention is based on early diagnosis and determining individuals "at risk" of committing offenses. The task of the expert is to identify and correct or fix the pathology.

Psychological and biological theories of crime and criminality are contentious and problematic owing to classificatory ambiguity, lack of physical/organic evidence and the highly subjective nature of notions such as risk, threat and dangerousness. To date, no known biological or genetic factors have been determined to cause crime, yet the popularity of this approach appears to be growing in both the academy and everyday culture. Pathological theories of crime causation have been criticized on numerous grounds. The long and controversial history of individualist theories, the lack of theoretical and disciplinary consensus on the mind-body relationship, the political history of its use and implications, etiological uncertainties, the long list of human rights abuses by the authorities and inconclusive empirical data highlight the problematic nature of individually based theories of crime and criminality. Theories that argue criminality is a pathological condition remain questionable and highly controversial, not least of all because of the implications these conceptions have on criminal justice policies that affect many individuals in custodial and noncustodial settings. The return of biogenic explanations signals the need to understand their histories, for those who do not learn from the past are destined to repeat the worst of it.

References

Beccaria, C. (1819). [1754]. *An essay on crime and punishment*. Philadelphia: Philip H. Nicklin.

Becker, P., & Wetzell, R. F., (2006). *Criminals and their scientists: The history of criminology in international perspective*. Cambridge: Cambridge University Press.

Eysenck, H. (1984). Crime and personality. In D. Muller, D. Blackman, & A. Chapman (Eds.), *Psychology and law*. New York: John Wiley and Sons.

Farrington, D. P., Biron, L., & LeBlanc, M. (1982). Personality and delinquency in London and Montreal. In J. Gunn & D. P. Farrington (Eds.), *Abnormal offenders, delinquency, and the criminal justice system* (pp. 153–201). Chichester, UK: Wiley.

Foucault, M. (1987). *Mental illness and psychology*. (A. Sheridan, Trans.). Berkeley: University of California Press.

Foucault, M. (1988). *Madness and civilization*. New York: Vintage.

Foucault, M. (1978). About the concept of the "dangerous individual" in nineteenth century legal psychiatry. *International Journal of Law and Psychiatry, 1*, 1–18.

Gabor, T. (1994). *Everybody does it!* Toronto: University of Toronto Press.

Garland, D., & Sparks, R. (2000). Criminology, social theory, and the challenge of our times. In D. Garland & R. Sparks (Eds.), *Criminology and social theory*. Oxford: Oxford University Press.

Hay, D. et al. (1977). *Albion's fatal tree: Crime and society in eighteenth century England*. Harmondsworth, UK: Penguin.

Hollin, C. R. (2002). Criminological psychology. In M. Maguire, R. Morgan, & R. Reiner (Eds.), *The Oxford handbook of criminology* (3rd ed.) (pp. 144–74) Oxford: Oxford University Press.

Ingleby, D. (1985). Professionals as socializers: The "Psy Complex." *Research in Law, Deviance and Social Control, 7*, 79–109.

Lombroso, C. (1911). *Crime: Its causes and remedies*. Boston: Little, Brown.

Newburn, T. (2007). *Criminology*. Cullompton, UK: Willan.

Pfohl, S. J. (1985). *Images of deviance and social control: A sociological history*. New York: McGraw-Hill.

Rafter, N. (2004). The unrepentant horse-slasher: Moral insanity and the origins of criminological thought. *Criminology, 42*, 979–1008.

Rafter, N. (2005). The murderous Dutch fiddler: Criminology, history and the problem of phrenology. *Theoretical Criminology, 9*, 65–96.

Rafter, N. (2007). Somatotyping, antimodernism and the production of criminological knowledge. *Criminology, 45*(4), 805–33.

Raine, A. (1993). *The psychopathology of crime: Criminal behavior as a clinical disorder*. San Diego: Academic Press.

Rimke, H. (2000). Governing citizens through self-help literature. *Cultural Studies, 14*(1), 61–78.

Rimke, H. (2003). Constituting transgressive Interiorities: 19th-century psychiatric readings of morally mad bodies. In A. Aldama (Ed.), *Violence and the body: Race, gender and the state* (pp. 403–28). Indianapolis: Indiana University Press.

Rimke, H. (2008). The development of the sciences of the mind. In R. Lawson (Ed.), *Research and discovery: Landmarks and pioneers in American science*. New York: M. E. Sharpe.

Rimke, H., & Hunt, A. (2002). From sinners to degenerates: The medicalization of morality in the C19th. *History of the human sciences, 15*(1), 59–88.

Rose, (1979). The psychological complex: Mental measurement and social administration. *Ideology & Consciousness, 5*, 5–68.

Rose, N. (2000). The biology of culpability: Pathological identity and crime control in a biological culture. *Theoretical Criminology, 4*, 5–34.

Sampson, R. J., & Laub, H. H. (Eds.). (2005). *Developmental criminology and its discontents: Trajectories of crime from childhood to old age*, special issue of *The Annals of the American Academy of Political and Social Science*. Thousand Oaks, CA: Sage.

Sheldon, W. H. (1949). *Varieties of delinquent youth: An introduction to constitutional psychiatry*, with the collaboration of E. M. Hartl & E. McDermott. New York: Harper & Brothers.

Szasz, T. (1971). *The manufacture of madness*. London: Routledge.

Taylor, K. A. (2001). On the explanatory limits of behavioural genetics. In D. Wasserman & R. Wachbroit (Eds.), *Genetics and criminal behaviour*. Cambridge: Cambridge University Press.

Taylor, I., Walton, P., & Young, J. (1973). *The new criminology*. London: Routledge & Kegan Paul.

Turner, R., & Edgley, C. (1983). From witchcraft to drugcraft: Biochemistry as mythology. *Social Science Journal, 20*(4), 1–12.

Valverde, M. (1998). *Diseases of the will: Alcohol and the dilemmas of freedom*. Cambridge: Cambridge University Press.

Walsh, A. (2002). *Biosocial criminology*. Cincinnati: Anderson Publishing.

Wasserman, D., & Wachbroit, R. (2001). *Genetics and criminal behaviour*. Cambridge: Cambridge University Press.

CHAPTER 6

Sociological Theories of Crime and Criminality

Kirsten Kramar, University of Winnipeg

INTRODUCTION

In this chapter, you will be introduced to a range of sociological ideas about crime and criminality published in Europe and the United States, beginning in the late 19th century. These ideas were created by social scientists who sought to describe and understand crime as one among a range of **social problems**. Their work was very much tied to the intellectual revolution called the **Enlightenment**, which began in Europe in the late 17th century. Enlightenment thinkers believed that human reason would promote human emancipation and social progress. The growth of modern science and technology, and modern systems of economic exchange, are associated with the Enlightenment, and throughout the 18th and 19th centuries, the societies of Western Europe and North America were undergoing rapid industrialization and the establishment of commodity-based capitalist economies. These societies witnessed massive social upheavals along with the growth of new industrial and colonial powers.

The Enlightenment had other significant aspects. This historical period saw the development of democratic governments and the establishment of the rule of law and the rights and responsibilities of citizens, all of which were seen as fruits of human reason deployed to provide rational political philosophies. In addition, social scientists, relying on the resources of human reason, aimed to contribute to the positive development of society by informing the government (or state) around questions of **social order**. Disorder was seen as destabilizing to the overall happiness of the population because it interfered with the smooth operation of society. Good government would be based on scientific knowledge about social change and social order and disor-der rather than on traditional ideas drawn from religious morality, with the state and social science working hand-in-hand to seek solutions to social problems, including the problem of crime. This idea that good government producing a harmonious society should be based on a sound scientific understanding of society and its history is called **sociological positivism**.

EARLY SOCIOLOGICAL POSITIVISM AND THE EMERGENCE OF SOCIOLOGICAL CRIMINOLOGY

Sociological positivism developed as an element of a broader positivist movement which rejected philosophical speculation in favour of scientific investigation and the empirical testing of scientific theories. We looked at biological and psychological theories of crime in the previous chapter. These reflect an individualistic variant of positivism which emerged a few decades after sociological positivism. Early sociological positivism was largely based on the premise that the social world functions like a machine or an organism—in predictable and regular patterns. The early sociological positivists believed they could "uncover" these predictable, regular patterns, which were often obscured by the apparent chaos and strife associated with rapid social change, thereby revealing enduring truths about human societies.

The first positivist is considered to be Auguste Comte (1798–1857), a French social philosopher who introduced the idea that society could be transformed using the techniques of the natural sciences (controlled observation and verification). Comte believed that the problems of society that resulted from the massive upheaval caused by the industrial revolution could be solved by social science. As such, Comte was also considered the founder of the discipline of sociology. A key idea of the early positivists is that social scientists could develop a deep understanding of historical trends, which would enable them to locate the problems associated with social upheaval in a broader context. As a result, they would be able to identify the sources of disorder and the possibilities for a more harmonious but still distinctly modern social order. The positivists saw themselves as progressives who rejected conservative nostalgia for the "good old days" before the Enlightenment and industrialization. The conceptual frameworks developed by early social scientists to understand and solve the problem of social order included "crime" as a measure of social upheaval and disorder. Social instability of this sort was thought to interfere with the newly developing market economies as well as the good order of society more generally.

You will see as you read this chapter how the basic approach of sociological positivism has influenced sociological ideas about crime and criminal justice up until the present day. Over the course of the 20th century, there was a general shift in sociological studies of crime from the identification of the social causes of crime to the investigation of the nature and operation of the criminal justice process, including the development of criminal law. Despite the shift of focus, for many social scientists the positivist goal of scientifically understanding society in order to enhance government has remained constant. Some of these social scientists have seen themselves as gentle reformers who identify and understand social problems such as crime so that they can be solved by tweaking basically successful social arrangements. Others, influenced by Marxism, feminism or antiracism, for instance, have seen modern societies as requiring more fundamental changes in order to achieve true justice and harmony. Whether reformist or revolutionary, the approach has been to grasp, through scientific research and theory building, the underlying dynamics of society and to understand crime and to an increasing extent the operation of the criminal justice system in that broader context with the aim of eventually achieving a more harmonious social order.

In the period after the Second World War, especially from the mid-1960s, the dominant ideas of the Enlightenment have been rejected by "postmodern" or "postpositivist" thinkers who insist that the Enlightenment, rather than guiding society and its members toward greater social justice and personal fulfilment, has produced new forms of human domination and suffering. These critics have argued that the principles of democratic government, the rule of law and human rights and citizenship established during the Enlightenment are a fiction that facilitated the colonization and domination of vast numbers of people according to group identities along the lines of class, race, religion, sex and sexuality. For example, in *Wretched of the Earth* (1961), Franz Fanon pointed out that France's colonial history in relation to Algeria demonstrates that Enlightenment principles were not extended to African Muslims, who were denied the rights of citizenship and equality extended to other French citizens. These denials of rights and freedoms cloaked beneath the principles of freedom, democracy and human rights worked to facilitate the colonial rule of Northern Africa by the French Republic and the exploitation Muslims of North African descent living in France.

Peter Fitzpatrick argued in *The Mythology of Modern Law* (1992) that even the conceptual foundations of Enlightenment law and citizenship relied on racist contrasts between the "civilized" and "savage." French social philosopher Michel Foucault (1926–1984) influentially identified negative outcomes of the Enlightenment as being closely associated with the development of the human sciences, including criminology, psychology and sociology.

Contemporary criminological thinking is a complex mixture of positivist theories, in both reformist and radical variants, and postpositivist commentaries informed by thinkers such as Foucault. Many academic sociologists and criminologists try to chart their own courses through these complex and contradictory possibilities, incorporating some of the postpositivist suspicions about the role of social science in modern government with a continuing commitment to understanding crime and criminal justice processes through sociological research. Reading this chapter will enable you to understand their debates and dilemmas and help you think about these complex and challenging issues.

In the first section of this chapter, you will read about the different sorts of problems the early sociological positivists observed along with the concepts they developed to assist the authorities in solving certain kinds of social problems. These early ideas focus on examining and providing empirically based solutions for social problems, with the solutions presented in the form of ambitious social theories. You will see how a strand of criminological thinking subsequently emerged which focused on the operation of the criminal justice system rather than on crimes and criminals. Later in the chapter, you will read about the critiques of positivism. These theorists focus on how particular social processes become defined as social problems and as objects of enquiry for social scientists. In other words, the focus shifts from the scientific examination of social problems to showing how social problems are "constructed" using social science.

GERMAN SOCIOLOGICAL POSITIVISM: CLASSICAL MARXISM

Karl Marx (1818–1883)

Major Works

The Communist Manifesto (1848) with Friedrich Engels (1820–1895)

Das Kapital (1867)

Main Concepts

Social Classes, Modes of Production, Means of Production, Dominant Ideology, Praxis, Alienation, Historical Materialism, State, Repressive Law

Karl Marx (1818–1883)

Like Comte, Marx himself did not offer a systematic analysis of crime. In relation to the question of crime and social order, Marx instead focused on the role of the state (and the legal system) in the emergence of a capitalist industrial society. His ideas have been enormously influential among academics, in world politics and, as we will see, among criminological theorists who would later take up his ideas. Writing in the middle decades of the 19th century, when European societies were still making the transition from **feudalism** to **capitalism**, Marx sought to explain the human suffering he observed around him. Influenced by early 19th-century writers such as Comte, as well as German philosophers G.W.F. Hegel and Ludwig Feuerbach, who sought to grasp the broad out-lines of human historical development, Marx developed a distinctive account of the changing foundations of societies. But unlike Comte and Hegel, Marx insisted that his historical insights showed the need for a revolutionary transformation of society under-taken purposefully by those who had grasped the unjust nature of contemporary social arrangements. Marx began by examining the ways in which people have produced the things they require to live (food, clothing, shelter, etc.). He therefore sought to describe the various **modes of production** that have existed in history to show that how we make things will be reflected in all other aspects of social life. Feudalism and capitalism are two such modes of production. According to Marx, all social relations are bound up with productive forces. When societies change their mode of production by changing the manner in which people earn a living, they also change their social relations (Marx & Engels, 1848).

The mode of production has two key components: the **means of production** and the **social relations of production**. The means of production are those material things (tools, machinery, land, raw materials or resources) used to produce goods and services. One's ability to secure these goods and services is defined by the social relations of pro-duction, specifically whether one owns and controls the means of production, or whether one has to sell one's labour power to acquire the products of the economy. In a capitalist society, all goods and services tend to become **commodities** which are priced for and purchased within a market, while labour is organized through a labour market. Those who own and control the means of production are the capitalist class (bourgeoisie) and those who have only their labour power to sell are the working class (proletariat). For Marx, one's social class is determined by one's economic position within a given mode of production, and because class interests are mutually exclusive, one class (the bour-geoisie in capitalism) exists and thrives by exploiting the other class (the proletariat). Marx expended much effort on his proof that this relationship was objectively exploita-tive. These two classes, the capitalist class and the working class, exist in a perpetual state of class struggle because they having opposing interests and seek to achieve oppo-site goals. The capitalist class seeks to maximize its profit through what Marx insists is the partly the unpaid labour of the working classes (also termed "surplus labour"), while the working classes seek to maximize their wages. Marx believed that the only way of re-solving these conflicts is the creation of a new mode of production in which there was only one class; that is, where the means of production are owned collectively. This would be a communist system. Achieving it would require a social revolution, and it would ob-viously be opposed by the capitalist class, whose exploitation of the workers, and hence, profits, would be brought to an end.

In part because the social arrangement of capitalism is premised on exploitation, the maintenance of class relations requires coercion. It is in this that Marx provided the outlines of a theory of the state that would influence later criminologists. Marx argued that the economic arrangements structured every aspect of society, including the political and legal systems. For Marx, the legal system under capitalism is a means of class domination. However, the system is organized so that the inequities of economic life, the law and politics are disguised and only perceived, by the working class at least, when economic and social crises make them obvious, or through the effort of careful scientific reasoning of the kind Marx was attempting. The cloaking of exploitation and class rule in the guise of fairness and equity is called *ideology* by Marx and his followers. Dominant ideologies such as the idea that crime is the product of individual pathology serves the interests of the capitalist class by drawing attention away from the class-based nature of crime and its control by the state. Ideology conceals the extent to which the dominant class interests are served and perpetuated by individualized and pathologized definition of crime and its causation.

Although Marx himself had a somewhat typical Victorian attitude to criminal elements, seeing them as dangerous sections of the working class with little revolutionary potential, his view of the operation of the state and law as mechanisms that operate to preserve the capitalist status quo and are thus fundamentally unjust because society is fundamentally unjust has been hugely influential. Many Marxist criminologists and sociologists have seen crimes as largely the products of inequity and impoverishment and the reactions of the criminal justice system as mechanisms to control the lumpen proletariat (the working and non-working class), contain class tensions and persuade members of both classes that the social system and its processes of government are basically just. The criminal law and the broader criminal justice system thus have an ideological as well as a more straightforwardly repressive function.

FRENCH SOCIOLOGICAL POSITIVISM

Émile Durkheim (1858–1917)

Major Works

The Division of Labour in Society (1893)
The Rules of Sociological Method (1895)
Suicide (1897)

Main Concepts

Consensus, Order, Anomie, Collective Conscience, Social Solidarity

Émile Durkheim (1858–1917)

Émile Durkheim, a French intellectual writing at the turn of the 20th century, was one of the founders of sociological criminology. His work shifted the focus of criminological thinking away from the individual toward the study of society. Durkheim was deeply influenced by Comte, taking up Comte's idea that the purpose of sociology was to grasp the underlying dynamics of social change, which he saw as largely positive, to provide the context within which contemporary social problems should be understood. Durkheim did not accept Marx's view that history pointed toward the need for a revolutionary transformation of the foundations of society. According to Durkheim, social evolution was largely taking care of itself, with the sociologist working to understand this evolutionary process so that it can be guided in relatively minor ways.

Whereas many of his contemporaries who studied crime were concerned with explaining social disorder, Durkheim shifted the focus toward an examination of how society maintains order. In his book *The Division of Labour in Society* (1893), Durkheim examined the role of the legal system (law) as a source of social order in modern industrial societies. Durkheim thought that social order reflects a deep lying pattern of social organization he referred to as *social solidarity*, by which he meant an integrated system of social relations, social practices and social norms. Durkheim called the shared mental outlook organized around social norms the *"conscience collective,"* usually translated as **collective conscience** or collective consciousness.

Because his work addressed difficult questions about order and stability during a time of considerable social change in Europe during the 19th century, Durkheim described how societies undergo changes in the form of social solidarity during times of evolution. During this period, European societies were shifting from ones defined by a preindustrial social structure to ones that were industrialized and more complex. In the face of this upheaval, Durkheim sought to understand how society maintains order and stability. He devised a conceptual framework for understanding the social changes he observed during his lifetime, which he saw as a transformation in the nature of social solidarity. This framework conceived of social development along a continuum with primitive societies of **mechanical solidarity** and more complex modern societies of **organic solidarity**. Societies characterized by mechanical solidarity are those with little or no division of labour while societies characterized by organic solidarity are those with complex divisions of labour. Durkheim believed that when organic solidarity was fully developed, society would be characterized by a fairly high degree of order, but society was undergoing a painful transition. In modern industrial societies with complex divisions of labour, situations exist where societal rules and values or social norms are unclear or not present, and people will not have a sense of how to behave. Durkheim referred to this as **anomie**, or a state of **normlessness**, in which a society in transition lacks the moral values and beliefs that produce social order.

Durkheim theorized that punishment serves the important function of reinforcing the collective conscience; crime provides the opportunity for a ritualistic celebration of social solidarity and therefore has a positive social function. He went so far as to suggest that different kinds of punishment—that is, different kinds of celebration—correspond to the different modes of social solidarity, with brutal "repressive" punishments occurring under mechanical solidarity and "restitutive" punishments typical of advanced organic solidarity. Even in the transitional state of anomie he was witnessing, crime and punishment had, he believed, positive benefits, with crime and disorder evoking an emotional and even vengeful response in the form of punishment. This response reinforces the collective conscience and teaches members of society its norms and values. The reinforcement of these shared norms through collection action counteracts anomie. In this way, society is seen as largely self-correcting. The normlessness associated with social transition gives rise to crime and thus to punishment reactions, which help to combat normlessness as society moves toward a new normative order.

Durkheim's writings on crime and law are unique in that crime is understood as a normal and necessary feature of properly functioning modern society for the first time. According to Durkheim (1895, p. 67), "Crime is normal . . . it is a factor in public health, an integral part of all healthy societies." In this sense Durkheim's views differed from the theorists writing about the same time we reviewed in the previous chapter because they viewed crime as a reflection of an inferior body or a diseased mind.

According to Durkheim, crime contributes to social solidarity in several ways, by: 1) setting moral boundaries; 2) strengthening in-group solidarity; 3) allowing for adaptation or change and 4) reducing internal societal tensions. Each of these will be discussed in turn.

1. **Boundary-Setting Function.** According to Durkheim, crime is functional to society because it performs an important boundary-setting function. When we sanction the criminal (or rule-breaker), society informs its members about **moral boundaries** that we should not cross. The act of sanctioning symbolizes what we are to avoid and reminds us of the punishments we will face if we break the rules. By sanctioning the rule-breaker, moral boundaries are set, helping us understand what it means to live normally.

2. **Group Solidarity Function.** Crime is also a necessary feature of a healthy society because it unites us against a common enemy. Durkheim argued that collective opposition to threats from criminals strengthens the social bonds of the community. Our collective reactions against crime result in a stronger sense of community and therefore a stronger, better society.

3. **Adaptation (Innovation) Function.** Durkheim also sought to provide an explanation for changes in attitudes toward crime. He believed that crime also functioned to move society forward—to adapt and become flexible to a changing environment. Therefore, the adaptive function of crime allows society to change its rules—to revise its moral boundaries—in the face of innovative crimes occurring in times of complex social change.

4. **Tension-Reduction Function.** Durkheim also conceptualized what he termed a tension-reduction function of crime. This function allowed society to reduce internal tensions by projecting social problems onto some criminal or rule-breaking group such as youth or minorities. The tension-reduction function of crime allowed society to maintain a kind of natural equilibrium by dealing with internally produced social tensions.

In these ways and others, Durkheim envisioned crime and punishment as a means of reinforcing the collective conscience to produce social solidarity. For Durkheim, the collective conscience, the shared moral values and beliefs that are common to a given society, is the glue that holds society together.

In the society envisioned by Durkheim, phenomena such as crime are therefore necessary features of society because they are **functional** to society. Because Durkheim's work emphasizes how crime offends **shared moral values** which in turn produces a collective response, his explanations of how societies produce social order and maintain stability is often referred to as a **functionalist approach**. This theme of an underlying potentially functional social order exhibiting some transitional normlessness or anomie is later picked by the American sociological positivists we discuss below. Functionalists are reluctant to see their own society as somehow characterized by structural inequity and conflict. As a result, functionalist theorists have a very difficult time explaining enduring inequalities such as those that persist around group identities of class, race, gender, sex and sexuality.

Durkheim and the American sociological positivists are able to see order and consensus in the midst of classes divided by chaos—this vision is less fundamentally conflictual than the Marxist vision we discuss below. Functionalists want to see society moving in the direction of greater harmony, with sociologists playing an important role in tweaking that harmony through sociological empirical knowledge. For the functionalists, the creation of social harmony does not require a fundamental reorganization of society but rather an understanding of and appreciation for the largely self-correcting processes associated with large-scale social change and careful interventions aimed at accelerating and guiding these processes. For instance, sociologists might be able to suggest reforms to ensure that laws and punishments precisely reflect organic solidarity.

EARLY AMERICAN SOCIOLOGICAL POSITIVISM

Robert E. Park (1864–1944)
Ernest W. Burgess (1886–1966)
Clifford Shaw

Henry McKay
Edwin Sutherland (1893–1950)
Robert King Merton (1910–2003)

HISTORY OF EARLY CRIMINOLOGY IN THE UNITED STATES (1895–1920)

Questions about crime and criminality began to emerge during what was known the Progressive Era in American political history. In 1901, Theodore Roosevelt, leader of the Republican Party and the Progressive movement, became president of the United States of America. The Progressive movement was a broad social reform program of the early 20th century focused on alleviating the human suffering caused by rapid industrialization and urban expansion. In this context, newly emerging social problems became an important topic for social reformers of all kinds, doctors, psychiatrists, prison reformers, social workers, Christian charity groups and temperance organizations such as the Women's Christian Temperance Union (1873), the Anti-Saloon League (1893) and the American Social Hygiene Association (1913). Issues such as crime and punishment were framed within the context of broader social problems such as alcohol use, prostitution, vice, juvenile delinquency and so-called racial and moral degeneracy among the expanding immigrant working classes, including single young women. These groups of people were popularly referred to as the "dangerous classes" whose minds were deemed to be more susceptible to the negative influence of drugs and alcohol which inevitably led to crime and degeneracy.

In the context of these moral reform movements, a less theoretical and more applied strand of sociology (and what would eventually become social work) began to emerge in the United States beginning with the development of the Chicago School in the late 19th century.

CHICAGO SCHOOL OF SOCIOLOGICAL CRIMINOLOGY

Robert E. Park   Henry McKay
Ernest W. Burgess   Clifford Shaw

Major Works

Robert Park and Ernest Burgess, *The City* (1925)
Clifford Shaw and Henry McKay, *Juvenile Delinquency in Urban Areas* (1942)

Main Concepts

Social Disorganization, Urban Ecology, Social Control, Delinquency, Community

Robert E. Park and Ernest W. Burgess

Early Chicago School research took the form of urban ecology research and relied on the concept of social disorganization in understanding social problems. This research focused on inner city neighbourhoods and other geographical areas near the newly established University of Chicago. The sociology department was established at the University of Chicago in 1892 and soon began to conduct urban sociological research that focused on the disorganizing force of urban expansion. Those Chicago School sociologists who focused on urban areas collected quantitative data to map the geographical distribution of social problems within the city. Using these maps, which were divided into zones, Chicago School urban sociologists were able to show how social problems concentrated in certain areas. This led to a focus on the larger urban contexts out of which **social disorganization** emerged.

Robert Park's early work focused on the conflicts between racial groups in America and emphasized the importance of assimilation. Park and colleagues such as Ernest Burgess used an ecological approach to explain the effects of urban expansion. This approach was modelled after the ecological approach in biology in which the relationships among plants, animals and their natural habitats are studied. These relationships are seen as a part of a natural web in which each part depends on the other for every aspect of its survival. Using this ecological approach to the study of urban development, Robert Park, Ernest Burgess and Roderick MacKenzie developed a concentric ring model of the city. The model, published in their book *The City* (1925), illustrated five concentric zones which were an ideal type representation of the effects of economic growth on the city. Beginning with the central business district, the city expands radially outward in rings of increasing affluence from the middle to the periphery (Valier, 2002, p. 44).

Zone of Transition

It was the zone of transition between the working-class district and the manufacturing district that was the focus of interest for criminologists. This is the locale in and out of which the city's poor residents would migrate, creating what Burgess called a process of influx and exodus which made the area particularly prone to disorder. This idea was based on a sociological consensus model which assumed that racial and ethnic heterogeneity (or differences of norms and values) produced social disorder and high rates of crime. This can be seen as a geographic model of anomie. It was only through assimilation that stability could be achieved. Once immigrants assimilated to the American way of life, they would move out of the zone of transition, therefore making the zone of transition the least likely to stabilize. These locales were also characterized as "moral regions" characterized by different and competing moral values and social disorganization. By providing an ecological mapping of these areas, early Chicago School sociologists sought to contribute to social harmony through assimilationist efforts directed at these zones of transition.

Clifford Shaw and Henry McKay

The kind of social disorganization identified by early Chicago School sociologists was picked up Clifford Shaw and Henry McKay, who argued that the deterioration of the inner city led to the disintegration of community which ultimately contributed to juvenile delinquency. In *Juvenile Delinquency and Urban Areas* (1942), Shaw and McKay argued that geographic areas with higher levels of shared moral values had the lowest rates of juvenile delinquency:

> In general, . . . in the areas of low rates of delinquents there is more or less uniformity, consistency, and universality of conventional values and attitudes with respect to child care, conformity to law, and related matters; whereas in the high-rate areas systems of competing and conflicting moral values have developed. (p. 164)

Therefore, Shaw and McKay and other Chicago School sociologists connected juvenile delinquency with low-income geographical areas and connected criminal behaviour to different systems of values and poor social control. The juvenile delinquent was seen as a product of communities that lacked conventional mechanisms for controlling its youth.

Like Durkheim, Shaw and McKay (1942) believed that shared moral values (or social solidarity) is the glue that holds communities together creating effective social controls which prevent rule-breaking by youth. They also echoed Merton's (1938) idea that crime and delinquency are caused when boys in low-income areas lack the opportunities and skills to achieve socially desirable goals because the low-income boys lacked the institutional means to achieve economic success and socially desirable goals that were idealized by American society. The juvenile delinquent boys relied upon acts of delinquency and crime to achieve that success.

SOCIAL STRAIN AND ANOMIE

Robert Merton (1910–2003)

Major Works

Robert King Merton, "Social Structure and Anomie" (1938)

Main Concepts

Anomie, Social Strain, Institutionalized Means, Socially Desirable Goals

Robert Merton (1910–2003)

> . . . Capone represents the triumph of amoral intelligence over morally prescribed "failure," when the channels of vertical mobility are closed or narrowed *in a society which places a high premium on economic affluence and social ascent for all its members.* (Merton, 1938, p. 679)

According to Piers and Messerschmidt (2006), the idea that crime and delinquency are caused when youth in low-income areas lack the opportunity to achieve socially desirable goals implies that juvenile delinquent boys are not antisocial or maladjusted. Instead, their delinquency was understood by Chicago School theorists as rational activity employed by people attempting to achieve the idealized expectations of society through nonconventional means. These ideas were first articulated by Robert Merton, who was a contemporary of the Chicago School sociologists. Merton received his PhD from Harvard University under the direction of the Russian-American sociologist Pitirim A. Sorokin, who founded Harvard's first Department of Sociology. Merton published his most significant contribution to sociological criminology, "Social Structure and Anomie," in 1938 while teaching at Harvard but spent most of his career at Columbia University.

Merton's work is best appreciated in the context of New Deal America (1933–1937). The New Deal was a name President Franklin D. Roosevelt gave to a series of economic and social programs designed to provide relief to the economy during the Great Depression. In a political climate in which the need to defend and enhance the situations of the most economically vulnerable through robust government activity had become broadly accepted, Merton's emphasis on social and economic exclusion as a cause of crime was resonant. Like the work of Chicago school sociologists, Merton's work was a marked departure from biological and individualistic explanations of crime. However, unlike Shaw and McKay and other Chicago School sociologists, Merton did not locate the causes of crime to disorganized neighbourhoods. He sought to provide a purely sociological account of the criminogenic culture of American society, which stressed the idea that the American dream was universally available to members of all social classes. Relying on Durkheim's concept of anomie, Merton linked the pressures exerted by these universal success symbols to nonconforming behaviour. According to Best, "Merton associated anomie with a broad range of troubling behavior, including criminality, drug addiction, and political radicalism . . ." (2004, pp. 3–4). Although Merton outlined and carefully conceptualized a range of possible responses to exclusion, for criminologists, it was obviously the response of criminal conduct which was most interesting.

Merton argued that American culture stressed the cultural goals of accumulation of wealth and prosperity but failed to provide adequate institutional means to all social classes to achieve those **socially desired goals**. This disconnect between socially valued goals and the **institutional means** available to achieve those goals created an anomic society. In well-integrated societies, the goals and means are readily available and socially accepted by all classes of society. Unstable societies, or those characterized by social disorder, are ones in which the means of achieving socially desirable goals are unavailable to members of certain classes, which causes **social strain** on those who are denied the means to achieve society's definition of success. In this way, antisocial behaviour is "called forth" by both the conventional values of culture and by the class character of a society which fails to provide universal access to legitimate opportunities to achieve social successes (Merton, 1938, pp. 678–9). Those denied access to institutionally acceptable means are pressured

> to rely on illegitimate, but more or less effective, expedients of vice and crime. The cultural demands made on persons in this situation are incompatible. On the one hand, they are asked to orient their conduct toward the prospect of accumulating wealth and on the other, they are largely denied effective opportunities to do so institutionally. The consequences of such structural inconsistency are psychopathological personality, and/or antisocial conduct, and/or revolutionary activities. The equilibrium between culturally designated means and ends becomes highly unstable with the progressive emphasis on attaining the prestige-laden end by any means whatsoever. (Merton, 1938, p. 679)

Thus, social strain exists in societies that place emphasis on universal goals without providing the legitimate means for all social classes (also divided by race and ethnicity) to achieve those goals.

It may be tempting to view simple poverty as the primary predictor of strain within Merton's analysis. However, Merton was careful to emphasize the strain caused by the ideology of the American dream coupled with lack of opportunity within class structures. Therefore, in addition to examining the goals and means of a given society, Merton also emphasized the impact of strong cultural expectations of material success in the context of rigid class structures (or castes) in producing high rates of crime and disorder in American society:

> A comparatively rigidified class structure, a feudalistic or caste order, may limit such opportunities far beyond the point which above all else, certain *common* symbols of success *for the population at large* while its social structure rigorously restricts *for a considerable part of the same population*, that antisocial behaviour ensues on a considerable scale. In other words, our egalitarian ideology denies by implication the existence of noncompeting groups and individuals in the pursuit of pecuniary success. (Merton, 1938, p. 681)

Therefore, it is the combination of "poverty, limited opportunity and a commonly shared system of success symbols" that explains "the higher association between poverty and crime in [American] society than in others . . ." (Merton, 1938, p. 682). Merton goes on to stress that in Southwestern European societies, poverty and associated disadvantages are less highly correlated with crime. Crime is reduced in cultures which stress "differential class symbols of achievement" but which nonetheless have rigidified class structures and limited opportunities (Merton, 1938, p. 682). For Merton, it was not so much poverty and disadvantage leading to limited opportunities for the achievement of success that produced social strain toward crime. Rather, it is the overemphasis upon a universalized definition of success for all class structures that leads to higher rates of criminality in a given society. Therefore, within the Mertonian framework, crime reduction must necessarily involve more diversification of success symbols so that each class within society may achieve some kind of socially valued success.

DIFFERENTIAL ASSOCIATION AND WHITE-COLLAR CRIME

Edwin H. Sutherland (1883–1950)

Major Works

Edwin Sutherland, *Principles of Criminology* (1947, originally published 1924)

Main Concepts

Differential Association, Social Organiza-tion, Interaction, White-Collar Crime

Edwin H. Sutherland (1883–1950)

Like Merton, Sutherland rejected the idea that criminality is biologically inherited. Sutherland sought to develop a general sociological theory of crime applicable to all situations and events. In doing so, he emphasized patterns of interaction and learned behaviour. Sutherland argued that people were influenced by those around them. According to Best (2004, p. 6), Sutherland's theory is basically "an academic version of the classic parents' warning against their children associating with bad companions."

Sutherland's propositions insist upon the ordinariness of disorderly conduct; criminal behaviour is just like any other behaviour because it is *learned* through association (and interaction) with one's peers. In this regard, crime is also conceived of as the product of normal social and psychological processes rather than any kind of biological weakness or mental illness. The idea that crime is learned through interaction within small group settings (differential association) can also be understood as a kind of social anthropology of disorder (Downes & Rock, 2003). In *Principles of Criminology* (org. pub. [1924] 1947), Sutherland set out nine principles of differential association to explain his very general sketch of the manner in which criminal behaviour is learned. These are:

1. *Criminal behavior is learned behavior.* Negatively, this means that criminal behavior is not inherited, as such; also, the person who is not already trained in crime does not

invent criminal behavior, just as a person does not make mechanical inventions unless he is trained in mechanics.

2. *Criminal behavior is learned in interaction with other persons in a process of communication.* This communication is verbal in many respects but includes also "the communication of gestures."

3. *The principal part of the learning of criminal behavior occurs within intimate personal groups.* Negatively, this means that the impersonal agencies of communication, such as picture shows and newspapers, play a relatively unimportant part in the genesis of criminal behavior.

4. *When criminal behavior is learned, the learning includes (a) techniques of committing the crime,* which are sometimes very complicated, sometimes very simple; *(b) the specific direction of motives, drives, rationalizations, and attitudes.*

5. *The specific direction of motives and drives is learned from definitions of legal codes as favorable and unfavorable.* In some societies an individual is surrounded by persons who invariably define the legal codes as rules to be observed, whereas in others he is surrounded by persons whose definitions are favorable to the violation of the legal codes. In our American society these definitions are almost always mixed, and consequently we have culture conflict in relation to the legal codes.

6. *A person becomes delinquent because of an excess of definitions favorable to violation of law over definitions unfavorable to violation of law.* This is the principle of differential association. It refers to both criminal and anti-criminals associations and has to do with counteracting forces When persons become criminals, they do so because of contacts with criminal patterns and also because of isolation from anti-criminal patterns. [. . .]

7. *Differential associations may vary in frequency, duration, priority, and intensity.* This means that associations with criminal behavior and also associations with anti-criminal behavior vary in those respects. [. . .] "Priority" is assumed to be important in the sense that lawful behavior developed in early childhood may persist throughout life, and also that delinquent behavior developed in early childhood may persist throughout life. "Intensity" is not precisely defined, but it has to do with such things as the prestige of the source of a criminal or anti-criminal pattern and with emotional reactions related to the associations. [. . .]

8. *The process of learning criminal behavior by association with criminal and anti-criminal patterns involves all of the mechanisms that are involved in any other learning.* Negatively, this means that the learning of criminal behavior is not restricted to the process of imitation. A person who is seduced, for instance, learns criminal behavior by association, but this process would not ordinarily be described as imitation.

9. *Though criminal behavior is an expression of general needs and values, it is not explained by those general needs and values since non-criminal behavior is an expression of the same needs and values.* Thieves generally steal in order to secure money, but likewise honest labourers work in order to secure money. The attempts by many scholars to explain criminal behavior by general drives and values, such as the happiness principle, striving for social status, the money motive, or frustration, have been and must continue to be futile since they explain lawful behavior as completely

as they explain criminal behaviour. They are similar to respiration, which is necessary for any behavior but which does not differential criminal from non-criminal behavior. (Sutherland, 1947, pp. 5–7)

Rather than get bogged down in the details of each of these nine propositions, it is perhaps better to understand Sutherland's contribution to criminology more generally as one that sees criminal behaviour as no different from noncriminal behaviour—both are expressions of general needs and values and the product of the same kinds of learning processes. Sutherland argued that nonconformity is a way of life, just like any other, that is learned and passed on through successive generations.

In later works such as *The Professional Thief* (1937) and *White Collar Crime* (1949), Sutherland made a radical departure from earlier works on crime by examining the activities of professional thieves and white-collar criminals (nowadays referred to as corporate criminals). In these works, he shifted the focus away from the relations among inner-city poverty, working- class immigration and criminality toward an examination of criminal conduct across class structures. In *White Collar Crime* in particular, Sutherland demonstrated that crime is socially distributed across all class structures. He was able to show that by relying on official statistics, other Chicago School sociologists had provided a distorted picture of the social distribution of criminality. These statistics gave the inaccurate impression that poverty was the primary predictor of crime (Bierne & Messerschmidt, 2006, p. 337).

MID-CENTURY AMERICAN SOCIOLOGICAL POSITIVISM

Howard Becker	Robert Seidman
Richard Quinney	Jock Young
William Chambliss	Ian Taylor
Robert Seidman	Paul Walton
Edwin Schur	Stanley Cohen
Erving Goffman	

THE LABELLING PERSPECTIVE

Major Works

Erving Goffman, *Stigma* (1963)

Howard Becker, *Outsiders* (1963)

Edwin Schur, *Crimes without Victims* (1965)

Main Concepts

Labelling, Deviant, Deviance, Social Reaction, Victimless Crimes, Deviance Amplification

Howard Becker (1928–)

The labelling perspective emerged in the 1960s in the context of various kinds of rebellion against established political authority. U.S. foreign policy in Vietnam was widely rejected, and radical intellectuals, civil rights groups and the women's movement challenged sex-, gender- and race-based forms of discrimination. The so-called sexual revolution also emerged in the 1960s with the decriminalization and subsequent widespread availability of the birth control pill and the increased availability of sexually explicit materials with the publication of *Playboy* and *Penthouse* men's magazines. Along with this, U.S. antipornography statues were struck down by the courts as violations of freedom of expression. Marijuana and drug use, particularly LSD, by middle-class youth and young adults became newsworthy when otherwise respectable individuals were charged by police and subject to harsh legal penalties. In this context, studies of social problems shifted from the lower classes toward political authority and power structures. Political authority and oppressive power structures were increasingly seen as illegitimate:

> All of these developments had the effect of making police, and social control generally, seem unsympathetic in many eyes. The upbeat functionalist vision of social order, in which social-control agents somehow maintained order and protected a smoothly functioning society, now seemed naïve. The police were the ones beating non-violent protesters against segregation and busting good kids who smoked harmless weed. (Best, 2004, p. 26)

The labelling perspective offered a way of understanding these phenomena by shifting the focus away from crime and disorder toward the reactions that certain kinds of behaviours and political activities provoked. Becker and others challenged the Durkheimian worldview relied upon by both Chicago School theorists and Robert Merton because they were able to demonstrate that modern societies did not reveal themselves to be organic structures in which there was a consensus around rules and how they should be enforced.

By shifting the focus away from crime, the labelling framework examined **social reaction** and its effects upon individuals and groups subject to the process of **labelling** acts and people as **deviant**. This is summed up in Howard Becker's now famous quote from *Outsiders* (1963):

> *Social groups create deviance by making the rules whose infraction constitutes deviance,* and by applying those rules to particular people and labeling them as outsiders. From this point of view, deviance is not a quality of the act the person commits, but rather a consequence of the application by others of rules and sanctions to an "offender." The deviant is one to whom that label has successfully been applied; deviant behavior is behavior that people so label. (p. 9)

Because the labelling framework focused on social reaction to deviant behaviour, it fit well with the counterculture politics of the 1960s. Rather than focus on the causes of crime, the labelling framework allowed researchers to examine the effects of deviant labels. These researchers tended to portray those labelled deviant in sympathetic, even romanticized terms (Best, 2004). They tended to focus almost exclusively on the social control of **victimless crimes**, ignoring crimes of violence altogether. Informed by the labelling perspective, intellectuals and the public alike called for the decriminalization of abortion, the reform of drug laws and an end to the discriminatory laws and sometimes police brutality aimed at gays and lesbians. Thus, the tendency of the labelling perspective was to challenge the social control of exchanges between consenting adults (which also included the consumption of pornography and prostitution).

This style of social enquiry revealed that perhaps there were underlying power relations that gave rise to particular kinds of deviance depending upon the actions of those in political power who made and applied the rules. By demonstrating that political power was applied unevenly, labelling revealed that the idea of a consensual moral order prominent within the functionalist research of Durkheim, Merton and the Chicago School sociologists was largely fictional.

The labelling research contributed to the **decriminalization** of certain kinds of consensual behaviour, the **diversion** of victimless crimes and petty theft out of the criminal courts and the movement toward the decarceration of correctional inmates and the mentally ill into the community for rehabilitation and healthcare. It also provided support for restitution to victims and associated movements toward reintegrative shaming of offenders and other systems of restorative justice (Piers & Messerschmidt, 2006).

The insights of the labelling framework established the intellectual groundwork for social constructionism in sociological criminology. **Social constructionist** scholars highlight the social and political processes involved in the social construction of "social problems" and moral panics. In the United States, sociologists such as Philip Jenks and Joel Best have drawn attention to the role of the mass media and "moral entrepreneurs" in framing "the public perception of the causes, prevalence, and seriousness of crimes such as serial murder, child abuse, drug use, prostitution, drinking and driving, and terrorism" (Piers & Messerschmidt, 2006, p. 386). In drawing attention to the exaggeration of certain social problems, social constructionists develop the concept of **deviance amplification** from labelling theory to highlight the role of the mass media in the sensationalization of various issues.

NEO-MARXISM: NEW LEFT AND RADICAL CRIMINOLOGY

Richard Quinney	Ian Taylor
William Chambliss	Paul Walton
Robert Seidman	Stanley Cohen
Jock Young	

NEW LEFT CRIMINOLOGY IN THE UNITED STATES

Richard Quinney
William Chambliss
Robert Seidman

Major Works

William Chambliss and Robert Seidman, *Law, Order and Power* (1971)
Richard Quinney, *Class, State, and Crime* (1977)

Main Concepts

Crimes of Accommodation, Crimes of Domination, Criminalization

Scholars influenced by Marx extended the analyses of political authority developed within labelling theory and social constructionism. "New Left" scholars in the United States picked up on and extended orthodox Marxism to provide analyses of the role of law, policing and punishment in modern capitalist societies. New Left scholars such as Richard Quinney, William Chambliss and Robert Seidman in the United States continued to focus on the nature of social order but in a manner quite different from the scholarship discussed thus far. New Left criminologists argued that **criminalization** and **social control** were central to the maintenance of an oppressive capitalist social order. Using Marxist theory, Richard Quinney argued that law, and criminal law in particular, secures the interests of the capitalist class and preserves the existing economic and social order. In *Class, State, and Crime* (1977), Quinney identified several sorts of crime committed either by the capitalist ruling class or the working class. He divided these sorts of crimes in two categories, crimes of domination and crimes of accommodation. The sorts of crimes committed by the ruling class are located in economic exploitation and are **crimes of domination**. These crimes committed in the furtherance of capitalist economic exploitation go largely unregulated:

1. *Crimes of Control*—these crimes such as illegal surveillance and violations of civil liberties are committed by the police and law enforcement agencies;

2. *Crimes of Government*—these include political crimes such as the Canadian Federal Sponsorship Scandal in which $100 million of public funds were paid by the Liberal Party to private ad firms in Quebec purportedly to promote federalism but from which Canadian taxpayers derived no benefit;

3. *Crimes of Economic Domination*—these include corporate crimes such as price fixing, syndicated crime and pollution;

4. *Social Injury*—these involve the denial of basic human rights, sexism and racism, which are not deemed criminal offences.

In contrast, the sorts of crimes committed by the working class are located in the context of capitalist oppression and are **crimes of accommodation**. These are the sorts of things that are done as a way of adapting to or accommodating the oppressive conditions of capitalism by the working classes:

1. *Predatory Crimes*—burglary, robbery and drug dealing, which are part of a survival strategy;

2. *Personal Crimes*—murder, assault and sexual assault, which are a product of being brutalized by capitalism;

3. *Defensive Crimes*—such as industrial sabotage committed by alienated workers.
   (Quinney, 1977; Jones, 2001, p. 245; Piers & Messerschmidt, 2006, pp. 397–8)

Quinney revealed that crimes of domination are not criminalized or policed in the same way that crimes of accommodation are criminalized and policed. Crimes of accommodation are a normal response to the contradictions of capitalism. He argued that crimes of domination are much more harmful to society but that they are ignored because it benefits the ruling class that this be so. In this regard, Quinney took an instrumentalist view of the state to argue that law is a weapon of class rule and, as such, the capitalist class is largely immune to criminal sanction (Comack, 2006, p. 37). In other words, the criminal law should be viewed as an instrument or tool of the ruling class relied upon to control the exploited class for the benefit of the ruling class.

Instrumental analyses of law cannot account for those instances in which law benefits the working classes such as workplace health and safety law or when the capitalist classes are prosecuted by the state for price fixing or polluting. In response to this inadequacy, structural analyses of law and crime emerged which viewed the state (and law) as providing the capitalist class with the means of reproducing the long-term interests of the capitalist class. The structuralist account of the role of the law (administered by the state) provides the opportunity to account for those instances when the crimes of the capitalist class are policed and prosecuted as well as those instances when laws are enforced to the overall benefit of the working class. Their analyses point to the ideological nature of law. According to Comack (2006, p. 40), structural neo-Marxists argue that in its ". . . ideological form, law acts as a legitimizer of capitalist social relations." This is often achieved when the law advances such notions as formal legal equality of all before the law but fails to acknowledge the uneven application of the law or to call into question exploitative class relations. Structuralists provide a more nuanced description of the role of the law under capitalism by assessing how the law ensures both the symbolic legitimacy of the capitalist economic system and its long-term reproduction. For the most part, both the instrumental and structural analyses argue that crime control (and mainstream criminal justice policy) fails to address or question the exploitative structure of the power base of capitalist society. As a result, governmental criminology addresses only the symptoms of capitalism rather than the root causes of both crimes of domination and crimes of accommodation.

NEW LEFT CRIMINOLOGY IN BRITAIN

Ian Taylor   Stan Cohen

Paul Walton   Stuart Hall

Jock Young

Major Works

Ian Taylor, Paul Walton and Jock Young, *The New Criminology* (1973); *Critical Criminology* (1975)

Stanley Cohen, *Folk Devils and Moral Panics* (1972)

Stuart Hall, *Policing the Crisis* (1978)

Main Concepts

Criminalization, Correctionalism, Moral Panic, Social Construction

In the British context, New Left scholars such as Taylor, Walton and Young (1973) sought to move beyond the insights of the labelling perspective to provide a more nuanced

Marxist-based analysis of the direct role played by the ruling class in the creation of deviance and the enforcement of criminal law. Their arguments moved beyond the labelling framework to identify the ruling class as those who do the "labelling" of working class patterns of individual behaviour as deviant. They argued that those with the power to criminalize will do so in a manner that protects their own long-term economic interests. In capitalist societies marked by inequalities of class, expressions of ruling class interests extend to the realm of crime control. Those acts of deviance committed by the working class will inevitably be subject to greater social control efforts on the part of the authorities who individualize and pathologize crime, thereby drawing attention away from the oppressive relations of the capitalist social structure that give rise to crimes of accommodation such as theft and violence.

Taylor, Walton and Young (1973) were also very critical of the work of earlier criminologists. They argued that these "mainstream" scholars failed to grasp the realities of wealth and power in the policing of crime. They also said that "any criminology which was not normatively committed to the abolition of the inequalities of wealth and power was inevitably bound to fall into correctionalism" (Taylor, Walton, & Young, 1973, p. 281). This stance toward **correctionalism**, or what we have already discussed in Chapter 1 as administrative criminology, is based on the observation that mainstream criminology was rooted in a conservative theory of values. According to Valier (2002, p. 111), "[t]hey objected that strain theory took the existing society for granted and that labelling theory left aside questions of whose interests the definers represented, as well as the ways in which their actions reinforced the nature of capitalist society." The "New Criminology" of Taylor, Walton and Young (1973) was committed to the development of more comprehensive descriptions of the root causes of social disorder in an effort to bring true and lasting harmony to society, and in this they were critical of the work of criminology itself. This new approach was steadfastly opposed to the science of social control, which they believed took shape within criminal justice policy advanced by earlier mainstream administrative criminologists. They insisted on a commitment to radical social change through struggles for social justice.

Also during this time, Stanley Cohen picked up on the notion of societal reaction to examine in more detail the processes involved in the **social construction of social problems**. Cohen's (1972) research revealed how the media, police and various moral entrepreneurs are able to create what Cohen called a **moral panic** around two rival youth styles (the Mods and the Rockers) in southern England in the 1960s. Cohen argued that the mass media did not report or create news of a particular crisis; instead, they reproduced and sustained dominant interpretations of and solutions for those crises. In this regard, the media was also seen as an agent of social control that helped frame political reaction to social problems and, in so doing, functioned to reproduce the dominant power relations of capitalism.

The unfortunate tendency in New Left scholarship was to romanticize the crimes committed by the working class as political acts engaged in as a response to capitalism. As a reaction, this branch of criminology very quickly developed a new strand of neo-Marxist theorizing called Left Realism. After all, it was pointed out that the victims of working-class criminality are other members of the working class, including women and children. Left Realism is mainly associated with British criminologists such as Jock Young, who published a chapter in *Critical Criminology* (1975) which was the follow-up book to Taylor, Walton and Young's *New*

Criminology (1973). Here Young reframed his earlier position to argue that crime, particularly violent crime, has real effects mainly upon women and that this must be taken seriously both by the authorities and by New Left criminology.

FRENCH POSTPOSITIVISM

Michel Foucault

Major Works

Michel Foucault, *Discipline and Punish: The Birth of the Prison* (1975)

Main Concepts

Moral Regulation, Discipline, Discourse, Power/Knowledge, Subjectivity, Genealogy, Governmentality, Poststructuralism, Post-modernism, Postpositivism

Michel Foucault (1926–1984)

The suspicion of correctionalism which informed the work of the New Left criminologists only went so far. Poststructuralist scholars such as Michel Foucault saw in the doctrines of Marxism the same kind of claims to authority and hence to social domination as the claims of administrative criminology. Foucault sought just as vigorously as the New Left to expose the dangers of administrative criminology, as well as of other "human sciences" such as psychiatry, penology and sexology, but he did not seek to replace these sciences with a new, better science like the New Criminology. Rather, he encouraged the suspicion of all such psychological and social scientific **discourses**.

In Chapter 1, we introduced a range of concepts developed by Foucault to understand power. Here we examine Foucault's critiques of the human sciences and the systems of **regulation** and control that emerged throughout the 19th century. Foucault's work on the emergence and operation of modern forms of power is very closely linked to a critique of the Enlightenment and of the kind of knowledge produced by the sociological positivists we have discussed thus far. For Foucault, the Enlightenment contained within it a sinister element that had gone relatively unnoticed but which has had a significant impact upon how in the modern world we understand ourselves and our history. Rejecting the positivist view that social science can identify the true nature and potential of modernity so that so-ciety can be improved, Foucault claimed that the positivist human sciences, developing within and organizing our systems of government, construct modernity; *Foucault views modernity as a product of human sciences which includes the sociological knowledge about the causes of crime and social disorder we have discussed in this chapter*. In books such as *Madness and Civilization* (1961), *The Birth of the Clinic* (1963), *The Archaeology of Knowledge* (1969) and *Discipline and Punish* (1975), Foucault sought to show that ideas and professional practices developed in universities, prisons and clinics provided the foundation of the modern social order. Through critical research he called **genealogy**, Foucault examined the production of positivist knowledge that emerged within these institutional settings. His aim is to use this historical work to make his readers aware of ways of thinking about themselves that they have absorbed from the positivist knowledge which has influenced all institutions of society.

For Foucault, the discipline of criminology and the institutions of the criminal justice system produce knowledge that frames human subjects in distinctive ways and then subjects them to disciplinary norms and standards. Especially significant for criminological study are the arguments Foucault made in relation to changing forms of punishment, particularly the development of the prison in the early 19th century, which coincided with the industrial revolution. Foucault argued that modern states emerged alongside the development of prisons, hospitals and even army barracks, which were engaged in techniques of management and control that transformed the population into a newly disciplined citizenry and workforce.

Foucauldian research does not aim to substitute a more complete theory of society and deviance for the academic and professional theories it analyzes. Rather, Foucauldians want to show us that positivist social theories and the systems of government they produce construct society and its members in a particular way. In this view, there is no deep truth about human nature or human history to discover; all such claims are just vehicles for the organization of society. Whereas the New Left is engaged in perfecting neo-Marxist theories to inform radically inclined government about the proper causes of and responses to social disorder based on their vision of society, Foucauldians want us to see that these new ideas are merely variants on the same theme.

References

Becker, H. (1963). *Outsiders: Studies in the sociology of deviance*. New York: Macmillan.

Best, J. (2004). *Deviance: The career of a concept*. Florence, KY: Wadsworth Cengage Learning.

Beirne, P., & Messerschmidt, J. W. (2006). *Criminology* (4th ed.). Los Angeles: Roxbury Publishing.

Chambliss, W., & Seidman, R. B. (1971). *Law, order and power*. Reading, MA: Addison-Wesley.

Cohen, S. (1973). *Folk devils and moral panics*. St Albans, UK: Paladin.

Comack, E. (Ed.) (2006). *Locating law: Race, class, gender, sexuality connections*. (2nd ed.). Toronto: Fernwood.

Durkheim, É. (1997 [1893]). *The division of labour in society*. New York: Free Press.

Durkheim, É. (1982 [1895]). *The rules of the sociological method* (W.D. Halls, Trans.). New York: The Free Press.

Durkheim, É. (1967 [1897]). *Suicide*. Paris: Presses universitaires de France.

Fanon, F. (1961). *Les damnés de la terre*. [*Wretched of the earth*]. Paris: Librairie François Maspero.

Fitzpatrick, P. (1992). *The Mythology of modern law*. London: Routledge.

Foucault, M. (1975/1991). *Discipline and punish: The birth of the prison*. London: Penguin.

Goffman, E. (1963/1990). *Stigma*. London: Penguin.

Hall, S., et al. (1978). *Policing the crisis: Mugging, the state and law and order*. London: Macmillan.

Jones, S. (2001). *Criminology* (3rd ed.). Oxford: Oxford University Press.

Marx, K. (1867). *Das Kapital*. New York: L.W. Schmidt.

Marx, K., & Engels, F. (1967). *The communist manifesto*. London: Penguin.

Merton, R. (1938). Social structure and anomie. *American Sociological Review, 3*, 672–682. Reprinted in Stompka, P. (Ed.). (1996). *On Social structure and science: Essays by Robert K. Merton*. Chicago: University of Chicago Press.

Park, R., & Burgess, E. (1925). *The city.* Chicago: University of Chicago Press.

Quinney, R. (1977). *Class, state, and crime.* New York: Longman.

Shaw, C., & McKay, H. (1942). *Juvenile delinquency in urban areas.* Chicago: University of Chicago Press.

Schur, E. (1965). *Crimes without victims: Deviant behavior and public policy.* Englewood Cliffs, NJ: Prentice Hall.

Sutherland, E. H. (1947/1924). *Principles of criminology.* Chicago: University of Chicago Press.

Sutherland, E. H. (1937). *The professional thief.* Chicago: University of Chicago Press.

Sutherland, E. H. (1949). *White collar crime.* New York: Dryden Press.

Taylor, I., Walton, P., & Young, J. (1973). *The new criminology.* London: Routledge & Kegan Paul.

Taylor, I., Walton, P., & Young, J. (Eds.). (1975). *Critical criminology.* London: Routledge & Kegan Paul.

Valier, C. (2002). *Theories of crime and punishment.* Harlow, UK: Longman.

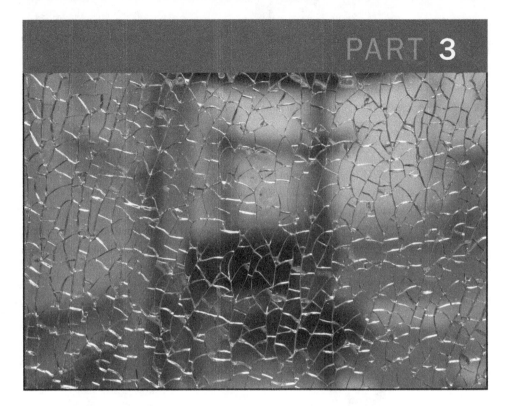

PART 3

Contemporary Conceptual Tools

Chapter 7 Feminist Contributions to Criminology
Kirsten Kramar, *University of Winnipeg*

Chapter 8 Critical Realist Criminology
Jon Frauley, *University of Ottawa*

Chapter 9 On Postcolonialism and Criminology
Renisa Mawani, *University of British Columbia,* and
David Sealy, *York University*

Chapter 10 Governmentality and Criminology
Randy Lippert, *University of Windsor,* and
Grace Park, *York University*

CHAPTER 7

Feminist Contributions to Criminology

Kirsten Kramar, University of Winnipeg

INTRODUCTION

This chapter focuses on the contributions made by feminists in the field of criminology. It describes and assesses the impact of feminism in three main areas of criminology: theories of women's deviance; the criminal law as it relates to women victims and offenders; and policy and practice in women's prisons. Nineteenth and early 20th-century "first-wave" feminists focused primarily on officially mandated inequalities and on those public issues such as suffrage, equal access to professions and their schools and the reform of property rights for women. In the 1960s and 1970s, "second-wave" feminists identified women's sexuality as the main target of the coercive and violent power exercised by men over women. Because male violence and coercion is largely directed at women in the domestic sphere, feminists' reform efforts focused on those issues directly connected to the control of women's sexuality in the home. However, they also pointed out that the violent oppression of women which occurred "in private" was supported by wider societal norms and institutions, including the criminal law. This generation of feminists used their earlier sisters' language but proclaimed that, for them, the "private is public." In this way, they were able to continue the discussion of feminist principles while expanding the domain of their critical engagement.

Seeking to reconceptualize the state's response to violence against women, second-wave feminists challenged a broad spectrum of laws and policies that controlled sexuality and authorized violence against women and female children (Valier, 2002, p. 128). They worked to decriminalize abortion, reform rape law, police wife-battering and censor violent, degrading and dehumanizing pornography. The issue of violent abuse of women by intimate partners was championed with especially strong and coordinated campaigns by women's groups, both in Canada and internationally. The victimization of women by patriarchal and capitalist structures was the central organizing feature of the second-wave feminist movement. At the same time during the 1970s and 1980s, French feminists such as Julia Kristeva, Hélène Cixous and Luce Irigaray focused on the concept of "writing from the body" or "feminine writing" (écriture féminine) to challenge male-centred philosophy of knowledge that was rooted in male experience.

Third-wave feminism began to appear in the 1990s in the writing of antiracist feminists as a response to second-wave feminism's tendency to assume that gender is a monolithic category. The idea that there was a universal women's experience predated the third-wave feminist movements' critiques in the writings of some late 19th-century critics such as anarcha-feminist Emma Goldman (1869–1940). Goldman distanced herself from first-wave feminist suffragettes who fought for the right to vote only for white women of privilege and because they sought to criminalize prostitution rather than support the fight to end the economic exploitation of women by capitalism, slavery and patriarchy (Rimke, 2009, pp. 1411–1412).

In the 1980s, antiracist feminists revived these criticisms of feminism and began to criticize white mainstream feminists' tendency to assume that their experiences could be universalized to include all women (Pinterics, 2001). Third-wave feminist was also a response to the backlash against second-wave feminism that gained considerable strength in the fiscally conservative era toward the end of the 20th century in Canada, the United States and the United Kingdom. Unlike postfeminism, which some argue is apolitical because it abandons structural analyses of patriarchal power (Genz, 2006), third-wave feminism extends second-wave feminism in new and interesting ways. In many ways, the second-wave–third-wave designation is an artificial divide. Third-wave feminists are also sometimes called Gen-X feminists because they were born in the 1960s and 1970s and have benefited from the gains made by both first- and second-wave feminism. This new generation of feminists also reacted against the perceived elitism and rigid morality of second-wave feminists who connected a rejection of consumer culture and the trappings of feminine beauty with patriarchal oppression. Third-wave feminists embraced this consumer culture wholeheartedly, but they also campaigned against violence against women, the rights of gays and lesbians, healthcare for those infected with HIV, affordable and accessible childcare, and global and environmental awareness (Pinterics, 2001). This new generation of feminists is sometimes inaccurately portrayed as criticizing their mothers as being stone-faced, hairy-legged man-haters who embraced victimhood. In fact, this image is largely constructed by an antifeminist media which attempts to undermine feminism by picking up on debates and disagreements about violence against women and sexual expression within feminist debates about pornography. Third-wave feminism has been critical of the some of the second-wave feminists' rules for being a "real feminist," relying on poststructuralist theory to argue that these "feminist discourses" are as restrictive for women as the "sexist discourses," that continue to be challenged by both second- and third-wave feminism. Third-wave feminism made a unique contribution to the feminist struggles for political freedom by situating itself firmly within popular culture and embracing all aspects of 21st-century consumer oriented culture. Third-wave feminism also offered more advanced theoretical critiques of the oppression of women which also rejected the discourse of victimization embraced by second-wave feminism to mobilize political action. They examined the ways in which the lasting effects of colonialism impacted women of colour differently than white women, and they also provided more sophisticated theoretical analyses of various expressions of power. As Genz (2006, pp. 340–341) argues, third-wave feminism is "founded on second wave principles" but offers a "more complex theorization of multiple forms of oppression that received relatively little attention within the second." Even though each of these waves of feminist activism and scholarship focuses on different social issues at different points in history, they share a common focus on women's social, legal, political and sexual freedom from the exploitative conditions that contour women's lives.

FEMINIST CRIMINOLOGY

It is within this context that feminism has, not surprisingly, made significant contributions to the field of criminology, with Canadian feminists at the forefront of these developments. Feminist contributors to criminology have sought to address the failure of the law and the courts to protect women from male violence and oppression. They have also challenged the sexist and otherwise inappropriate treatment of (the relatively small number) of women offenders by the courts and especially the correctional system. Both of these problems derive in part from the influence of sexist assumptions, and feminists have constantly drawn attention to the law's tendency to reinforce sexist institutions. As one aspect of this, second-wave feminists have exposed sexist assumptions underlying first-wave feminist ideas regarding criminal justice, ideas which were influential during the early to mid-20th century, especially in women's corrections. In addition, feminists have challenged a range of established criminological theories as reflecting similar sexist assumptions. Now, both second- and third-wave feminism have become highly influential within academic criminology. Writing in the early 1990s, Mariana Valverde (1991, p. 241) argued that among academic criminologists "it is no longer true that women's issues are being ignored, for there are entire shelves of work on women as victims of male violence, women offenders and women police officers. The more extreme examples of sexism found in criminological theory have been discredited – at least in the eyes of those who read feminist works." This influence is felt, to a considerable degree, beyond academia in the criminal justice system itself.

In examining the impact of second- and third-wave feminism on theories of women's deviance, the criminal law as it relates to women victims and offenders, and policy and practice in women's prisons, the focus of the next section of this chapter will be on key feminist ideas which have influenced mainstream criminology. Certainly, some theoretical schools of feminism have had more direct impact on criminal law and justice policy than others. Although it is a simplification, commentators often divide academic second-wave feminism into "liberal," "socialist" and "radical" versions. Liberal feminists believe that feminist goals can be achieved through the reform of the existing political and economic system. Their feminist agenda is more or less seen as an extension of liberal democratic ideals of equality of legal and political rights and social opportunities. Socialist feminists insist that feminist goals can only be achieved through the development of a socialist political and economic system. This is due in part because existing patriarchal oppressions are products of the existing economic system. Radical feminists view men and women as more fundamentally at odds than do either liberal or socialist feminists. They insist that the foundation of contemporary and historical societies is their patriarchal character and that women's interests cannot be secured without unqualified confrontation with those of men. Third-wave feminism is informed by academic poststructuralism and a multiculturalist or postcolonial sensibility to point out that our diverse experiences are sometimes contradictory and always complex. Despite their differences, which will be discussed in this chapter, all second- and third-wave feminists have shared concerns about male violence and the control of women's sexuality through criminal law, which have had such an impact on mainstream criminology.

CHALLENGING SEXISM WITHIN CRIMINOLOGICAL THEORY

The broad range of criminological theories developed in the hundred or so years since Cesare Lombroso first proposed his "positive criminology" were presented in Chapter 5 of Part Two of this text. While there are contemporary versions of even the earliest criminological theories, they are open to devastating criticisms, often appearing to be mostly products of the prejudices and preoccupations of their times. Not surprisingly, the history of criminological theory is replete with instances of extreme sexism in relation to women as both victims and offenders. A major contribution of feminism to mainstream criminology has been to expose and challenge this legacy.

According to Loraine Gelsthorpe, early criminological theorizing around female offenders was often confusing and contradictory:

> On the one hand, a female offender or delinquent is seen as 'weak,' 'submissive' and 'dependent,' and, therefore, in need of protection. On the other hand, her offending is associated with 'uncontrollable sexuality' or with the rejection of prescribed feminine roles (e.g. through aggressive behaviour) and therefore, she is an object of condemnation and contempt. In both cases, however, there is perhaps a further tendency to perceive the female as a creature of impulse,

easily swayed by emotion and, in the extreme cases, incapable of fully intending her own actions. This frequently leads to the interpretation of her behaviour as mentally abnormal or unstable. (1989, p. 1)

The critical analyses of feminist criminologists such as Gelsthorpe is more than just "cleaning house" because criminological theories have an impact outside academia, fusing with and influencing other currents of thought and practice in the criminal justice system and even in wider society. Indeed, from this perspective, criminology has from the time of Lombroso been as much a part of the criminal justice as an external observer of it (Garland, 1985). As a result, exposing and challenging sexism within criminology can ultimately improve the experiences of women victims and perpetrators of crime. In particular, feminist criminologists have challenged the notion that women who commit crimes are mentally unstable. Instead, their analyses focus on the ways in which structural inequality and oppression compel women to commit economic and other crimes. Nevertheless, women in conflict with the law have a tendency to appeal to psychological mitigation frameworks to explain their offending behaviour because the law indicts individual rather than societal forces.

The close historical relationship between criminological theories regarding women and the treatment of women by the criminal justice system is reflected in two key critical concepts developed by feminist analysts. First, feminists claim that women offenders are often regarded, and sanctioned, as **"doubly deviant,"** being seen to have simultaneously transgressed both the criminal law and societal norms for appropriate feminine behaviour. The contrast is with male offenders, whose criminal actions are seen as violations of criminal law but as more or less consistent with the willful, assertive, self-pleasing ways in which boys and men are expected and encouraged to behave. Second, feminists draw attention to a tendency they call the **"medicalization of women's deviance."** Women who break the law or act in ways otherwise defined as deviant tend to be viewed as suffering from some kind of physical or psychological pathology, as if "normal," "healthy" women could never act so badly. In criminological theory, this produces an emphasis on individual and psychological explanations of women's criminality, an emphasis which has persisted long after theories of this kind became marginal in the explanation of male crime. This same emphasis extends to the treatment of women in the legal and correctional systems. Overall, women offenders seem to have been understood, and to some degree to still be understood, through a subjective manner based on persistent sexist ideas and feelings rather than the scientific approach of sound, appropriate reasoning.

FEMINIST CRITIQUES OF SEXISM IN EARLY THEORIES OF WOMEN'S CRIMINALITY

Rarely is a woman wicked, but when she is she surpasses the man. As a double exception, the criminal woman is consequently a monster.

C. Lombroso and G. Ferrero, *The Female Offender* (1895)

The modern age of girls and young men is intensely immoral, and immoral seemingly without the pressure of circumstances. At whose door we may lay the fault, we cannot tell. Is it the result of what we call 'the emancipation of woman', with its concomitant freedom from chaperonage, increased intimacy between the sexes in adolescence, and a more tolerant viewpoint towards all things unclean in life? This seems the only logical forbear of the present state.

W. I. Thomas, *The Unadjusted Girl* (1967)

Before the publication in 1976 of Carol Smart's influential book *Women, Crime and Criminology: A Feminist Critique*, there were only a few papers that challenged the sexist assumptions reproduced in the above quotes by early criminologists commenting on female criminality. In 1968, Frances Heidenson published "The Deviance of Women: A Critique and an Enquiry" in which she focused on the omission of this topic from sociological literature (Heidenson, 1968, p. 162). Heidenson accounts for this exclusion of deviant women in the literature in two ways. First, she notes that "women *appear* to be remarkably conformist" with "consistently lower rates of deviance than men" (1968, p. 161). Second, Heidenson (1968, p. 162) argued that "deviant women may have benefited far more than their male counterparts by the extension of the concept of the sick role and its more widespread application, in that women who might once have been adjudged 'delinquent' may now be defined as 'sick' and hence excluded from the population of 'deviants.'"

In addition to the lack of scholarly interest in women, whether sick or deviant, the early frameworks for understanding women's criminality were profoundly sexist. Klein explains that early theories of female criminality such as those of Lombroso and Ferrero (1895), Thomas (1907, 1923), Freud (1933), Pollak (1950) and Davis (1961) all saw criminality in women as biological or psychological characteristics of individual women only marginally influenced by "economic, social and political forces" (Klein, 2004, p. 325, originally published 1973). The early bio-psychological models of women's criminality reflected profoundly sexist assumptions about the inherent nature of women. Smart (1977, p. 91) argued that these theorists provided "a scientific gloss for common-sense understandings." Early criminological ideas about women's criminality were especially problematic because they almost always connected bodily processes (such as menstruation, childbearing and menopause) to criminality in women. They also depicted women's biological capacity for childbearing as determining "the temperament, intelligence, ability and aggression of women" (Smart, 1977, p. 91). Smart's critique of early mainstream criminological theories about female crime and deviance set the tone for feminist criminology for the next three decades after the work was published (Downes & Rock, 2003, p. 293).

Lombroso and Ferrero and the "Passive Female Criminal"

Lombroso, a criminal anthropologist and the founding father of the biological-positivist school of criminology, considered women to be biologically and intellectually inferior to men. Lombroso and Ferrero viewed criminals in social Darwinian terms as "degenerates" or "atavistic." By this Lombroso and Ferrero meant that criminals were evolutionary throwbacks who had retained "primitive" traits which they said explained most criminal behaviour. However, Lombroso and Ferrero had trouble fitting women into the typology of this "born criminal" because the women they studied failed to exhibit the signs of "degeneration" required to fit their model of **criminal atavism.** To account for this anomaly, Lombroso and Ferrero argued that women had evolved far less than men and were therefore already more "primitive." Since women exhibited fewer outward signs of degeneration, their criminality was harder for the criminal anthropologist to detect. However, the idea that criminality in women was harder to detect had more to do with Lombroso and Ferrero's own weak model of crime than female criminality.

To account for the relative lack of female criminality, Lombroso and Ferrero argued that women were naturally more passive than men and that this passivity was rooted in biology (Smart, 1976, pp. 32–33). This passivity they argued could be explained by "the immobility of the ovule compared with the zoosperm" (Lombroso & Ferrero, 1895, p. 109). They believed that female criminals lacked maternal feeling or instinct because they are more like men than women. According to Lombroso and Ferrero, "[h]er maternal sense is weak because psychologically and anthropologically she belongs more to the male than to the female sex" (1895, p. 153). For Lombroso and Ferrero, then, criminal women are harder to detect because they lack the visible signs of degeneracy, making it difficult for the expert to differentiate criminal women from normal women. Because women are constructed as naturally passive, they are rarely engaged in criminal activity. According to Comack (2004, p. 165), Lombroso and Ferrero's criminal women are "cast as excessively vile and cruel in their crimes" because they "combined the qualities of the criminal male with the worst characteristics of the female: cunning, spite and deceitfulness." This sexist description attributes socially undesirable characteristics to women while assuming these characteristics are natural. Smart argues that this myth results in the situation where criminal women are "**doubly damned**" both for their law violations and transgression of social norms governing femininity (Smart, 1976, p. 34).

W. I. Thomas and the "Emancipation Hypothesis"

With the publication of W. I. Thomas's *The Unadjusted Girl* (1967, originally published 1923), we see the beginning of a shift from the purely biological explanation of women's criminality advanced by Lombroso and Ferrero to those that begin to look at the importance of the relationship between society and the individual for understanding crime. Smart (1976, p. 37) argues that Thomas's work represents an attempt to explain crime in terms of a "**socially induced pathology**" rather than the "**biologically induced pathology**" seen in work of Lombroso and Ferrero. Nevertheless, theorists such as Thomas continue to advance established sexist ideas about women's biological nature as being selfish and manipulative. Thomas argues that girls become "delinquent" because they crave stimulation, causing them to have intense desires to give and feel love in an inappropriate manner. This desire for response is derived from their maternal instinct and causes them to be drawn to crimes like prostitution where they can fulfill that intense need for stimulation (Klein, 2004, pp. 328–329; Smart, 1976, p. 39). Thomas argued that women had more varieties of love in their nervous system and therefore required greater social control to quell their natural desire for sexual stimulation and excitement. Furthermore, he believed that lower class delinquent girls committed more criminal acts than their middle-class counterparts because they were not socialized to repress their natural inclination toward sexual manipulation. Thomas believed that girls and women required the direct control of fathers and husbands in order to prevent criminal behaviour. The control of girls and women took place in the context of a traditional monogamous marriage in which the woman existed solely as a wife and a mother. As the quote at the beginning of this section illustrates, Thomas believed the cause of crime in girls and women was the loosening of these patriarchal social norms.

According to Klein's critique of Thomas, his theory of criminal women accepts and legitimizes a ruling class definition of femininity and expands the Victorian myth of criminal women. To achieve their wicked, selfish goals, these women seduce men who "are caught by helpless sexual desires" (Klein, 2004, pp. 328–329). Similarly, Smart (1976, p. 39) argued that Thomas' work is sexist because "it confused socio-culturally and historically produced features [with] supposedly inherent or 'natural' characteristics" of women. Here, Smart is suggesting that Thomas sees criminality in women as being largely the product of biology. This is why Thomas resisted any progressive reform that led to the removal of traditional restraints on women. Even though he suggested that environment plays a role in women's deviance, he favoured early intervention by social welfare agencies into the lives of working class girls before they became "delinquent." Downes and Rock (2003) argue that Thomas's work was particularly problematic because it provided a strong argument against the emancipation of girls and women by connecting their emancipation to increased "juvenile delinquency" and "female criminality." This overall framework has remained highly influential with some criminological theorists. According to Downes and Rock:

> Thomas is seen as the most authoritative link in the chain of criminologists lending their voice to the resistance to female emancipation, on the grounds that it would inevitably entail an increase in female deviance. (2003, p. 298)

As Downes and Rock go on to suggest, this concern with the supposed dangers of female emancipation would resurface much later in sexist criminological theories developed in response to the second-wave feminist movement.

FEMINIST CRITIQUES OF SEXISM IN POST-WORLD WAR II THEORIES OF WOMEN'S CRIMINALITY

Some more recent theories of women's criminality are surprisingly similar to those of the earlier period. Otto Pollak's *The Criminality of Women* (1961) and Cowie, Cowie and Slater's *Delinquency in Girls* (1968) continue to rely on variants of biological determinism, much like the early theorists, while Freda Adler's *Sisters in Crime* (1975) picks up where Thomas left off by suggesting that women's criminality is connected to their emancipation.

Otto Pollak: Women's Deceitfulness and the "Chivalry Hypothesis"

According to Smart (1976, p. 46), Pollak's ideas, published in *The Criminality of Women* (1961, originally published 1950), do not move much beyond the obvious sexism of Lombroso and Ferrero and Thomas. Pollak continues to advance common sense ideas about women's inherently flawed character, intelligence and capacity for engaging in deceitful and criminal activities such as prostitution. Furthermore, he links these qualities to women's reproductive biology, albeit through the mediation of cultural factors. For Pollak, female criminals were much worse than male criminals because their law violations were much more difficult to detect. Women's deviance is well hidden because of their position in the private sphere of the family. Pollak attempted to account for differences between men's and women's recorded involvement in criminal behaviour by arguing that female crime is "masked" crime. Pollak argued that women do not commit less crime than men, only that women's crime is hidden or masked because women are by nature more manipulative and devious than men. Pollak believed that menstruation, which he termed the "generative phase," was the cause of female criminality because it weakens women's inhibitions and causes women to be more unbalanced than men:

> Particularly because of the social meaning attached to them in our culture, the generative phases of women are bound to present many stumbling blocks for the law-abiding behaviour or women. Menstruation with its appearance of injury must confirm feelings of guilt which individuals may have about sex activities which they have learned to consider as forbidden. As a symbol of womanhood, it must also, because of its recurrent nature, aggravate many feelings of irritation and protest which women may have regarding their sex in a society in which women have had, and still have, to submit to social inequality with men. In both instances, it must lead to a disturbance of the emotional balance of the individual and this becomes potentially crime-promoting. (Pollak, 1961, pp. 157–158)

Within Pollak's model of female criminality there is recognition of the impact of culture on female criminality similar to that of Thomas. However, Pollak (1961) argues that because women are oppressed by men, they look for ways of getting back at those men whom they see as the cause of their misery. Therefore, women's criminality is connected to the cultural subordination of women which gives them a second rate social status vis-à-vis men. Pollak (1961) believes that criminality in women is rooted in their inherent deceitfulness, which is in turn understood as rooted in women's ability to hide their orgasms (or lack of orgasm) during sexual intercourse; Pollak's theory of women's criminality relies on stereotypes of women as deceitful, manipulative and evil, all of which, equally stereotypically, have a biological basis:

> Through sexual intercourse, women are able, according to Pollak, to discover and acquire confidence in their ability to deceive men in all respects. As a result Pollak endows all women with the master-status of liars and deceivers because of their ability to conceal a lack of sexual arousal. (Smart, 1976, pp. 47–48)

Smart's critique of Pollak challenges his acceptance of conventional sexual politics. She points out that inheritance and property laws required women to sacrifice their rights to sexual self-determination and that refusal to have intercourse with one's husband was considered adequate grounds for a divorce. As a result, women might often submit to intercourse without pleasure or enjoyment (Smart, 1976, pp. 48–49). Smart also points out that there is no evidence to suggest that female crime is more (or less) hidden than male crime. According to Smart (1976, p. 49) Pollak provides no empirical evidence that female criminality is more 'masked' than men's "and relies instead upon tenuous assumptions about the behaviour of men and women," which is not a social scientific basis for that kind of claim. In fact, Smart (1976, p. 49) argues that research on the widespread occurrence of wife-battering is more "indicative of the 'masked' nature of assaults by men."

Finally, in attempting to account for the higher numbers of men involved in recorded criminality, Pollak argued that women have benefited from male "chivalry." This idea was known as the "**chivalry hypothesis.**" The chivalry hypothesis rests on the notion that police and courts respond in a more lenient manner to women and girls than to men and boys, which is then claimed to account for the lower crime rate among women. But Pollak's thesis ignores the overall nature and extent of the crimes women commit. Women tend to commit petty property offences and are more likely to be first-time offenders. While there is some evidence to suggest that white women with dependant children benefit from more lenient treatment by the police and the courts (Spohn, 1999; Grabe, Trager, & Lear, 2006), the extent to which the lenience can be attributed to patriarchal attitudes toward women, rather than the nature of the crimes women commit and the conditions under which they commit them, is an under-researched topic in criminology. However, research using anonymous self-reports strongly suggests that overall, women commit fewer, and less serious, crimes than men (Morris, 1990, p. 415). Kramar (2005) argues that both men and women who commit serious crimes like homicide have access to special defences that take into account the social circumstances within which the crimes are committed. Women who commit "infanticide" by killing their newly born babies are punished less severely not because of chivalry but because the courts have always recognized that social conditions faced by single mothers should mitigate responsibility for infant homicide. Nevertheless, the move by courts toward greater and greater formal legal equality has meant that women are being charged more frequently with murder rather than infanticide (Cunliffe, 2009).

Cowie, Cowie and Slater: A Contemporary Degeneracy Theory of Women's Criminality

Like Lombroso and Ferrero, Cowie, Cowie and Slater (1968) search for outward physiological signs of delinquency in girls and women. According to Smart (1976, p. 55):

> . . . they look for signs of 'defective' intelligence, abnormal central nervous function and impaired physical health. Their findings reveal that 'Delinquent girls more often than boys have other forms of impaired physical health; they are noticed to be oversized, lumpish, uncouth and graceless, with a raised incidence of minor physical defects' (Cowie, Cowie, & Slater, 1968, p. 166–7, quoted in Smart 1976, p. 55).

Smart argues that Cowie et al. reproduce the notion that ruling class standards are the physiologically (and biologically) based norm and set a normative ruling class standard for appearance and behaviour against which they measure a sample of institutionalized girls:

> Cowie, Cowie and Slater give virtually no attention to the socio-cultural basis of definitions of criminal and deviant behaviour nor do they appear to recognize the significance of power in the framing and enforcement of laws and social norms. They are aware of the existence of a double-standard of morality but this awareness in no way informs their analysis of female delinquency, which in fact they accept as being mainly sexual in character. (Smart, 1976, p. 57)

Cowie et al. assumed that girls' nonconformity to the ruling class standards of femininity which required girls to be quiet, clean, chaste and eventually wives and mothers amounted to juvenile delinquency. Feminist criminologists criticize Cowie et al. for believing that there is only one way of being feminine which Cowie et al. viewed as the "true" nature of the female sex. For Cowie et al., identifying any sort of nonconforming behaviour in girls will prevent criminality in the future.

Cowie et al. go on to argue that female criminality has genetic origins. Much like Lombroso and Ferrero, they argue that criminal women are simply more masculine than non-criminal women; they must be genetic abnormalities because they will have exhibited masculine characteristics by engaging in criminal conduct (Smart, 1976, p. 57). However, as Smart (1976) observes, there is no medical evidence for this argument. Cowie et al. blend sex and gender because "They do not perceive gender roles to be at all fluid, insisting that femininity is a *natural* attribute of the female and that masculinity is similarly *natural* for the male" (Smart, 1976, p. 58). Feminist criminologists want it acknowledged that feminine and masculine characteristics are culturally sanctioned behaviours. Different cultures authorize different kinds of conduct as gender appropriate through laws and norms which define normal feminine and normal masculine behaviour. Indeed, Cowie et al. contribute to the cultural definition of certain kinds of non-deviant and non-criminal behaviour as feminine through the very theoretical ideas they advance. The feminist critique of this criminological theory insists that we understand the social structures within which "unfeminine" behaviour on the part of women is responded to as criminal and deviant behaviour, and brought back into line through law and punishment. For example, Cowie et al. would consider young women going to a bar for drinks and socializing as "deviant" behaviour because it is "unfeminine," while for young men the same activity would not be considered deviant because it is culturally sanctioned as "masculine" behaviour.

The "Emancipation Hypothesis" Revisited

In the later decades of the 20th century, crime statistics seemed to indicate an increase in women's involvement in crime. In an attempt to explain this rising crime rate among women, some old ideas, including the **"emancipation hypothesis,"** have been recycled. The emancipation hypothesis is the idea that the women's movement has led to changes in women's social and economic opportunities, and as those opportunities have increased, so have women's opportunities to commit crime. As we saw earlier, this thesis was first advanced by Thomas (1967, originally published 1923), who cautioned against allowing women more freedom because with that would come increased crime rates. According to Smart (1976, pp. 70–71), Thomas blamed the women's movement for a variety of "social ills" and urged others to resist the emancipation of women which brought with it **"immorality"** in the form of social and sexual freedom for unmarried women and girls. For Thomas's generation, this new freedom signaled the demise of bourgeois life, social disorganization and crime.

In the 1970s, the work of Rita Simon (1975) and Freda Adler (1975) popularized the idea that women are committing more crime because they are becoming more like men. The emancipation hypothesis is rooted in sex role theories, which highlight the changing nature of gender roles. As women become "emancipated" and thus more like men, they will exhibit behaviour, including criminal behaviour, similar to men's. The problem with these assumptions is that they fail to challenge cultural standards of masculine, and by contrast feminine, behaviour. The emancipation hypothesis also lacks strong evidence in support of its claims, as has been revealed by Stephen Box. According to Downes and Rock (2003, p. 302):

> In the most rigorous review of the available evidence, Box concludes that when trends in crime are properly related to social and economic indictors of liberation on the one hand and economic marginalization on the other, it is the latter which best accounts for the modest convergence in property crime rates between the sexes.

In other words, women's increased participation in property crime has more to do with their continued economic marginalization than their emancipation. Downes and Rock cite further research which shows that between 1959 and 1979 there were no changes in rates of violent crime among women. They argue that the " 'new violent' female offender is a myth" (Downes & Rock, 2003, p. 302). More recently, Doob and Sprott (2005, p. 127) have analyzed slight increases in crime rates among girls between 1991 and 1996. Relying on data from Statistics Canada, Doob and Sprott (2005, p. 128) argue that "girls are more likely to be involved in less serious violence." Doob and Sprott (2005) argue that the increases are mainly in the category of minor assaults. However, there has been an increase in the number of cases in which girls have been involved in violence as well as the rate at which those cases are brought to youth court. Doob and Sprott (2005, p.128) have noted that the rate at which girls were convicted remained relatively stable between 1991 and 2000 (19 per 1,000 in 1991 and 18 per 1,000 in 2000). However, the rate at which boys were convicted decreased between 1991 and 2000 (85 per 1,000 in 1991 and 64 per 1,000 in 2000). They conclude that the increases in convictions for girls (vis-à-vis boys) because boys are being found guilty in court at much lower rates (Doob & Sprott, 2005, pp. 129–130) rather than any real increase in girls overall rates of violence.

Doob and Sprott (2005) and Downes and Rock (2003) agree that changes in rates of female offending are an effect of changing police policy (either to charge or deal with informally) and prosecution practice that are the result of changed attitudes on the part of agents of the criminal justice system to female criminality. The claim that the emancipation of women and girls accounts for their increased recorded involvement in crime is not borne out by the evidence.

THE MEDICALIZATION OF WOMEN'S DEVIANCE IN CRIMINOLOGICAL THEORY

We have seen how important criminological theorizations have tended to depict women offenders as physically or psychologically abnormal and pathological, and specifically as being abnormally and pathologically masculine. Mainstream psychiatry has made its own contributions to this tendency, developing diagnoses applicable only to women which attempt to explain specific behaviours that are either themselves crimes or otherwise relevant to the criminal law. It is here that the medicalization of women's deviance is most obvious. The impact of psychiatric and psychological ideas on judicial and correctional practices make these diagnoses of prime interest to feminist criminologists. In addition, some feminist theorists have claimed that psychiatry, as opposed to the criminal justice system, is the primary mode of patriarchal social control of women (Smart, 1976, pp. 146–175). This has been argued to explain the greater rates of diagnosed mental illness, especially depression and various anxiety states, among women. Although Joan Busfield (1988) has cautioned that despite its important insights, the feminist criticisms of psychiatric and psychological ideas obscures the possibility that living with patriarchal oppression is bad for women's mental health. Whatever the complexities of the interaction between sexism in society and sexism in psychiatry, feminists have developed critiques of a range of psychiatric diagnoses, including those with direct relevance to criminal justice concerns. The modern feminist critique of the medicalization of deviance will be discussed below in relation to the battered woman syndrome. The early history of the medicalization of women's deviance is discussed in the following sections on nymphomania, kleptomania and infanticide. The sexism is revealed both in the categories used to describe women's behaviour and the explanations for the behaviours themselves.

Early Psychocriminology of Women:
Kleptomania, Nymphomania and Infanticide

There is reason to be suspicious of criminological theories that identify medical or biological conditions as the source of women's deviance and criminality. This is because there is an established sexism in early psychocriminology of women. Psychopathological categories such as kleptomania and nymphomania were categories of disease that were applied to women who violated the societal strictures that defined feminine modesty, passivity and domesticity. This is perhaps the beginning of what is known as the "medicalization" of women's unwanted behaviour.

According to Carol Groneman (1994, p. 341), the concept of nymphomania begins to appear in the medical literature at the very point in history when women begin to demand greater participation in public life. During the latter half of the 19th century, women demanded access to the professions through education and the right to vote, and they were joining the workforce in growing numbers. Woman were also marrying later in life, having fewer children and enjoying greater opportunities for sexual independence. According to Groneman (1994, p. 342), the newly established disease of nymphomania constructs female sexuality as completely out of control: ". . . out of control of their husbands, mothers and doctors; and out of control of the 'natural laws' that supposedly determined women's passive response to male desire." Case studies during that time described women as having "insatiable sexual appetites" or "enjoying intercourse greatly (with her husband)" with whom she "has had sex with every night for seven years of their marriage" (Groneman, 1994, p. 337). These women were further described as suffering from "ungovernable sexual excitement" and were instructed by 19th-century physicians to restrict their intake of meat and brandy and other stimulations to diminish sexual desire. Women were also instructed to replace feather mattresses and pillows with more uncomfortable ones made of hair, to take cold enemas and sponge baths and to swab their vaginas with harsh chemical solutions containing borax to cool their passions (Groneman, 1994, p. 338). In addition to nymphomania, other constructed psychopathologies such as sadism, masochism and lesbianism were thought to be inheritable by daughters. Constructing women's perceived sexual deviance from the socially proscribed norm as "psychopathology" in the form of inheritable nymphomania, allowed for greater control over girls and women. Nymphomania was a sign of moral delinquency, the outcome of which was thought to include prostitution, insanity, or both. "Nymphomaniacs were driven to prostitution to satisfy their desires; prostitutes were often lesbians" (Groneman, 1994, p. 356). Nymphomania buttresses those early criminological theories of Lombroso and Ferrero and Thomas, who link dangerousness and criminality in women to their emancipation. By seeing women's sexual desire and autonomy as a disease or psychopathology, the category of nymphomania helped to construct the normal Victorian woman as passive, virtuous and kind. Nymphomania extended and confirmed the early criminological theories about women's deviance by creating a psychopathological disease that defines woman's sexuality as dangerous and in need of control either by fathers and husbands or physicians. According to Groneman (1994, p. 356), "[l]esbians, nymphomaniacs, and prostitutes – and by extension, suffragists, feminists, and the modern woman – were considered not only diseased, but dangerous as well." That this illness was used to control women through sexuality can be directly linked to women's increasing sexual independence from men; where the private sphere of the family breaks down as a means of social control of women, the medical establishment picks up to rein in feminine sexual independence in various odd and painful ways.

Like nymphomania, kleptomania was thought to be an extreme expression of feminine desire for the department store commodities associated with the expression of feminine sexuality. Kleptomania, also called thieving mania, was seen as another addictive sexual disorder brought on by contact with the accoutrements of femininity, mass-produced and freely available for consumption by white middle- and upper-class women of the 19th century (Camhi, 1993). Again, this "illness" emerges during a historical period when women are beginning to achieve social and economic independence from men. Kleptomania was used to define theft in gendered as well as class-based terms in the context of burgeoning consumer capitalism. The diagnosis of kleptomania was used to defend the actions of a select group of privileged women (Abelson, 1989). In 1887, Dr. Orpheus Everts described the case of a 39-year-old kleptomaniac who was widowed, with children, and of "good society." Everts diagnosed the woman as suffering from "womb disease mania," which he described as "larceny and eroticism with hysteria" (cited in Abelson, 1989, p. 125). Here we see a direct link being made between the reproductive system and women's shoplifting as a means of providing an excuse for upper-class women's deviant behaviour. Similarly, the infamous case of Mrs. Ella Castle, which unfolded in London in 1896, reveals the extent to which medical diagnoses provided legal excuses for women of "good society." Castle was a wealthy American tourist traveling in London with her husband when she was caught stealing a sable muff from a fashionable department store. Leading medical experts described Castle as neither mentally nor morally responsible for her crime. Her defence attorney described her as a pathetic kleptomaniac. "I have had her examined by some leading specialists in mental diseases, and have no doubt that the judge will admit that her symptoms are such as to warrant the defense of kleptomania (Abelson, 1989, p. 127). Upon her return to the United States, Castle was diagnosed by doctors in Philadelphia as suffering from an hysterical disorder of the mind connected to "long neglected uterine and rectal disease" (cited in Abelson, 1989, p. 129). It was typical for both the medical profession and the courts to diagnose women caught shoplifting with the disease of kleptomania, sometimes linking its onset to childbirth. The diagnosis of kleptomania was used to morally and legally "excuse" shoplifting by middle- and upper-class women. Unsettled by middle- and upper-class women stealing from department stores, physicians explained the behaviour in terms of reproductive pathology or "pelvic disease" (Abelson, 1989, p. 130). No attempts were ever made by these commentators to draw connections between women's legally enforced social and economic dependence upon men in the context of the rise of consumer-based capitalism in the United States and Canada.

Like nymphomania and kleptomania the defence of "infanticide" was used to legitimately excuse the unwanted behaviour of working-class women. The crime of infanticide was one in which women kill their newly born babies, usually directly following childbirth. Experts in mental medicine typically understood the root causes of infanticide in terms of "exhaustion psychosis" experienced by working-class women who were widowed with many children. These women made up a significant number of the women who committed infanticide (Morton, 1934). Unlike nymphomania and kleptomania, infanticide was a defence to murder were it could be shown that the accused woman was suffering from the effects of lactation and childbirth, which caused a "disease of the mind." Chiefly a legal category, infanticide functioned to diminish responsibility for a crime largely connected to women's lack of reproductive autonomy in the context of the death penalty for murder in Canada, England and Wales. Unlike nymphomania and klep-tomania, the category of infanticide provided a legal excuse based on women's **socioeconomic responsibility** for childrearing in the context of recent childbirth and the physical strains of lactation. Infanticide differed from nymphomania and kelptomania in that it was a special defence for homicide rather than a full-blown category of mental ill-ness, despite the strong psychological language written into the law itself. During the early years of the prosecution of infanticide cases, Crowns were unable to establish the mental element beyond a reasonable doubt because infanticide was not understood either by judges or juries within the context of a psychiatric framework. As a result, the law was amended so that Crowns now do not have to establish the mental element of the of-fence (a disease of the mind consequent pregnancy, childbirth and lactation) beyond a reasonable doubt (Kramar, 2005). Later, postpartum mental illness or psychosis would become an additional explanation for the killing of older children by women suffering acute psychosis postpartum and would be conflated with the infanticide defence. In the-ses cases, women typically kill older infants and suffer from extreme delusions about the child. For example, in the U.S. context, Andrea Yates drowned her five children in the bathtub in their Houston, Texas, home in June 2001. The law in the United States does not provide for any distinction between homicide and infanticide. Unlike most Western countries, the state of Texas has no defence for postnatal psychosis other than the formal insanity defence. Even though Yates was diagnosed with postpartum depression, which led to her psychosis, she was convicted of murder and sentenced to life imprisonment with no possibility of parole for 40 years. Her conviction was later overturned on appeal when she was found not guilty by reason of insanity. The fact that a woman who will-ingly drowned her five children in one hour would not have access to a formal insanity defence at her original trial illustrate a profound misogynist attitude toward women who deviate from the conventions of normative motherhood.

CHALLENGING CRIMINAL LAW AS A MEDIUM OF PATRIARCHY: RAPE, SPOUSAL ASSAULT, ABORTION AND PROSTITUTION

Feminists were, of course, not only intent on reforming academic views of women offend-ers. They campaigned for changes in the criminal justice system's treatment of women vic-tims and offenders. The concerns which animated the feminist analysis of criminological theories have been equally relevant to the criminal justice system; the identification of sex-ist assumptions underlying systemic practices, and the discriminatory and oppressive ef-fects of these practices. Here again, the views of women offenders as doubly deviant and physically and psychologically pathological were exposed and criticized. Through the study of crime and gender, feminist criminology maintains its commitment to working to-ward the abolition of the oppression of women.

In this section, we examine the challenges posed by feminists to established legal doc-trines and courtroom practices, and to the treatment of women by police. We look at cor-rectional policies and practices in the next section.

THE LAW'S TREATMENT OF WOMEN VICTIMS OF MALE VIOLENCE

Until the mid-1970s, victims of crime were essentially ignored by criminologists and sociologists. The second-wave women's movement brought the issue of violence against women and girls to the attention of social scientists and the public. In the early to mid-1970s, feminists established a number of rape crisis centres and battered women's shelters across the United States, Britain and Canada. They fought for reform of the law and criminal justice practices relating to rape and spousal assault. Evidence of serious abuse of women and their children by husbands or common-law partners forced the authorities to take the problem of domestic violence seriously. This lead to mandatory police charging policies, special Crown directives not to drop the criminal charges once laid, and the creation of specialized family violence courts for dealing with domestic violence. Victim-witness support services were established in Crown attorneys' offices to assist women and children through the criminal court process.

Reforming the Law of Rape

Second-wave feminists, including feminist criminologists, insisted that women complainants to the criminal justice system, especially in cases of sexual assault, "met parallel patriarchal and oppressive responses that brought about the 'secondary victimization' of the woman complainant by the criminal justice system" (Downes & Rock, 2003). Sexist ideas about women informed judicial decisions. For instance, in a Manitoba Court of Appeal case in which a defendant pled guilty to sexually assaulting his teenaged babysitter, the judge commented that:

> The [twelve-thirteen-year-old] girl, or course, could not consent in the legal sense, but nonetheless was a willing participant. She was apparently more sophisticated than many her age and was performing many household tasks including babysitting the accused's children. The accused and his wife were somewhat estranged. (Cited in Busby, 1999, p. 269)

In this statement from the court, we can see sexist attitudes about domestic work and women's sexual availability going hand in hand to justify a reduced sentence for sexual assault. According to the three-person panel of judges on the Manitoba Court of Appeal, the teenaged girl must have been a willing stand-in for the accused's wife because the girl was already performing most of the household and childrearing tasks reserved for women! Evidence of the girl's willingness to perform these domestic chores was used to mitigate the sexual assault sentence because the judges believed that because she performed domestic labour it meant that she must also have consented to sexual relations.

Throughout the 1990s, the rules of procedure and evidence in sexual violence law were changed (both by law reform and judges' reinterpretations of the law) to address the "**twin myths of rape**." These twin myths are first, that women and girls lie about sexual violence out of malice toward men, specifically, that women trick men into having sex with them and then complain to the authorities about it afterward to get back at the men; and second, that women and girls will say "no" to having sexual relations with men when they really want to have sex with them, and that they therefore mean "yes" when they say "no." We saw previously in this chapter how similar ideas found their way into early criminological theories; the idea that women and girls lie to manipulate men and are sexually deceitful has been a dominant theme in both the early and modern theories of women's criminality advanced by Lombroso, Pollak, and Cowie et al. According to Busby (1999) these myths underpin legal rules and procedures as well as the attitudes of judges and lawyers. Busby (1999, p. 261) tells us that, "these myths are sustained even though there is no evidence in Canada that the incidence of false reports is higher for sexual offences than for other offences." By the end of the 20th century, rules of evidence were amended so that a woman's past sexual history (her "chaste" character or lack thereof) could not be used against her at trial. The Supreme Court of Canada set fairly strict guidelines for a defence attorney's access to a complainant's personal records (medical or counseling) in an effort to balance the defendant's right to a fair trial and a woman's right to privacy (*R. v. O'Connor*, 4 [1995] SCR 411). Historically, defendants had been successful in convincing the courts that they mistakenly believed that their victims consented to sex because they had previously consented to sexual relations, either with them or some other man. This was known as the defence of "**mistaken belief**." In 1992, the *Criminal Code* was amended to limit the mistaken belief defence by requiring the defendant to take "reasonable steps to ascertain that the complainant was consenting" (Busby, 1999, p. 271). The amendments redefined "consent" so that it would be understood from the perspective of the woman to be her voluntary agreement to engage in sexual activity at that time. According to Busby (1999, p. 270):

> This amendment is intended to shift the factual and legal issue at trial away from what the defendant might have thought to what the complainant actually said or otherwise communicated at the time of the incidents. By this law, initiators of sexual activity should no longer be able to rely upon stereotypes or fantasies about women or even their knowledge of specific complainants' sexual lives to assume consent, but rather have the positive obligation of determining whether the real, present woman is agreeing on the particular occasion to sexual activity.

By shifting the perspective to what women actually say and do at that particular time, the 1992 law represented a major shift in the adjudication of sexual assault cases.

An important change in the law, dating from the amendment of the *Criminal Code* in 1983, was the shift from a traditional definition of rape as an act of penetrative intercourse forced on a woman who is not the wife of the accused to a gender-neutral category of "sexual assault." The *Criminal Code* now covers a broader range of criminal sexual acts but divides sexual assault into three levels of seriousness which reflect the violence with which the assault was pursued (*Criminal Code* sections 271–273). Now that no relationship between offender or victim is excluded, the old "marital exception" has been removed. Marital or **spousal sexual assault** is now seen by the law and the criminal justice system as feminists have insisted it should be: part of the spectrum of domestic violence and intimidation to which many women are subject.

Spousal Assault: Demanding Action from the Police and the Courts

Early in the 1970s, feminist activists identified wife assault as a serious social issue and established shelters for battered women and children. Out of that shelter movement came demands for better funding for shelters and other services that promote women's economic independence from men, as well as reforms in the area of criminal law. Alongside their sisters in the shelter movement, feminist academics revealed that the problem of violence against girls and women was hidden in the private or domestic sphere. These advocates for women sought to draw attention to the nature and extent of the problem of violence faced by women and children in their homes. Domestic violence came to be seen as an instance, and a crucial pillar, of the broader phenomenon of patriarchal oppression—a gendered phenomenon that could not be understood in the same way as the victimization of men.

By the 1980s and 1990s, feminists were demanding that the police and the courts take the issue of spousal assault seriously. The feminist movement pressed the government to see that women were victims of serious crimes of assault and that these crimes should be aggressively policed and prosecuted as part of an overall strategy to empower women. In addition, feminist criminologist Elizabeth Comack (1996) provided research data that revealed that women offenders were also victims of abuse. Comack's (1996) research on 24 women incarcerated in a provincial jail revealed the complex connections between women's violations of the law and their histories of abuse, with the official distinction between victim and offender often blurred. Self-report victimization surveys and other research by feminist criminologists revealed that spousal abuse was a systemic problem that had dire consequences for women of every class and background.

By the early 1990s, official measures of sexual and nonsexual assault painted a picture of rapidly increasing rates of violent crime (Johnson, 1996, p. 32). In 1993, Canada's Department of Health commissioned a national population survey conducted by Statistics Canada on male violence against women for which 12,300 women were interviewed by phone about their experiences of interpersonal victimization (Johnson, 1996, p. 46). Known as the "Violence against Women" survey, it revealed that 10% of women had been victims of violence in the year prior to the telephone interview. The survey also revealed that 51% of Canadian women had been the victim of at least one physical or sexual assault since the age of 16. The data provided the necessary tools for feminists to urge the government to adopt a "**zero tolerance**" policy for spousal assault. These included mandatory arrest, charge and prosecution policies in response to incidents of domestic violence. Shortly before the survey was conducted, the city of Winnipeg implemented a specialized Family Violence Court in 1990. The specialized court was established through the lobbying efforts of feminist sociologist Jane Ursel, who advocated the use of punishment to denounce the crime and deter offenders. In 1993, the Winnipeg Family Violence Court saw a 172% increase in its case load following the Winnipeg Police Service's decision to implement a rigorous charging protocol for the policing of domestic assault. Under the new guidelines, police were directed to lay charges when a complaint had been made, regardless of whether the victim wished for the charges to be laid and regardless of whether there were visible injuries on the victim. Other provinces in Canada soon adopted similar measures and the issue of domestic violence came to dominate governmental initiatives aimed at protecting women. In addition, police services adopted mandatory arrest policies for cases of domestic violence following widespread criticism that police officers were often reluctant to become involved in what they saw as "domestic disputes."

Seeking redress through punishment was not without its critics. Some feminist criminologists insisted that the punishment of men would not empower women and would only serve to extend the arm of the law (Snider, 1991, 1994). Many feminist criminologists and sociolegal scholars view the law as both historically and inherently patriarchal. The mandatory charge and prosecution ("no drop") policies were shown to disempower immigrant women, who often relied on their husbands' status in Canada for their own well-being, both as citizens of Canada and as economic dependants of their husbands (see Singh, Chapter 11). However, overall these policies contributed to a decline in domestic violence against women in Canada. Sadly, these declines have not been as significant for Aboriginal women in Canada. According to a report published in 2001 by the Canadian Centre for Justice Statistics titled *Family Violence in Canada: A Statistical Profile*, Aboriginal women are killed at a rate eight times that of non-Aboriginal women. This report is a summary of Statistics Canada's findings in the 1999 General Social Survey. This research revealed that almost one half of the Aboriginal women surveyed experienced severe, potentially life-threatening types of violence (being beaten, choked, threatened with a gun or knife or sexually assaulted). Approximately 49% of Aboriginal women victims reported physical injury, 23% received medical attention for their injuries and 39% feared for their lives as a result of the violence (Statistics Canada 2001). Fifty-seven percent of the Aboriginal women who experienced abuse indicated that children witnessed the violence (Statistics Canada, 2001). Aboriginal people also expressed higher levels of dissatisfaction with police performance than their counterparts in the general society. Fifty-four percent of Aboriginal women victims of spousal violence had contact with the police compared with 37% of non-Aboriginal women victims (Statistics Canada, 2001). Between 1991 and 1999, spouses were responsible for killing 62 Aboriginal women and 32 Aboriginal men (a rate that is eight times higher than for non-Aboriginal women and 18 times higher for Aboriginal men (Statistics Canada, 2001). In many cases, aboriginal women who kill their aboriginal spouses do so in response to domestic abuse; however, Aboriginal women have not had access to the battered woman syndrome defence. In 1995, Justice Lynn Ratushny of the Ontario Superior Court was appointed by the Ontario solicitor general and the federal minister of justice to conduct a self-defence review of 98 cases in which women had killed domestic partners in self-defence or in defence of their children. This review was undertaken following the landmark decision by the Supreme Court of Canada in *R. v. Lavalle* [1990], which significantly altered the law of self-defence in Canada as it relates to the issue of imminent danger (this will be discussed in detail in the next section).

According to the Elizabeth Fry Society (1998):

> Judge Ratushny was appointed by the Ministers to conduct an independent review of the cases of battered women convicted of murder or manslaughter while trying to defend themselves from abusive men. In order to fulfill her self defence review mandate, Judge Ratushny sought the assistance, input and analysis of legal counsel, provincial attorneys general, officials within the Department of Justice, Ministry of the Solicitor General, legal academics, independent equality-seeking and advocacy groups, front-line anti-violence rape crisis and shelter workers, as well as the allegedly wrongfully convicted women themselves.

After completing her extensive review in 1997, Justice Ratushny recommended that seven of the 98 women be given immediate relief. Unfortunately, the government bureaucrats charged with implementing the recommendations ignored Justice Ratushny's recommendations following input from the prosecuting authorities in the provinces were the seven women were convicted. These prosecutors were arguably in a conflict of interest vis-à-vis the self-defence review for the role they may have played in overseeing the original convictions. The Elizabeth Fry Society reported their disappointment when only one of the seven women was provided with relief from the government. The relief was granted following section 690 review, which is a provision in the *Criminal Code* that allows the minister to send a case to the Court of Appeal. In only one of the seven cases recommended by

Justice Ratushny did the government send the case back to the Court of Appeal for remedy (Canadian Association of Elizabeth Fry Societies, 1998). None of the women was released from prison as a result of the review.

Battered Woman Syndrome: The Thin Line between Survival and Offence

In terms of providing a self-defence for women accused of murdering their abuse intimate partners, battered woman syndrome provided an opportunity to diminish abused women's responsibility for the crime. In addition to battered woman syndrome, courts have also accepted testimony of premenstrual syndrome to excuse women's violent conduct. Feminists are critical of these kinds of special medico-legal defences for women because they appear to reproduce the early sexism of diseases such as nymphomania and kleptomania by linking criminal behaviour in women to irrationality caused by the reproductive system (Johnson & Kandrack, 1993). This is what is known as the contemporary "medicalization of deviance."

Before 1990, the defence of battered woman syndrome was not available to Canadian women who killed their intimate, yet abusive, partners. In May 1990, the Supreme Court of Canada heard the case of *R. v. Lavallee* in which it allowed testimony about the "battered woman syndrome" (BWS) to support a woman's self-defence pleas. A Winnipeg woman, Angelique Lyn Lavallee, was charged with the second-degree murder after she shot her common-law husband, Kevin Rust, in the back of head. She shot Rust as he was leaving her bedroom to return to a group of partiers in another room of the house. Evidence at the trial revealed that Lavallee had been the victim of severe battering at the hands of Rust and that he had threatened to kill her when he got back from the party if she didn't kill him first. Because Lavallee's actions in killing Rust did not fit within the traditional doctrine of self-defence; her lawyers attempted to introduce battered woman syndrome evidence.

For some, the court's decision in the case corrected the law's prior gender bias in self-defence (Bonnycastle & Rigakos, 1998). Because the self-defence law requires the danger to be *imminent*, and Rusk's threat to kill Lavallee was not imminent, there was a need to expand the court's understanding of imminent harm in the context of gendered violence. The law also asks what a *reasonable* person would do in a similar situation. Before *Lavallee*, that test of reasonableness had been based on male-to-male violence, such as in a barroom brawl. The introduction of psychological evidence of "battered woman syndrome" helped the courts to understand gendered violence. Because Lavallee had been the victim of severe abuse, she perceived the threat from Rust differently than would a women who had not been abused. In those circumstances, she subjectively believed she had no other course of action, and her actions were therefore *reasonable* given the circumstances and worthy of a claim of self-defence. Feminist law professor Martha Shaffer (1997) cautioned her feminist colleagues not to see the gender sensitivity of the provision as a victory for women. Shaffer cautioned that the *Lavallee* decision "could have negative consequences for women if it led to the view that women who live in domestic relationships marked by violence suffered from a 'syndrome' and were thus pathological" (Shaffer, 1997, p. 47).

The battered woman syndrome is based on the work of Lenore Walker and attempts to explain in psychological terms why a woman in an abusive relationship might fear for her life when not in any immediate danger from her spouse. Because the battered woman syndrome self-defence provides a medicalized framework for understanding women's conduct, many feminist criminologists have been skeptical of its ability to correct the male-centredness of law. Medicalization (and syndromization) refers to a process in which women's social conduct is explained (or excused) in medical or psychological terms. Feminist criminologists prefer for women's social conduct, including offending behaviour, to be explained in terms of social inequality or structural power imbalances between men and women. To the extent that the legal excuse of BWS fails to incorporate gendered power relations into its self-defence framework, it does not correct gender bias law. For example, feminist criminologist Elizabeth Comack, who is a leading scholar in this field, is critical of the "syndromization" of women's experiences because it does not adequately challenge the male-centredness of law. Instead, the syndromization of women's experiences of gendered violence individualizes and pathologizes women's experiences of violence. More recently, in *R. v. Mallot*, the Supreme Court of Canada recognized the problem of syndromizing women's experiences and importance of recognizing women's varied experiences of and responses to violence. In the words of Chief Justice Beverly McLachlin:

> It is possible that those women who are unable to fit themselves within the stereotype of a victimized, passive, helpless, dependent, battered woman will not have their claims to self-defence fairly decided. For instance, women who have demonstrated too much strength or initiative, women of colour, women who are professionals, or women who might have fought back against their abusers on previous occasions, should not be penalized for failing to accord with the stereotypical image of the archetypal battered woman. Needless to say, women with these characteristics are still entitled to have their claims of self-defence fairly adjudicated, and they are also still entitled to have their experiences as battered women inform the analysis. Professor Grant, *supra*, at p. 52, warns against allowing the law to develop such that a woman accused of killing her abuser must either have been "reasonable 'like a man' or reasonable 'like a battered woman'". I agree that this must be avoided. The "reasonable woman" must not be forgotten in the analysis, and deserves to be as much a part of the objective standard of the reasonable person as does the "reasonable man". (*R. v. Mallot*, para 40)

This recognition of the potential limitations of the defence of battered women syndrome seems to address the concerns raised by feminist law professors and criminologists. And certainly the Canadian Association of Elizabeth Fry Societies and other equality-seeking groups have continued to call for reforms to self-defence law to better recognize women's needs (Canadian Association of Elizabeth Fry Societies, 1998). Now we turn to an examination of the expression of male dominance in criminal law's attempts to regulate women's sexuality.

CRIMINAL LAW REGULATION OF WOMEN'S SEXUALITY

The second-wave feminist concern with the patriarchal control of women's sexuality was the centerpiece of their insistence that the "private is public." They wished to bring the intimate masculine control and subordination of women and their sexuality within the domestic sphere into the open. However, the criminal law provided certain public sanctions limiting women's sexual agency and thereby lent support to the regimes of control exercised by men over the women in their lives which, we have already seen, the law had failed to address. Not surprisingly, feminists challenged these laws, exposing the legal double standards operating against women and the harms to which they made women subject.

Contraception and Abortion: Our Bodies, Ourselves

Beginning in the mid-1960s, feminists challenged the sexist criminalization of birth control and abortion. In 1969, Pierre Trudeau's Liberal government decriminalized birth control and allowed abortions under limited circumstances, upon the approval of a hospital committee.

In 1988, The Supreme Court of Canada struck down the existing abortion law as unconstitutional (*R. v. Morgentaler* [1988] 1 S.C.R. 30). The Court found that the law requiring women to seek consent from a hospital-based therapeutic abortion committee violated section 7 guarantees to liberty and security of the person. An attempt to pass a new abortion law was later defeated in the Senate. Canada is one of the few countries in the world where there are no legislative or judicial restrictions whatsoever on abortions.

The following year, the Supreme Court was asked to consider whether a man had a right to veto a woman's decision to have an abortion. The courted ruled against the boyfriend of Chantal Daigle, who sought an injunction to prevent her from having an abortion under the guise of protecting the rights of the fetus (*Tremblay. v. Daigle* [1989] 2 S.C.R.). The court denied Jean-Guy Tremblay's petition for an injunction on the abortion. Under Canadian law, the fetus has no legal standing until it becomes a live born human being; this is also known as the "born alive" rule. The case presents another instance of an attempt to exert patriarchal control over women's sexuality by using the law to interfere with an individual woman's reproductive freedom under the guise of fetal rights.

Feminists understood these criminal laws as an extension of male dominance and control of women's sexuality. In particular, the criminalization of contraception represented one of the more extreme forms of male dominance in criminal law. By drawing attention to the inherent sexism of criminal laws the limited women's reproductive autonomy and working to decriminalize the provisions feminists engaged in law reform sought to promote women's freedom.

Prostitution: The Invisibility of Marginal Young Women

Like those laws that control women's reproductive freedom, criminal laws against prostitution are rooted in patriarchal attitudes about the ownership and control of women's sexuality. These laws are rooted in profoundly sexist ideas about dangers to society of women's sexuality. Although prostitution is found in every society, it is most pronounced among culturally and economically marginalized women. In Canada, prostitution is legal, but its practice is criminalized and rendered invisible.

The *Criminal Code of Canada* criminalizes any public communication and/or solicitation for the purposes of prostitution. The criminalization of communicating in public for the purposes of prostitution and the maintenance of brothels (or "bawdy houses") entrenches the invisibility of prostitution. The criminal law and its enforcement by police against the women (rather than the "johns" who demand their services) further perpetuates exploitation and violence toward "sex trade workers" who are themselves already a highly marginalized group of mainly young women. Tepperman (2006, p. 114) argues describing prostitution as "sex work" is a misnomer because it ". . . promote[s] the invisibility of prostitution's harm. The interconnectedness of racism, colonialism, and child sexual assault with prostitution is evident." While there is considerable debate among feminists on the issue of prostitution, feminist criminologists have argued in favour of the decriminalization of prostitution.

Pornography's Challenge to Women's Equality

In 1992, Canadian feminists had the opportunity to engage the law that criminalizes some kinds of pornography. In *R. v. Butler*, heard before the Supreme Court of Canada, feminists addressed the issue of the sexualization of violence in pornography and violence against women in both the public and private spheres. Here, feminist advocates were in the unusual position of defending an established and controversial legal provision despite their general suspicion of "patriarchal law" which had historically been used to repress sexual practices that failed to conform to the heterosexual monogamous norm. Depictions of homosexuality had long been criminalized by the *Criminal Code* obscenity provision which defined sexually explicit depictions of anal intercourse as "depraved" or "corrupt." The Women's Legal Education and Action Fund (LEAF) intervened at the Supreme Court to promote women's equality under the *Charter of Rights and Freedoms*. LEAF is a nonprofit organization made up of feminist lawyers and activists who are devoted to using the provisions of the *Charter* to promote women's equality. LEAF often relies on section 15(1) of the *Charter of Rights and Freedoms* which guarantees that "every individual is equal before and under the law and has the right to the equal protection and equal benefit of the law without discrimination and, in particular, without discrimination based on race, national or ethnic origin, colour, religion, sex, age or mental or physical disability." LEAF works to ensure that section 15(1) of the *Charter* is interpreted and applied by the Canadian courts to ensure that law promotes women's equality.

R. v. Butler: A New Harms-Based Interpretation of Obscenity

The events leading up the Supreme Court decision began in 1987 in Winnipeg, Manitoba, when police seized the entire inventory of a pornography store, Avenue Video Boutique, owned by Donald Butler. Butler was subsequently charged under section 163 of the *Canadian Criminal Code* for possessing and exposing "obscene" material for the purposes of distribution and sale. Section 163 criminalizes the sale, possession, distribution or display of "(8) . . . any publication a dominant characteristic of which is the undue exploitation of sex, or of sex and one or more of the following subjects, namely crime, horror, cruelty and violence." The Manitoba Provincial Court convicted Butler on eight of the original charges but threw out the rest. The Crown appealed the ruling to the Manitoba Court of Appeal, which overturned the lower court's decision and found Butler guilty on all of the original obscenity charges. Following that decision, Butler's lawyers appealed to the Supreme Court of Canada. They argued that the criminal law of obscenity violated section 2(b), the **"freedom of expression"** provision of the *Charter of Rights and Freedoms* and that the criminal law on obscenity was therefore unconstitutional. Section 2(b) of the *Charter* guarantees "(b) freedom of thought, belief, opinion and expression, including freedom of the press and other media communication." The Supreme Court of Canada was asked to consider whether section 163 of the *Criminal Code* violated Donald Butler's right to freedom of expression, as guaranteed by section 2(b) of the *Charter*.

LEAF represented a feminist voice to argue that pornography is not protected expression because it promotes violence and hatred toward women, which contributes in women's unequal position in Canadian society. LEAF argued that the Supreme Court should uphold the obscenity provision of the *Criminal Code* and attempted to persuade the Court that pornography is a practice of sex discrimination against women and that it should be subject to criminal penalty. LEAF's argument is that violent, degrading and/or dehumanizing pornography causes harm to women and girls because it allows for the circulation of certain kinds of sexualized ideas about women's social value which harms their equality rights. LEAF also argued that pornography harms gay men's rights because it "contributes to abuse and homophobia, as it normalizes male sexual aggression generally" (1991, p. 15).

Having listened to the various arguments and submissions on behalf of a variety of interest groups, including LEAF, the Supreme Court of Canada concluded that while section 163 of the *Criminal Code* does violate a citizen's right to free expression guaranteed under section 2(b) of the *Charter*, the violation of freedom of expression was **"justified"** under section 1 of the *Charter*. Section 1 of the *Charter* allows the government to place "reasonable limits prescribed by law as can be demonstrably justified in a free and democratic society." According to Kendall (2004, p. 6):

> The Court held that the over-riding objective of the *Criminal Code* provision is to prevent harm to society—specifically, the harms that result from the production and distribution of pornographic representations and pictures that undermine the right of other people to live equally, without fear of harassment, violence, and other discrimination. State-imposed limits on the right to sell pornography were found justified when inequality resulted from the sale of those materials.

The Supreme Court of Canada found that the obscenity law was a quite reasonable limit to free expression because certain kinds of pornography cause harm to women and to men in Canadian society. The Court then went on to define the kinds of pornography (called **"obscenity"**) which are forms of expression that promote harm and should be criminalized on the grounds that the materials would not be tolerated by the Canadian community as fit to circulate (**the community standards test of tolerance**). The Supreme Court decision divided pornography into three categories:

1. explicit sex with violence;
2. explicit sex without violence but which subjects people to treatment that is degrading or dehumanizing; and,
3. explicit sex without violence that is neither degrading nor dehumanizing. Violence in this context includes both actual physical violence and threats of physical violence. (*R. v. Butler* [1992] 1 S.C.R. 452)

According to the Court, pornography that falls into categories one and two should be considered "obscenity" because sex coupled with violence and sex that is otherwise degrading or dehumanizing amounts to the **"undue exploitation of sex"** and that pornographic representations in the first two categories violate the "community standards test for tolerance" for material of this sort. Once pornography fails this community standards test of tolerance, it becomes illegal, and defined as criminally "obscene." Obscene materials are sexually explicit materials (print and video) that pair sex with violence and sex with degrading and dehumanizing acts, typically toward women. By attempting to articulate a harms-based equality approach to obscenity, the Supreme Court of Canada radically redefined the concept of obscenity and upheld the criminal law to restrict harmful sexually explicit materials that undermine gender equality.

Throughout the *Butler* trials, debates among feminists who were either for or against state censorship of pornography led to fairly sharp divisions. These divisions were hardly surprising given the suspicion with which many feminists regarded the law and the criminal justice system and, in many ways, they mirrored the divisions discussed earlier in the chapter on the question of whether mandatory arrest, charge and prosecution policies relating to domestic assaults would promote the empowerment of women. However, the most significant critiques of state censorship came from academics working in gay and lesbian studies. Gary Kinsman (1987) pointed out very early on that obscenity laws regulate gay and lesbian sexually explicit materials in a manner that is heterosexist and homophobic. Judicial interpretations of obscenity would define gay and lesbian sexual practices and their representation as abnormal, deviant and criminal. Historically, the state has used obscenity laws to criminalize gay and lesbian expressions of sexuality because they do not conform to the heterosexual standard. In fact, obscenity laws have been used by the state to enforce a heterosexual norm. This process is known as **"moral regulation."** Obscenity laws have been used to construct gay and lesbian sexuality as immoral and, in the process, make very public statements about what amounts to normal versus abnormal sexuality. The gay and lesbian objection to obscenity law was informed by a history of criminalization of homosexuality through obscenity laws. Gays and lesbians had good reason to be concerned about homophobic state censorship because Canada Customs had for years been discriminating against sexually explicit materials imported for sale at Canadian gay and lesbian bookstores. Customs officers had regularly detained books such as *The Gay Joy of Sex*, bound for a gay and lesbian bookstore, Glad Day Books in Toronto, while the very same book could be bought down the street at Coles! Discriminatory customs practices would later become the subject of intensive litigation when Little Sister's, a bookstore located in Vancouver, took the Canadian government to the Supreme Court of Canada for its discriminatory homophobic customs practices. The Supreme Court of Canada ruled in favour of the bookstore stating that there were "grave systemic problems in the administration of the law" (*Little Sister's Book and Art Emporium v. Canada (Minister of Justice)* [2000] 2 S.C.R. 1120). The Supreme Court ruled that "the application of the Customs legislation has discriminated against gays and lesbians in a manner that violated s. 15 of the *Charter*" (*Little Sister's Book and Art Emporium v. Canada (Minister of Justice)* [2000] 2 S.C.R. 1120).

CHALLENGING PUNISHMENT PRACTICES IN THE CORRECTIONAL TREATMENT OF WOMEN

Women commit far less crime than men. The crimes women commit are also less harmful. Therefore, women make up only a small minority of adults in the Canadian correctional system. This is partly explained by the fact that girls and women are subjected to far more informal than formal modes of regulation (Carlen, 2002). Because women are a small minority of the prison population, their rehabilitation needs tended to be ignored, or it was assumed that women's needs were the same as men's. Early critics of the correctional treatment of women pointed out that the programs for women were sexist because they insisted on conformity to male patriarchal norms, which often meant that women in monogamous heterosexual relationships were more likely to be paroled from prison. Feminist criminologists and advocates for women in conflict with the law drew attention to the different experiences of female offenders and the need for women-centred approaches in the correctional treatment of women.

Feminist contributions to understanding women's offending links criminal behaviour to women's history of physical and sexual abuse (Comack, 1996; Balfour & Comack, 2006).

Many women in Canadian prisons report having been physically or sexually abused during their lifetime. In her study of women in provincial prison in Manitoba, Comack (1996, p. 37) found that 78% of the 727 women admitted to the jail between 1988 and 1993 reported having been the victims of sexual or physical violence during their lifetimes. A 1990 survey of federally sentenced women found that two thirds of the women reported being physically abuses as children, and more than half reported having been sexually abused. The problem is more acute for Aboriginal women in prison. Ninety percent of federally sentenced Aboriginal women reported physical abuse, while 61% reported having been sexually abused (Comack, 2006, pp. 15–16). Women are much more likely than men to be victims of violence such as sexual assault and property-related offences such as theft. They are also more likely to know their perpetrator. Women are more likely to be murdered by someone they know than by a stranger. Thirty-five percent of the women who were murdered in 1999 were murdered by a spouse or ex-spouse, whereas for men, this was the case in only 3% of cases for that year (Statistics Canada, 2001).

WOMEN IN PRISON

In 2002–2003, women sentenced to provincial or territorial sentenced custody made up 10% of the total admissions, while those sentenced to federal custody made up only 5% of admissions. The ratio of women admitted to custody has remained stable relatively stable since 1998–1999. The province of Alberta admitted the highest proportion of women to sentenced custody (12%) in 2002–2003.

In 1994, the Correctional Service Canada (CSC) sent an all-male emergency response team into the solitary confinement wing of the Prison for Women (P4W) in Kingston, Ontario. In the spring of 1995, a videotape of the event aired by CBC-TV's *The Fifth Estate* showed the women being forcibly removed from their cells, stripped naked, shackled and taken to a shower where they were subjected to body cavity searches by the men. Once searched, the women were returned to their cells with only blankets for clothing. Following the incident, some of the women were kept in prolonged segregation, denied access to lawyers, clothing, showers and sanitary products (Hannah-Moffatt, 2001, p. 3). The graphic video of women being strip searched by an all-male emergency response team in full riot gear caused considerable outrage among members of the public as well as advocates for women prisoners. According to Hannah-Moffatt (2001, p. 3), "In the wake of this videotaped evidence, the Canadian government was widely accused of inhumane and unconstitutional treatment of women prisoners." The Honourable Louise Arbour headed up an inquiry into the events that took place at P4W in April of 1994 which concluded that fundamental and systemic changes to the women's correctional system were needed.

What was troubling about the treatment of the women was that government of Canada had earlier established a Task Force on Federally Sentenced Women (TFFSW) which had recommended that P4W be closed. According to the CSC:

> Since the opening of this facility in 1934, numerous task forces and royal commissions have called for its closure. This is not surprising, given that the institution was geographically isolated (many women were incarcerated far away from their families, friends, and communities); it lacked programming specific to women's needs; it had limited space, ventilation, and privacy; it could not fully meet the cultural and spiritual needs of Aboriginal offenders; and its environment only supported the language requirements of its English-speaking majority.

The report of the TFFSW, *Creating Choices* (Correctional Service Canada, 1990) also suggested that women's unique needs could be better met by the creation of five new regional corrections facilities and a healing lodge for Aboriginal women. The report also called for the development of women-centred programs, including survivors of abuse and mother-child programming; and the establishment of a community strategy to expand and strengthen residential and nonresidential programs and services for women offenders who are conditionally released (Correctional Service Canada, 1990). Most important, the report recommended that the imprisonment of Canadian women should be guided by five important woman-centred principles:

1. empowerment;

2. the provision of meaningful choices;

3. treating women with respect and dignity;

4. the provision of a physically and emotionally supportive environment; and

5. the sharing or responsibility for women's welfare between institutional staff, community members and the women themselves. (Hannah-Moffat & Shaw, 2000, p. 21)

The new facilities began operating in 1995 and 1997, with the last female inmate at P4W being transferred in 2000. According to the Canadian Centre for Justice Statistics (2004), "These changes to the federal system have resulted in increased costs to incarcerate and care for federally sentenced women offenders. In 2001/02, the average cost of incarcerating a female offender in a federal prison was $155,589 annually, an increase of 37% since 1998/99 ($113,610)."

Many of the recommendations for reform and the guiding principles informing those changes were rooted in feminist ideas about the best ways to handle women prisoners. As a result of the connection to feminist ideas about women prisoners, *Creating Choices* represented a new and promising direction in women's corrections because they focused on being woman-centred.

References

Abelson, E. S. (1989). The invention of kleptomania. *Signs, 15*(1), 123–143.

Adler, F. (1975). *Sisters in crime: The rise of the new female criminal.* New York: McGraw-Hill.

Balfour, G., & Comack, E. (2006). *Criminalizing women.* Halifax: Fernwood.

Bonnycastle, K., & Rigakos, G. (1998). *Unsettling truths: Battered women, policy, politics, and contemporary research in Canada.* Vancouver: Collective Press.

Busfield, J. (1988). Mental illness as social product or social construct: A contradiction in feminists' arguments? *Sociology of Health and Illness, 10*(4), 521–542.

Camhi, L. (1993). Stealing femininity: Department store kleptomania as sexual disorder. *Differences: A Journal of Feminist Cultural Studies, 5*(1), 27–50.

Canadian Association of Elizabeth Fry Societies. (1998). *Annual report 1997–1998: Government again refuses to assist battered women who defend themselves.* Retrieved from http://www.elizabethfry.ca/areport/1998/gov.htm

Comack, E. (2006). *Women in trouble: Connecting women's law violations to their histories of abuse.* Halifax: Fernwood.

Correctional Service Canada, Task Force on Federally Sentenced Women. (1990). *Creating choices: The report of the Task Force on Federally Sentenced Women.* Retrieved from http://www.csc-scc. gc.ca/text/prgrm/fsw/choices/toce-eng.shtml

Cowie, J., Cowie. V., & Slater, E. (1968). *Delinquency in girls.* Cambridge: Institute of Criminology, Humanities Press.

Downes, D., & Rock, P. (2003). *Understanding deviance: A guide to the sociology of crime and rule-breaking.* Oxford: Oxford University Press.

Garland, D. (1985). *Punishment and welfare: A history of penal strategies.* Aldershot, UK and Brookfield, VT: Gower.

Gelsthorpe, L. (1989). *Sexism and the female offender: An organizational analysis.* Hampshire, UK: Gower.

Grabe, M. E., Trager, K. D., & Lear, M. (2006). Gender in crime news: A case study test of the chivalry hypothesis. *Mass Communication & Society, 9*(2):137–163.

Goneman, C. (1994). Nymphomania: The historical construction of female sexuality. *Signs, 19*(2), 337–367.

Hannah-Moffat, K., & Shaw, M. (Eds.). (2000). *An ideal prison? Critical essays on women's imprisonment in Canada.* Halifax: Fernwood.

Heidensohn, F. (1968). The deviance of women: A critique and an enquiry. *British Journal of Sociology, 19*(2),160–175.

Johnson, K., & Kandrack, M.-A. (1993). On the medico-legal appropriation of menstrual discourse: The syndromization of women's experiences. *Resources for Feminist Research/Documentation sur la recherche féministe, 24,* 1–2.

Kinsman, G. W. (1987). *The regulation of desire: Sexuality in Canada.* Montreal: Black Rose Books.

Klein, D. (2004). The etiology of female crime: A review of the literature. *Issues in Criminology, 8,* 3–30. (Original work published 1973.)

Kramar, K. J. (2005). *Unwilling mothers, unwanted babies: Infanticide in Canada.* Vancouver: University of British Columbia Press.

Little Sisters Book and Art Emporium v. Canada (Minister of Justice), 2000 SCC 69, [2000] 2 S.C.R. 1120.

Lombroso, C., & Guglielmo, F. (1895). *The female offender.* London: T. Fisher Unwin.

Morton, J. H. (1934). Female homicides. *Journal of Mental Science, 80,* 64–74.

Pinterics, N. (2001). Riding the feminist waves: In with the third?" *Canadian Women Studies, 20*(4), 15.

Pollak, O. (1961). *The criminality of women.* Philadelphia: University of Pennsylvania Press. (Original work published 1950.)

Rimke, H., & Goldman, E. (2009). In I. Ness (Ed.), *International encyclopedia of revolution and protest* (pp. 1411–1414). London: Blackwell Publishing.

Shaffer, M. (1997).The battered woman syndrome revisited: Some complicating thoughts five years after *R. v. Lavallee. University of Toronto Law Journal, 47*(1), 1–33.

Smart, C. (1976). *Women, crime and criminology: A feminist critique.* London: Routledge & Kegan Paul.

Spohn, C. C. (1999). The rape reform movement: The traditional common law and rape law reforms." *Jurimetrics, 39*(2): 119–130.

Sprott, J. B., & Doob, A. N. (2000). Bad, sad, and rejected: The lives of aggressive children. *Canadian Journal of Criminology–Revue canadienne de criminologie, 42*(2), 123–133.

Statistics Canada, Canadian Centre for Justice Statistics. (2001). *Family violence in Canada: A statistical profile 2001*. Retrieved from http://www.phac-aspc.gc.ca/ncfv-cnivf/pdfs/fv-85-224-x2000010-eng.pdf

Statistics Canada, Canadian Centre for Justice Statistics. (2004). *Adult correctional services in Canada 2002–2003*. Retrieved from http://dsp-psd.pwgsc.gc.ca/Collection-R/Statcan/85-211-XIE/0000385-211-XIE.pdf

Thomas, W. I. (1923). *The unadjusted girl with cases and standpoint for behavior analysis*. Boston: Little, Brown.

Valier, C. (2002). *Theories of crime and punishment*. Essex, UK: Pearson.

Valverde, M. (1989). Beyond gender dangers and private pleasures: Theory and ethics in the sex debate. *Feminist Studies, 15*(2), 237–254.

CHAPTER 8

Critical Realist Criminology[1]

Jon Frauley, University of Ottawa

INTRODUCTION

Criminology emerged at a time in the 19th century when **crime** was fast becoming a widespread social problem requiring a solution, as it was held to be threatening to the social, political and moral arrangement of society. This early criminology focused on the nature of crime and its causes. Subsequently, the attention of criminologists shifted to the means used to control crime. As Clifford Shearing (1989) points out, whether studying crime and criminals or responses to crime, criminologists have always been concerned with something beyond the sphere of crime; namely, the broad process of **social ordering**, of which crime and criminal justice are only aspects. This is more obvious in later criminology, which analyzes societal responses to crime, but even early criminology concerned social ordering in so far as crime was perceived as important because it was a problem of social order:

> Criminology was theoretically and politically relevant as a discipline because it studied this great threat to social order. As interest shifted from crime, and its sources, to the control of crime, it was still *order* that was the central topic; a topic that was approached through the study of the phenomenon most central to it—crime. Criminology, thus, has always been about ordering. (Shearing, 1989, p. 177)

Although criminology has always concerned these broader processes of social ordering, criminologists have usually embraced a conventional understanding of their discipline, which Shearing calls "crime-ology," a discipline "about crime, the people who do it and responses to it" (Shearing, 1989, p. 170).

The problem, as Shearing sees it, is that most criminologists do not fully appreciate that crime is part of something larger; that crime can be looked upon as an indication, a symptom or an index of something else that requires description and explanation. If we hold that crime is an outcome of complex social processes and relations that require elucidation and explanation, then such a conventional view can be seen as superficial and inadequate. Critical realist criminologists share a particular understanding of the broader processes of social ordering (e.g., criminalization, diffusion of norms, marginalization) and structural arrangements (e.g., stratification, integration) that interact to generate both crimes and responses to them as well as ideas about how these processes can be studied. Not all criminologists who accept with Shearing that their discipline involves the study of social ordering are critical realists (Shearing himself is not a critical realist criminologist), but all critical realists attempt to move beyond "crime-ology."

CRITICAL REALISM

What is the particular understanding of social ordering shared by critical realists like me? We are interested in the conditions that are necessary for crime to emerge. By "crime," critical realist criminologists are referring both to the events classified as crimes and to the criminal law categories (including their production) used to classify these events as crimes. We want to understand how the ways our society is organized (its overall social, political and economic forms), our institutions are arranged and our social practices are enabled or constrained within these contexts promote the emergence of particular categories and conceptions of crime as well as the application of these categories to material activities. In this way, we do not accept criminal law categories at face value, viewing both criminal activities and their criminalization as products of the broader conditions

---

1   This is a modified version of the original manuscript.

which are our main objects of enquiry. **Conditions** refers to the general context of broad processes and structural arrangements described above, including both the *presence* and *absence* of factors. For example, consider the presence of a law, which classifies particular actions as a crime combined with an absence of enforcement, which might encourage law-breaking; or the presence of exploitative working conditions combined with the absence of worker loyalty, which might encourage workers to engage in actions defined by our legal system as industrial crimes.

Perhaps the most distinctive aspect of critical realists' understanding of the social ordering producing "crime" is that we regard these "conditions" as *deep* and even as partially unobservable so that crimes and criminal justice responses are observable signs of something largely unseen. This might seem strange and complicated, but if we think of something such as gravity, we know it exists but we cannot see it; we infer its existence when we let go of an object and it falls to the ground. Making connections between what we can see (e.g., crime as an event) and the things that must exist which support and make crime possible but may be unobservable to us (e.g., criminalization, weak social integration, power relations), will aid in our understanding of how something such as "crime"—both as a category and as an event—emerges, is reproduced and can be transformed in our society. By shedding light on the conditions, as defined above, a criminology informed by critical realism will inevitably transform the conventional understanding of crime as well as criminology. This is especially so because critical realist criminologists typically identify the *same* deep conditions from which emerge both categories used to identify some activities as crimes and the possibility for criminal events themselves. For instance, we might identify both the definition of certain kinds of sexual activities by women as prostitution-related offences *and* the engagement of women in these activities as produced by the same underlying class/gender processes and structural arrangements, these being core underlying conditions which produce in contemporary society many of its observable characteristics. Critical realists would similarly argue that different kinds of crimes (e.g., theft, murder, fraud) are not discrete or unconnected events but rather products of these core underlying conditions. Thus, it is not the different kinds of crimes that are important to study; rather, it is the sorts of conditions or systems that must be in place for crime to exist, with this study contributing to the identification and elucidation of the most general processes of social ordering.

METATHEORY

Before we get to the point where we identify specific conditions from which emerge the categories and definitions of crimes, criminal activities, as well as crime control strategies and practices, critical realist criminologists believe it is possible and useful to talk more generally about the qualities social theories should have. Speaking in a general way about conditions and observable outcomes is not a specific theory of crime or criminal justice. It is not even a single general social theory which can be applied to crime and criminal justice. It is a "metatheory"; a more general set of postulates or "foundational assumptions" (Danermark *et al.,* 2002, p. 118) that can be used to both examine and also formulate a more specific or substantive theory of crime and criminal justice or any other aspect of social life. (It is important to note that "critical realism" is not the same as "criminological realism," also described as "left realism" in some criminology texts. Criminological realism is a specific descriptive theory, while critical realism is a metatheory.)

All criminological theories contain metatheoretical assumptions, whether or not these are made explicit, or, indeed, whether or not the proponents of a criminological theory appreciate this. A metatheory also offers a systematic way of understanding the relationship between us and the things we seek to describe and explain. A crucial aspect of metatheories is that they offer us conceptual tools and a particular mode of reasoning that allow us to conceptualize or picture the production of knowledge itself as well as our objects of investigation. Each metatheory thus has a number of interrelated elements. Broadly, these are:

An ontology—a theory of the nature of social reality and of the specific objects of investigation. A critical realist ontology, to overly simplify, holds reality to be stratified into differing but interacting domains. The specifics of this are not important at this point. What are important are the implications of this view. On this view, what we can readily observe is only one element of social life. Unobservable or partially unobservable elements of social life are also important, particularly for explaining what we can readily see. There is a difference between what we can observe (which is "transitive") and the important underlying structural features and processes that generate these observable features (that is, "relatively enduring" conditions). It is the latter that requires our attention if we are to go beyond a concern with describing outcomes and grasp the causes of these outcomes. Another important feature is the process called "emergence." Outcomes emerge only given the right conditions. There will be a tendency, for instance, for gunpowder to explode if we have the presence of a spark as well as dryness. An explosion can be described as an emergent outcome where the potential for an explosion has been realized. In some cases, potential for outcomes may exist but the outcome does not materialize because the conditions were not "right" (e.g., the presence of dampness impugns the explosion of gunpowder).

An epistemology—a theory about what knowledge is and how it can be attained. Critical realist epistemology embraces the idea that to adequately explain observable events we must go beyond simply describing these and begin with the ontological assumptions outlined above. We must begin with identifying crucial differences between what is transitive (our knowledge of things as well as observable outcomes) and the relatively enduring and causal features of social outcomes (which involve a complex intersection of things that may not be directly observable, such as social structure, power relations, racialization and patriarchy, among other things).

A methodology—which identifies appropriate modes of reasoning and research strategies. Methodologies involve much more than simply research methods (techniques of data collection). Methodology concerns the conceptual basis of not only how we go about producing "data" but also how this data is to be interpreted. Methodologies direct how we derive significance from what we observe. Critical realist methodology must facilitate the identification and analysis of relatively enduring aspects of social reality (conditions) that may be unobservable or only partially observable.

We find little discussion of metatheory in criminology and sociology. Such an aversion to metatheory stems in no small way from the traditional view of the social sciences as applied forms of enquiry that are to solve social problems (see Manicas, 1987). Criminology especially, as Shearing points out, originated as what we could call a "danger science," concerned with finding solutions to things deemed to be problems by the state (things defined by others as problems criminologists ought to be concerned with). A tension persists between what we can call, on the one hand, a "protective service" orientation and, on the other, a "social science" orientation to the study of crime and its control (see Frauley, 2005). Criminology tends to be dominated by the former, "administrative" or "governmental" kind of criminology which is oriented towards enhancing the management of crime in the service of institutions of social control (discussed in Chapter 1). Despite the rise of critical and radical positions in the 1970s, and their further development into the present, criminology has yet to break free of its technocratic, "protective service" roots, an orientation that forcibly maintains criminology as a "crime-ology" (see Frauley, 2005). Moreover, the epistemologies and methodologies dominating criminology do not explicitly raise the related questions of ontology; that is, questions regarding the *nature* of and *kinds* of things that exist in the social world which need to be studied. This means that the objects of criminological investigation are not routinely problematized but are largely taken for granted. This is precisely the problem with crime-ology and the widespread belief that "crime" is the object of investigation.

How we formulate an understanding of crime and criminality is shaped by metatheory, and this in turn shapes the research strategies for attaining knowledge of crime and criminality. Adopting one research strategy over another will in turn shape the kinds of questions that can be asked by researchers owing to the imported assumptions about the character of crime. This is because each strategy will advance a theory of the nature of social reality (ontology) and a theory of knowledge (epistemology). It will come replete with categories and concepts that operate as lenses through which researchers will picture not only crime but their own research practice. Depending on which set of lenses are adopted, our attention will be directed toward some issues and away from others: for example, toward "class" and away from "intention"; toward outcomes such as "fraud" and away from processes such as "criminalization"; toward "gender" and away from "sex"; toward "offenders" and away from "offences"; or, in Shearing's case, toward "social ordering" and away from "crime." The descriptions and explanations generated will be shaped by these lenses, and explicit metatheoretical theorizing is needed to refine them.

In addition, explicit consideration of metatheoretical questions is important because criminologists often unknowingly rely on and advocate particular epistemological and ontological positions and, as a result, sometimes frame their understandings of their practice in contradictory ways. For students and academics alike this can be quite confusing. Criminologists may disagree with one another without realizing that their disagreement is largely a product of metatheoretical differences. Conversely, scholarly debate may ensue between people who hold different substantive positions but are similar in terms of their underlying metatheoretical assumptions without anyone appreciating it. For instance, to cite examples I will discuss in detail later in this chapter, "rational choice theorists" and "cultural criminologists" may fail to appreciate that they share the ontological assumption that crimes are instances of individual agency, or Marxists and Durkheimians may debate one another without realizing that both their approaches are broadly realist. Greater theoretical clarity would flow from identification of metatheoretical differences and similarities between the various criminological theories. So, being able to make sense of the theory of knowledge and conception of reality that we commit to when we "do" criminology is more than a good idea; it is imperative if we want to be able to contribute to the development of criminology as a scholarly discipline, engage in critique, craft a coherent and forceful argument or attend to practical matters toward achieving social justice.

I will go on to examine critical realist metatheory in detail, arguing that it offers the most developed concepts for investigating the nature of social reality and hence crime and its control. I will begin, however, with a discussion of the metatheoretical approaches which are currently the most influential within criminology.

POSITIVIST AND CONVENTIONALIST METATHEORY

In contemporary North American social science, the dominant metatheories are **positivism** and a distinctive set of approaches underlined by what I will call **conventionalism**. Positivism and conventionalism are sometimes thought of in sociology as corresponding to "macro" and "micro" analysis, respectively, and both are thereby represented in research methods texts. It is worth discussing these here in brief as they are dominant positions that inform a wide variety of social science approaches and will help to highlight what is distinctive about critical realist social science.

Positivism is often associated with the "scientific method," which involves the search for regularly occurring events or patterns of events in order to yield predictions. Being able to predict what will happen under specific circumstances is often held to be the key to improving society. Positivist ontology holds that the universe, including the social universe, is ordered and composed of a series of atomistic and observable events that exist independently of our knowledge of them and that only observable things can be considered real. These observable events appear to us as regularities; one type of event is typically associated with another type of event. It holds that these regularities can be represented by universal truth claims which state these associations as "constants" involving "variables." Where one of these types of events is a type of human behaviour, cause is often thought to reside in observable regularly occurring events which can be shown to be associated with the behaviour. For instance, positivist criminologists might ask, How do incidences of certain crimes vary by age, sex, class and region?

The epistemology or theory of knowledge advanced by positivism holds that knowledge is to be attained through direct observation, ultimately sensory perception, via experiments or surveys, that our sensory perception of a thing corresponds to what that thing is really like, and that knowledge is gained toward prediction of outcomes. A distinction is made between theories that proffer explanation and which must be treated with scepticism and observations that can be established with certainty. Claims about observable regularities are thus held to be subject to verification or falsification.

Conventionalism comes under a variety of names and in a number of forms: interpretivism, constructivism, hermeneutic analysis, sociological phenomenology and postmodern research (see Benton & Craib, 2001; Blaikie, 1993; Delanty, 1997; Keat & Urry, 1975). Conventionalists argue that human beings' actions in the world are not, as positivists insist, the result of impersonal, objective social factors of which they may be unaware and which social science can identify but instead are based on their subjective perceptions and meaning systems. The ontology advanced by conventionalists holds that social reality comprises shared meanings and understandings; "social reality" is held to be a product of, indeed, to consist of, our interpretations. Thus, we would not, for instance, expect to see economic inequality directly correlated with crime because subjects' responses to relative poverty will depend on how, in a given social context, economic wealth is perceived by the relatively poor and the kinds of responses to relative poverty they, as individuals and communities, regard as rational and legitimate. The central task of the social researcher is to understand the worldviews of his or her subjects, and how these structure their actions, including the answer to the question, How do subjects understand and experience crime?

The epistemology advanced by conventionalism holds that knowledge is derived using the everyday concepts and meanings of those we are studying. Researchers seek to understand the shared meanings about what is of interest and then attempt to "translate" this into social scientific language using specialized categories (see Blaikie, 1993). Verification and falsification, in the senses advocated by positivism, are rejected as inadequate for determining validity because it is held that there is no one single truth but rather multiple truths and realities. Social researchers can gradually come to appreciate these truths and realities and thereby see the world more or less as their subjects see it. The human capacity for cultural and linguistic understanding, rather than our capacity to observe the physical world through our senses, is central.

CRITICAL REALIST METATHEORY

The outlines of critical realist ontology have already been established. Critical realists understand the production of observable effects in terms of underlying conditions. Critical realist criminologists may be interested in the events categorized as crimes, but they take these as outcomes that are indicative of deeper and in many cases unobservable conditions that must be identified. Critical realists argue that positivist or conventionalist social scientists fail to take basic ontological depth sufficiently seriously, with positivist and conventionalist ontologies developing implicitly and taken for granted rather than through explicit attention and developed argument.

There are a number of important similarities and differences between critical realist ontology and the more implicit ontologies associated with positivism and conventionalism. Like positivist ontology, critical realist ontology holds that objects of enquiry exist independently of our knowledge of them but, unlike positivist ontology, it does not limit its account of the production of observable events to identifying patterned regularities. Like conventionalist ontology, critical realist ontology regards the categories and meanings used by subjects as crucial to the production of subjects' actions, but it insists this is only part of the story and that deep, unobservable structures can be identified which produce these categories and meanings. Viewed as an outcome that indicates the existence of deeper and perhaps unobservable features of social reality, events such as crime cannot be explained by searching for recurring patterns (positivism) or by only attending to the self-understandings of participants (conventionalism). These strategies produce descriptions, albeit rich and interesting ones, rather than explanations, and they advance an implicit view of social reality as rather shallow rather than as having depth. Because of the similarities with some aspects of positivism and conventionalism, critical realism is often said to be third way "in between" each.

Critical realists such as Roy Bhaskar (1975, 1979) and Andrew Sayer (1992) have developed a technical philosophical language to describe this third way. Social reality is stratified into three intertwined domains: "the empirical," "the actual" and "the real." The empirical refers to subjects' perceptions and understandings of the events in which they are involved. The actual refers to the entire range of observable events, which, in the social world, involves but is not limited to the empirical because subjects may not gain direct experience of these. The real is the realm of tendencies and potential from which observable events emerge and thus also includes the actual and the empirical. Social explanation requires consideration of all three.

In light of the above, social fields are conceptualized as having a vertical dimension; that is, they are conceptualized as having depth. One influential way of thinking about social reality as consisting of layers or different interconnected domains, of taking account of the empirical, the actual and the real, is provided by Derek Layder (1993). His model was developed partly as an attempt to provide a practical guide for doing realist social science. Figure 8.1 is a schematic presentation of his model, modified to bring out its relevance for criminology. A critical realist criminology would be concerned with how all four of the domains outlined in Figure 8.1 are *interconnected* and how together they constitute the conditions and potential for crime to emerge. Positivists largely but not exclusively concentrate on large-scale structural attributes. In doing so, study is confined to context and setting. Conventionalism largely focuses on interactions between individuals, confining analysis to situated activity and self. As conventionalism and positivism cannot and do not provide for one to conceptualize the interconnection between all four domains, especially in how the relations between each form the conditions for the emergence of activities and events, research strategies built upon these metatheories tend toward examination of surface features of crime and its control.

Let us take the example of fraud. Fraud is not simply an outcome of individual wrongdoing. What makes this outcome possible in the first place? Critical realists' attention is directed, not primarily to fraud, but to the "larger thing," the conditions from which fraud emerges. What sorts of things might make up these conditions? All four levels outlined in Figure 8.1 would combine to constitute the social conditions under which fraud might emerge. The conditions for "credit card fraud" might include the structured "interactions" (e.g., exchange) between social "subjects" (e.g., consumers and merchants), within some "field" or another (e.g., economic markets) organized toward reproducing a larger "context" (e.g., capitalism). Critical realism also helps us to understand and explain that if a fraud is not committed, this does not negate that the *potential* for fraud to emerge is real and exists. Whether this potential is realized is a different matter. The potential is real given the structure that each of these four elements in Figure 8.1 comprises.

As a third way "between" positivism and conventionalism, critical realism has the capacity to yield knowledge that would not be arrived at if working from either a positivistic or conventionalist research strategy. Realism's ontologically focused research questions have the potential to highlight new directions and forms of substantive research in criminology. It is highly unlikely that such questions would be generated or could be adequately answered by positivist or conventionalist approaches because these do not explicitly attend to ontology.

Because critical realist metatheory requires us to identify the often unseen arrangements and processes that could generate observable events such as "crimes," and because it does not take official categorizations and responses to these crimes at face value, it is an inherently critical research practice. This does not mean that every critical realist analysis must say that criminal justice categorizations and responses are wrongheaded or unjust. It means that critical realists are always asking searching questions about conditions, nature and structure of our criminal justice system, and about wider processes of social ordering; questions which positivist and conventionalist criminologists are not led to pose. If we are to think critically, we should also be thinking metatheoretically about what our objects of investigation consist of and how we might go about attaining knowledge of those objects. This is one of the reasons why the kind of metatheoretical thinking presented in this chapter, which may seem highly abstract and speculative to many criminologists, is so important.

FIGURE 8.1	Stratification of Social Reality (adapted from Layder, 1993, pp. 8, 72)	
Ontological Stratum	**Research Focus**	**Example**
SELF	*Self-identity and individual's self experience* Subjectivity and identity. As these are influenced by situated activity, setting and context and as they interact with the unique psychobiography of the individual. Focus on life career.	• politicians, public servants, experts • criminals, victims, witnesses • peace officers, judges, defence counsel, Crown prosecutors • professors, researchers, students • producers, consumers, merchants • men, women, poor, affluent, subordinates, superordinates
SITUATED ACTIVITY	*Social activity* Face-to-face activity involving symbolic communication by skilled, intentional participants implicated in settings and contexts. Focus on emergent meanings, understandings and definitions of the situation as these affect and are affected by dispositions of individuals and settings and contexts.	• lawmaking, criminalization • criminal activities • crime control activity—policing, adjudication, punishment/rehabilitation • higher education activity—application of metatheoretical principles, construction of research strategies and descriptive theories, learning • market activities—production, consumption, exchange
SETTING	*Intermediate social organization* Immediate environment of activity: e.g., schools, family, factory. Work: industrial, military and state bureaucracies, hospitals, social work agencies, penal and mental institutions, domestic labour, labour markets. Nonwork: leisure activities, sports and social clubs, religious and spiritual organizations.	• legislature/Parliament • justice system—police, courts, corrections • economic markets • education—universities, colleges • community • for above categories: character of position—subordinate, superordinate
CONTEXT	*Macro social forms: e.g., class, gender, ethnic, economic and legal-political relations* Values, traditions, normative forms of social and economic organisation and power relations—e.g., legally sanctioned forms of ownership, control and distribution, interlocking directorships, state intervention. These elements as they are implicated in settings.	• democratic society • capitalism—exploitative relations, inequality, poverty/affluence

The Italian Marxist thinker Antonio Gramsci is especially instructive as to why criminologists, or any social scientists, would want to understand their practice on a metatheoretical level:

> [I]s it preferable to 'think' without having critical awareness, in a disjointed and irregular way, in other words to 'participate' in a concept of the world 'imposed' mechanically by external environment, that is by one of the many social groups in which everyone is automatically involved from the time he enters the conscious world . . . or is it preferable to work out one's own conception of the world consciously and critically, and so out of this work of one's own brain to choose one's own sphere of activity, to participate actively in making the history of the world, and not simply accept passively and without care the imprint of one's own personality from outside? (1957, pp. 38–39)

Gramsci is stipulating that it is important to consider what the very act of conceptualizing entails and how this is possible; how we go about working out our conceptions of the world or of crime and crime control. What are the tools that are available to us that can help us do this? We would do well to accept Gramsci's entreaty and to see beyond the crime-ology understanding of criminology and to avoid the constraints externally imposed in taking "crime" to be the thing that the discipline is organized around. Crime-ologies tend to adopt an ideological or taken for granted understanding of crime and criminality. If, for example, we hold crime to be activities that violate the criminal law, we accept a state definition of crime, which is one that is defined externally to criminology. Social workers, state agencies, police officers, journalists, big business and industry may all have a hand in shaping the dominant understanding of what the categories "crime" and "criminal" refer to, but social scientists need not accept this. If they do, they run the risk of accepting an externally defined understanding of what criminology ought to take to be as its main and legitimate problem and focus. In addition, because these values underlie such a definition of crime, they are an important part of why and how classifications of crime are generated and applied and should be subjected to scrutiny rather than imported into the discipline unchallenged.

WAYS OF THEORIZING: INDUCTION, DEDUCTION AND RETRODUCTION

Sociology and criminology students seldom study metatheory or theorizing, instead learning about various descriptive theories of crime and criminality. Although theory is situated at the core of contemporary social science curricula, there is little or no agreement on its role or place in research and pedagogy. Social science methods texts, for instance, present "theory" as a set of variables to be measured or applied in data interpretation or as a hypothesis to be falsified or verified. Social and criminological theory texts, on the other hand, often portray theory as one of many perspectives on the world, as a description of social objects or events, or as a school of thought (e.g., Marxism, labelling theory, governmentality theory, rational choice theory, strain theory). What is important here is that the prominent understanding of theory within social sciences such as criminology, criminal justice studies and sociology is one that holds theory is something that is made reference to. As Lopez (2003, pp. 1–2) instructively observes, most theory texts tell us what theorists have said, but little about the "practice of social theory" itself. As Ian Craib (1984, p. 5) puts it, "Since we start with the result [the end product of thinking theoretically] it is too easy for students and teachers to imagine that the whole process is a matter of learning what various theorists have said, of learning theories." Because the evaluation of theories necessarily requires the interrogation of categories and the "capacity of seeing the effects of categorization, measurement and competing research protocols on research findings" (Curtis & Weir, 2002, p. 6), learning to think theoretically is vitally important. This, as Craib (1984, p. 5) suggests, "is less a matter of learning theory than of learning to think theoretically."

Critical realists advocate explicit attention to the relationship between the process of systematic conceptualizing and empirical research. This is in part because criminological and sociological theories are the outcome of processes of conceptualizing or thinking theoretically which adhere to the logic of one or another metatheoretical position. As Sayer (1992) argues, the most crucial moment in any discussion of method is how we conceptualize. Our methods (e.g., surveys, participant observation, discourse analysis) and theories (e.g., Marxism, strain theory, labelling theory, etc.) espouse epistemological and ontological positions whether or not researchers intend this or are even aware of it. These assumptions inform how we conceptualize and thus how we approach what we are studying. Because most criminology and sociology curricula do not emphasize this important aspect of how theories, as sets of interconnected concepts, are constructed and then deployed in social science research, students (and dare I say some academics) very seldom are exposed to the differences between metatheories, their relationships to descriptive theories and the implications of advocating one descriptive theory over another. It is not that students and researchers are prevented from thinking theoretically but that they are not informed about *how* they go about this and the different ways they might do it.

Thinking theoretically requires us to use one or another, or some combination, of a range of available research logics. Critical realist methodology adheres to an overall research logic called *retroduction*. Many social science methods and philosophy of social science texts do not discuss retroduction, restricting their accounts of research logics, where this is discussed at all, to the better known research logics of *induction* and *deduction*. As cornerstones of methodology, these three research logics have an important place in the positivist, conventionalist and critical realist metatheories. Before I describe retroductive reasoning, I will describe induction and deduction, explain how they are used in positivist and conventionalist research and analyze their limitations.

Induction is the logical process involved in generalizing from observations. It works on the assumption that something observed in one situation will hold in more or less similar situations. Let us use the example of criminological research on street gangs. A positivist criminologist may show through research on a number of street gangs that the greater the relative poverty of the community from which a gang is drawn, the higher the rate of criminal convictions among the gang members. The criminologists may then infer that this is a statistical relationship which will be found in street gangs generally. This inference is inductive. Inductions by conventionalists tend to be more tentative, but the logical process is the same. A conventionalist may get to know a few members of a street gang and come to understand some of the categories they use to interpret the world and guide their conduct. If the conventionalist then suggests that these same categories will be used by other members of the same gang, or perhaps that similar categories may be used by members of related gangs, this would generalize the observations and thus involve induction.

Deduction is the logical process involved in applying a theoretical claim to a particular instance or instances. This process is involved when hypotheses are derived from general ideas or theories and are then tested. The theories or general ideas can be products of induction, but this is not necessarily the case. Let us return to our criminologists studying street gangs. Having discovered in a sample that the greater the relative poverty of the community from which a gang is drawn, the higher the rate of criminal convictions among the gang members, and having inferred that this finding will hold generally, the positivist criminologist may attempt to test the theory or generalization by developing new sample of street gangs, predicting which gangs will have the highest rate of criminal convictions on the basis of their relative poverty and then finding out whether this is so. The logical process through which a hypothesis is derived from a general set of ideas or a theory is called deduction. Deduction characterizes as well the procedure of beginning from a general and tentative claim and then moving toward a confirmation of this claim. A conventionalist criminologist may similarly deduce that members of the gang being studied will share the categories of the informants already consulted, a claim that can be tested by getting to know and interviewing more members of the gang. Again, the logical process of identifying specific new informants as likely using certain categories is deduction. However, not all theories which are applied to particular cases through deduction are products of induction in this way. Rational choice theorists and cultural criminologists share the view that crime is an outcome of an individualistic process (see above), but they differ in the qualities they ascribe to this process. Crime, for a criminologist who subscribes to rational choice theory, is described, based on the available categories, as the outcome of a process of reasoning where a rational person weighs the advantages and disadvantages of committing a criminal act. The commission of a crime is held to be a voluntary act of one's free will. Crime, however, for those who are working within the relatively new field of cultural criminology is described as the outcome of a productive and creative process. Crime is held to be what we could call a "cultural artefact" and is regarded as the product of the manipulation of signs and symbols toward the communication of resistance and expression of a subcultural style that undermines authority. Note that very different expectations about gang crime would be deduced from these theories, with rational choice theory predicting crimes where there is a rational expectation of advantage for the criminal, and cultural criminology expecting this to be largely irrelevant and predicting crimes which exploit opportunities for gestures of resistance. Note also that that rational choice theory and cultural criminology are not, in any simple sense, the products of observation and induction. Rather, they are broad intuitions about "human nature."

Induction and deduction are logics of justification. A general claim made through induction (e.g., the greater the relative poverty of the community from which a gang is drawn, the higher the rate of criminal convictions among the gang members) is said to be justified by the logic of induction. A specific claim made through deduction (e.g., the members of a specific gang from a relatively very poor community will have a high rate of criminal convictions) is said to be an expectation justified by logical deduction. Despite the apparent value of such justified inferences, induction and deduction direct us to surface events and relationships because they both emphasize description of patterned regularities.

Retroduction, advocated by critical realists, is described as a logic of discovery rather than of justification. Starting from both a theory of social reality (ontology) and with particular observations of our object if interest, critical realists attempt to infer the kinds of conditions that must be present for the observed events to occur; a retroductive analytic is used to create a theoretical model of what might exist and would broadly consider context, setting, situated activity and self. The idea is that if true, this hypothetical model can help us explain the existence of that which is observed. Realists would then search for evidence that this model is accurate. This retroductive inference aims to illustrate how something *might* be and is therefore concerned with making something intelligible and finding *a* plausible explanation to a puzzle. It requires some imaginative and creative conceptualizing. Because our knowledge of reality is held, by realists, to be subject to change, we cannot claim with certainty to have found the single right answer. Conventionalists would not claim certainty either, but this is because they assert that there are multiple realities rather than the possibility of multiple interpretations of one reality (as realists hold). Positivists assert the existence of one reality but believe that certainty or near certainty is possible if the correct procedures are followed.

Going back to our example of criminological study of gang crime, critical realists would make observations about the relationship between relative poverty and criminal convictions, as well as the categories employed by gang members to interpret and act in their world, as well as the official categorizations that define crimes and identify criminals, and attempt to develop models of the conditions which might plausibly produce all these observable events and categorizations. This procedure cannot be said to justify the inference of the existence of these deep, unobservable social processes and relations because the primary objective is to take a "leap in logic" to formulate a hypothetical model that then can be borne out through further observation. The primary focus is on ontology, or *what* can be known, rather than on epistemology or *how* we might attain knowledge. Likewise, there will always be plausible competing inferences of this kind, and choosing between them is a matter of thoughtful judgement. As Blaikie (1993, p. 168) outlines, retroduction requires "a disciplined scientific imagination" meaning the conclusion then is an attempt to formulate a plausible premise that, if correct, could explain what is observed, which includes positing the existence of underlying things that may not be directly observable (e.g., social cohesion or mode of production). This is to reveal something new, unlike deduction and induction, which cannot produce new ideas. Critical realists insist that this is how science must develop; gravity was not discovered through generalizing the observation of objects falling to the ground or through an intuition about the universe from which the falling of objects to the ground can be deduced but by the application of disciplined imaginative powers to the observation of objects falling to the ground to produce a new idea about the underlying forces which make this happen.

Because positivism and conventionalism, including their inductive and deductive methods, are the dominant metatheories for criminology and sociology, the dominant questions asked and conceptualizations produced have been shaped accordingly. It should be pointed out, however, that some Marxist and Durkheimian scholars have been able to provide criminology with a retroductive analysis because both these positions are underwritten by a form of realism (see Erhbar, 2007; Marsden, 1998; Pearce, 1989; Woodiwiss, 2001). Many, however, have dismissed these positions as dated, reading Marx dogmatically as an economic determinist and Durkheim as a positivist. As a result, the influence of these positions has waned over the past few decades, especially with the rise to prominence in the 1980s of postmodern theory (which is a form of conventionalism).

We can draw on classical sociological theory for illustrative purposes since both Marx and Durkheim employed what could be characterized as retroductive reasoning. Marx *inferred* from empirically observable class conflict the existence of an inherently contradictory process of capitalist production. That is, if Marx's elaboration of what he termed the capitalist mode of production were correct, this could explain the emergence and reproduction of class conflict. Crime, it should be noted, would itself be an indication of class conflict and in turn a symptom of the contradictory process of capitalist production (including distribution of resources).

Durkheim held that a social fact, such as crime, is the crystallization of constitutive and obfuscated social relations (the connections between various structured positions within a society) and that these relations were what social scientists should be concerned with. Along these lines, the amount of crime in a society would refer to or indicate the presence of deeper constitutive relations; for Durkheim, levels of crime would refer to or indicate the level of social cohesion and the complexity of the division of labour (i.e., degree of specialization) in a society. We may not be able to directly observe "social cohesion," but we can observe the amount of legal regulation and the various crime control strategies implemented as a response to what is held to be crime, all indicating to us whether there is strong or weak social cohesion (that is, how "integrated" into a society its members are). The idea that empirically observable phenomena are effects that are related in a complex way to underlying and sometimes obfuscated conditions and that these outcomes can themselves generate further effects is something that a critical realist criminology, unlike positivistic and conventionalist research strategies, would be explicitly concerned with.

Conclusion

We have seen that difficult issues of ontology, epistemology and methodology, largely ignored in criminological methods and theory texts, must be identified, understood and addressed. Why we pose one criminological question rather than another, how we can conceptualize crime, the sorts of descriptions we can produce and the explanations we can arrive at all depend on our metatheoretical position. Pawson (1989, p. 139), taking a critical realist position, says it best when he stipulates that "research cannot simply dwell at the level of events and if we were to confine observations solely to the business of monitoring events, we will end up with endless descriptions of more or less random sequences." The point he is making is that neither positivism nor conventionalism can provide a description or explanation of the conditions that are necessary to the emergence of outcomes and events such as crime or the practices of crime control. Critical realism provides the metatheoretical foundation for a criminology that can meet these requirements.

References

Benton, T., & Craib, I. (2001). *Philosophy of social science: The philosophical foundations of social thought*. New York: Palgrave.

Bhaskar, R. (1975). *A realist theory of science*. Leeds, UK: Leeds Books Ltd.

Bhaskar, R. (1979). *The possibility of naturalism: A philosophical critique of the contemporary human sciences*. Brighton, UK: The Harvester Press.

Blaikie, N. (1993). *Approaches to social enquiry*. Cambridge, MA: Polity Press.

Craib, I. (1984). *Modern social theory: From Parsons to Habermas*. New York: Harvester Wheatsheaf.

Curtis, B., & Weir, L. (2002). The succession question in English Canadian sociology. *Society/Société, 26*(3), 3–13.

Danermark, B., Ekstrom, M., Jakobser, L., & Karlsson, J. (1997). *Explaining society: Critical realism and the social sciences*. New York: Routledge.

Delanty, G. (1997). *Social science: Beyond constructivism and realism*. Buckingham, UK: Open University Press.

Ehrbar, H. G. (2007). The relation between Marxism and critical realism. In J. Frauley & F. Pearce (Eds.), *Critical realism and the social sciences: Heterodox elaborations*. Toronto: University of Toronto Press.

Frauley, J. (2005). Representing theory and theorising in criminal justice studies: Practising theory considered. *Critical Criminology: An International Journal, 13*(3), 245–265.

Gramsci, A. (1957). The study of philosophy and of historical materialism. In *The modern prince and other writings* (pp. 58–75). New York: International Publishers.

Keat, R., & Urry, J. (1975). *Social theory as science*. London: Routledge & Kegan Paul.

Layder, D. (1993). *New strategies in social research: An introduction and guide*. Cambridge MA: Polity Press.

Lopez, J. (2003). *Society and its metaphors: Language, social theory and social structure*. New York: Continuum.

Manicas, P. T. (1987). Capitalism, science, and the university: The Americanization of the social sciences. In *A history and philosophy of the social sciences* (pp. 193–212; 213–237). New York: Blackwell.

Marsden, R. (1998). The unknown masterpiece: Marx's model of capital. *Cambridge Journal of Economics, 22*, 297–324.

Pawson, R. (1989). *A measure for measures: A manifesto for empirical sociology*. New York: Routledge.

Pearce, F. (1989). *The radical Durkheim*. Winchester, MA: Unwin Hymen.

Sayer, A. (1992). *Method in social science: A realist approach*. New York: Routledge.

Shearing, C. (1989). Decriminalizing criminology: Reflections on the literal and tropological meaning of the term. *Canadian Journal of Criminology, 31*(2), 169–178.

Woodiwiss, A. (2001). *The visual in social theory*. New York: Athlone Press.

CHAPTER 9

On Postcolonialism and Criminology*

Renisa Mawani, University of British Columbia

and

David Sealy, York University

INTRODUCTION

Recently, a growing awareness has developed among criminologists regarding the broad impact of colonial ideas and practices upon modern Western conceptualizations of criminality and practices of crime management. **Colonialism** refers to the practice of settling or controlling land that belongs to others and is a specific outcome and form of imperialism. Imperialism refers to a dominating metropolitan power, such as Britain, ruling over distant territories. British imperial expansion took various forms including territorial acquisitions and settlements that resulted in coercion and violence against colonial populations (including Africans, Aboriginal peoples, South Asians and others). British settlers migrated to diverse regions across the empire. Some of these locales became white settler colonies and sites of long-term resettlement (Canada, Australia, New Zealand), whereas others were ruled from afar (India and East Africa). The British continued to maintain their allegiance to their country and relied upon the land, natural resources and populations in the colonies to generate personal and imperial wealth. Some observers have argued that crime management techniques were first put into practice in colonial contexts by British administrators who developed techniques such as fingerprinting in order to manage and regulate colonial populations (Cole, 2002). In many cases, colonial administrators also criminalized the beliefs and rituals of Indigenous communities and in so doing were better able to subjugate these populations and rule over their

territories (Ross, 2006). The theories of 19th-century criminologists such as Cesare Lombroso (discussed in Chapter 5), whose ideas were deeply rooted in anthropological concepts of racial degeneration and atavism, drew upon the experiences of European colonialism and established an early connection between racial identity and criminality in Europe. Despite these influences, the relationships between colonial and racial domination and criminological knowledges and practices have not been fully analyzed through the insights of postcolonial theory.

The objectives of this chapter are twofold. First, to discuss the ways in which colonial knowledges inform criminology as a discipline, and second, to consider the analytical possibilities of postcolonial theory. **Postcolonial theory** refers to a body of knowledge which addresses the harmful and lasting effects of colonial rule on cultural practices and knowledge production. Edward Said's *Orientalism* (1978) is seen to mark the emergence of **postcolonial studies**. Here Said (1978) argued that colonial knowledges were central to the production of literary, political and administrative ideas in Britain, France and later the United States because empire figured prominently in the ideas advanced by iconic European thinkers including, for example, Voltaire and Flaubert.

In this chapter, we consider how postcolonial theory might reveal the centrality of race and colonialism to criminology as a discipline, even when these processes are not the object of inquiry. We argue that colonial knowledges of racial inferiority are rooted in the 19th century and reemerged in

* This chapter has been the product of over two years of conversation and collaboration. David Sealy passed away suddenly on December 26, 2009, and did not see the chapter or book in its final stages or in print. Although this is the first official collaboration between us, resulting in a publication, David inspired, questioned and challenged me for many years; his thoughts have left a deep imprint on many of my own. This chapter is dedicated to David's memory and to his critical visions for criminology.

what David Garland (2001) calls the modern "culture of control." Specifically, the mass incarceration of racialized minority populations, including Aboriginal peoples and African-Canadians, is located in these historical colonial narratives linking race and criminality. The idea that Aboriginal peoples and those of African ancestry have propensities toward crime has been discounted through empirical research, yet contemporary crime control narratives continue to connect racial identity with criminality, albeit in more subtle ways.

The chapter is organized as follows: In the first section, we offer brief critiques of both conventional and critical perspectives in criminology. Some criminologists argue that the historical distribution and enforcement of crime is influenced by colonial histories of criminality that link crime and race. Ultimately, perceptions of some communities as more prone to crime results in higher rates of incarceration (especially for African-Canadian and Aboriginal peoples in Canada). However, little attention has been given to how these older colonial ideas continue to inform contemporary debates within law and criminology. In the second section, we offer two related examples to highlight the lasting influences of colonial knowledges of criminality. The first example centres on race and punishment and the second on Aboriginal crime. In both cases, we demonstrate the contradictory ways in which 19th-century ideas are reactivated in contemporary debates over race and crime. Finally, we argue that postcolonial theory can usefully problematize the racial categories that have been so foundational to the discipline of criminology and to the practices of crime control deployed by police and other criminal justice agents.

CRIMINOLOGY AND THE PERSISTENCE OF THE COLONIAL IN THE "CULTURE OF CONTROL"

Perhaps no issue has come to represent the crisis of contemporary Western crime control than the connection between **race, racialization** and punishment. From South Africa to Canada and in other Western industrialized nation-states, there is a growing awareness that the overrepresentation of racialized minority populations in prisons is an urgent social problem. Just at the point when it appeared as though crime rates in Western Europe, the United States, and Canada were declining, there emerged a marked increase in incarceration rates, as well as a growth in prison-related private industries. As Malcolm Feeley (2003, p. 112) argues, "[t]he historical trajectory of . . . crime control over the last three decades has been almost exactly the opposite of what was anticipated in 1970." This mass incarceration has in no way been democratically distributed. On the contrary, this increase in incarceration rates, which began in the United States and followed in Canada and other democratic nations including South Africa, has resulted in an unprecedented imprisonment of **racialized** minorities, foreigners or both. This fact raises an important question: Why in societies where racial inequality has been formally eliminated through law and policy do race and racism continue to play such pivotal roles in crime control and penal practices?

In the United States, Canada, South Africa and other Western democratic regimes, there is some consensus that legally sanctioned racist practices were aimed at keeping racialized minorities in their place, especially after the demise of more formal segregationist processes. In keeping with these arguments, we could assess the overincarceration of African-Americans in the United States as the endpoint of a continuum that began with lynching during slavery and expanded to the incarceration and the establishment of chain gangs in the Jim Crow period (see Wacquant, 2000).[1] There appears to be a similar continuity between the emergence of the reservation system for Aboriginal peoples in Canada, Australia, South Africa, New Zealand and the United States with their more recent overincarceration in contemporary periods. To put it differently, the mass containment of these racial populations that emerged during the colonial period (including slavery and the reservation system) have been reconstituted in our contemporary context but in ways that still draw upon and are situated in colonial knowledges. It might be relatively uncontroversial to state that there is a continuity between ideas of criminal subjects that emerged out of colonial slavery and those that surfaced during the postslavery postcolonial period up to the civil rights era. A controversy emerges, however, in thinking of the overimprisonment of racialized minority subjects in our recent multicultural or "postracial" period as connected to these earlier practices. The governments and citizens of Western liberal democracies assume there is a clean break between the colonialism of the past and the multiculturalism of the present.

Before we turn to the literatures that explore the ways in which race figures in the discourses of punishment, we should first briefly explore Garland's (2001) understanding of the culture of control. Our argument is that prevailing understandings of penal modernity, like dominant approaches to understanding the effects of race on punishment, ignore the historical role of colonial knowledges in shaping conceptualizations of the relationship between race, crime, and punishment. Garland's work is no exception here. Broadly speaking, the literatures that engaged with questions of race and punishment from the post-civil rights period, beginning with the Reagan regime in the United States, then the Thatcher regime in Britain through to the postapartheid period in South Africa and beyond, can be said to have emerged and developed within the parameters of what Garland has termed a modern culture of control. For Garland, this period witnessed shifts in the political cultures of late modern Western societies, from welfare statism to neoliberalism, leading to what he argues are corresponding shifts in the penal cultures; from what he terms "penal welfarism," with its core strategy of rehabilitation, to "neoliberal penalty" with its core strategy of mass incarceration. Further, Garland notes in his discussion of mass incarceration that the imprisonment of racial minorities does figure in these shifts and developments. Despite the strengths of his work, Garland neglects to connect the mass incarceration of racialized minorities in recent times to the European ideas of colonized peoples that facilitated their oppression and subordination. By glossing over the role of race and colonialism in the transformations that mark the culture of control of late modernity, he obscures other important developments including the shift away from welfare state centered policies and a movement towards new modes of governing race through a discourse of "antiracist multiculturalism" (Goldberg, 2002). More important, Garland does not adequately problematize the relationship between this culture of fear of the racial other and nineteenth century colonial narratives of race. Contemporary knowledges of race in the North American context that informed slavery and residential segregation were indeed derived from a longer legacy of European colonialism. This legacy provides an important historical and racial context

---

1   The Jim Crow period or Jim Crow laws refer to a period between the late 1870s and mid-1960s when state laws were enacted in the southern United States which mandated "separate but equal" status for black Americans. These were segregationist laws that required blacks to attend separate schools and provided for separate "whites only" areas in public places such as trains, buses and restaurants.

for the social organization of penality, which today includes the mass incarceration of African-Americans in the United States and Aboriginal peoples in Canada. By fore-grounding this history, we argue that the racialization of crime and criminality are not the ancillary effects of a "culture of control" as Garland suggests but a central and constitutive feature of penal modernity.

RACE AND INCARCERATION

Within the criminological literature, we identify four dominant ways of exploring how the concept of race figures in theories of overincarceration. First, there is criminological research founded in positivist social science with an explicit and/or implicit public policy orientation (we saw in Chapter 1 that this is what is known as administrative criminology or correctionalism). Much of this research suggests that racialized minority citizens are negatively affected by the unduly discretionary policies of criminal justice authorities. Discretion enables police officers and legal officials to make decisions based on factors other than those relevant to the case (race, gender, sexual orientation). As critics of discretion have pointed out, the effects include differential rates of arrest and conviction and amplified police surveillance of racial minority populations.

The more recent scholarship in this field has focused directly on the problem of racial profiling (Kalnuta-Crumpton, 2000, 2006; Hood, 1992; Wortley & Tanner, 2005). In particular, these scholars argue that the arrest, prosecution and incarceration of racial minorities are founded in prejudice, racial bias and stereotyping, all of which are pervasive problems within the administration of justice. These inequalities, many assume, can be addressed and even remedied through better criminological knowledges of discretionary processes. The arguments advanced by much of this literature is to demonstrate that "from the point of arrest to the sentencing stage the weight of criminal justice practices falls on the lower classes in general and on black people in particular" (Kalnuta-Crumpton, 1998, p. 321; see also Kalnuta-Crumpton, 2000; Kellough & Wortley, 2002; Miller, 1997; Tonry, 1997). The solution for many of these scholars includes more in-depth research and the implementation of antiracist criminal justice policy initiatives. These types of solutions ignore a larger problem: Racial differences inform not only the work of the police and other criminal justice personnel but are deeply entrenched in the types of knowledges produced by the social sciences more generally. Colonialism relied on scientific and other forms of racism to justify the systematic oppression of Indigenous populations in Canada and elsewhere. These ideas of racial difference were often tied to criminality as a way of justifying coercive laws and policies, including antipotlatch legislation, restrictions on alcohol use and legislation aimed at racial segregation. Thus, our very understanding of what it *means* to be Aboriginal cannot be undone simply through a liberal affirmative action campaign that promotes formal equality. Underpinning these sensibilities are deeply rooted notions of Aboriginal people as "criminal" and "in need of correction."

Much of this criminological research addresses racial differences through visual identification. As several scholars have noted, racism derives its power from the multiple registers upon which racial difference operates (Goldberg, 1993; Stoler, 1997). While racism may be connected to cultural oppression, as is often the case with Aboriginal offenders, in its most recent manifestations, religious affiliations have become significant markers in establishing racial difference and exclusion (Goldberg, 2006). By focusing on the visual alone, positivist research on racial profiling often ignores the ways in which other modes of racial difference that rely on nonvisual qualities also work to construct racialized minority populations as criminally predisposed. In addition, these approaches obscure the histories of particular constructions of race and thus do not consider how, for example, the present situation facing the increased profiling of African-Americans and African-Canadians is in fact a re-articulation of earlier ideas established during colonial times (evident in the enforcement of Jim Crow laws in the United States, for example).

The second set of criminological scholarship is what we would call the **culture of violence** literature. This work emerges out of earlier forms of social anomie and social disorganization theory discussed in Chapter 6. The overwhelming theme that characterizes the culture of violence literature centers on the ways in which a so-called culture of violence has come to dominate the civic space of urban neighborhoods in major cities throughout the West. According to many scholars working along this line of thought, a violent subculture is created out of continuing cycles of poverty. Some scholars have traced this condition to the failure of neoliberal policy initiatives such as the "war on drugs" and major welfare cuts. The effects of both have been used to explain increasing violent crime rates in inner cities. Some of the early 20th-century theorists of deviance argued that these subcultures exist because the residents of these neighborhoods are not properly socialized into the mainstream; here, violence is viewed to be a coping strategy or problem solving technique. Thus, the culture of violence is rooted in a set of antisocial and informal rules governing interpersonal public behavior, which relies on the use of violence and has become the major socializing agent in these already marginalized minority communities. Importantly, these ideas have only solidified and exacerbated existing racial segregation in inner city communities. The problem is made worse when these urban locations become racialized through the culture of violence narratives made popular through media reports of individual incidents of interpersonal violence in the inner city. These communities, which are already marginal, become increasingly marginalized. The media focus on the inner city rather than on interpersonal violence that occurs in the suburbs serves to amplify a generalized fear of crime and violence in urban locales in Canada and the United States. The inner city thus becomes a location to be feared, avoided and overpoliced.

The third set of criminological research literatures includes multiple versions of critical sociology that emerged out of Marxism (discussed in Chapters 6 and 8). These literatures tend to collapse race-based oppression into class-based oppression when addressing questions of crime and deviance. This approach connects the overincarceration of Aboriginal peoples, people of African ancestry, and South Asians in Canada, the United States and Britain to the political economy of capitalism and slavery founded in and perpetuated by European colonialism. These analyses shift attention away from the specifics of crime, punishment and criminal justice and instead view punishment to be an integral part of the organization of capitalist relations of production (and in the case of feminism, reproduction). These discussions locate crime and punishment in the context of capitalism's control of marginalized racial minority populations through the use of incarceration. Thus, these literatures conceptualize the over incarceration of African-Americans in the United States as rooted in processes that are much more complex than racial prejudice or class domination. The overincarceration of racial minority populations is linked to historical processes of domination and control that become integral to the management of freed black slaves that began with the demise of plantation slavery and culminated with the unemployment crises of the inner city ghettos. The mass incarceration of African-Americans in the United States is understood to be about the *management* of a redundant population whose labor power is no longer necessary for the capitalist production of surplus value.

French scholar Loïc Wacquant (2000, 2003) describes this to be a process whereby the penal system is used to address a middle-class fear of crime and is mobilized to warehouse those at the bottom of the class structure. These social problems are the products of neoliberal social policies, which include massive cuts in social welfare and a downsizing of government. There is a political if not structural convergence between the concern to warehouse a surplus population, and the overincarceration of racialized communities. Goldberg (1999) argues that the prison–industrial complex is now an integral feature of American social and economic life. Like Wacquant, he sees the convergence of a racial and spatial politics of exclusion and containment within the building of more prisons to warehouse those racially excluded. Following Foucault, Goldberg (2002) argues that prisons are modern institutions of control which are an integral feature of modern life. Goldberg (2002) goes further to explain that prisons also define and reproduce our concepts of race by marking out which types of people belong behind bars and which do not.

While this scholarship is useful for documenting the connections between race, plantation slavery and mass incarceration, its beginning points remain anchored in several problematic assumptions of race. For instance, the structural Marxist literature tends to ignore the ways in which black criminality is assumed from the start. Agonzio (2000) argues that these criminological literatures reinforce rather than contest racist discourses because they emerge from theories of relative deprivation which position all citizens in relation to their class position. The point for Agonzio (2000) is that research grounded in theories of relative deprivation neglect the institutional racism that is an integral feature of black life. From Agonzio's perspective, there is no way to isolate the race effect from the variables that help predict the decision to incarcerate as these processes that enable prediction (such as relative deprivation) are themselves racialized.

Questions of methodology are central to the discussion above. Attempts to scientifically discover or decipher the race effect of criminal justice practices are steeped in the development of knowledges that are then used to reform those practices. Thus, there is an assumption that through carefully developed social science research we can get behind and move beyond these racist practices and new knowledges can then be used in governmental reformist agendas. But if the process of knowledge production is itself racialized, then even our best efforts will only reproduce ideas of race within different parameters. In so doing, it becomes easier to speak of antiracist strategies aimed at democratizing punishment but remains difficult to challenge the idea that prisons are the best ways of "solving" social problems (Davis, 2000).

Wacquant (2000, 2002, 2003) also views the mass incarceration of African-Americans and other racialized communities in our contemporary context within the broader patterns of increases in carceral practices during late modernity. Wacquant agrees that the welfare state tolerated poverty in previous eras and that the current neoliberal state penalizes poverty. For Wacquant, the criminalization of poverty renders the prison to be an important strategy for the containment, management and control of those disreputable elements and classes. Here Wacquant's description of the American prison system and its governance of African-Americans is instructive. Although the criminalization of African-Americans in the United States is similar to the criminalization of the poor and dangerous classes that has occurred throughout North America, Western and Eastern Europe, and even South Africa, Wacquant argues that "blacks are the only category to have experienced ghettoization in American society" (Wacquant, 2002, p. 52). While European and non-European immigrants of other ethno-racial origins may initially have lived in poor ethnic neighborhoods, this was viewed as a transition toward their "integration into the composite of white society" (Wacquant, 2002, p. 52). Like the Jews of medieval Europe, African-Americans were legally segregated and ghettoized. The implication of Wacquant's observation for our purposes is that he demonstrates how ideas of African-Americans as "unfit," "degenerate," and "criminal" are constitutive of the American social imaginary.

In our present neoliberal era of global government, for example, the stark comparisons between the ways in which race and poverty are deeply embedded in the spatial make up of major American cities is both troubling and revealing, especially in terms of how racial segregation concentrates certain types of crime in specific urban areas. Here, it is noteworthy that in both Toronto and Halifax, the Canadian cities with the largest African-Canadian populations, there are distinctive areas known for producing black crime and social problems. The extent to which these areas have assumed structural characteristics similar to American-style ghettos and to other racialized, peripheralized spaces in Britain and elsewhere is in need of further research. However, we do see some troubling trends. The recent moral panic surrounding American-style gangs in Toronto urban neighborhoods, for example, is revealing. What is important here is that in a time of decreasing crime rates, the marked increased in the fear of crime, or more specifically, the fear of criminal victimization by an unknown racial other, echoes the fears of a black masculinity that has been an important aspect of American life from the early colonial period to the post-Emancipation era (Richardson, 2007; Wilson, 2005).

Finally, there is a race and punishment literature that takes as its starting point ideas of Enlightenment rationality, which were to enable not only better and more comprehensive knowledges of the "criminal" but also the "criminal act" and its appropriate punishment (Dumm, 2000; Lichtenstein, 2001). The questions raised by this work centres on the ways in which Enlightenment narratives concerning the value of more humane forms of punishment were also racially inflected and focused on the containment of racialized minorities and those others who remain socially marginalized. The goals of this literature are to challenge ongoing debates regarding race and punishment and to push scholars to critically question the assumptions underlying their own research. For Thomas Dumm (2000), the governmental rationality of prisons today has given up on the original individualized disciplinary notions of individual reform and rehabilitation that led to the creation of prisons in the first place. Prisons have now become an integral feature of new forms of symbolic, economic and geographical racial segregation.

Like Dumm, Lichtenstein (2001) raises questions concerning the problems inherent within Enlightenment narratives. He too points to specific racial histories as a way to argue that the move toward a supposedly more humane form of punishment was nothing more than the institutionalization of a far reaching and all-encompassing mode of racial control. For Lichtenstein (2001), the history of race and penalty in the United States is not about the shift from rehabilitation to retribution but about "the struggle on the part of rationalizing 'experts' to overcome forms of punishment more traditionally rooted in the patriarchal family, the ownership of slaves, vigilantism, and employer–employee contract relations than in state sanctions" (Lichtenstein, 2001, p. 191).

The point is that sentiments about controlling badly behaved black subjects are inscribed into more institutionally centre and therefore more precise forms of social control. Lichtenstein contends that arguments made in the United States for ending the illegal practice of punishing African-Americans through lynching were not motivated by calls for more humane methods of punishment but were underpinned by a growing movement to legally institutionalize lynching through the more politically legitimate state practices of the death penalty (Lichtenstein, 2001).

In our view, these arguments made by Dumm (2000) and Lichtenstein (2001) aim to productively challenge prevailing discussions of race and punishment that pervade the discipline of criminology. In light of the unexpected increase in the incarceration of racialized minorities, the lessons we should learn from this literature points beyond a return to the welfare state and away from calls to develop more rigorous social science tools. Rather, the implications of these poststructuralist arguments may redirect us toward the ways in which colonial knowledges continue to persist in modern times. To be clear, we are suggesting that colonial knowledges figure in the very conceptual frameworks of criminology as a discipline and that we as researchers and students rely upon them to articulate arguments about justice and punishment. Postcolonial scholars have long pointed to the continuities and mutations between the past and present (see Chakrabarty, 2000; Mehta, 1999; Said, 1978, 1993) but this observation has largely been ignored by mainstream criminology. To continue our discussion, let now explore how the colonial surfaces in the most foundational of all Canadian relationships: that between Canada and its Aboriginal peoples.

COLONIAL KNOWLEDGES AND ABORIGINAL CRIME

Scholars writing on Aboriginal people and the criminal justice system in Canada and elsewhere (most notably Australia and New Zealand) have long observed that Aboriginal women and men are vastly overrepresented in the criminal justice systems of former white settler colonies. According to Correctional Services Canada (2007), Aboriginal people make up approximately 3.3% of the Canadian population yet account for 18.7% of those federally incarcerated. These vast discrepancies have produced a number of different explanations. Some scholars have argued that the disproportionate involvement of Aboriginal peoples in the Canadian criminal justice system is evidence of what James Waldram (1997) describes to be a function of "cultural oppression, social inequality and the loss of self government, and systemic discrimination which are the legacies of the Canadian governments treatment of Aboriginal peoples" (22). Others insist that overrepresentation is a product of racism and colonialism. In both cases, the point is not to deny the existence of high rates of Aboriginal criminality but to cast our understanding of these crises within a broader political, cultural and for some colonial context. While Waldram and others have aimed to dispel myths of Aboriginal people as criminogenic and dysfunctional, we argue that gestures toward "cultural oppression" and Canada's "colonial legacy" point to the importance of historical context but are not useful explanations in and of themselves. To attribute the mass incarceration of Aboriginal peoples to a "colonial legacy," for example, provides us with few insights as to how racial knowledges that emerged during the period of British colonialism are themselves an ongoing legacy that has been reactivated and legitimized in our present context.

Some scholars have attributed the overrepresentation of Aboriginal peoples in Canada's criminal justice system to a type of culture conflict or "clash of civilizations." According to Waldram (1997), Aboriginal peoples, unlike Westerners, have religious and healing practices that are deeply intertwined (see also Ross, 2006). Thus, the civilization project of the early French and English colonizers that sought to convert Aboriginal peoples to Christianity meant that some forms of indigenous healing practices were lost and even criminalized (Backhouse, 1999). With the formation of the Canadian nation-state in 1867, the government set up a policy aimed at creating reserves, a process that was intended to both exclude and assimilate Canada's Aboriginal peoples. Assimilation thus meant that pressure was placed on Aboriginal peoples to give up not only their religions practices but also other cultural expressions and ceremonies including the potlatch and Sundance, which were deemed to be illegal according to Western law (Backhouse, 1999). With the passing of the *Indian Act* in 1876 there emerged a policy which directed Indian agents, missionaries and others working closely with Aboriginal groups and communities to discourage and suppress these ceremonies, restrictions that figured centrally in the colonial processes of civilizing and improving "the Indian." As we saw in Chapter 1 of this text, this suppression was so extensive that by the turn of the century, many Aboriginal peoples who were incarcerated in Stony Mountain Penitentiary in Manitoba were imprisoned simply for practicing their religious and traditional beliefs (Waldram, 1997, p. 8). For Waldram and others, the current mass incarceration of Aboriginal peoples is not a contemporary phenomenon but one which must be traced to European contact and colonization.

Those scholars writing about Aboriginal people in conflict with the law have argued that the suppression of indigenous customs and spirituality combined with the displacement of Aboriginal peoples from their traditional land and resources meant that many of these communities living on reserves were functioning in a kind of anomic situation created by what some scholars have called "cultural deprivation" (see Doob *et al.,* 1994; LaPrairie, 2002). This cultural deprivation then produced conditions of poverty and intensified social problems creating conditions in which Aboriginal peoples routinely come into conflict with the law. These arguments about relative deprivation have been so pervasive and powerful that they have informed not only criminal justice policy (for example, the new sentencing guidelines contained in section 718.2e of the *Criminal Code*) but also Canadian jurisprudence. In the recent Supreme Court of Canada decision in *R v. Gladue* (SCR, 1999, p. 688), we see the court adopting a mitigation framework for Aboriginal criminality rooted in cultural deprivation wrought through colonialism. According to this decision, in all cases involving Aboriginal persons charged with criminal offences "the court requires sentencing judges to consider the unique systemic factors that may have brought a particular Aboriginal offender before the courts and to consider 'the types of sentencing procedures and sanctions which may be appropriate in the circumstances for the offender because of his or her particular aboriginal heritage or connection.' [Gladue, 1999]" (Roach & Rubin, 2002, p. 358). Here it is interesting and important to note that culturally sensitive criminal justice programming grounded in healing, including healing lodges and circle sentencing, are now deemed to be the most appropriate ways of rectifying the historical and contemporary problems that contribute to high rates of incarceration for Aboriginal offenders (LaPrairie, 2002; Roach & Rubin, 1999). As we discuss below, the problem with these ideas of cultural difference, while reparative and thus progressive in their immediate effects, in the long term only reproduce colonial notions of Aboriginality as a form of essential racial difference.

Even among Aboriginal scholars, arguments of cultural difference and colonial legacy have had a certain scholarly purchase that obscures the role of colonial knowledges. Many Aboriginal scholars have rightfully argued that their people's involvement with the criminal justice system has not often been discussed within the past and ongoing effects of racism. Writing of the Donald Marshall Inquiry, Mary Ellen Turpel (1992) has insisted that the false imprisonment of Donald Marshall must be understood against a larger backdrop of colonialism and racism. One "must understand that racism does not exist in a vacuum," she writes. "The context of colonization and broader subjugation of Aboriginal peoples by the British, French, and later 'Canadian' states is the antecedent of its appearance in an in-stitutionalized form in the criminal justice system" (Turpel, 1992, p. 93). Earlier in her essay, Turpel explains this point in detail:

> The Aboriginal experience of institutionalized racism in Canada, resulting in a web of mistrust of non-Aboriginal officials, is one which flies in the face of a legal system theoretically premised on the rule of law and equal access to justice. It is frequently said that the rule of law is the soul of the modern state. . . . . Aboriginal perspectives on the criminal justice system in Canada reflect concerns which one would expect to find in South Africa, El Salvador, or elsewhere, not in an os-tensibly 'progressive' Western liberal democracy such as Canada. (Turpel, 1992, p. 86)

Turpel's arguments raise some important conceptual and political questions. By position-ing law and justice with Canada's liberal democracy and by placing these in opposition to the "undemocratic" and racial states (Goldberg, 2002) of South Africa and El Salvador, countries that are well known to be marked by racial violence, Turpel suggests that institu-tionalized racism is somehow antithetical to democracy and to the liberal notion of progress. Yet, as we hint above, in our discussion of the literatures on race and punishment, and as postcolonial scholars have long argued, colonialism and liberalism have long worked together, facilitating the extension of imperial control through liberal notions of humanitarianism, equality and progress. Uday Mehta (1999), among others, has provided us with critical insights on liberalism, racism and empire-building that might help us to re-think the situation facing Aboriginal peoples in Canada, the connections between the pres-ent and the colonial past and our own methodological shortcomings and inabilities. Let us address each of these points in turn below.

Empire and colonial racism, as postcolonial scholars have long argued, are constitutive of liberalism and not antithetical to it. Mehta's (1999) elegant analysis of 19th-century lib-eral thought, for example, details not only how the experience of British imperialism deeply shaped and contoured liberal ideas but also how the inclusionary ideals of liberal-ism were reconciled with its exclusionary racial impulses (see also Arneil, 1996). Imperialism, Mehta (1999) argues, did not contradict liberal idioms and ideals but on the contrary was central to these doctrines (6). While the European proselytized Enlightenment humanism in theory, he frequently denied it in practice. John Stuart Mill, among others, wrote prolifically on the ideals of liberalism at the very same time he deliberated and con-templated the merits of colonialism. Mill had personal experiences with and was deeply in-vestment in these questions as he worked within the administrative machinery of the British colonial bureaucracy. For Mill and his contemporaries, liberalism and colonialism were not antithetical, nor were they contradictory. In the introduction to his famous essay, "On Liberty," Mill reconciled his two positions by characterizing liberty to be a principle applicable "only to human beings in the maturity of their faculties." Thus, for Mill, there were set limits to liberty; it could not be extended to children or to "those backward states of society in which the race itself may be considered in its nonage" (Mill, 1968, p. 73). It was precisely through these arguments that liberalism coexisted with and even justified imperial expansion, colonial occupation and its illiberal and violent impulses.

In Canada, as was the case elsewhere in the British Empire, the tensions between universal freedom and colonial exclusion were routinely legitimized through discourses of incivility and improvement. To be sure, there are countless examples that document and illustrate the ways in which colonial agents across the country perceived Aboriginal peoples to be childlike and culturally and developmentally primitive (see Francis, 1992). For liberal thinkers like Mill and for colonial administrators who subscribed to these ideals, imperial rule in all of its illiberality was necessary to bring those "backward populations in line with European modernity." Thus, Aboriginal peoples needed to be closely governed, disciplined and segregated precisely because they were lacking in reason and rationality. The reserve, as an exemplary site of racial segregation and exclusion, was deemed to be a necessity, a place where Aboriginal peoples would eventually be enfranchised and assimilated and thus would cease to be "Indians" (Mawani, 2009).

Through this brief discussion, we make two points. First, that the "culture of deprivation" that has so often been linked to Aboriginal peoples and evoked to explained their involvement with and overrepresentation in the criminal justice system has deep roots that emerged through the logics of colonialism. Contemporary knowledges of Aboriginal criminality which move to culturalize law breaking and incarceration are not new ideas but are folded into older knowledges in which Indigenous peoples were historically represented as socially and culturally deprived. Those scholars, including Waldram (1997), who insist on a framework of cultural deprivation do not adequately problematize how these populations have been historically constituted through similar discourses. What these logics accomplish is the reinscription of an Aboriginality that does not know how to exist in a modern liberal democracy and thus remains in what Mill termed "those backward states of society" (1968, p. 73).

Second, through our discussion of liberalism, we emphasize the insights of postcolonial thinkers that race is not outside or antithetical to the modern nation, but constitutive of it. Thus, we should not be looking for racism in South Africa or El Salvador, as Turpel (1992) suggests in her discussion of the Donald Marshall Inquiry. What we need to do is to hone our analytical tools to think more carefully as to how colonial racisms and their contemporary formations have been constituted through the ideals of law, liberty and equality that have not only been central to the ethic of liberal thought but also to the Canadian nation-state. Although the Canadian criminal justice system does claim in theory to be a site of justice and equality for all, we need to work through its exclusions, the logics through which Aboriginal peoples are deemed to be simultaneously outside of law and justice (as having their own, for example) and in need of tutelage (similar to the civilizing missions of the late 19th and early 20th centuries), a process of improvement that will enable them to become rational and law- abiding peoples.

Our contention with the literature on Aboriginal criminality, as with the scholarship on race and punishment, thus centers on its foundational ideas of Aboriginality. By failing to historicize and thus problematize ideas of cultural deprivation, criminologists, social policy advocates and the courts continue to reinscribe incivility, disorder and chaos onto Aboriginal communities, tropes which are remarkably reminiscent of late 19th- and early 20th-century colonial truths that were generated in Canada and elsewhere (see Brown, 2002; Mawani, 2009). By constituting racism as something that is external to the Canadian nation rather than foundational to it, critics also miss important connections and continuities between colonial knowledges and contemporary ones.

CRIMINOLOGY AND THE POSSIBILITIES OF POSTCOLONIAL CRITIQUE

Let us now conclude with a brief discussion of the possibilities that bringing the insights of postcolonial theory to criminology might avail. Although the question of a postcolonial criminology has not often been contemplated, above we suggest that encounters between postcolonial critique and criminological theories may open important opportunities to understanding how colonial pasts continue to reside in our contemporary present. There is now an emerging interest in these questions from outside the discipline of criminology. Recently, anthropologists John and Jean Comaroff (2006) have made these connections, albeit on different registers. They observe that postcolonial societies in Africa and elsewhere have seen an upward surge in crime rates since official decolonization. "Lawlessness and criminal violence," John and Jean Comaroff explain, "have become integral to depictions of postcolonial societies, adding a brutal edge to older stereotypes of underdevelopment, abjection, and sectarian strife" (Comaroff & Comaroff, 2006, p. 6). If the colonies were constitutive of Europe (and North America) as so many postcolonial thinkers have argued (see Said, 1978, 1993), then this surge of lawlessness and criminal violence that the Comaroffs' detail in their recent book, tells not only of the colonies per se but of the western metropolis as well. We need to rethink the rise of crime rates in the former colonies and the mass incarceration of African-Americans and Aboriginal peoples as inextricably linked. Our task is to trace how these processes and their underlying knowledges converge in ways that render such violence rational and justified both in Western liberal democracies and in the (post)colonies.

Our discussion above has been more speculative than conclusive. What this brief chapter intimates, we hope, is that colonialism is deeply implicated in the developments of both criminological knowledges and techniques of crime control. As our chapter highlights, older knowledges of the colonial are not only reinvigorated in conservative explanations of crime but also in more progressive, liberal and critical ones. If spectres of the colonial are indeed haunting contemporary criminological knowledges, then what analytic insights can we derive by reading North American criminology against postcolonial critique? Here, we make some provisional and fragmented observations. To begin with, Canadian scholars need to remember that Canada was once a British and French colony that has since forged a long-standing colonial relationship with Aboriginal peoples and a more recent set of imperial relations with the United States. The colonial narratives that were created and evoked to classify racial groups into observable and understandable hierarchies did not dissipate with confederation.

Rather, these taxonomies have been reshaped and recontoured from the late 19th century onward, as our discussions of Aboriginal crime suggests. The objective for a critical criminology should be to unravel the ways in which these older colonial ideas of race are folded or recycled into new ones and in ways that create a series of (dis)continuous trajectories. Exploring how the past inhabits the present might open important insights into the criminalization of racialized minority populations as well as our ethical investments and responsibilities.

References

Agonzio, B. (2000). Theorizing otherness, the war on drugs and incarceration. *Theoretical Criminology, 4*(3), 359–376.

Arneil, B. (1996). *John Locke and America: The defense of English colonialism.* Oxford: Oxford University Press.

Backhouse, C. (1999). *Colour-coded: A legal history of racism in Canada, 1900–1950*. Toronto: Published for the Osgoode Society for Canadian Legal History by University of Toronto Press.

Brown, M. (2002). Crime, governance and the company Raj: The discovery of Thuggee. *British Journal of Criminology, 42*, 77–95.

Chakrabarty, D. (2000). *Provincializing Europe: Postcolonial thought and historical difference*. Princeton: Princeton University Press.

Cole, S. (2002). *Suspect identities: A history of fingerprinting and colonial identification*. Cambridge, MA: Harvard University Press.

Comaroff, J., & Comaroff, J. (2006). Law and disorder in the postcolony: An introduction. In J. & J. Comaroff, (Eds.), *Law and disorder in the postcolony*. Chicago: University of Chicago Press.

Correctional Service Canada. (2008). *2007/2008 estimates. Part III. Report on plans and priorities*. Ottawa: Queen's Printer.

Davis, A. (2000). The challenge of prison abolition: A conversation. *Social Justice 27*(3), 212–218.

——— (1999). From the convict lease system to the supermax prison. In J. James (Ed.), *States of confinement: Policing, detention and prisons*. New York: St. Martin's Press.

——— (1996). Race and criminalization: Black Americans and the punishment industry. In W. Lubiano (Ed.), *The house that race built*. New York: Random House.

Doob, T., Grossman, M. G., & Auger, R. (1994). Aboriginal homicides in Ontario. *Canadian Journal of Criminology, 36*, 29–62.

Dumm, T. (2000). Enlightenment as punishment. *Social Justice, 27*(2), 237–251.

Feeley, M. (2003). Crime, social order and the rise of neoconservative politics. *Theoretical Criminology, 7*(1), 111–130.

Francis, D. (1992). *The imaginary Indian: The image of the Indian in Canadian culture*. Vancouver: Arsenal Pulp Press.

Garland, D. (2001). *The culture of control: Crime and social order in contemporary society*. Oxford: Oxford University Press.

Goldberg, D. T. (2006). Racial Europeanization. *Ethnic and Racial Studies 29*(2), 331–364.

——— (2002). *The racial state*. Malden, MA: Blackwell Publishers.

——— (1999). *The political economy of prisons and policing*. In J. James (Ed.), *States of confinement*. New York: St. Martin's Press.

——— (1993). *Racist culture: Philosophy and the politics of meaning*. Malden, MA: Blackwell Publishers.

Hood, R. (1992). *Race and sentencing*. Oxford: Oxford University Press.

Kalnuta-Crumpton, A. (2006). *Drugs, victims, and race: The politics of drug control*. Hampshire, UK: Waterside Press.

——— (2006). The criminalization of "black deprivation" in the United Kingdom. *Social Justice, 27*(1), 76–102.

——— (1998). Drug trafficking and criminal justice. *International Journal of Sociology of Law, 26*, 321–338.

Kellough, G., & Wortley, S. (2002). Remand for plea: Bail decisions and plea bargaining as commensurate decisions. *British Journal of Criminology, 42*, 186–210.

LaPrairie, C. (2002). Aboriginal overrepresentation in the criminal justice system: A tale of nine cities. *Canadian Journal of Criminology, 44*(2), 128–181.

Lichtenstein, A. (2001). The private and public in penal history: A commentary on Zimring and Tonry. *Punishment and Society, 3*(1), 189–196.

Mawani, R. (2009). *Colonial proximities: Crossracial encounters and juridical truths in British Columbia, 1871–1921*. Vancouver: University of British Columbia Press.

Mehta, U. S. (1999). *Liberalism and empire: A study in nineteenth-century British liberal thought*. Chicago: University of Chicago Press.

Mill, J. S., (1968). *Utilitarianism, liberty, and representative government*. New York: Everyman's Library, 1968.

Miller, J. (1997). *Search and destroy: African American males in the criminal justice system*. New York: Cambridge University Press.

Richardson, R. (2007). *Black masculinity and the U.S. South: From Uncle Tom to gangsta rap*. Athens: University of Georgia Press.

Roach, K., & Rubin, J. (2000). Gladue: The judicial and political reception of a decision. *Canadian Journal of Criminology, 42*(3), 355–386.

Roberts, J., & von Hirsch, A. Racial disparity in sentencing: Reflections on the hood study. *Howard Journal of Criminal Justice, 36*(3), 227–236.

Ross, R. (2006). *Returning to the teachings: Exploring Aboriginal justice*. Toronto: Penguin.

Said, E. W. (1978). *Orientalism*. New York: Verso.

Said, E. W. (1993). *Culture and imperialism*. New York: Vintage Books.

Stoler, A. L. (1997). Racial histories and their regimes of truth. *Political Power and Social Theory*, 11, 183–206.

Tonry, M. (1997). *Sentencing matters*. New York: Oxford University Press.

Wacquant, L. (2003). The penalisation of poverty and the rise of neoliberalism. *European Journal of Criminal Policy and Research, 9*(4), 401–412.

——— (2002). From slavery to mass incarceration: Rethinking the question in the US. *New Left Review, 13*, 41–60.

——— (2000). The new peculiar institution: On the prison as surrogate ghetto. *Theoretical Criminology, 4*(3), 377–389.

Waldram, J. B. (1997). *The way of the pipe: Aboriginal spirituality and symbolic healing in Canadian prisons*. Peterborough, ON: Broadview Press.

Wilson, D. (2005). *Inventing black on black violence: Discourse, space and representation*. Syracuse, NY: Syracuse University Press.

Wortley, S., & Tanner, J. (2005). Inflammatory rhetoric? Baseless accusations? Responding to Gabor's critique of racial profiling research in Canada. *Canadian Journal of Criminology, 47*(3), 581–609.

CHAPTER 10

Governmentality and Criminology

Randy Lippert, University of Windsor
and
Grace Park, York University

INTRODUCTION

Criminology arose as a discipline in the 19th century. Only in 1979 was the English translation of French philosopher and historian Michel Foucault's lecture, "On Governmentality," published as an essay in an obscure and soon after defunct British journal. Barely noticed at the time, this new accessibility of Foucault's ideas on "governmentality" to Anglo-American criminologists was—in retrospect—a highly significant development. Indeed, this **Foucault effect** has seriously altered criminology's trajectory (see Introduction). While Michel Foucault was not a criminologist (he would have actively resisted the label) of the disciplines (see Lippert, 2005, p. 3), criminology may well be the one he most profoundly influenced. Criminology's affinity for governmentality may be because since at least the 1960s criminologists have turned their attention to understanding policing, punishment, and social control, fields that are also inseparable from governmentality. By the mid-1990s, governmentality concepts were actively informing criminological and related sociolegal studies in United Kingdom, Australia and Canada (see Stenson, 1993; O'Malley, 1992, 1997; Smandych, 1999). At this juncture, one of the most respected criminologists in the United Kingdom, David Garland (1997, p. 173), wrote that "the governmentality literature offers a powerful framework for analyzing how crime is problematized and controlled." By the first decade of the 21st century, a sizeable body of research had accumulated. Criminologists used these concepts to make sense of vital elements of crime control and criminal justice policies and practices in ways that revealed aspects previously taken for granted. It is not an exaggeration to say an entire cohort of criminologists, including many of those hired as

professors at Canadian universities in the past decade, have been profoundly inspired by these concepts. Although not without opposition and further refinement, this body of work continues to grow. It is therefore ironic that few if any Canadian criminology textbooks currently dedicate space—let alone a chapter—to governmentality. For this reason, and because we have both conducted research under governmentality's banner, we especially welcome the opportunity to discuss this compelling perspective here.

The purpose of this chapter is to introduce students to governmentality and how it informs criminology. We discuss governmentality's features first since they will be unfamiliar to most readers and then define and describe its three major concepts. Using Canadian examples, we then illustrate these features and concepts within two traditional areas of criminological interest: the prison and crime prevention. We conclude by discussing criticisms and merits of governmentality-informed criminological inquiry.

WHAT IS GOVERNMENTALITY?

Governmentality (government-mentality), as this text's introduction notes, refers to the reasons why populations are governed in particular ways, or the mentalities of government (Foucault, 1991; Dean, 1999). In "On Governmentality" Foucault was referring to how populations in modern Western societies were subjected to rule. Rather than adopting the traditional focus on the state to understand rule (Foucault once compared state theory to an indigestible meal), he instead set out to provide concepts to allow exploration of how conduct is shaped by various authorities through myriad means to shape conduct. Foucault provides a historical analysis, or genealogy, of the development of different forms of rule beginning in the 16th and 17th centuries, when sovereign power, or the monarchy, typified the form of rule. Earlier, in his famous book *Discipline and Punish* on the historical emergence of the prison as a dominant institution, Foucault (1977) showed that the exercise of sovereignty (or sovereign power) had an affinity for spectacles of which public punishment was the epitome. He described in detail the horrific dismembering as the "spectacle of the scaffold" during which the monarch's power was literally inscribed onto the offender's body for all to witness. Yet Foucault also noted that as grandiose and visible to the public was the monarch's occasional withholding of the power to punish by granting last-minute pardons (see Foucault, 1977; Lippert, 2005, p. 68). Sovereign power can thus best be described not as a monopoly to punish but instead as a monopoly to decide the exception (Lippert, 2005, p. 69). Yet in his governmentality essay Foucault observes a shift away from this form of rule, which also entailed a concern with territory whereby more emphasis was placed instead on subtle forms of regulation of the population. There is a "transition which takes place in the eighteenth century from . . . a regime dominated by structures of sovereignty to one of rule by techniques of government, [which] turns on the theme of population . . ." (Foucault, 1991, p. 101). The population was increasingly deemed to have its own characteristics and thus needed to be understood and governed in special ways (Rose, O'Malley, & Valverde, 2006). Population and mundane governance are seen to emerge alongside and at least to some degree to displace sovereign power's territorial, spectacular and exceptional nature. However, Foucault (1991, p. 102) makes the point that while there is a shift toward governmentality, sovereign power continues to have influence (e.g., U.S. President Bush suddenly and without explanation pardoned his former White House aide Karl Rove, who had been convicted of serious crimes), a point to which we later return.

To understand governmentality, governance (sometimes referred to as government) needs to be defined. For Foucault, governance is simply the "conduct of conduct" (Gordon, 1991, p. 2), or any attempt to guide, direct or shape behaviour, as an orchestra conductor would guide how an orchestra's musicians play the necessary instruments. Governance is thus about how actions are directed with a specific goal in mind. Actions are shaped based on a set of norms put in place, approved and reproduced by governing agencies and authorities (Dean, 1999). Governance, then, includes laws, policies and practices of the municipal, provincial and federal levels of the state but also efforts of countless private authorities and organizations (e.g., private corporations, business organizations, churches, condominium corporations, sports clubs and so on) as well as those who do not easily fit into public or private categories (Williams & Lippert, 2006, p. 296). Governance also encompasses self-governance or the reflection on one's own behaviour that can lead to efforts to change it for the better.

GOVERNMENTALITY'S FEATURES AND CONCEPTS

Governmentality-informed criminology has several basic features that distinguish it from positivist, administrative and related mainstream criminologies. While the latter focus on patterns of criminal behaviour, crime rates and the like, the former attends to the programs and practices of those (e.g., police, correctional personnel, legal professionals, citizens, as well as the criminalized themselves) who seek to shape and control conduct defined as criminal. A related distinctive feature of governmentality-informed criminology, with which we need to be aware, is its attention to discourse or the discursive realm rather than to what is known as "the real" or reality. A major focus is the language found in what are called programmatic texts of various kinds (policy statements, operational manuals, mission statements and so on), as will be clearly seen in two examples later in this chapter. This language is viewed not as a perfect representation of reality nor as obscuring reality or masking what is really going on. Rather, language is assumed here to be performative and constitutive; it makes actions of agencies and agents possible and constitutes (or makes up) their reality. There is an assumption that the social world is experienced through language, that it constitutes ways of acting and being (what are called subjectivities) and the social spaces in which they occur and exist. Therefore, discourse is the key here. It is presumed to structure what can be experienced and limits what can be done or said by institutions and their representatives, including those public, private and other institutions concerned about crime and related behaviour. In these ways, governmentality-informed criminology differs from critical realist perspectives while sharing philosophical underpinnings with some social constructionist studies (see Chapter 8).

A third basic feature is the presumption in governmentality studies that governance is always accompanied by the production of knowledge (Rose & Miller, 1992). For instance, the action of gathering statistics about known offenders allows criminologists to create profiles of potential criminals. In this way, governmentality-informed criminology is reflexive; it sees criminology itself as one form of knowledge used to govern populations. Interestingly, one effect of this kind of criminological knowledge production is to create a "criminal other" (Garland, 1997). Other members of society are then governed through their desire to stay clear of this risky "criminal other" (e.g., by avoiding certain parts of a city at night, purchasing a home security alarm or ensuring their children are equipped with cell phones to report criminal "stranger danger"). In this way, criminology plays a key role in informing individuals about how to act upon themselves and others. Though sometimes in proportion to the threats revealed by criminological profiling, and perhaps well-intentioned, this can also become what Simon (2007, p. 4) aptly calls "governing through crime" whereby institutions and individuals "deploy the category of crime to legitimate interventions that have other motivations." Whether reforming public schools or reconfiguring the workplace, Simon (2007) argues that this practice is evident in an array of institutions. One of these is the family, which he suggests is increasingly treated as a flash point of suspicions about crime (Simon, 2007, p. 9). He points out that parents are increasingly enlisted to indirectly work on behalf of law enforcement (Simon, 2007, p. 9) in that they are more and more often held morally or legally responsible if they overlook their children's use of illicit drugs; fail to prevent them from joining youth gangs that might engage in minor criminal acts; or more generally fail to identify and manage criminal risks to their children or spouses (Simon, 2007, p. 178). Simon also notes that criminal law increasingly intervenes in divorce proceedings that become more like battles between two parents in that if one parent is shown to have a single criminal conviction, this has become reason to cancel that parent's rights to child custody in favour of the other parent (Simon, 2007, p. 9).

A final feature to be aware of is that governmentality is neither a theory of society nor a theory of governance or power. Rather, research informed by governmentality attempts to avoid such totalizing aspirations. Analyses avoid reducing their specific findings to general (if not grandiose) theories about capitalist society, patriarchal society, risk society, information society, postmodernity and the like (Garland, 1997). In this way, criminologists enamoured with governmentality concepts tend to differ sharply from many sociological and social theorists who have traditionally used crime and crime control as sites to ground their theorizing about society and social relations, suggesting, for example, that what is observed in the criminal courts can reveal much about the nature of an entire society. Instead, the governmentality analytic in criminology and elsewhere calls for the detailed analysis of specific phenomena consistent with Foucault's own historical research to—quite simply—make these institutional domains and practices understandable (Rose, O'Malley, & Valverde, 2006).

Central to governmentality analysis are three major concepts: rationalities, programs and technologies. These are the tools with which to examine how various efforts undertaken to do something about crime and criminals are shaped and made possible. Each is discussed in turn. First, a rationality is "any systematic way of thinking about government" (Dean, 1999, pp. 210–211). Rationalities include questions about how to govern and serve to call into question existing governmental arrangements. They are justifications for how conduct is conducted and are based on "problematizing" conduct (i.e., seeing conduct as a problem) in order to change that behaviour in some manner. These are the mentalities of government informed by the human sciences, such as criminology, but also medicine, geography, psychology and so on (Dean, 1999). Through these knowledges normative assumptions are created about what is good, proper, ideal, appropriate or responsible conduct (Rose & Miller, 1992, p. 179). Rationalities are translated into programs which seek to address the problems of governance and create an illusion of governance as self-evident or taken for granted (Dean, 1999, p. 16). These questions provide us with the possible language in which to think about and practice governance. Questions of rationalities are based in the past; they are typically a response to problems of past forms of rule.

Programs, the second concept, are prescriptions, plans or schema for acting on some element of social conduct. They "constitute a space within which the objectives of government are elaborated, and where plans to implement them are dreamed up" (Miller & Rose, 1990, p. 14). Programs are created to try to "make things better" (Dean, 1999, p. 33) and are informed by knowledge (including criminological knowledge) about to how to overcome a problem (e.g., a rash of break and enters in an urban retail strip) that requires a response (introduction of an "open-street" CCTV surveillance program to watch pedestrians on the street at night (see Lippert, 2007). As a consequence, programs aim to reform and shape conduct. Programs are not limited to those initiated by the state and instead tend to include those of various other governing agencies. The common denominator, however, is a goal to manage conduct.

Technologies, the third and final concept, are intellectual and material means that make different forms of rule possible (Dean, 1994, p. 188). Technologies develop and become arranged within particular programs by rationalities; they are the means through which rationalities are carried out or made possible. They are the practical features of governance that put rationalities into place and bring programs into effect (Valverde, Levi, Shearing, Condon, & O'Malley, 1999). When linked to specific rationalities, they can serve different purposes. Examples of technologies might include different statistical and calculation measures—for instance, crime statistics (see Chapter 3). They might also include architectural strategies such as spatialization—for instance, the design of a special handling unit in a Canadian penitentiary. They range from risk management involving attention to future loss or danger to what Foucault called "technologies of the self," that is, technologies used to guide the self, by the self (Dean, 1995). We will discuss examples of these technologies in relation to prisons and crime prevention shortly.

Governance can additionally enlist "abstract things" (Foucault, 1991). Examples are the physical objects associated with criminal justice, ranging from the mundane safety on a police officer's side-arm, which serves as but one technology to prevent the firearm from going off inappropriately and resulting in deadly force, to the sophisticated CCTV cameras mounted in police cruisers that record activity in the immediate vicinity. Technologies possess a capacity to shift functions. For instance, while CCTV cameras in cruisers are aimed at making crime control more efficient by visually recording police encounters with vehicles owners who, for example, might suddenly drive away owing to outstanding arrest warrants, these devices also serve to govern police conduct. If officers wish to engage in police deviance (e.g., illegally threatening a driver to gain information about an offence, planting evidence in the vehicle or receiving a bribe in lieu of issuing a ticket) and avoid being caught and disciplined, officers must ensure they do so outside the camera's gaze. Thus a CCTV camera erected to deter crime and drivers from resisting arrest can become a tool of the police administration to watch officers' conduct and to potentially provide evidence to discipline them accordingly. The list of possible technologies is infinite, but a key aspect to remember is that they do not appear precisely as they are imagined. As such, they are not always identical to their blueprint set out in a program (Dean, 1999). This analysis of technologies also reminds us that governance is not merely repressive but is productive, even in the most mundane or seemingly insignificant sense (Hunt & Wickham, 1994, pp. 81–83). This creates the constant need for reflexivity and experimentation with new technologies and programs. Governance is reliant on the use of multiple technologies (new and old) informed by prevailing rationalities and translated into programs (Rose & Miller, 1992).

ADVANCED LIBERALISM

Central to liberal governmentality is the notion of individual freedom. Thus, while governance aims to shape individuals' action, in liberal governance this is ideally to be accomplished through a subject's freedom. As Dean (1999, p. 14) states: "To govern, in this sense, is to structure the field of possible action, to act on our own or others' capacities for action." Freedom is the cornerstone of liberal rationalities, distinguishing them from other historical rationalities.

One such liberal rationality that governmentality scholars have elaborated is social liberalism (sometimes also called liberal welfarism or welfare liberalism) or the government of "the social." Social liberalism as a rationality advocates sharing responsibility between the state and individuals, where the state has a responsibility to provide the general means for the population's well-being and the population is responsible for behaving as good citizens (Rose, 1999, p. 139). The objectives of social liberalism became translated into fiscal policies which establish security for the population "from the cradle to the grave" through programs such as national public health care, education, and welfare (Dean, 1999, p. 150). These policies are generally spoken about as the welfare state. This goal of security was coupled with an economic policy that adhered to the ideas of John Maynard Keynes and demanded state intervention in the economy. The welfare state, however, was criticized due to a sense that the state had too much control over society and traditionally private matters. As well, the Keynesian style of economics was increasingly thought to be unable to deal with inflation and recession. The result was a gradual shift to an advanced liberal rationality (Rose, 1999), which has become dominant in a number of policy domains, including those related to criminal justice and crime control.

There are several key features of advanced liberalism. One is that expertise in the management of specific populations is no longer assumed to be located within the state (Rose, 1993). Expertise is now to be "purchased" by careful consumers exercising their choice in a marketplace. This is true of policing, for example, whereby consumers are increasingly imagined to purchase protection not only from neighbourhood break-ins by choosing from an array of advertised expertise from private security firms but also from "paid-duty" policing offered by local police services (Brown & Lippert, 2007; see also Chapter 12).

Other key features of advanced liberal governance are "localization" (Crawford, 1997) and "responsibilization" (Garland, 1996, pp. 452) or movement of responsibility to more local levels (O'Malley & Palmer, 1996, pp. 141–142). Localization has taken the form of a new emphasis on the language of "community" (Stenson, 1993). Here community comes to displace the social as the field through which conduct is both thought about and governed (Rose, 1996, pp. 331–337). There is also a shift to the local level of subjects themselves, perhaps best exemplified—as will be seen later—by empowerment (Rose, 1996, pp. 336). This advanced liberal rationality therefore presupposes more active or enterprising actors (Rose, 1992), that is, "subjects of responsibility, autonomy, and choice" (Rose, 1996, pp. 53–54). Further, responsibilization also requires that the citizenry increasingly be given the tools through which to take responsibility for and govern themselves. As such, we see an increasing number of programs that motivate responsibility based on individual choices, empowerment and encouraging entrepreneurship (e.g., Cruikshank, 1999; Kesby, 2005). Thus, advanced liberalism has a normative aspect in that it creates categories of deserving and undeserving citizens. Rather than depending on the state to provide for his or her well-being, the deserving citizen is one who tries to improve his or her capacity to be productive and to be responsible for his or her own fate. This individual responsibility is exemplified in the types of programs and strategies which have the goal of sustaining market relations that resemble business transactions (Rose & Miller, 1992, p. 199).

Advanced liberal rule generally involves the introduction of more distance between decisions of formal political authorities and the conduct of a variety of authorities and actors (Rose, 1996, p. 53). It shifts the responsibility for conditions that are risky to the citizen to the private market and away from the state. This has the effect of creating forms of risk management and government "at a distance" (O'Malley, 1992; Simon, 1994). In the realm of crime control, these include the use of crime prevention through environmental design knowledge, which shows a disinterest in the psychological and social causes of crime and a preference for manipulating urban and other environments instead.

To be sure, advanced liberalism is not the only rationality relevant to criminology (Williams & Lippert, 2006; Park & Lippert, 2008). Another, for example, is pastoralism, which Foucault described as targeting an individual's salvation and needs that are laid bare through producing intimate knowledge of their souls (see Lippert, 2005). It has been found to be relevant in, among other areas, the contemporary Canadian context of church-affiliated groups illegally providing sanctuary to illegal migrants facing imminent arrest and deportation by police and immigration authorities (Lippert, 2005). We return to this point at the chapter's end, but to provide a sense of governmentality-informed criminology for now we shall limit our attention in what follows to advanced liberalism. The examples we discuss below clarify and more vividly illustrate the uses of the foregoing governmentality themes and concepts in two key criminological realms: prisons and crime prevention. There we pay special attention to the technologies of empowerment and risk management.

PRISONS AND EMPOWERMENT

Since its origins in social movements of the 1960s, empowerment has been used as a technology across a variety of domains (Cruikshank, 1999). Like other technologies—as noted above—it has shifted its functions. Recently, it has been taken up as a governance technology through which particular types of individuals, or subjectivities, are created so that they can be more easily governed via their needs and desires. The powerless are to be mobilized to actively participate in their own improvement, in the development of their own interests and actions (Cruikshank, 1999). Empowerment strategies, therefore, aim to enhance the power individuals can exercise in their daily lives. A vital technology of self-governance through empowerment is self-esteem discourse (Cruikshank, 1999). Guided and supported by social scientists and social service professionals, self-esteem has come to be seen as a way to solve all manner of social problems stemming from capitalism, racism and inequalities (Cruikshank, 1999). Cruikshank (1999) states that self-esteem is a technology in that "it is a specialized knowledge of how to esteem our selves, how to estimate, calculate, measure, evaluate, discipline and judge our selves" (89). The result is a connection of personal achievement to the governance of much broader policy domains.

A definitive example of the use of empowerment as a technology of governance is in Hannah-Moffat's (2000) study of the advanced liberal governance of women's prisons in Canada (she uses the related term "neo-liberal"—see Lippert, 2005, pp. 5–6). Prior to 1990, there was only one federal penitentiary for women in Canada, the Prison for Women (P4W) in Kingston, Ontario. Since its inception in 1934, the P4W has been marked by ongoing problems, including poor programming, an absence of community resources, unnecessarily strict security and a neglect of prisoners' cultural differences, especially where Aboriginal and francophone women were concerned (Hannah-Moffat, 2000, p. 512).

In 1989, due to increasing criticism, the Task Force on Federally Sentenced Women (TFFSW) was created to address these issues. It is here that Hannah-Moffat's analysis begins. Cochaired by the Elizabeth Fry Society and a deputy commissioner from Correctional Service Canada, the TFFSW was created in partnership with community organizations and included women who were previously federally sentenced (Hannah-Moffat, 2000, p. 512). The result of the TFFSW was a programmatic statement called *Creating Choices*, a report that outlined findings and recommended a series of changes based on a women-centred correctional model. This model encompassed five principles found throughout the report: "empowerment, meaningful and responsible choices, respect and dignity, supportive environment, and shared responsibility" (Hannah-Moffat, 2000, p. 514).

What is significant for our purposes is how, according to Hannah-Moffat, the TFFSW represents a shift to advanced liberal governance, a change which is particularly evident in the way responsibility came to be assigned in this domain. The state no longer remained responsible for the problems related to female imprisonment. Rather, the responsibilization strategy mobilized women's prisons and the community to more actively participate in finding a solution. This befits advanced liberal governance "at a distance" and is legitimated through a related language of "partnerships," shared responsibility and, above all, empowerment.

These technologies require that new programs be created as a result of the input and organization of community members who volunteer their experiences and expertise. This emphasis on community is also consistent with advanced liberalism as described earlier. Participation from the community rather than state officials within initiatives is foreseen allowing programs to become more relevant to women who will come face-to-face with the federal penal system. However, as Hannah-Moffat points out, these advanced liberal strategies are not without benefit to those who activate them. The state gains from partnership initiatives by quelling criticisms from advocacy groups who in the past were excluded from these decisions, as well as increased confidence and trust from citizens that the state is actively making strides to solve the problem of federal women's imprisonment (Hannah-Moffat, 2000, p. 516).

Through her discourse analysis, Hannah-Moffat reveals a shift to advanced liberalism evident in the language of the *Creating Choices* report. For example, in the report's preface, phrases such as "responsible partnerships" and "essential in order to foster independence" and "women must be supported by a coordinated comprehensive effort" (Hannah-Moffat, 2000, p. 515) are illustrative. An explicit link is made in the report between community partnerships and mutual responsibility to federally sentenced women's ability to make responsible choices. The report proceeds to state that this strategy for women's prisons is essential to the production and implementation of solutions to issues affecting federal women inmates in Canada (Hannah-Moffat, 2000, p. 515). The report also criticizes past imprisonment strategies for concentrating too narrowly on the correctional system itself. This is plainly a move away from state intervention.

An element of this responsibilization strategy evident in the report is the mobilization of the technology of empowerment. What is interesting about empowerment here is how women prisoners are enlisted in the problem's solution. In the past, what was seen as a state function is placed on the shoulders of women and the community (Hannah-Moffat, 2000). Women prisoners are encouraged to become functioning members of the population by attending programs that enhance their life skills and optimize the quality of their lives. This form of empowerment, while perhaps with good intention, reinforces the existing power structure that P4W had come to represent. Thus, while the TFFSW and the subsequent *Creating Choices* report were meant as a strategy which challenged structural barriers facing women inmates, empowerment was taken up as a technology consistent with advanced liberalism. It also legitimated the shift away from rehabilitation ideals (see Cullen & Gilbert, 1982) and ultimately the removal of state responsibility for the management of needs and risks (Hannah-Moffat, 2000). Such risk management that is consistent with advanced liberalism will also be seen in the second case study below.

The success of women's prisons relies upon the willingness of female inmates to participate in these governing strategies, whether wittingly or not. This brings us back to the idea that liberalism is based on individual freedom. However, prisons provide an interesting case as the individuals subject to governance are not actually free to make choices based on what they believe is to their own benefit, as typical advanced liberal subjects would do. Rather, the state makes their choices, which sometimes results in resistance in the form of suicide attempts and escapes (Hannah-Moffat, 2000, p. 526). Hannah-Moffat found that in instances where advance liberal technologies failed to govern the inmates, their subjectivities were redefined as "difficult to manage," "disruptive," "risky" and "potential escapees" (2006, p. 526). A discourse of the "criminal other" noted earlier is enacted here, legitimating alternative governing strategies such as the use of "enhanced security cells" which are high security units in which inmates must remain for 23 hours a day (Hannah-Moffat, 2000, p. 527; see also Martel, 2006). This form of punishment, it should be noted, is reminiscent of sovereign power.

In a more recent study of Canadian provincial women's prisons, Martel (2006, p. 608) found that segregation policies in which women were excluded from the general population for conduct deemed improper can be seen as instances of sovereign power but also befit advanced liberalism. Segregation was performative in that it taught inmates responsible self-governance and to "make-the-same" as other inmates in the general population. This aspect of excluding in order to include the inmate, while drastically different from empowerment, is consistent with advanced liberal governance. Segregation here seeks to reshape inmates' conduct to befit advanced liberal subjectivity. What this alludes to is the coexistence rather than the replacement of sovereign power by governmentality, a point mentioned at the beginning of the chapter. Advanced liberalism therefore is not totalizing in its strategies and has the potential to exist alongside other forms of power.

CRIME STOPPERS

With more than 1,000 programs in 20 nations, Crime Stoppers (CS) is the most popular community crime prevention program in the world (Crime Stoppers International, 2009). First launched in 1976 in the United States, CS came to Canada in 1982 and has since grown rapidly in this country. By 1985, there were 20 (Carriere, 1987, p. 112n) and by 2007, 118 programs (Crime Stoppers, 2007). The dominant image of CS is an arrangement among police, mass media outlets and the community that foresees average citizens anonymously calling in tips in response to unsolved crimes advertised in media, usually as Crimes of the Week. A coordinator distributes these tips to police investigators with the explicit purpose of solving the advertised crime. If a tip leads to any arrest or seizure of property or illegal drugs by police, the "tipster" is to be granted a monetary reward and instructed how to anonymously retrieve it (Crime Stoppers, 2001a, p. 4).

Lippert (2002) studied one major Canadian CS region containing more than 10 programs by analyzing a wide array of CS texts and conducting interviews with CS coordinators, partners, and board members. To study promotions, 640 Crimes of the Week from 10 CS programs were also analyzed for content. The study revealed that CS promotions and partnerships, anonymization (the act of making a person or place anonymous by masking identity) and rewards were key technologies that help permit CS to operate along risk management lines consistent with advanced liberal governance.

CS Promotions and Partnerships

For CS to work, the means of reporting specific kinds of risky people or situations must be promoted, along with offers of anonymity and rewards. This is primarily sought through the vehicle of Crime of the Week advertisements that appear in four media formats: television, radio, newspaper and Internet sites (including YouTube). Lippert found that the primary aim of the Crime of the Week is promotion, specifically of anonymity, rewards and how to report particular types of crime, rather than generation of tips about specific unsolved crimes. For instance, the CS coordinators select specific criminal acts to be Crimes of the Week, yet they admit that in some weeks no significant crimes occur that can conceivably become such. Much earlier events and "generics" promoting one type of crime rather than a specific act are then periodically used. In some programs, Crime of the Week television reenactments are filmed one day a month, up to three at a time, and then spread out in weekly succession over the course of the subsequent month. In these ways, Crime of the Week discourse portrays crime as a continuous and spatially immediate danger that demands an active, ongoing community response rather than as an unpredictable distant problem easily handled by police alone. The central message of this discourse is that significant crimes are occurring in your community every week, and your tips are required to do something about them. This emphasis is further evident, for example, in the CS manual, in which there is a focus on "making communities aware" to allow them to "better protect themselves" (Crime Stoppers, 2001a, p. 4). However, according to the CS coordinators, less than 10% of Crimes of the Week are solved as a result of tips (cf. Carriere & Ericson, 1989, p. 103). Yet this consistently low clearance rate has not curtailed use of Crime of the Week promotions, thereby suggesting their primary purpose is not tactical. Indeed, within CS, effectiveness is not measured by the clearance rate at all. Instead, only the absolute number of arrests or value of property or drugs recovered as a result of tips is typically tracked and reported for this purpose. This measure is impressive on the surface, which is likely the reason it is prominently displayed in CS promotions, but it is a dubious indicator of program effectiveness (see Carriere & Ericson, 1989). Thus, it is evident that CS is concerned mostly with identifying and managing risk.

Much information regularly received as tips as a result of a promotion concerns persons and situations thought to pose a risk of some kind. This attention to risk is being carried out more and more on behalf of CS partners. Sponsors have provided free advertising for promotions or contributed to the general reward funds for years, but a significant development beginning in the 1990s was the addition of specific regional and federal "partnerships." The newer partnership ideal foresees mostly private entities entering into intimate, well-defined arrangements with CS to yield more practical and less symbolic payoffs for both parties. In most instances, these take the form of rewards for a tip that signals reduction of specific kinds of offences that represent a risk to the partner. Such partnerships lend insight into the content of Crimes of the Week noted above. In particular, the Crime of the Week is more a practical, promotional effort to reduce loss along property lines through offering rewards under cover of anonymity and less a tactical effort to solve crime. Through CS promotions and special reward arrangements, new partners stand to satisfy requirements to manage risk to their property. The practical requirements of partners to manage risk of property loss via CS undoubtedly contribute to the kinds of crime selected as Crimes of the Week. For instance, of the 640 analyzed advertisements, Lippert found that several types of crime were conspicuously absent. White-collar crimes, crimes by police and corporate crime were not present. Only one Crime of the Week referred to domestic violence that mostly affects women. In addition, barely one fifth had a violent component. Across CS programs, the vast majority of Crimes of the Week (89%)—including those with a violent component—described property loss, mostly to businesses and citizens' residences. It was also found that CS has few if any partnerships that would encourage featuring the types of crime neglected in Crimes of the Week. For example, regarding corporate crime, it may well be that corporate partners would not approve of featuring such crimes. Yet given the way CS is organized, another factor is undoubtedly an absence of regulatory agencies or consumer groups that normally police corporate crime as CS partners. This is also true of other types of crime that are absent. For example, no civil liberty organizations (crimes by police) presently serve as CS partners, either.

This emphasis of Crimes of the Week on property loss more broadly suggests involvement of the private insurance industry in CS. A factor contributing to the growth of CS in the 1990s has been the "problematization" of fraud within this industry (see Ericson, Barry, & Doyle, 2000). Insurance representatives tend to sit on local CS boards and donate thousands of dollars for advertising. The private insurance industry seeks friendly connections with CS to generate tips about insurance fraud and to encourage a broader reduction of property loss. Crimes against businesses, nonprofit and public institutions and residences involving property loss are often insured against in the form of commercial property, homeowner and other forms of insurance. Promotion of property crime in Crimes of the Week therefore indirectly benefits private insurance. In some instances CS identifies risk by sending the tip to the insurance partner who then manages risk by, for example, denying an insurance claim. These tips about insurance fraud promise to benefit private insurance directly to the extent that fraud is reduced by increasing their profits. Establishing links with CS in these ways is among the best examples of "governing through crime."

Governing and Deploying Anonymity

From the birth of CS, anonymity has been its lynchpin and without it the program would collapse like a house of cards. Anonymization is a technique of governance that promises to camouflage subjects' identity, effectively hiding them from those who govern. But subjects are not relocated so far away that they are unknowable. CS attempts to render only legal name, "locatability" and potential pseudonyms of tipsters unknown. Anonymization in CS, therefore, involves some forms of identity knowledge, but tipsters are nonetheless still known in some manner (such as through their voice or the hours they tend to call CS). Without this "pattern" knowledge, CS would cease to function. Anonymization requires constant vigilance. Befitting this arrangement, the anonymity of these tips is represented in moral terms such that a tip that is anonymous is "clean," whereas a "dirty" tip is one that identifies the caller and needs to be "cleaned up" before distribution.

Anonymity promises to reduce CS tipsters' fear, but it also seeks to protect police from moral spoilage in a way that mere confidentiality used with traditional registered police informants cannot. Confidentiality presumes trustworthiness; anonymity presumes suspicion. Because of increasing association with wrongful conviction of innocents across Canada during the 1990s (e.g., McLean-Candis, 2000), the "jailhouse" informant has been problematized and the registered informant continues to reveal considerable potential for moral contamination of police. Anonymization undertakes to protect police from this moral risk. CS coordinators may have been morally tainted through direct, albeit brief, transactions with the criminal element, but no one knows for sure whether this has occurred. Therefore in CS, anonymization seeks to "demoralize" the relationship between police (and their new partners) and criminal subcultures in the course of identifying and managing risk. If anonymity is maintained, the need for elaborate witness protection programs is avoided. It also reduces risk of civil lawsuits launched by victims of police informants who can claim police had knowledge of the criminal intentions of an informant but failed to prevent the informant's commission of a criminal offence (e.g., Abbate, 2002).

While anonymization creates uncertainty about tipsters' identity, enough is still known about the tipster to permit determination of appropriate rewards to manage risk. Befitting these arrangements, rewards are supposed to depend on offence type and seriousness and increasingly on the institutional priorities of partners, as well as the level of tipster risk-taking. While monetary rewards are calculated and offered for all useful tips, moral rewards in the form of relaying specific information to the "good citizen" tipster about tip outcomes (e.g., whether the perpetrator was arrested and convicted) also occur in CS. Reward determination is therefore about risk management and moral categorization.

Rewards, Risk and Tipsters

Given an attention to risk in CS, how are rewards to be understood? In CS, a standing reward varies in value from $50 to $1,000. These monetary rewards from the perspective of CS boards and coordinators target specific tipsters' past efforts that eventually led to arrest or recovery of stolen property or illegal drugs. In addition, tips called into CS do not always refer at the time of the call to specific unsolved criminal acts of the past. Rather, many tips are future oriented and lead to, for example, future police stings and public alerts.

A further sign of an emphasis on managing risk through rewards and a means of governing their use is a graduated point system now used in some programs to determine reward levels (Crime Stoppers, 2001b, p. 2.9). If an arrest is made due to a tip, the CS board is to consider the number and severity of the charges it generated, or with recovery of illicit property or drugs, their estimated value. Points are assigned for each. CS coordinators send information about a case to a designated partner representative who then decides whether to reimburse CS. The reward decision is plainly not about management of risk posed by the individual criminal, but instead that posed by the number and types of crimes to which the tip pertains.

Significantly, one program's reward point system includes, besides the aspects above, "risk to caller" and "repeat caller" as factors to be considered. The 2001 manual similarly recognizes both practices. In this case the tipster that takes more risk is to be rewarded accordingly. Being a repeat tipster, that is, continually patrolling for certain kinds of risky situations or persons is therefore also encouraged through rewards. An important result of these arrangements is that information has to flow both ways in CS. Tips come in and are directed to police and partners, but it is essential the tip's fate be gleaned and relayed to the tipster when he or she calls back to inquire and to otherwise determine appropriate rewards. Here the advanced liberal strategy of responsibilization of individuals to reduce risk to property is evident, too.

Moral Categorization and Tipsters

Inseparable from promotions, anonymization and rewards are imaginings of the tipster. It is the tipster who is deemed potentially governable in CS, not the criminal, though the two entities at times overlap. Crimes of the Week do not discriminate among types of tipsters. In CS, tipsters' fear is to be reduced through anonymization and apathy transformed into risk-taking through promise of reward.

In CS discourse "tipster" and "caller" largely replace the morally spoiled "narc," "rat" and "snitch" identities that connote a breach of trust. Yet, CS tends to foresee at least two tipster types when granting rewards, "good citizen" and "criminals themselves" (Crime Stoppers, 1983, pp. iv–7). The "good citizen" tipsters are deemed more prevalent and apparently "aren't usually motivated by cash rewards" (Crime Stoppers, 1983, pp. iv–7). This aspect conveniently justifies the CS program by preventing the appearance of rewarding mostly the criminal element. Otherwise, such a situation might prevent private corporations and others from wanting to partner with CS.

In CS, the "good citizen" comes to be linked with fear and is presumed to be in pursuit only of moral rewards such as learning from the CS coordinator what became of their tip. Yet, the "criminal" tipster is associated with the pursuit of monetary rewards and revenge. In CS, the knowledge produced during interactions between coordinators and tipsters and then used in reward determinations permits such moral classifications. The imagined "criminal" tipster is deemed morally inferior, calling in tips due to the basest of motivations. It is association with this type from which anonymization seeks to prevent police from becoming morally tainted.

CS therefore is consistent with and lends insight into advanced liberalism. The rise of CS partnerships, exemplified by private insurance, that entails new reward criteria and risk management requirements, suggests an increasing abandonment of efforts to govern through "the social" for the public good. CS is more concerned with risk to property, often to the practical benefit of partners who are interested mostly in reducing risk associated with only *their* kind of crime. By creating social distance, anonymity is a technology that is plainly consonant with advanced liberalism. Despite an emphasis on risk to property, moral aspects are also evident in CS. The technology of anonymization, for example, seeks not only to promote tips about property crime, but also to demoralize police (and partners') relationships with tipsters. Other such efforts include creating and displaying moral categories such as the "good citizen" tipster. CS suggests that attention to risk in advanced liberal governance is intertwined with moral discourse. It may be precisely because CS techniques encounter obstacles that moral discourse cannot be eliminated from risk management, especially when their source can be easily assigned to partners and a necessarily unfamiliar community upon whom CS is reliant for tips.

Consistent with localization under advanced liberalism, CS promotions seek to continuously carve out paths in the community from a morally safe distance while anonymity and rewards, in tandem, promise to activate and steer tipsters as they take to these freshly paved streets to patrol for potential property loss. In CS, community is necessarily "imagined," not because of its sheer size, but due to carefully governed efforts not to know it. The community can only ever be imagined in the most impoverished ways. Reciprocity here is limited to calling in and receiving tips about, and to granting and receiving rewards to and from, people in the community whom one can never meet or know by name.

CRITICISMS OF GOVERNMENTALITY

Thus, far in this chapter we have discussed governmentality concepts and themes and illustrated their use in two areas of criminological interest. Yet it is necessary to note that like all perspectives, governmentality studies have not developed without criticism. We will conclude the chapter by considering three areas of concern.

One common criticism is that by focusing on discourse and the discursive realm governmentality studies ignore reality. Curtis (1995, p. 583) charges that governmentality studies neglect "situated social relations and relations of causation" (see also Garland, 1997, pp. 199–201; Kerr, 1999, p. 196; Stenson, 1998, p. 334). Essentially it is suggested that implementation and the real effects of programs are ignored in place of attention to language and texts. However, in perhaps the most sympathetic critique to date, O'Malley, Weir and Shearing (1997, p. 512) note that "many programmes exist only in the process of messy implementation," thereby suggesting there is no clear division between the discursive and the real; between what is imagined and what is put into action. Nor is such a division plainly evident in actual governmentality-informed studies within criminology, including those pertaining to the two foregoing areas of interest. We suggest that when actual governmentality-informed studies are scrutinized it is often more a matter of emphasis than a categorical denial of "the real." Governmentality-informed studies do not so much deny the real effects of programs as focus attention on the crucial components (i.e., rationalities and technologies) that come from the past to make up particular domains.

A second criticism related to the first is the rather simplistic claim that governmentality-informed criminology and other scholarship is without reference to normative theory; that governmentality studies say little about how the specific domains upon which they shed light *ought* to be organized. This is a well-worn (we think worn-out) criticism originally stemming from Fraser's (1989) critique of Foucault's work. At its best, governmentality-informed criminology can reveal the detailed workings of specific criminal justice and crime control policies and practices, how they are changing and how they are made possible by new strains of criminological knowledge and technologies, thus making these regimes more amenable to progressive intervention and reform. The two cases detailed above reveal contradictory, even perverse, arrangements that much broader or microlevel perspectives simply cannot. Here these two programs are shown to entail, on the one hand, *imprisoning* women disadvantaged by class and race or ethnicity while claiming to *empower* them and, on the other hand, ignoring harmful domestic violence and corporate crime, while exerting tremendous effort to the benefit of private interests *not to know the local community*, all the time claiming to engage in *community* crime prevention. A close reading of the two studies primarily referred to within these cases (Lippert [2002] and Hannah-Moffat [2000]) reveals nuanced normative claims (see also Williams & Lippert, 2006); indeed, we suggest the normative implications of much governmentality-informed criminology—in practice—are present without being preachy and prescriptive.

A final criticism suggests that for all the talk in governmentality circles about avoiding totalizing claims associated with neo-Marxist and some feminist perspectives, the way advanced liberalism is at times invoked can adopt a similar totalizing look (Lippert, 2005). A focus on the possible presence of alternative rationalities and forms of power, or what has been aptly called "governance from below" (Stenson, 2005; cf. Lippert & Stenson, 2007), is neglected. Governmentality scholars claim to assume plurality and to move away from seeking a general theory of power and governance, but at times it is unclear whether they are truly doing so. Of the three criticisms, we think this may be the most trenchant. In our own recent research on illegal sanctuary practices (Lippert, 2005) and legal aid provision for criminal and other proceedings (Park & Lippert, 2008), we found clear evidence of the presence of other rationalities operating alongside advanced liberalism. And as we implied at the chapter's outset, also neglected by most governmentality advocates is closer scrutiny of sovereign power in contemporary crime control and criminal justice domains, not as a return to a grand and archaic form of rule, but instead in relation to specific contemporary programs (Lippert, 2005). The question of how the sovereign monopoly to decide the exception will be enacted as arbitrary bodily punishment, coercive punishment, or both (as seen in segregation in women's prisons) or the equally unjustified sudden withholding of justice, as well as other rationalities operative within these domains, needs attention. Perhaps this will be the Foucault effect on the next cohort of criminologists.

Conclusion

Governmentality studies emerged following the English translation of a lecture by Michel Foucault and have since had a profound influence on criminology and criminologists. Three main concepts—rationalities, programs and technologies—show great promise in revealing the detailed workings of crime control and criminal justice policies and practices. Although they are not without criticisms, when put to good use these concepts can potentially reveal where and when progressive intervention in existing programs is possible or might best occur, as well as help reveal programs, agencies and authorities that are really only "governing through crime."

References

Abbate, G. (2002, January 12). Judge okays suit by informant's victims. *Globe and Mail*, p. A7.

Canadian Coalition Against Insurance Fraud. (2000). Crime Stoppers results. *Challenges and Champions, 2*, 8.

Carriere, K. (1987). Crime Stoppers critically considered. *Canadian Criminology Forum, 8*, 104–115.

Carriere, K., & Ericson, R. (1989). *Crime Stoppers: A study in the organization of community policing*. Toronto: Centre of Criminology, University of Toronto.

Crawford, A. (1997). *The local governance of crime: Appeals to community and partnership*. Oxford: Clarendon Press.

Crime Stoppers. (1983). *Crime Stoppers manual: How to start and operate a program*. (Revised edition). Albuquerque, NM: Crime Stoppers USA, Inc.

Crime Stoppers. (2001a). *Operational and administrative standards manual*. (Spring edition). Albuquerque, NM: Crime Stoppers International, Inc.

Crime Stoppers. (2001b). *Operational and administrative standards manual*. (Unabridged version). Arlington, TX: Crime Stoppers International, Inc.

Crime Stoppers. (2007). Crime Stoppers programs: Canada. Retrieved July 8, 2007, from http://www.c-s-i.org/list.php?area=2.

Crime Stoppers. (2009). Programs. CS International. Retrieved from http://www.c-s-i.org/Programs.aspx.

Cruikshank, B. (1999). *The will to empower: Democratic citizens and others*. Ithaca, NY: Cornell University Press.

Cullen, F. T., & Gilbert, K. E. (1982). *Reaffirming rehabilitation*. Cincinnati: Anderson Publishing Company.

Curtis, B. (1995). Taking the state back out: Rose and Miller on political power. *The British Journal of Sociology, 46*(4), 575–589.

Dean, M. (1995). Governing the unemployed self in an active society. *Economy and Society, 24*, 559–583.

Dean, M. (1999). *Governmentality: Power and rule in modern society*. London: Sage.

Ericson, R., Barry, D., & Doyle, A. (2000). The moral hazards of neo-liberalism: Lessons from the private insurance industry. *Economy and Society, 29*(4), 532–558.

Foucault, M. (1977). *Discipline and punish: The birth of the prison*. New York: Random House.

Foucault, M. (1991). Governmentality. In G. Burchell, C. Gordon, & P. Miller (Eds.), *The Foucault effect: Studies in governmentality* (pp. 87–104). Chicago: University of Chicago Press.

Fraser, N. (1989). *Unruly practices: Power, discourse and gender in contemporary social theory.* Minneapolis: University of Minnesota Press and Polity Press.

Garland, D. (1996). The limits of the sovereign state: Strategies of crime control in contemporary society. *British Journal of Criminology, 36*(4), 445–471.

Garland, D. (1997). Governmentality and the problem of crime: Foucault, criminology, sociology. *Theoretical Criminology, 2*(1), 173–214.

Gordon, C. (1991). Governmental rationality: An introduction. In G. Burchell, C. Gordon, & P. Miller (Eds.), *The Foucault effect: Studies in governmentality* (pp. 1–51). Chicago: The University of Chicago Press.

Hannah-Moffat, K. (2000). Prisons that empower: Neo-liberal governance in Canadian women's prisons. *British Journal of Criminology, 40*, 510–531.

Hunt, A., & Wickham, G. (1994). *Foucault and law: Towards a sociology of law as governance.* London: Pluto Press.

Kerr, D. (1999). Beheading the king and enthroning the market: A critique of Foucauldian governmentality. *Science and Society, 63*, 173–202.

Kesby, M. (2005). Re-theorizing empowerment-through-participation as a performance in space: Beyond tyranny to transformation. *Signs: Journal of Women in Culture and Society, 30*(4), 2037–2065.

Lippert, R. (2002). Policing property and moral risk through promotions, anonymization and rewards: Crime Stoppers revisited. *Social & Legal Studies, 11*(4), 475–502.

Lippert, R. (2005). *Sanctuary, sovereignty, sacrifice: Canadian sanctuary incidents, power, and law.* Vancouver: UBC Press.

Lippert, R. (2007). Open-street CCTV, Canadian Style. *Criminal Justice Matters, 64*, 31–32.

Lippert, R., & Stenson, K. (2007). Introduction, urban governance and legality from below, *Canadian Journal of Law & Society, 22*(2), 1–4.

Martel, J. (2006). To be, one has to be somewhere: Spatio-temporality in prison segregation. *British Journal of Criminology, 46*, 587–612.

McLean-Candis, A. (2000). No more "father confessor": Manitoba, B.C., Alberta, Ontario and Newfoundland have strict rules around the use of jailhouse informants at criminal trials. *Report-Newsmagazine, 27*, 21.

Miller, P., & Rose, N. (1990). Governing economic life. *Economy and Society, 19*(1): 1–31.

O'Malley, P. (1992). Risk, power and crime prevention. *Economy and Society, 21*(3), 252–275.

O'Malley, P. (1997). Policing, politics and postmodernity. *Social & Legal Studies, 6*, 363–381.

O'Malley, P., & Palmer, D. (1996). Post-Keynesian policing. *Economy and Society, 25*(2), 137–155.

O'Malley, P., Weir, L., & Shearing, C. (1997). Governmentality, criticism, politics. *Economy and Society, 26*(4), 501–517.

Park, G., & Lippert, R. (2008). Legal aid's logics. *Studies in Law, Politics, and Society, 45*, 177–201.

Rose, N. (1987). Beyond the public/private division: Law, power and the family. *Journal of Law and Society, 14*(1), 61–76.

Rose, N. (1992). Governing the enterprise self. In P. Heelas & P. Morris (Eds.), *The values of the enterprise culture: The moral debate* (pp. 141–164). London: Routledge.

Rose, N. (1993). Government, authority and expertise in advanced liberalism. *Economy and Society, 22*(3): 263–299.

Rose, N. (1996). The death of the social? Re-figuring the territory of government. *Economy and Society, 25*(3), 327–356.

Rose, N. (1999). *Powers of freedom: reframing political thought.* Cambridge: Cambridge University Press.

Rose, N., & Miller, P. (1992). Political power beyond the state: Problematics of government. *British Journal of Sociology, 43,* 173–205.

Rose, N., O'Malley, P., & Valverde, M. (2006). Governmentality. *Annual Review of Law and Social Sciences, 2,* 5.1–5.22.

Simon, J. (1994). In the place of the parent: Risk management and the government of campus life. *Social & Legal Studies, 3,* 15–45.

Simon, J. (2007) *Governing Through Crime: How the War on Crime Transformed American Democracy and Created a Culture of Fear.* New York: Oxford University Press.

Smandych, R. (1999). Introduction: The place of governance structures in law and criminology. In *Governable places: Readings on governmentality and crime control* (pp. 1–14). London: Ashgate.

Stenson, K. (1993). Community policing as a governmental technology. *Economy and Society, 22*(3), 373–389.

Stenson, K. (1998). Beyond histories of the present. *Economy and Society, 27*(4), 333–352.

Stenson. K. (2005). Sovereignty, biopolitics and local government of crime in Britain. *Theoretical Criminology, 9*(3), 265–287.

Valverde, M., Levi, R., Shearing, C., Condon, M., & O'Malley, P. (1999). *Democracy in governance: A socio-legal framework.* Ottawa: Law Commission of Canada.

Williams, J., & Lippert, R. (2006). Governing at the margins: Exploring the contributions of governmentality studies to critical criminology in Canada. Special issue of *Canadian Journal of Criminology and Criminal Justice, 48*(5), 703–720.

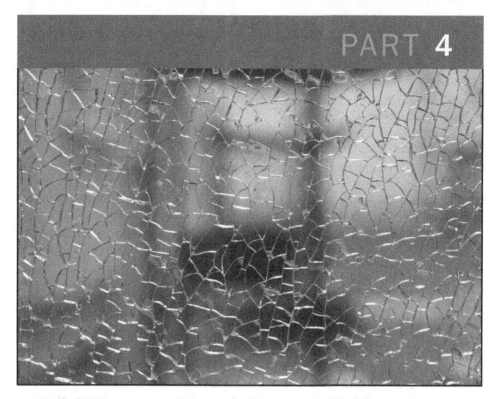

PART 4

Critical Perspectives on Current Issues

Chapter 11 Immigrant and Refugee Women and the Unintended
Consequences of Domestic Violence Policy
Rashmee Singh, *University of Toronto & American Bar Foundation*

Chapter 12 Governing Security
Benoît Dupont, *Université de Montréal*

Chapter 13 "Speaking for the Dead": Forensic Science and Wrongful Convictions
Kirsten Kramar, *University of Winnipeg*

Chapter 14 Talking Trash with the Supreme Court of Canada:
The Reasonable Expectation of Privacy under the Charter
Richard Jochelson, *University of Winnipeg*

CHAPTER 11

Immigrant and Refugee Women and the Unintended Consequences of Domestic Violence Policy

Rashmee Singh, University of Toronto & American Bar Foundation

INTRODUCTION

On International Women's Day in 1996, Arlene May, a mother of five children, was fatally shot by her ex-boyfriend, Randy Iles. At the time of the murder, Iles was under a court order to stay away from May and to surrender his firearms. Iles breached both conditions of the court order. As is often the case in domestic homicides, Iles killed himself following the murder. The murder of Arlene May raised several important questions about the effectiveness of the criminal justice system in preventing domestic abuse. Prior to murdering his ex-girlfriend, Iles had been in court on several occasions for failing to comply with his court orders following convictions for domestic assault. The criminal justice system overlooked the noncompliance and failed to incarcerate Iles for breaching the conditions of the court orders. Despite the addition of stalking legislation designed to address the kind of criminal harassment to which Iles subjected May, police failed to lay charges.

In response to the failure of the criminal justice system to prevent domestic homicides, the Office of the Chief Coroner for Ontario announced an inquest into May's death. The purpose of the inquest was to determine where the police and courts went wrong and how the system could respond more effectively to prevent the murder of victims at the hands of their abusers. The inquest's jury responded with 216 recommendations which were subsequently implemented in July 1998.

Despite these efforts, domestic violence continues to be a major social problem in Canada. In fact, just 4 years after the May–Iles inquest, a woman by the name of Gillian Hadley was murdered by her estranged husband, who was under a court order preventing him from contacting her. An inquest into Hadley's death followed. The tragic deaths of May and Hadley along with the changes implemented in the wake of both the May–Iles and the Hadley inquests highlight the continuing problem of domestic violence and the ongoing struggles to develop strategies aimed at properly addressing and preventing violence against women.

The purpose of this chapter is to provide an understanding of one of the most contentious of criminal justice policies to be administered in response to domestic violence in recent years: the mandatory charging and aggressive prosecution policy. Also known as the "zero tolerance" approach, mandatory charging directs police officers to lay charges in all cases of domestic violence, regardless of whether victims want their partners to be arrested. These policies work in tandem with aggressive or "no drop" prosecution strategies, which instruct Crown attorneys to pursue the prosecution of all domestic violence cases rather than drop charges, even if victims are reluctant or afraid to testify.

Mandatory charging and prosecution are controversial due to the fact that they are widely perceived to be extremely coercive. The interventions prevent victims from making choices about whether they want to press and pursue charges against their abusers. What is considered most interesting about this approach is that it was initially a feminist intervention. Mandatory charging and prosecution practices emerged throughout Canada in the early 1980s following years of organized liberal feminist activism. Reacting to decades of police negligence, the women's movement put considerable pressure on the provincial and federal governments to take domestic violence seriously and to treat it just like any other violent crime. Although they acknowledged the potential problems associated with removing police discretion and victims' choices, feminist reformists believed that this approach was the only way to ensure the protection of abused women.

Although zero tolerance approaches appeared to be a good idea in theory, once they were put into practice, whether they helped or harmed women was no longer clear. In many cases, mandatory charging and prosecution actually hurt rather than helped women. Most harmed were immigrant and refugee women, who experienced considerable hardship after the intervention, often because the sudden removal of their abusive partners from the home jeopardized their immigration prospects. The unprepared loss of abusive partners also increased their social isolation and deprived them of financial resources. The few available studies on the issue suggest that whether mandatory charging and prosecution offer protection to victims is contingent upon an abused woman's social location, particularly her race, class and citizenship status.

In what follows, I will discuss the emergence of and controversies surrounding mandatory charging and aggressive prosecution strategies particularly in relation to their impact on immigrant victims of violence. After reading this chapter, you will have a sense of the context in which these intervention policies emerged, feminist understandings of violence against women and the complications associated with developing criminal justice policies on domestic violence. In addition, you will gain an understanding of some of the negative consequences of "no drop" policies on immigrant and refugee women which will allow for critical reflection upon the limitations of relying on the criminal law to protect women and prevent domestic violence. Before discussing studies on immigrant victims' experiences with mandatory charging and prosecution, I will first review the emergence of zero tolerance approaches in order to provide you with an understanding of the feminist struggles that led to their incorporation into the criminal justice system.

THE EARLY YEARS: FEMINIST ACTIVISM AND VIOLENCE AGAINST WOMEN

Societal and Criminal Justice Responses

In order to fully understand why mandatory charging and aggressive prosecution strategies were considered necessary for the safety of abused women and the prevention of domestic violence, we must look back to the early 1970s when the women's movement was in full swing and the issue of violence against women was generally ignored by criminal justice authorities. At that time, domestic violence was not considered to be a social problem. Prevailing explanations assumed that it occurred very infrequently at the hands of individual men who were suffering from psychological or emotional problems. The cause(s) of domestic violence were thus assumed to be individual; there was little understanding of it as a systemic or social problem.

Individualized explanations generally assumed that the batterers were mentally ill or pushed to their limits by stress (Pence & Paymar, 1993). Just as common were theories which attributed male violence to alcohol abuse, "natural" male aggression and the failure of men to come to terms with the changes associated with women's liberation

(MacLeod, 1980). Even more problematic for victims was the general belief that woman abuse was a man's right or that abused women were somehow deserving of the violence. A survey conducted in 1970 by the National Commission on the Causes and Prevention of Violence on a cross-section of the population in the United States found that one out of four men and one out of six women approved of a husband slapping his wife under certain conditions (Stark & McEnvoy, 1970 in Strauss et al., 1980). Similar findings were reported in a 1976 study involving a sample of 2,143 families in the United States. Researchers found that one out of three husbands and a little under one out of four wives believed that "couples slapping each other" was "necessary, normal and good" (Strauss et al., 1980).

Accompanying these sorts of justifications for violence in intimate relationships was also the general sentiment that violence against women was comedic. To illustrate this observation, Buzawa and Buzawa (2003) refer to examples of representations of domestic aggression in popular 1950s televisions comedies. Scenes of Ricky Ricardo "spanking" Lucille Ball were considered funny in episodes of *I Love Lucy* and were always followed with canned audience laughter. In the television comedy *The Honeymooners*, arguments between Ralph Kramden, played by Jackie Gleason, and his wife, Alice Kramden, played by Audrey Meadows, were typically ended by Gleason's pithy phrase: "One of these days, Alice . . . pow, zoom, right to the moon" (Buzawa & Buzawa, 2003, p. 61).

These examples illustrate the degree to which cultural norms throughout most of the 20th century trivialized and justified the corporal punishment of women at the hands of their husbands. Not surprisingly, the police and courts neglected the problem and in many ways reinforced the male dominance over women and children. In her review of several studies examining police attitudes toward domestic violence, Hilton (1993) revealed that officers were often reluctant to arrest men given their view that offenders may not be entirely responsible for the assault (Hilton, 1993, p. 43). She notes a study conducted by Saunders and Size in the mid-1980s in which the researchers compared the perceptions of police officers, abused women and other victims in relation to the degree to which they viewed violence against women as a crime and arrest as the best response. It was found that the police were least likely to believe that "the best way to deal with marital violence is to arrest the offending party" (Hilton, 1993). In addition, during this time, police officers were far more likely to think that abuse was justified if female victims had been unfaithful to their husbands.

Fears that intervention would divide families also contributed to the general police reluctance to arrest abusers. Although laws prohibiting domestic violence had existed as early as 1909 in Canada, the police and courts rarely enforced them. The reason for this systemic neglect was largely due to the belief that violence in the home was a private family affair (MacLeod, 1980). Consequently, police preferred to respond to incidents by encouraging reconciliation through informal mediation (Mosher & Martin, 1995).

Finally, police culture also played a role in the general reluctance amongst officers to lay charges in domestic violence cases (Buzawa & Buzawa, 2003). Research on police attitudes and practices shows that officers tend to prefer cases in which they can act as crime fighters rather than counsellors. The general belief that intervening in domestic violence cases was akin to social work placed the crime on the bottom of their agendas. This combination of factors normalized police neglect and made it permissible for police to caution and warn, rather than arrest, abusive men.

Feminist Theorizations of Domestic Violence

The lackadaisical approach of the police, the cultural normalization of domestic violence and the prevailing sexist beliefs about violence against women formed the core of feminist campaigns in the 1970s to address the problem of male violence. Feminist launched critiques of conventional explanations of domestic violence and fought to replace them with new ones that understood violence as both rooted in and critical to the maintenance of patriarchal social relations. According to this analysis, male violence was both a consequence of and a tool to ensure that men exercised supreme authority in the home and in wider society. For instance, feminist analysis made links between men's ability to control the physical movement and emotional lives of women to unfair labour market practices that did not recognize domestic labour as paid work and marginalized women in low paying part-time employment. Such an understanding was revolutionary, as prevailing explanations at the time did nothing to illuminate the social causes of violence against women. Feminists thus inspired a shift from understanding the issue as a biosocial or psychological abnormality to a social and cultural problem.

This shift in thinking had profound implications for potential solutions to domestic violence. While feminists believed that it was important to hold individual men accountable for their use of violence, the reframing of domestic violence from an individual abnormality to a crime that "normal" men were capable of necessitated social reform to alleviate the problem. Thus, in contrast to micro or individual rehabilitative strategies that advocated solutions such as alcohol abuse prevention programs such as Alcoholics Anonymous or anger management seminars, feminists urged for changes to socioeconomic and cultural structures that systematically placed men in positions of privilege in the first place. The movement rejected individualized or "Band-Aid" approaches because they failed to address the way in which social institutions supported power imbalances and tacitly authorized the problem.

However, despite consensus among feminists regarding the root causes of male violence, considerable conflict emerged over how best to address the problem. Most feminist debates centred on whether the state and criminal justice system should be employed as a solution in the fight against male violence. The next section will discuss these debates in more detail. A discussion of the specific events that led to the incorporation of mandatory charging and "no drop" prosecution policies into the criminal justice system in Canada will follow.

Violence Against Women, the State and Feminist Praxis

Initially, feminist interventions were primarily community based on and aimed at ensuring victims had access to safe houses and services to assist them in escaping domestic violence. In 1972, the first volunteer-run shelters for battered women were opened in British Columbia and Alberta (MacLeod, 1980). Consciousness-raising and public education were also common practices. However, the movement's grassroots initiatives began to disintegrate when activists increasingly began to look to the state and the criminal justice system for support. While much of this change in orientation was done out of necessity to finance an overextended shelter system, many were drawn to the symbolic gesture of criminal justice support for their cause.

Feminists, however, were not at all in agreement about whether, or how, to involve the state in their struggle to dismantle patriarchal relations contributing to domestic violence.

While all agreed that the systemic neglect was problematic, not all felt comfortable about allying themselves with the police and the courts. Many feminists questioned whether it was possible to rely on the state as an ally given its longstanding complicity in the perpetuation of sexist as well as racist and classist practices. They feared that once the system was engaged, the original intentions and social justice focus of the movement would dissolve. Specifically, many activists anticipated that criminal justice involvement would promote individualized solutions to domestic violence, such as tougher penalties for abusers. As a consequence, the primary objective of the feminist movement—to transform the wider socioeconomic structures that led to the abuse of women—would be sacrificed (Morrow, 2005). Those opposed to criminal justice involvement insisted on addressing the problem through grassroots interventions and remaining outside the realm of the state.

The feminists who hoped to engage the police and courts as allies, however, believed that criminal justice reform was not entirely at odds with the movement's objectives. Those embracing this strategy drew attention to what they considered to be the transformative potential of the law and its ability to influence social attitudes and norms. This perspective was echoed in the work of Linda MacLeod (1980), who wrote the first feminist informed government report on the incidence and prevalence of domestic violence in Canada for the Canadian Advisory Council on the Status of Women (CACSW). In *Wife Battering in Canada: A Vicious Circle*, she argues:

> A man may no longer have the legal right to beat his wife under the letter of the law, but many legal procedures still support the power of the husband over his wife, and so help encourage the societal acceptance of violence in the family. . . . It is undeniable that laws have a considerable influence in shaping the values of society as well as reflecting the attitudes of those who framed them. When these values are in question, the law must also be put under scrutiny. (1980, p. 42)

Advocates of criminal justice intervention thus demanded that the criminal justice system respond to the abuse of women as they would any other assault. Doing so, they argued, would ensure that individual victims as well as all women were protected given the capacity of the law to educate the public on what was right and wrong.

Campaigns for the increased criminalization of domestic violence thus brought two key issues into focus, which eventually led to the incorporation of mandatory charging and prosecution: systemic discretion and the pressure abused women experience from their partners to drop charges. With regards to the former, advocates were hesitant to leave decisions about arrest and prosecution to individual officers and Crown attorneys, since neither group had demonstrated much commitment to intervening in the problem historically. In relation to the latter, feminists argued that the legal system should act as a buffer between the victim and abuser and alleviate victims of the pressure to make decisions about whether or not to pursue charges. Doing so would bar abusers from the ability to coerce victims to drop charges. As MacLeod notes in her CACSW report: "By allowing the wife to be persuaded by her husband to withdraw her complaint, the legal system again is giving official recognition to the powerlessness of the woman in the home and to the acceptance of wife battering as a private matter" (MacLeod, 1980, p. 43). While MacLeod's work does not explicitly advocate the adoption of mandatory charging and prosecution, the symbolic importance of mandated criminal justice intervention is reiterated.

"Just Like Any Other Crime": The Emergence of Mandatory Charging and Aggressive Prosecution Policies

As the decade progressed, it was the liberal feminist reform efforts rather than the more radical grassroots activists' efforts that gained currency with the state. Just as essential in convincing the federal government of the need to mandate the policing and prosecution of domestic violence, however, was a research project conducted by the London Coordinating Committee on Family Violence (LCCFV) in 1981 (Department of Justice, 2005). The LCCFV was a committee composed of service providers from a variety community and victim service agencies that had joined forces to review the community and criminal justice supports for abused women. With funding from the solicitor general, the committee analyzed the police response to domestic abuse victims in a variety of divisions in London (Jaffe et al., 1993). Having found that the police only laid charges in less than 3% of woman abuse cases, despite the fact that close to 20% of victims in their study required medical attention, they recommended the implementation of a mandatory charge policy (Jaffe et al., 1993). Due to its longstanding relationship with the LCCFV, the London police department took the findings seriously. Accordingly, the London City Police Force issued the following directive in May 1981:

> Commencing immediately, charges are to be laid by our Force in all cases where there are reasonable and probably grounds [to believe that an assault has taken place] revealed in the investigation. The practice of directing the victim to lay private informations is to cease. (Hilton, 1988, p. 328)

Both of these initiatives triggered a series of events that would prove to be central in the eventual incorporation of zero tolerance strategies throughout Canada. In 1982, the recommendations found in *Wife Battering in Canada*, along with other government reports such as *Towards Equality for Women* led to the formation of an all-party parliamentary standing committee during which women's groups, transitional housing staff and feminists advocated for mandatory charging, the prosecution of all woman abuse cases through criminal rather than family courts, more severe punishments and the creation of new legal categories to address the issue (Currie, 1990). The standing committee eventually agreed to adopt a mandatory charge policy similar to the one in effect in London, Ontario (Hilton, 1990, p. 329). Despite the fact that it was initially ridiculed in Parliament on May 12, 1982, by July of the same year, members of Parliament expressed their unanimous support for the policy and passed a motion to ensure its implementation. A few days later, on July 15, 1982, the federal Ministry of the Solicitor General endorsed mandatory charging and directed the Canadian Association of Chiefs of Police to comply with this directive. In February 1983, the Royal Canadian Mounted Police (RCMP) developed a national charging policy (Jaffe et al., 1993). Eventually, in 1986, attorneys general and solicitors general attempted to standardize mandatory policing and prosecutorial practices across Canada through a series of federal directives instructing the police to lay charges "where investigation reveals reasonable and probable grounds to believe a serious indictable offence has been committed as part of a domestic dispute" (Department of Justice, 2005). Thus, by the mid-1980s feminist reformists had succeeded in their attempts to make domestic violence "just like any other crime." The negligence that had for so long characterized the criminal justice response was to be a thing of the past.

Good Intentions and Misguided Assumptions: The Promises of Mandatory Charging and Prosecution

Unfortunately, feminist reformists had not at all predicted the various problems that criminalization solutions would produce for certain groups of women. In order to fully understand how and why the well meaning intentions of feminist reformists backfired, it is necessary to examine the underlying assumptions of mandatory policing and prosecution. First, a brief discussion of the various incarnations of the policy throughout Canada is necessary.

Currently, all jurisdictions employ some form of mandatory charging and prosecution in cases of domestic violence. The *Ontario Policing Standards Manual* (2000) includes the most comprehensive description of the policy to date. It indicates: "The procedures should provide that in all domestic violence occurrences an officer is to lay a charge where there are reasonable grounds to do so."[1] Further to this, it notes, "a decision to lay charges should not be influenced by any of the following factors," including, among others, "the victim's unwillingness to attend court proceedings or the officer's belief that the victim will not cooperate," as well as "the officer's concern about reprisals against the victim by the suspect."[2]

Police mandates throughout Canada are similar to Ontario's approach. However, some variations do exist. In Quebec, for example, the decision to charge rests with the Crown attorney. Similarly, in New Brunswick, the police lay charges only after securing the approval of Crown attorneys (Department of Justice, 2005, p. 11). In British Columbia, although the mandatory charge policy is currently under review, the revised approach will continue to emphasize that the "decision to charge or continue to prosecute should not be determined by the victim's wishes" (British Columbia Ministry of Attorney General, 2004). British Columbia also allows for precharge diversion measures in exceptional cases, per the consent of a Crown attorney. A similar program exists in the Northwest Territories. According to this protocol, cases can only be diverted if the RCMP, the criminal justice committee and the regional director for the Department of Justice Canada agree on this measure (Department of Justice, 2005, p. 12).

Working in tandem with mandatory charging, "no drop" prosecutorial strategies ensure victims participate and testify in the trial process. This policy asserts that the decision to pursue prosecution should be made independently of the wishes of the victim. However, it is important to note that Canada has what is known as "soft" mandatory prosecutorial measures. This means that although the courts and the police technically have the authority to arrest victims who defy subpoenas and refuse to testify, this practice is generally not encouraged and is only to be done in the most exceptional circumstances (Department of Justice, 2005). In 2000, the Manitoba provincial government passed the *Victims' Bill of Rights*, which includes a provision ensuring victims the right to be consulted about prosecution. This section also requires that the director of prosecutions consult victims when laying charges or staying charges. Yet, it should be made aware that it is standard practice for court-based victim services in some provinces to inform victims of the possibility of arrest should they express a reluctance to testify.

Having detailed how these policies direct police officers and Crown attorneys, it is necessary to explore more fully the assumptions of zero tolerance approaches, in order to understand why some feminists believed that the removal of the victim's voice or rights would be empowering for abused women. Earlier, it was noted that many considered a punitive criminal justice response critical to ensuring that the system sent out the message that domestic violence is an intolerable criminal offence. This argument assumes that arrest in all cases will not only help individual victims but will also benefit women as a group. It also assumes that all women view the police as protectors. Although they acknowledge that undermining a victim's autonomy and infringing on her liberty is problematic, proponents of this policy claim it is also justified, given the protection is offers to women as a whole (Hanna, 1996).

Another assumption of mandatory charging and prosecution is that victims of abuse would much rather have the police and courts decide on their behalves whether or not to proceed with their cases. As noted earlier, feminists advocating for this strategy believed that the criminal justice system would help abused women resist pressures from abusive partners to drop assault charges. Indeed, when the dynamics of abusive relationships are considered, along with the reality that victims are most at risk of further abuse and homicide after phoning the police, it is clear to see how mandatory criminal justice interventions could be perceived as a positive solution. However, those who question this approach note that many victims could have many valid reasons for not wanting their partners to be arrested.

This point leads us to the third assumption of mandatory charging and aggressive prosecution policies. Implicit in the notion that victims prefer to have the police and courts make decisions on their behalves are related ideas about the capacities of abused women to make "reasoned" arrest decisions. Specifically, some proponents of this policy assume that victims are helpless and unable to do what is best for them and their children. Consider the following, written by an advocate of aggressive intervention: "Due to the inherent imbalance of power in an abusive relationship, isolation, and fear, all of which are present in domestic violence situations, the victim is often incapable of making an independent informed decision about arrest" (Wanless, 1996, p. 547). The suggestion that abused women lack the ability to make "reasoned arrest decisions" is paternalistic and has the added effect of pathologizing women who do not wish to press charges against their abusers. Thus, when victims express reluctance to charge partners, they are immediately regarded as helpless or working against their own interests.

In sum, aggressive policing and prosecutorial strategies are laced with an array of assumptions. First, arrests in all cases will unequivocally benefit and protect abused women individually and as a whole. Second, all victims welcome criminal justice intervention and appreciate being relieved of decisions to press charges. Third, any victim preference for noncriminal justice intervention is illegitimate or a product of learned helplessness.

When examining these assumptions and the reasons for this policy backfiring, it is important to remember that mandatory charging and prosecution are indeed helpful to some victims. Many also support the zero tolerance approach. For instance, after surveying abused women residing in 150 shelters throughout Canada, MacLeod (1987) found that 72% of her interviewees supported zero tolerance strategies (MacLeod, 1987, p. 85). Landau (2000) found that of the 94 abused women that she had interviewed, 60% were satisfied with the criminal justice response to their cases. Unlike the victims who did not want their partners to be arrested, those who supported the policy indicated that they appreciated being relieved of the decision to proceed with their cases. Proponents also felt that arrest was necessary in order to teach their partners a lesson (Landau, 2000).

However, whether victims *want* to end relationships is not the most critical factor in assessing whether or not mandatory policies help or harm abused women; more important is whether victims actually have the necessary supports and resources, such as friends, family and finances, to even consider leaving as a possibility in the first place. The focus on supports and resources alerts us to the role socioeconomic position and legal status plays in shaping the impact of zero tolerance approaches. Nowhere are the assumptions underlying these interventions more challenged than in cases involving immigrant, refugee and racialized women.

The next section will review the few available empirical studies on abused immigrant women's experiences with zero tolerances approaches in Canada and will explore in detail why criminalization strategies have failed them. The following factors have been implicated in the failure of these policies to enhance the safety of immigrant victims: precarious immigration status; heightened fears and distrust of the police; isolation; and linguistic and financial dependence. Each immigrant-specific factor will be discussed individually.

FORGOTTEN VOICES: THE EXPERIENCES OF IMMIGRANT VICTIMS OF DOMESTIC VIOLENCE

Immigration Status

Legal status is a critical issue for immigrant victims of abuse. Without permanent residence status or citizenship, abused women may experience dire consequences following mandatory arrest. For women who lack status entirely, the police are anything but the guardians that proponents of mandatory charging imagined them to be. Instead of protecting victims, officers may arrest or deport them for lacking the requisite documentation to reside in Canada legally. The issue of abuse in sponsorship relationships is also a serious problem that questions whether mandatory criminal justice intervention is indeed the best way to proceed (Mosher, 2009).[3] If a woman is dependent on her husband for permanent residence status and her sponsor is abusive, mandated arrest may compromise her immigration prospects. Although neglecting these cases is not at all a favoured approach, since nonstatus victims are among the most vulnerable of abused women, any criminal justice intervention that is negligent of these factors will inevitably hurt rather than help victims.

Distrust and Fear of the Police

Fear of the police and the criminal justice system more generally is another factor that complicates abused immigrant women's experiences with mandatory charging. Negative experiences with the police both in Canada and in home countries are generally the sources of this fear. The racism and xenophobia immigrant communities encounter in host countries are also a factor. In their study on immigrant women's perceptions of mandatory charging in New Brunswick, Wachholz and Miedema (2000) found that many abused women were reluctant to call the police owing to fears that officers would abuse their authority and physically threaten them and their partners (Wachholz & Miedema, 2000, p. 309). All of the women who had expressed this concern had previously lived in countries with authoritative police regimes. Similarly, in her exploratory study on South Asian immigrant victims' experiences with domestic violence in Toronto, Shirwadkir (2004) found that many women did not view the police as protectors. Fears that they would be blamed for the abuse or that the police would not believe them were also prevalent.

The reasons abused immigrant women give for distrusting the police based on their experiences of integration in Canada are multilayered, often stemming from concerns of racism and xenophobia. The general acceptance of "culturalized" narratives of domestic violence which assume that immigrant men are more violent and patriarchal than Canadian or Western men play a considerable role in preventing many women from coming forward (MacLeod & Shin, 1990; Crenshaw, 1991; Smith, 2004). Immigrant victims considering police assistance often choose not to disclose for fear of invoking stereotypes and hostility toward their communities. Concerns that they might be stereotyped as passive and oppressed victims of their own traditions also prevent women from calling police.

Isolation

The lack of family and community supports is a key factor that distinguishes immigrant victims' experiences of violence from those of their Canadian-born counterparts. This is an important point to note given the fact that abusers often engage in a variety of isolation tactics in order to ensure that victims are entirely dependent on them and have little contact with the outside world (Pence & Paymar, 1993). Thus, while all victims are generally isolated, for newly arrived victims who have left family, friends and community supports in their home countries, experiences of isolation are compounded.

Not surprisingly, abused immigrant women often fare much worse than Canadian women following mandatory arrest given that they have few people to rely on when their partners are removed from the home (Menjívar & Salcido, 2002; Smith, 2005). Wachholz and Miedema (2000) found that over half of the women in their study worried about the extreme loneliness they would endure if their partners were arrested (Wachholz & Miedema, 2000, p. 308). While all victims consistently report that they want the abuse to stop, at the same time, few want their families to be separated and their partners to be criminalized (Martin & Mosher, 1995). Concerns regarding family separation are legitimate considering that mandatory policing and prosecutorial strategies can sometimes result in the removal of the accused from the household for up to 9 months to even a year, depending on whether he pleads guilty or proceeds with charges through trial.[4] Such consequences of state intervention have led one victim in Wachholz and Miedema's (2000) study to remark, "This help from the government or whatever; it is not really solving your problems, it's just splitting [up families]" (Wachholz & Miedema, 2000, 313).

In the event that community networks have been forged, the arrests of partners can still trigger a loss of supports. Immigrant victims report concerns that invoking the police would "bring dishonour and shame" to their families and communities and would consequently "sever their relationships with those who could assist and support them" (Wachholz & Miedema, 2000, p. 308). Calling the police carries considerable stigma in some immigrant communities, largely owing to pressures to appear law abiding and respectable. Not surprisingly, many immigrant victims report that they would prefer to address the violence in their lives in private through some form of mediation rather than through arrest and formal prosecution (Martin & Mosher, 1995; Wachholz & Miedema, 2000; Shirwadkar, 2004).

Linguistic and Financial Dependence

A final issue that proponents of zero tolerance approaches did not consider is the fact that many abused immigrant women may be dependent on their partners both linguistically and financially. In situations where this is the case, mandatory charging may cause more harm than good. The sudden loss of financial support following the unexpected removal of abusers from the home leaves many women unprepared for managing households, rent and mortgages on their own (Martin & Mosher, 1995).

While many economically disadvantaged Canadian-born victims of woman abuse may also share these financial consequences, immigrant women are in a far more restrictive bind given the barriers they experience when accessing state resources and the labour market. The employment difficulties newcomers and immigrants endure are well known: Discriminatory workplaces, racist hiring practices and the Canadian government's refusal to recognize foreign qualifications and degrees coupled with, in some cases, limited fluency in English, all have the effect of marginalizing them in low-wage and unstable employment sectors (Smith, 2004; Martin & Mosher, 1995). Without the financial resources from their partners and with few economic opportunities and employment prospects owing to systemic racism, immigrant victims have much to lose should the police and courts intervene in their lives, remove them from decision-making processes and arrest their partners without notice.

Conclusion

In sum, interviews with immigrant victims who have experienced the effects of mandatory charging and prosecution strategies stand in stark contrast to the assumptions of safety that feminist reformers promised would follow from the incorporation of these policies. As opposed to the imaginings of the police and courts as protectors, mandatory criminal justice interventions appear to offer very little to immigrant victims by way of support and assistance. Empirical research shows that rather than providing a solution to the violence in immigrant victims' relationships, these policies have backfired. As has just been illustrated, for those victims who do not have permanent residency rights, zero tolerance strategies have the potential to jeopardize immigration prospects. For those who have secured the legal right to remain in Canada, economic vulnerability is still a concern owing to employment and linguistic barriers. Alongside these material factors, policies that remove victim choice do little to allay fears of tyrannical policing that appear to circulate widely within immigrant communities, nor do they quell concerns of losing control over decisions related to abusive partners.

Although mandatory arrest and prosecution policies appeared to be good ideas when they were initially thought through, it is clear that feminist reformers made a critical oversight in their assumptions that all victims want and have the requisite social and economic resources to end their abusive relationships. Reformists had also erred in presuming that victims are not capable of making "reasoned" arrest decisions and would consequently appreciate having the state decide on their behalves how to address the violence in their relationships. Although in theory this approach makes sense given what we know about the dynamics of abusive relationships, in reality it is clear that reluctant victims have several legitimate reasons for not wanting criminal justice intervention in their lives. The experiences of abused immigrant women are case in point. The fears and the consequences that they report are very material in the sense that the arrest of partners could have a profound impact on their economic and social well-being. Considering the detrimental consequences that are likely to follow mandated arrest and prosecution for abused immigrant women, it is clear that preferences to avoid the criminal justice system should not be interpreted as indicative of masochism or learned helplessness.

The most important thing to remember when considering the effectiveness of zero tolerance strategies is that not all abused women will experience mandated state intervention in the same way. There is no doubt that mandated criminal justice intervention does help some victims. However, it is generally safe to conclude that the victims these policies work for, or harm less, tend to be white, Canadian born and middle class.[5] As Martin and Mosher note:

> It is important to observe that the potential for harms and thus the experience of fear, are not evenly distributed among women. Rather, their distribution is demarcated along class, race, ethnicity and citizenship status lines. The various reasons identified suggest that it is racial minority women, poor women and immigrant women who are likely to be exposed to the greatest risk of harm. (1995, p. 35)

Thus, although radical in their sensitivity to and theorizations of gender oppression, feminist reformist were neglectful of the inequalities associated with immigration, class and race. By advocating a "one size fits all" punitive state approach, they overlooked the fact that not all abused women experience relationship violence similarly, nor do they all view the police and courts as protectors. In so doing, proponents failed to account for the "often violent ways the state enters the homes and lives of marginalized women" (Mosher, 2009, p. 1). Consequently, they could not predict the differential impact that mandatory charging and prosecution could potentially have on abused immigrant women.

The story of the rise and failures of mandatory criminal justice intervention is a perfect illustration of the concerns that both feminist activists and scholars have raised in relation to relying on the criminal justice system to forward the interests of women. As noted earlier, from the beginning of the movement, feminists who favoured grassroots approaches to ending domestic violence worried that a reliance on the law would result in individualized, Band-Aid solutions to the problem and do little to disturb the socioeconomic and cultural conditions that led to the problem in the first place. Building on these insights, feminist legal scholars such as Carol Smart (1989) have raised similar concerns. Smart devised the term "juridogenesis" to capture the commonplace occurrence in which the "legal cure is frequently as bad as the original abuse" (Smart, 1989, p. 161). In her warnings to feminists about employing the law as a means of social reform, she cites two central problems: the inability to predict the actual effects of laws once they are put in practice and the law's tendency to distil complex problems into black and white, adversarial frameworks.

As this discussion illustrates, there is no simple or easy solution to the problem of domestic violence. While it is clear that current criminal justice interventions are too coercive, the systemic negligence that characterized historical responses to violence against women, particularly in relation to its policing, is not ideal, either. Perhaps a more moderate approach is required to deal with the intricacies of the problem of violence in intimate relationships, one that considers differences among abused women. Although some feminist reformers wanted domestic violence to be treated "like any other crime," in hindsight, this may not have been the best approach. One thing that is certain is that victims do require more autonomy than current state interventions offer them. If the criminal justice system is serious about protecting all victims of violence, a reform of mandatory policing and prosecution is imperative.

References

British Columbia Ministry of Attorney General. (2004). *Crown counsel spousal assault policy.* (Discussion paper). Vancouver: Queen's Printer.

Buel, S. M. (1988). Mandatory arrest for domestic violence. *Harvard Women's Law Journal, 11,* 213–226.

Buzawa, E., & Buzawa, C. (2003). *Domestic violence: The criminal justice response.* Thousand Oaks, CA: Sage.

Crenshaw, K. (1991). Mapping the margins: Intersectionality, identity politics, and violence against women of color. *Stanford Law Review, 43*(6), 1241–1299.

Currie, D. (1995). Battered women and the state: From the failure of theory to a theory of failure. *Journal of Human Justice, 1,* 77–96.

———. (1998). The criminalization of violence against women: Feminist demands and patriarchal accommodations. In Bonnycastle & Rigakos (Eds.), *Unsettling truths: Battered women, policy, politics and contemporary research in Canada.* Vancouver: Collective Press.

Davis, R., et al. (2001). Access to justice for immigrants who are victimized: The perspectives of police and prosecutors. *Criminal Justice Policy, 12*(3), 183–196.

DeKeseredy, W., & MacLeod, L. (1997). *Woman abuse: A sociological story.* Toronto: Harcourt Brace.

Department of Justice Canada. (2005). *Final report of the ad-hoc federal-provincial-territorial working group reviewing spousal abuse policies and legislation.* Retrieved from www.justice.gc.ca/en/ps/fm/reports/spousal_e.pdf

Hanna, C. (1996). No right to choose: Mandated victim participation in domestic violence prosecutions. *Harvard Law Review, 109*(8), 1857–1909.

Hilton, N. Z. (1988). One in ten: The struggle and disempowerment of the battered women's movement. *Canadian Journal of Family and the Law, 7,* 313–336.

———. (1993). "Police intervention and public opinion." In Hilton (Ed.), *Legal responses to wife assault: Current trends and evaluation.* Newbury Park, CA: Sage.

Jaffe, P. G., Hastings, E., Reitzel, D., & Austin, G. W. (1993). The impact of police laying charges. In Hilton (Ed.), *Legal responses to wife assault: current trends and evaluation.* Newbury Park, CA: Sage.

Landau, T. (2000). Women's experiences with mandatory charging for wife assault in Ontario, Canada: A case against the prosecution. *International Review of Victimology, 7,* 141–157.

MacLeod, L. (1987). *Battered but not beaten: Preventing wife battering in Canada.* Ottawa: The Canadian Advisory Council on the Status of Women.

———. (1980). *Wife battering in Canada: The vicious circle.* Ottawa: The Canadian Advisory Council on the Status of Women.

MacLeod, L., & Shin, M.Y. (1990). *Isolated, afraid and forgotten: The service delivery needs and realities of immigrant and refugee women who are battered.* National Clearinghouse on Family Violence: Health and Welfare Canada.

Martin, D. L., & Mosher, J. (1995). Unkept promises: Experiences of immigrant women with the neo-criminalization of wife abuse. *Canadian Journal of Women and the Law, 8,* 3–44.

Menjívar, C., & Salcido, O. (2002). Immigrant women and domestic violence: Common experiences in different countries. *Gender and Society, 16*(6), 898–920.

Ministry of the Solicitor General. (2000). *Ontario policing standards manual.*

Ministry of the Attorney General. (2004). *British Columbia policy on the criminal justice response to violence against women and children*. Vancouver: Queen's Printer for British Columbia.

Ministry of the Solicitor General. (2000). *Ontario policing standards manual*. Toronto: Queen's Printer for Ontario.

Morrow, M., Hankivsky, O., & Varcoe, C. (2005). Women and violence: The effects of dismantling the welfare state. *Critical Social Policy, 24*(3), 358–384.

Mosher, J. (2009). The complicity of the public state in the intimate abuse of immigrant women. In V. Agnew (Ed.), *Racialized migrant women in Canada: Essays on health, violence, and equity*. Toronto: University of Toronto Press.

Pence, E., & Paymar, M. (1993). *Education groups for men who batter: The Duluth model*. New York: Springer.

Shirwadkar, S. (2004). Canadian domestic violence policy and Indian immigrant women. *Violence Against Women, 10*(8), 860–879.

Smart, C. (1989). *Feminism and the power of law*. New York: Routledge.

Smith, E. (2004). *Nowhere to turn? Responding to partner violence against immigrant and visible minority women*. Ottawa: Canadian Council of Social Development.

Strauss, M., Gelles, R., & Steinmetz, S. (1980). *Behind closed doors: Violence in the American family*. New York: Anchor Books.

Wachholz, S., & Baukje, M. (2000). Risk, fear, harm: Immigrant women's perceptions of the 'policing solution' to woman abuse. *Crime, Law and Social Change, 34*(3), 301–317.

Wanless, M. (1996). Mandatory arrest: A step towards eradicating domestic violence, but is it enough? *University of Illinois Law Review, 2*, 533–587.

Endnotes

1. *Policing Standards Manual* (2000), Ontario, Ministry of the Solicitor General. Guideline 15, 7.

2. *Policing Standards Manual* (2000), Ontario, Ministry of the Solicitor General, Guideline 16c and 16g, 7.

3. Although the majority of those seeking to obtain residency through sponsorship relationships enter Canada having already obtained permanent status, recent changes to the Immigration and Refugee Protection Act (IRPA) now allows for sponsored individuals to arrive without status and to apply for residency within Canada (Mosher, 2009). This discussion relates to victims in this latter category.

4. When police lay charges, a "no contact" condition is implemented through bail to ensure that the victim and accused do not interact until the matter has proceeded through the system and has been resolved. Depending on how backlogged a court is, the wait time for trial can be considerable. In Toronto, for instance, the wait time for a trial can be close to 7 or 8 months from the first appearance of the accused in court.

5. Although not all immigrants are people of colour, the categories of race and immigration tend to overlap.

CHAPTER 12

Governing Security

Benoît Dupont, Université de Montréal

INTRODUCTION

The aim of this chapter is to explore the debate over whether the state ought to have the primary responsibility for policing. In recent years, there has been a rise in the use of private and community security arrangements (including policing) that are arguably more effective than the state-run police services. This has led to a debate about who best can provide effective security. Two perspectives animate this debate: a majority of scholars firmly believe that the provision of security is one of the core functions of the state and, as such, should be mainly the concern of public institutions. On the other side, a growing number of scholars question the state monopoly, claiming a trend toward more effective private and community-based security. These scholars propose a more flexible framework where the state would only be one actor among others.

In order to explore this debate, the concept of "governance" and its relationship to "security" need to be understood. In the field of security, governance is a much broader concept than government. It allows us to move beyond the myth of a state monopoly over the legitimate use of physical force (Brodeur, 2003; Zedner, 2006). The working definition of the "governance of security" used here is: "the constellation of institutions, whether formal or informal, governmental or private, commercial or voluntary, that provide for social control and conflict resolution and that attempt to promote peace in the face of threats (either realized or anticipated) that arise from collective life" (Dupont, Grabosky, & Shearing, 2003, p. 332).

The security of its citizens is of course of paramount importance to the state, as constitutive of its own legitimacy (Loader & Walker, 2006). In both democratic and authoritarian states, governments that are unable to provide a modicum of security quickly experience an erosion of their capacity to

administer. Such states are commonly referred to as "weak or failing" (Dupont, Grabosky, & Shearing, 2003; Agamben, 2003). It is also important to remember that in oppressive regimes the security of the people (human security) and the security of the state are rarely aligned: the latter is often obtained by compromising the former.

But even in the strongest states, security cannot remain the sole responsibility of a central actor when risks associated with human activities and their impact on social, technical and natural environments increase, often seeming to grow exponentially (Beck, 1992). The globalization of exchanges also creates new flows of private governance secured through their own private arrangements. These are not linked to local sovereign governments and, indeed, are capable of evading their control. The growth of private military companies (Singer, 2003), forensic accounting institutions (Williams, 2005) and other private security outfits that operate at the higher end of the industry spectrum to protect their clients' informational and intellectual assets (O'Reilly & Ellison, 2006) attest to the high demand from wealthy customers for specialized services. These private providers are not staffed by minimum-wage uniformed guards. They rely instead on experts with a background in risk management, investigation, intelligence, negotiation, logistics, forensic accounting or computing and armed response.

Study of the public police alone cannot capture the entire range of policing functions, which are undertaken through a constellation of public, private and community auspices and providers (Bayley & Shearing, 2001). In this sense, approaching security from a governance perspective provides a powerful antidote to a simplistic institutional focus by controlling the intellectual bias that systematically favors one particular form of social organization as a cure-all solution to the broad array of security challenges experienced by late-modern or developing societies.

Acknowledging that security is delivered by a plurality of actors forces us to consider the definition of "security" itself more carefully. Roché (2004) highlights the historical and theoretical problems associated with the fact that security is predominantly understood as a public good embedded in a social contract between the state and its citizens. This dominant approach never discusses situations where one party to the contract fails to meet its obligations, as, for example, when the state cannot maintain order and protect its citizens. It also underestimates the capacity of the private sector to deliver public services and overrates the capacity of the state to serve as the repository of the public good (Roché, 2004, p. 249). After considering the multiplicity of practices and interests associated with the *term* "security" in a plural governance environment, Manning (2006, p. 83) suggests that we should recognize the situational and contextual nature of the use of the term. What is covered by "security" is defined through negotiations between actors for whom it represents, among other possibilities, a want or a need, or a task framed by legislation, a profitable opportunity or any action that implies the use of coercive force. The lack of a precise agreed definition within the contemporary academic literature can be seen as a deliberate reflection of the elasticity and plasticity of the concept and its ability to be used by innovators adjusting to new threats and norms.

At this stage, it is important to note that the concept of governance cannot explain everything. Its range is much more modest, and its value much greater as a result: It provides us with a theoretical and empirical toolbox that can illuminate the complexity (and messiness) of security delivery mechanisms as they exist in real life. The various governance perspectives presented in the following pages should not be seen as elegant self-sustaining intellectual constructions but as windows that reveal a fairly disorganized—and rarely deterministic—reality.

This chapter follows a typological approach in order to capture the different dimensions and manifestations of the governance of security. In the first section, the three dominant social structures of state, market and networks and their impact on security governance will be examined. The second section focuses on the broad range of actors that authorize and deliver security at the local, national and international levels. The ties that bind these actors must also be considered and are analyzed in the third section. Finally, the fourth section adopts a more normative approach and delineates the challenges associated with the governance of security in terms of effectiveness and accountability.

GOVERNANCE STRUCTURES: STATE, MARKET AND NETWORKS

Three main social structures are usually mentioned with regard to governance: the state, the market and networks. This "unholy Trinity" (Fleming & Rhodes, 2005) reflects major shifts in modes of public service delivery, with the monopoly of the state being replaced by more decentralized mechanisms in which bureaucracies assume a steering function while the rowing is delegated to private and community interests (Osborne & Gaebler, 1992). These three structures are ideal types that are never found in a "pure" form in real life, where, to a large extent, they hybridize and overlap. However, in specific historical and political contexts each of them has been considered to be the most effective tool for designing and implementing public policy, more effective than the other two not only in the field of security but also in health, education, housing or transport.

For example, the Keynesian welfare state model forged in the 1930s in the United Kingdom and implemented in the rest of the Western world after World War II supported the professionalization of policing that occurred roughly at the same time in the United States (Roberg & Kuykendall, 1997), in Canada (Marquis, 1993), in the United Kingdom (Emsley, 2003) and in Australia (Finnane, 1994). The political features of each country gave these reforms a distinctive organizational flavour, but in most cases large investments were made in police institutions in an attempt to increase their human and technological capital. On this institutional configuration, private security was relegated to a marginal position and publicly denigrated by state institutions, which claimed a monopoly on the provision of protection and security expertise to the public and on the fulfillment of the public interest (Morn, 1982; Kalifa, 2000).

In the early 1980s, this state-centric model lost its appeal and declined, mainly because of the fiscal crisis precipitated by the two oil crises and their repercussions on world economies. The regulatory state model that emerged allowed the market to assume greater responsibilities for the implementation of policies, while design and coordination of these policies remained in the hands of the state (Braithwaite, 2000). Osborne and Gaebler's (1992) nautical metaphor was forged in this context to convey the idea of a leaner and smarter state that could govern at a distance (Rose, 2000) and focus more on outcomes than on outputs.

This transition led to a renewed interest in private security, the exponential growth of which seemed to compensate for the inability of the state to contain the crime epidemic that engulfed Western societies during the 1970s and 1980s. Following Shearing and Stenning's (1981) seminal work, scholars from around the world attempted to assess the size of the private security market (Cunningham & Taylor, 1985; De Waard, 1999; Ocqueteau, 2004; Sanders, 2005) and identify the causes of such a rapid shift. This new-found faith in the market was not only limited to offering more diverse and expanded services but also resulted in police organizations adopting management techniques borrowed directly from the private sector and business schools (Leishman, Cope, & Starie, 1996; McLaughlin & Murji, 1997; Dupont, 2003; Murphy, 2002). Because of the important differences between Western countries, it is impossible to make general statements about the diffusion of the New Public Management model. Nevertheless, the idea of a more responsive public administration that could be made more effective and accountable became the ideal for supporters of this model. The business jargon of "mission statements" "best practices," "customer service delivery" and "management by objectives" soon became a staple of police annual reports. Despite these good intentions, the limits of the market logic of competition and adjustments based on the law of supply and demand rapidly became apparent. The first issue is one of equity, where access to security becomes constrained by financial means. While wealthy individuals and communities can afford additional private security, the alternatives for disadvantaged groups are much more limited although their needs are equally pressing. The inequalities created by these new arrangements and the disparities in regulatory regimes for various security providers have not yet been satisfactorily resolved (Law Commission of Canada, 2002). Furthermore, efforts to rationalize police functions have often been thwarted by the incommensurability of public security. Police work—more precisely, its uniformed patrol component—is characterized by three features that make it impractical on even the most robust econometric models: its emergency dimension, its unpredictability and the wide discretionary powers exercised by police officers.

More recently, a third structure, which seems to offer a compromise between the state and the market, has attracted a great deal of interest. Networks can hardly be described as a new social structure, as Tilly (2005) reminds us, but their flexibility compares favourably with the rigidities of state hierarchies, and the reciprocity that sustains their members' ties appears more desirable than the ruthless competition that is characteristic of markets. The general trend toward networks has also been observed in the security field, where local, institutional, international and informational security networks that go beyond the informal and personal dimensions have appeared (Newburn, 2001; Dupont, 2004; Lippert & O'Connor, 2006). These networks transcend the public–private dichotomy and blend bureaucratic and market rationalities. The following table, borrowed and adapted from Rhodes (2006), summarizes the features of the three governance structures described above.

	The Bureaucratic State	The Market	Networks
Basis of relationships	Employment and law	Contract	Resource exchange
Degree of dependence	Dependent	Independent	Interdependent
Medium of exchange	Authority	Prices	Trust
Means of conflict resolution and coordination	Rules and commands	Haggling, arbitrage, and the courts	Diplomacy and mutual adjustments
Culture	Subordination	Competition	Reciprocity

Again, it is important to remember that these structural layers are ideal types and as a result they are not mutually exclusive in their expressions. The state, for example, is an avid consumer of private security (Crawford, Lister, Blackburn, & Burnett, 2005; Sanders, 2005), and local security networks are often used by equipment vendors as hunting grounds for new customers (Dupont, 2006). A constant hybridization process is at work, which forces actors to operate simultaneously under the three modes of governance and generates a tangled overlapping of practices, technologies, cultures and rationalities that are not without tensions and contradictions.

ACTORS AND LEVELS OF GOVERNANCE

There is a high level of functional and structural differentiation among the three dominant modes of governance. A broad and diverse range of social actors undertake security functions at the local, national and international levels and these two typologies—actors and levels of governance—provide a useful tool for the empirical study of security delivery.

The typology of actors designed by Bayley and Shearing (2001) quickly became a standard reference because it was able to capture both the nature of the institutions involved in the production of security and their role. These authors identified two main security functions. First, an authorization function corresponds to the process through which the needs of a community and the appropriate means to meet them are defined. A second more instrumental function is focused on the implementation of security solutions. Although these two functions are complementary, they can be assumed by discrete actors, such as public institutions, private companies, community groups or individuals. The security matrix derived from this typology then helps us to conceptualize the increasing number of security actors and functions and the virtually unlimited number of permutations and arrangements designated by the deceptively simple term "security governance." On this approach, private security is, for example, what results when a public or private client, after having conducted a "needs and means" analysis, makes use of the services of a security provider, with the choice of services dependent on the options the provider makes available. The decision to use the expertise of an external provider and the choice of this provider will be dictated by a number of factors and contingencies that go beyond a simple economic calculus. This matrix also takes into account illegal actors such as organized crime groups or militias, which in weak and failing states can act as substitutes for public institutions and provide summary justice and basic services to poor communities (Dupont, Grabosky, & Shearing, 2003). Gambetta (1993), Varese (2001) and Volkov (2002), for example, have argued that the Sicilian and the Russian mafias provided an effective protection system to many entrepreneurs in the absence of a reliable state during transitional political periods. The following table sums up the possible configurations under this plural perspective.

Security Functions	
Auspices	**Providers**
Governments	Governments
National	Police organizations
Regional	As a public service
Local	Pay duty (for a fee)
Economic interests	Crime prevention initiatives
Legal business	Other law enforcement bodies
Independently	Corporate security (in house)
Collectively	Private security companies (contract)
Criminal groups	Individuals (self-help)
Residential communities	Criminal groups
Open	
Gated	
Communities of interest	
Political	
Ethnic	
Religious	
Cultural	
Individuals	
Adapted from Bayley and Shearing (2001, p. 6 & p. 13)	

Rigakos (2005, p. 272) proposed an alternative typology based on policing activities: (1) polemic ("war-like" or paramilitary); (2) sentry-dataveillant (monitoring and intelligence-gathering activities); (3) investigative; (4) patrol-based; and (5) civic-sumptuary (involving regulation of various matters of social life "necessary for good administration and order maintenance," such as sanitation, public health and morals, etc.). While Rigakos's typology is very useful in understanding the many facets of security work, it is less helpful in conceptualizing why and how some activities are—exclusively or collectively—assigned to certain categories of actors rather than others.

Finally, two other major actors should be added to any typology used to explain the governance of security. These actors do not directly authorize or provide security but have a significant influence on the decision processes. The first group is the media, which plays the role of public opinion amplifier. Its responsiveness to dramatic security issues and its capacity to capture the attention of policy makers give it an important role in the governance of security (Ericson, Baranek, & Chan, 1989; Doyle, 2003). Police unions constitute a second group of very influential actors. As Murphy (2002, p. 34) stated, "most police unions are fiercely resistant to managerial initiatives that may affect traditional occupational privileges and established working practices." In several cases unions have not hesitated to enter the political arena and lobby in favour of law and order policies, going as far as publicly opposing reelection bids of politicians perceived as unfriendly to their cause (Forcese, 1999; Finanne, 2002).

The variables that influence the participation of certain categories of actors in governance processes are not limited to the legal or moral legitimacy, capacity or solvency of these actors. Their influence is also determined by their structural compatibility with the three political levels of security governance: micro- or local governance, interinstitutional governance at the nation/state level, and international governance. Microgovernance implies the direct involvement of communities and individuals in the production of security. The community policing philosophy, which emphasises citizen consultation and mobilization through beat-meetings (Skogan & Hartnett, 1997), neighbourhood watch schemes (Bennett, 1992; McConville & Shepherd, 1992), and police volunteer programs (Gill & Mawby, 1990; Murphy, 2002, p. 23), epitomizes the rediscovery of microgovernance's virtues in the field of security. The rationale behind microgovernance associates high levels of community participation with the reinforcement of collective efficacy and informal social controls (Lemieux & Sauvêtre, forthcoming). Local communities are believed to possess vast reservoirs of untapped knowledge about the problems they face and the best ways to solve them. Microgovernance mechanisms encourage communities to become co-producers of their own security, helping state institutions better adjust their offer of services. Some critics have questioned the motives of the state in adopting this model, noting unrealistic expectations placed on weak communities (Loader & Walker, 2006), but the Zwelethemba model of peacemaking and peace-building developed and implemented by Shearing and his colleagues in South African and in Argentinean shanty towns provides a promising example of deprived communities that have been able to mobilize local resources in order to efficiently, creatively and noncoercively improve their access to security (Johnston & Shearing, 2003; Shearing & Wood, 2003).

At the nation state level, interinstitutional governance is focused mainly on organizational effectiveness and is therefore dealt with exclusively through formal structures, both public and private. Pooling of resources and establishment of partnerships in the areas of training, investigative, information management, order maintenance or forensic science represent the most common forms of interinstitutional governance. The growing complexity of large-scale organized crime and terrorist networks, which often exceeds the investigative capacity of separate police organizations, has been instrumental in the creation of integrated teams and joint task forces such as the Integrated National Security Enforcement Teams in Canada or the Joint Terrorism Task Forces in the United States. These semiautonomous operational entities bring together investigators and crime analysts from each member organization in order to increase coordination and avoid the duplication of resources that has often limited the scope of major investigations. The trend toward working this way is strongest in decentralized countries that maintain large numbers of small- to medium-sized police organizations, but countries with unified national police forces, such as France, have also found it necessary to find ways to better integrate their law enforcement bodies. According to Ericson and Haggerty (1997), use of interinstitutional governance has also been reinforced by the advent of the risk society and its insatiable appetite for personal data to produce profiles and dangerousness scores. Information sharing arrangements between public and private actors thrive in such a risk management environment: Insurance companies obtain accident data from police organizations (Ericson & Haggerty, 1997), air transport security authorities routinely access Passenger Name Records (PNR) provided by airlines and reservation systems to screen for terrorists (Bennett, 2005), intelligence agencies are given access to client transaction databases by telephone companies (Wait, 2006) or international banking institutions (Lichtblau & Risen, 2006) in the hope of uncovering suspicious patterns, and so forth. In these cases, security is governed through data flows. The elusive search for zero-risk outcomes can also extend interinstitutional governance arrangements to fields such as military affairs (Kraska & Kappeler, 2005), health (Burris, 2006) or even social work and education. Such colonization of every sphere of public life by security concerns risks the corrosion of democratic values, especially if it is not preceded by proper debate.

The third level of governance reflects the globalization of exchanges and the declining relevance of physical borders. International or transnational security governance mainly involves large institutional actors such as international organizations (Interpol, Europol, United Nations Office on Drugs and Crime), bilateral regional initiatives (Canada–US Smart Border Declaration, Integrated Border Enforcement Teams), high-end security companies operating on behalf of multinationals, and nongovernmental organizations promoting human security issues. International security governance arrangements existed long before air travel and the Internet. Deflem (2002), for example, traced the origins of Interpol to 19th-century Europe, and Morn (1982) showed how the Pinkerton detective agency acted as an exchange platform between its international network of police contacts and an embryonic U.S. government. For the past two decades, however, the increased density of this institutional space has resulted in heightened tension between the bureaucratic and commercial autonomy of actors that interact directly at the international level, on one hand, and the erosion of political oversight mechanisms designed to guarantee citizens' rights and states' sovereignty (Deflem, 2002) on the other.

These three levels of governance frequently overlap: International security governance can become an arena where national conflicts between competing law enforcement institutions are played out (Alain, 2001), while in border zones and the virtual world, the demarcation between the local and the global becomes blurred.

A RELATIONAL TYPOLOGY OF GOVERNANCE

Strictly speaking, there are no intrinsic links between the three levels of governance and the types of tangible ties and modes of exchange that connect security auspices and providers. While private security companies operate according to a business rationale, they must also develop trusted relationships with police services, often trading information without financial compensation. In the current context of fiscal frugality, police organizations are being pressed to diversify their sources of revenue and to open "commercial units" that market some of their services to private buyers. A relational typology of security governance is therefore needed to map the various connections that hold contemporary security assemblages together. Five main categories of interaction (Grabosky, 2004) play a significant role in the governance of security:

- Third-party policing or conscription
- Delegation
- Sale
- Gift
- Swap (exchange)

These five categories are to a large extent contingent on historical, political, economical and regulatory forces. Conscription, for example, is most likely to be found in strong states with centralized police organizations, while sale will be more frequent in societies where the welfare state has declined. Gift, swap and delegation thrive in environments where security networks are already part of routine functions.

Third-party policing (Mazerolle & Ransley, 2005), or policing by command (Ayling and Grabosky, 2006a), refers to the imposition of mandatory requirements on institutional actors by another security organization, either public or private. This covers, for example, the obligation imposed on financial entities to report suspicious transactions to the Financial Transactions and Reports Analysis Centre of Canada (FINTRAC) or on airlines to communicate their PNR lists to border authorities. Compliance is obtained through a variety of direct and indirect levers that range from financial incentives to the threat of large fines and other regulatory penalties. Insurance companies have, for example, adopted a softer approach by offering lower premiums to clients who purchase accredited security systems for their houses or cars. In the early 1990s, the British government embraced the "naming and shaming" approach by making public the list of most frequently stolen vehicles. Automakers promptly equipped newer models of these cars with more robust antitheft devices (Laycock, 2004). Other third-party mechanisms make the delivery of permits and license conditional on compliance with security guidelines. For instance, in their study of French protest policing, Fillieule and Jobard (1998) showed that social movement organizers need to satisfy their police counterparts that they will have adequate security measures (such as marshals) in order to obtain the permission to march. Those in command can seek to eliminate unsafe practices, to force the implementation of security measures or to regulate recordkeeping for future audits and investigations. The Sarbanes-Oxley Act of 2002, voted into law in the United States to reassure investors after a string of major accounting scandals, makes the failure of company executives to maintain a wide range of records (work papers, memoranda, e-mails, correspondence and other documents) for a period of 5 years a felony punishable by 10 years of imprisonment (section 802(a)(1) and (a)(2)). This obligation to retain data for an extended period is intended to facilitate investigations.

Delegation of responsibility reflects the transfer of functions from the state to private or hybrid actors who act on its behalf and receive the corresponding resources. Sometimes the delegate must generate its own revenues by imposing a fee on users. In many countries, for instance, air transport security duties are assumed in part by the companies that own or manage the airports, and these companies are responsible for preboarding screening of passengers and their luggage and for controlling access to restricted areas. Following the 9/11 terrorist attacks, the effectiveness of this system was questioned and new public authorities were created in the United States and Canada to reintegrate these functions into the state's sphere of responsibility. In a number of Australian states and in France, automated cameras systems that register automobile speed are managed and operated by private companies, which receive a percentage of the fines paid by motorists (2% in France) or a flat fee (Clapaud, 2003; Department of Justice Victoria, 2004). In Japan, police organizations have delegated parking enforcement to private security companies (Economist, 2007). This type of relationship is attractive to public institutions that want to make significant savings in infrastructure investments (the burden of the initial outlay is carried out by the delegate in exchange for commensurate profits). It can also be more economical for institutions to outsource devalued tasks to the private sector. This form of relationship is often criticized because it is difficult for public security organizations to monitor and supervise the performance of external providers.

Sale constitutes the most frequent form of governance relationship in a market structure economy, and Loader (1999) even employs the term "commodification of policing and security" to describe the trend that sees security treated as a consumer good, like any other product or service. It is important to note, however, that private security does not always involve a commercial transaction, since many businesses protect themselves through in-house (also known as proprietary) security units. In this case, the same organization authorizes and delivers its security needs through vertical hierarchical integration. Public institutions are increasingly involved in commercial exchanges, both as buyers and, more recently, as providers. In Montreal, visitors to the headquarters of the municipal police (SPVM), provincial police (SQ), and federal police (RCMP) are welcomed by private security guards who control access to the buildings where public security policies and operations are designed and implemented. In a number of SQ districts, private security employees man detention facilities and handle surveillance of inmates waiting to see a judge, replacing constables who are then free to answer calls from the public (Dupont & Pérez, 2006). More recently, a number of police services in Canada and elsewhere have entered the security market as commercial providers in order to raise additional revenues. According to Murphy (2002), over 70% of Canadian police organizations charge user fees for a broad range of services. In 2006, the Montreal police service even printed and distributed a 47-page colour catalogue of the services it markets to other police organizations, private security companies and individuals, including training modules, technical support for telephone interception (restricted to police clients), uniformed officers for traffic duties or as extras for movie shoots. In the United Kingdom, chief police officers (Blair, 1998) have expressed their ambition to become significant players in the "for profit" security sector. Many have created the position of "business development manager" or "external funding coordinator" and offer the services of police auxiliaries known as "community support officers" to local merchant associations and to residential communities for a fee (Crawford & Lister, 2006). Similar arrangements are routine in the United States (Reiss, 1988; Gans, 2000) and elsewhere. While this has become an accepted type of relationship between private actors, the involvement of the public police in commercial transactions raises a number of issues. As a purchaser, making the distinction between "core" and "non-core" police services, which is an intrinsic part of the procurement process, is not easy (Murphy, 2002; Ayling & Grabosky, 2006b) and can have potentially dire consequences for the delivery of public policing. Who should be held accountable, for example, when a detained person commits suicide in her cell under the sole supervision of a private guard? Another potential risk is the sale of a public service that is already in short supply. Unless transparent systems are put in place to ensure that only excess capacity is sold (such as unused facilities or off-duty volunteers) and that fairness cannot be bought, trust in the police is likely to decline.

The gifts received (and often solicited) by police organizations obey the same rationale as income diversification in a time of fiscal parsimony. Under this type of arrangement, a private company donates cash, equipment or services to a public institution and expects in return to be acknowledged (Grabosky, 2004). Many British police services have established charitable trusts to receive such donations (Crawford & Lister, 2006). In Canada, police organizations have received computer equipment, software and even helicopters (Murphy, 2002, p. 23; Law Commission of Canada, 2006); and it is not uncommon for community policing units to be given exotic cars for outreach programs with young automobile enthusiasts. In order to avoid any accusation of impropriety and favouritism, Australian police services have implemented a disclosure policy that requires that their annual reports include the origin, nature and monetary amount of every gift received. Far from being the exclusive domain of public policing, sponsorship schemes are also frequently used to support crime prevention initiatives, with the bulk of the contributions being made by insurance companies. Mauss, in his classic work (Mauss, 1967) emphasized the fictional aspects of gift-giving, which in many contexts conceal a tacit contract made up of deferred obligations. It can sometimes be difficult to determine whether a particular gift is a disinterested contribution or a more reciprocal exchange. This aspect of gift-giving should not, however, be used to obscure the fact that governance of security can involve altruistic conduct that does not require compensation.

Finally, swaps denote formal or informal nonmonetary collaborative agreements that facilitate the equal exchange of information, knowledge, human resources, hardware and so forth. Swaps are characterized by a weak degree of constraint and a strong level of reciprocity between parties and occur on a routine basis among actors from the public and private spheres. The ethnographies of Rigakos (2002) and Huey, Ericson and Haggerty (2005) clearly show the constant flow of exchanges that link the Toronto and Vancouver police to a constellation of private security providers. As central players, police organizations retain a dominant position in these transactions but often play down the hierarchical dimension of the relationship in order to sustain productive mutual arrangements with their partners. This form of horizontal integration is also used frequently (and sometimes clandestinely) within networks of public security institutions in order to overcome bureaucratic rigidity. Managers and investigators build "relational portfolios" (Gatto & Thoenig, 1993) in which personal affinities play an important role in order to trade on the "market of favours." Exchanges usually provide additional resources and increased efficiency, at least up to a point. When used too frequently, paralysis can eclipse effectiveness because of the high transaction costs and the efforts needed to reach consensual decisions (Crawford, 1997).

These five types of relationships are not mutually exclusive. Crime prevention and law enforcement programs usually thrive on complementary relationships (delegation-gift, for example). Also, two institutional actors can sustain various forms of relationships simultaneously depending on the specific activities in which they are jointly involved and their respective aims. Furthermore, the motives behind the choices of partners and the predilection for a particular form of relationship need to be considered in relation to the constant power plays at work in the governance of security. Not all actors in this field are equal in their access to resources and their legitimacy. Their position depends to a large extent on the various forms of capital they can mobilize (Bourdieu, 1986), which allows them to dictate the terms of the exchanges in which they take part or forces them to accept more unfavourable conditions when their assets are not relevant to the "rules of the game." The state, for example, can still claim a central role in the governance of urban security, but its position is not as prevalent in other fields, such as the investigation of large financial frauds (Williams, 2005) or the control of cybercrime, which are largely regulated by hybrid authorities and private companies. The relational density of the security field also leads to numerous collisions between competing rationalities (Espeland, 1998); for instance, the utilitarian rationality of private security seeks to minimize losses and preserve the reputa-tion of its authorizers, while the justice rationality of public security institutions leads to a symbolic function of retribution—and sometimes restoration. Whether the governance of security is considered analytically or normatively, it can be understood only in relation to these frictions and the way they are empirically resolved.

THE NORMATIVE IMPLICATIONS OF SECURITY GOVERNANCE: EFFECTIVENESS AND ACCOUNTABILITY

The pluralization of security governance makes it difficult to determine how to assign re-sponsibility for effectiveness and accountability. How are we to assess the contribution of multiple actors to composite results? How can we ensure that the fragmentation of security functions does not facilitate the emergence of real (or virtual) institutional spaces where democratic values of equity and justice are made subordinate or are even absent?

When evaluating effectiveness, fluctuations in crime statistics are systematically at-tributed to police activities or to macroeconomic factors that are difficult to control. Technological or programmatic innovations have often played a significant role in increas-ing the effectiveness of policing but are rarely given credit for it. An exception is the Lojack car-tracking system, which has been associated with reductions in car thefts of up to 50% in cities where the service was made available and has also contributed indirectly to the protection of many more vehicles than those initially equipped with it (Ayres & Levitt, 1997). The exponential growth of private security and the omnipresence of its employees in mass private properties (Shearing & Stenning, 1981) and public spaces has also cer-tainly had a deterrent effect on several categories of crime and deviant behaviour, but this hypothesis has never been tested empirically at a general level. Evaluation methodologies able to map the effectiveness of the multiple contributors to the provision of security need to be designed and developed. These multi-institutional protocols would also be able to identify institutional actors that benefit disproportionately from the governance arrange-ments in which they are involved (free riders) and those that are either exploited or margin-alized. Looked at from this perspective, it is possible to argue that some part of the profits of private security companies derives from the existence of the public police as a last-resort guarantor. For instance, residential alarms installed by private companies for a monthly fee would not find nearly as many customers if the police stopped responding to alarms. The problem is compounded by the fact that more than 95% of activations are false alarms, at a cost of $150 to $300 per police response (Rush & Leeder, 2007). In this case, taxpayers' in-vestments are being mobilized by private interests that do not return part of their revenues to the police. The "blue drain" phenomenon, which refers to the massive transfer of public expertise to consulting firms offering risk management, competitive intelligence, forensic accounting or cybercrime services, reflects the same opportunistic exploitation of public resources by the private security sector (Erickson, 2001; Decorte, Van Laethem, & Van Outrive, 1999). This differential capacity of certain actors to mobilize public goods to fulfill private ends can be better understood by looking at the concept of club goods (Cornes & Sandler, 1996; Crawford, 2006). Club goods are nonrival (consumption by one consumer does not prevent consumption by others) and are also said to be indivisible and excludable (consumers who have not paid or who do not meet certain criteria can be prevented from enjoying their benefits). They are generally opposed to public goods, which are nonrival and nonexcludable. Making security a club good and its governance a Hobbesian enterprise where auspices and providers are free to satisfy private interests with minimal regulation would undoubtedly weaken the constitutive social contract that guarantees the citizens of most democracies collective and equitable access to security.

The pluralization of security creates similar dilemmas with regard to accountability. Current police oversight mechanisms are monoinstitutional, meaning that they usually examine only isolated cases of misconduct within a single organization. Private security cannot claim even this level of regulatory integration (Burbidge, 2005) because it uses several uncoordinated contractual and legal levers to extract compliance (Stenning, 2000). The fluidity of new forms of security governance and the relationships that sustain them offer a stark contrast to the rigidity and fragmentation of the regulatory regimes that are imposed on them. The narrowly defined mandate of regulatory regimes is proving to be increasingly irrelevant in the joined responsibility environment of the new forms of security governance, and the few institutional innovations attempted in this domain have been disappointing. In 2000, a national commission for security ethics was created in France with jurisdiction over all employees of public or private security institutions. In its first 5 years of activity, it investigated only four complaints related to private security employees. Even if more complaints had been lodged, the commission's financial resources are limited and barely allow it to properly examine cases involving police or correctional officers (Dupont & Pérez, 2006). In Northern Ireland, the Patten Commission's recommendation that a policing board be established signalled a shift from previous accountability mechanisms—under police authority—toward a more open governance model where the contributions of nonpolice actors to security could be considered. District policing partnership boards were also envisaged at the local level and were supposed to be allocated funds for the purchase of "additional services from the police or other statutory agencies or from the private sector" (Independent Commission on Policing for Northern Ireland, 1999, p. 35). Unfortunately, the current accountability system is a watered-down version of the commission's recommendations that focuses on public security providers (Kempa & Johnston, 2005). More recently, in Canada, the Arar commission recommended the creation of a new integrated review process for six national security agencies in order to better supervise information sharing as well as the joint operations of national and international intelligence organizations (O'Connor, 2006). As the sad tale of Maher Arar shows, the accountability problems created by the inability of democratic governments to understand the governance of security in all its complexity and to adjust their policies accordingly can have tragic repercussions for their citizens. Moreover, as it becomes increasingly difficult for laypersons to make sense of the decisions taken in this domain given all the interests at stake, their participation in public debates on security issues is curtailed.

To conclude, the governance of security generates a broad range of theoretical and normative interpretations. None of these interpretations, however, heralds the disappearance of the state. At most, we are witnessing a redeployment of its security resources and functions that could be described as an institutional tango between the private sector and civil society. If the state has withdrawn from several areas where other actors are more competitive, it has also assumed new mandates, such as the regulation of private security providers and the coordination of an expanding constellation of actors in the field of security. Only the state, through its ability to act for the common good, is capable of dealing with these conflicting interests. But in order to do so, it will need to appreciate the scope of the changes described above and will have to relinquish its centralized approach. Faced with a plurality of actors, it must learn to diversify its governance toolbox for the security of all.

References

Agamben, G. (2003). *State of exception* (K. Attell, Trans.). Chicago: University of Chicago Press.

Alain, M. (2001). The trapeze artist and the ground crew: Police cooperation and intelligence exchange mechanisms in Europe and North America. A comparative empirical study. *Policing and Society, 11*(1), 1–27.

Ayling, J., & Grabosky, P. (2006a). Policing by command: Enhancing law enforcement capacity through coercion. *Law & Policy, 28*(4), 417–440.

Ayling, J., & Grabosky, P. (2006b). When police go shopping. *Policing: An International Journal of Police Strategies & Management, 29*(4), 665–690.

Ayres, I., & Levitt, S. (1997). *Measuring positive externalities from unobservable victim precaution: An empirical analysis of Lojack.* Cambridge, MA: National Bureau of Economic Research.

Bayley, D., & Shearing, C. (2001). *The new structure of policing: Description, conceptualization and research agenda.* Washington, DC: National Institute of Justice.

Beck, U. (1992). *Risk society: Towards a new modernity.* London: Sage.

Bennett, T. (1990). *Evaluating neighbourhood watch.* Aldershot, UK: Gower.

Bennett, C. (2005). What happens when you book an airline ticket? The collection and processing of passenger data post-9/11. In E. Zureik & M. Salter (Eds.), *Global surveillance and policing: Borders, security, identity* (pp. 113–138). Cullompton, UK: Willan.

Blair, I. (1998, July 16). *The governance of security: Where do the police fit into policing?* Speech to the annual conference of the Association Chief Police Officers, Birmingham, UK.

Bourdieu, P. (1986). The forms of capital. In J. Richardson (Ed.), *Handbook of theory and research for the sociology of education* (pp. 241–258). New York: Greenwood Press.

Braithwaite, J. (2000). The new regulatory state and the transformation of criminology. *The British Journal of Criminology, 40*(2), 222–238.

Brodeur, J.-P. (2003). *Les visages de la police.* Montreal: PUM.

Burbidge, S. (2005). The governance deficit: Reflections on the future of public and private policing in Canada. *Canadian Journal of Criminology and Criminal Justice, 47*(1), 63–86.

Burris, S. (2006). From security to health. In J. Wood & B. Dupont (Eds.), *Democracy, society and the governance of security* (pp. 196–216). Cambridge: Cambridge University Press.

Clapaud, A. (2003, December 30). La prolifération programmée des radars automatiques. *01 Réseaux*, retrieved February 22, 2007, from http://www.01net.com/article/227107.html.

Cornes, R., & Sandler, T. (1996). *The theory of externalities, public goods and club goods.* (2nd ed.). Cambridge: Cambridge University Press.

Crawford, A. (1997). *The local governance of crime: Appeals to community and partnership.* Oxford: Clarendon Press.

Crawford, A., Lister, S., Blackburn, S., & Burnett, J. (2005). *Plural policing: The mixed economy of visible patrols in England and Wales*. Bristol, UK: The Policy Press.

Crawford, A., & Lister, S. (2006). Additional security patrols in residential areas: Notes from the marketplace. *Policing & Society*, 16(2), 164–188.

Crawford, A. (2006). Policing and security as 'club goods': The new enclosures? In J. Wood & B. Dupont (Eds.), *Democracy, society and the governance of security* (pp. 111–138). Cambridge: Cambridge University Press.

Cunningham, W., & Taylor, T. (1985). *The Hallcrest report: Private security and police in America*. Portland, OR: Chancellor Press.

Decorte, T., Van Laethem, W., & Van Outrive, L. (1999). Des tâches policières privatisées à une police grise. In J. Shapland & L. Van Outrive (Eds.), *Police et sécurité: Contrôle social et interaction public-privé* (pp. 71–100). Paris: L'Harmattan.

Deflem, M. (2002). *Policing world society: Historical foundations of international police cooperation*. Oxford: Oxford University Press.

Department of Justice Victoria. (2004, November 29). *History of safety cameras in Victoria*. Retrieved February 22, 2007, from http://www.justice.vic.gov.au/

De Waard, J. (1999). The private security industry in international perspective. *European Journal on Criminal Policy and Research*, 7(2), 143–174.

Doyle, A. (2003). *Arresting images: Crime and policing in front of the television camera*. Toronto: University of Toronto Press.

Dupont, B., Grabosky, P., & Shearing, C. (2003). The governance of security in weak and failing states. *Criminal Justice*, 3(4), 331–349.

Dupont, B, & Pérez, E. (2006). *Les polices au Québec*. Paris: Presses Universitaires de France.

Dupont, B. (2003). The new face of police governance in Australia. *Journal of Australian Studies, 78*, 15–24.

Dupont, B. (2004). Security in the age of networks. *Policing and Society*, 14(1): 76–91.

Dupont, B. (2006). Delivering security through networks: Surveying the relational landscape of security managers in an urban setting. *Crime, Law & Social Change*, 45(3), 165–184.

Emsley, C. (2003). The birth and development of the police. In T. Newburn (Ed.), *Handbook of policing* (pp. 66–83). Cullompton, UK: Willan.

Erickson, B. (2001). Good networks and good jobs: The value of social capital to employers and employees. In N. Lin, K. Cook & R. Burt, *Social capital: Theory and research* (pp. 127–158). New York: Aldine de Gruyter.

Ericson, R., Baranek, P., & Chan, J. (1989). *Negotiating control: A study of news sources*. Toronto: University of Toronto Press.

Ericson, R., & Haggerty, K. (1997). *Policing the risk society*. Oxford: Clarendon Press.

Espeland, W. (1998). *The struggle for water: Politics, rationality and identity in the American Southwest*. Chicago: University of Chicago Press.

Fillieule, O., & Jobard, F. (1998). The policing of protest in France: Toward a model of protest policing. In D. Della Porta & H. Reiter (Eds.), *Policing protest: The control of mass demonstrations in Western democracies* (pp. 70–90). Minneapolis: University of Minnesota Press.

Finnane, M. (1994). *Police and government*. Melbourne: Oxford University Press.

Finnane, M. (2002). *When police unionise*. Sydney: The Federation Press.

Fleming, J., & Rhodes, R. A. W. (2005). Bureaucracy, contracts and networks: The unholy Trinity and the police. *Australian and New Zealand Journal of Criminology*, 38(2), 192–205.

Forcese, D. (1999). *Policing Canadian society*. Scarborough, ON: Prentice Hall.

Gambetta, D. (1993). *The Sicilian mafia: The business of private protection*. Cambridge, MA: Harvard University Press.

Gans, J. (2000). Privately paid public policing: Law and practice. *Policing and Society, 10*(2), 183–206.

Gill, M., & Mawby, R. (1990). *Volunteers in the criminal justice system*. Milton Keynes, UK: Open University Press.

Grabosky, P. (2004). Toward a theory of public/private interaction in policing. In J. McCord (Ed.), *Beyond empiricism: Institutions and intentions in the study of crime* (pp. 69–82). Piscataway, NJ: Transaction Books.

Huey, L., Ericson, R., & Haggerty, K. (2005). Policing fantasy city. In D. Cooley (Ed.), *Re-imagining policing in Canada* (pp. 140–208). Toronto: University of Toronto Press.

Independent Commission on Policing for Northern Ireland (1999). *A new beginning: Policing in Northern Ireland*. Belfast: ICPNI.

Johnston, L., & Shearing, C. (2003). *Governing security: Explorations in policing and justice*. London: Routledge.

Johnston, L. (2006). Transnational security governance. In J. Wood & B. Dupont (Eds.), *Democracy, society and the governance of security* (pp. 33–51). Cambridge: Cambridge University Press.

Kalifa, D. (2000). *Naissance de la police privée: Détectives et agences de recherche en France 1832–1942*. Paris: Plon.

Kempa, M., & Johnston, L. (2005). Challenges and prospects for the development of inclusive plural policing in Britain: Overcoming political and conceptual obstacles. *The Australian and New Zealand Journal of Criminology, 38*(2): 181–191.

Kraska, P., & Kappeler, V. (1997). Militarizing American police: The rise and normalization of paramilitary units. *Social Problems, 44*(1), 1–18.

Law Commission of Canada. (2002). *In search of security: The roles of public police and private agencies*. Ottawa: LCC.

Law Commission of Canada. (2006). *In search of security: The future of policing in Canada*. Ottawa: LCC.

Laycock, G. (2004). The UK car theft index: An example of government leverage. In M. Maxfield & R. Clarke (Eds.), *Understanding and preventing car theft* (pp. 25–44). Cullompton, UK: Willan.

Leishman, F., Cope, S., & Starie, P. (1996). Reinventing and restructuring: Towards a 'new policing order.' In F. Leishman, B. Loveday & S. P. Savage (Eds.), *Core issues in policing* (pp. 9–25). Harlow, UK: Longman.

Lemieux, F., & Sauvêtre, N. (Forthcoming). Incivilities: The representations and reactions of French public housing residents in Montreal city. In J. Mosher & J. Brockman (Eds.), *Creating crime through law-in-action*. Vancouver: UBC Press.

Lichtblau, E., & Risen, J. (2006, June 23). Bank data sifted in secret by U.S. to block terror. *The New York Times*, p. A1.

Lippert, R., & O'Connor, D. (2006). Security intelligence networks and the transformation of contract private security. *Policing & Society, 16*(1), 50–66.

Loader, I. (1999). Consumer culture and the commodification of policing and security. *Sociology, 33*(2), 373–392.

Loader, I., & Walker, N. (2006). Necessary virtues: The legitimate place of the state in the production of security. In J. Wood & B. Dupont (Eds.), *Democracy, society and the governance of security* (pp. 165–195). Cambridge: Cambridge University Press.

Manning, P. (2006). Two cases of American anti-terrorism. In J. Wood & B. Dupont (Eds.), *Democracy, society and the governance of security* (pp. 52–85). Cambridge: Cambridge University Press.

Marquis, G. (1993). *Policing Canada's century.* Toronto: University of Toronto Press.

Mauss, M. (1967). *The gift: Forms and functions of exchange in archaic societies.* New York: Norton.

Mazerolle, L., & Ransley, J. (2005). *Third party policing.* Cambridge: Cambridge University Press.

McConville, M., & Shepherd, D. (1992). *Watching police, watching communities.* London: Routledge.

McLaughlin, E., & Murji, K. (1997). The future lasts a long time: Public policework and the managerialist paradox. In P. Francis, P. Davies, & V. Jupp (Eds.), *Policing futures: The police, law enforcement and the twenty-first century* (pp. 80–103). London: Macmillan.

Morn, F. (1982). *The eye that never sleeps: A history of the Pinkerton National Detective Agency.* Bloomington, IN: Indiana University Press.

Murphy, C. (2002). *The rationalization of Canadian public policing: A study of the impact and implications of resource limits and market strategies.* Ottawa: The Police Futures Group.

Newburn, T. (2001). The commodification of policing: Security networks in the late modern city. *Urban Studies, 38*(5–6), 829–848.

Ocqueteau, F. (2004). *Polices entre État et marché.* Paris: Les Presses de Science Po.

O'Connor, D. (2006). *A new review mechanism for the RCMP's national security activities.* Ottawa: Commission of Inquiry into the Actions of Canadian Officials in Relation to Maher Arar.

O'Reilly, C., & Ellison, G. (2006). Eye spy private high. *British Journal of Criminology, 46*(4), 641–660.

Osborne, D., & Gaebler, T. (1992). *Reinventing government.* Reading: Addison-Wesley.

Pierre, J., & Peter, B. G. (2000). *Governance, politics and the state.* London: Macmillan.

Reiss, A. (1988). *Private employment of public police.* Washington, DC: National Institute of Justice.

Rhodes, R. (1997). *Understanding governance: Policy networks, governance, reflexivity and accountability.* Maidenhead, UK: Open University Press.

Rhodes, R. (2006). The sour laws of network governance. In J. Fleming & J. Wood (Eds.), *Fighting crime together: The challenges of policing & security networks* (pp. 15–34). Sydney: University of New South Wales Press.

Rigakos, G. (2002). *The new parapolice: Risk markets and commodified social control.* Toronto: University of Toronto Press.

Rigakos, G. (2005). Beyond public-private: Towards a new typology of policing. In D. Cooley (Ed.), *Re-imagining policing in Canada* (pp. 260–319). Toronto: University of Toronto Press.

Roberg, R., & Kuykendall, J. (1997). *Police management.* (2nd ed.). Los Angeles: Roxbury.

Roché, S. (2004). La métropolisation et la privatisation de la sécurité en France: Quel avenir pour les acteurs publics de la sécurité? In S. Roché (Ed.), *Réformer la police et la sécurité: Les nouvelles tendances en Europe et aux Etats-Unis* (pp. 241–265). Paris: Odile Jacob.

Rose, N. (2000). Government and control. *The British Journal of Criminology, 40*(2), 321–339.

Rush, C., & Leeder, J. (2007, January 6). Flood of false alarms plagues police. *The Toronto Star*, retrieved February 25, 2007, from http://www.thestar.com/printArticle/168458.

Sanders, T. (2005). Rise of the rent-a-cop: Private security in Canada, 1991–2001. *Canadian Journal of Criminology and Criminal Justice, 47*(1), 175–190.

Shearing, C., & Stenning, P. (1981). Modern private security: Its growth and implications. In M. Tonry & N. Morris, *Crime and justice: An annual review of research* (pp. 193–245). Chicago: University of Chicago Press.

Shearing, C., & Wood, J. (2003). Governing security for common goods. *International Journal of the Sociology of Law, 31*(3), 205–225.

Sheptycki, J. (2004). Organisational pathologies in police intelligence systems. *European Journal of Criminology, 1*(3): 307–332.

Singer, P. (2003). *Corporate warriors: The rise of the privatized military industry.* Ithaca, NY: Cornell University Press.

Skogan, W., & Hartnett, S. (1997). *Community policing, Chicago style.* New York: Oxford University Press.

Stenning, P. (2000). Powers and accountability of the private police. *European Journal on Criminal Policy and Research, 8*(3), 325–352.

The Economist. (2007, January 6). Highway robbery. *The Economist, 382*(8510), 36.

Tilly, C. (2005). *Trust and rule.* Cambridge: Cambridge University Press.

Varese, F. (2001). *The Russian mafia: Private protection in a new market economy.* Oxford: Oxford University Press.

Volkov, V. (2002). *Violent entrepreneurs: The use of force in the making of Russian capitalism.* Ithaca, NY: Cornell University Press.

Wait, P. (2006, May 22). Too much for NSA to mine? *Government Computer News.* Retrieved February 19, 2007, from http://www.gcn.com/print/25_13/40827-1.html.

Williams, J. (2005). Reflections on the private versus public policing of economic crime. *The British Journal of Criminology, 45*(3), 316–339.

Zedner, L. (2006). Policing before and after the police: The historical antecedents of contemporary crime control. *British Journal of Criminology, 46*(1), 78–96.

CHAPTER 13

"Speaking for the Dead"

Forensic Science and Wrongful Convictions[1]

Kirsten Kramar, University of Winnipeg

Judge: but we've got to verify it legally

To see . . .

Mayor: to see . . .

Judge: if she . . .

Mayor: if she . . .

Judge: is morally, ethically

Munchkin 1: spiritually, physically

Munchkin 2: positively, absolutely

Munchkin men: undeniably and reliably dead

Coroner: as coroner I must aver, ?

I thoroughly examined her . . . ?

and she's not only merely dead,

but really most sincerely dead.

The Wizard of Oz (1939)

This scene from *The Wizard of Oz* portrays the citizens of Oz appealing to coronial expertise. By examining the crushed body of the Wicked Witch of the East, the coroner confirms for the public her untimely accidental death. Only when he officially declares her death, underscored by the production of an oversized "Certificate of Death," is Dorothy free from her fear of retaliation by the witch. Ding, dong, the witch is dead . . .

How should we understand the work of the coroners and their mobilization of forensic-scientific expertise in relation to the criminal justice system's need to categorize and explain deaths? Despite the endless cultural depictions of forensic scientists as mediators of truth in television programs such as *CSI: Crime Scene Investigation*, *CSI: Miami*, *CSI: New York* and *Crossing Jordan*, forensic medicine is, in practice, an inexact science.

A sort of forerunner to these morbid programs that fetishize death investigations were public dissections by anatomy professors for public audiences. But, unlike the television programs, public autopsies introduced medical students to the uncertainty of forensic medicine. According to professor Tony Walter:

> Whereas dissection teaches a general knowledge of anatomy, autopsies aim to determine the cause of death of a particular individual. . . . the popular television image of the pathologist as hero (often heroine) scientist who reads the interior of the corpse for the benefit of an otherwise medically untrained society can be very different from what actually goes on at an autopsy. Fox (1979, pp. 68–72) shows how witnessing their first autopsy is, for medical students, a key part of their training in uncertainty. They had expected pathological investigation of the corpse to reveal the truth about previously uncertain diagnoses but discover only that pathology too is an uncertain science. (2005, p. 395)

Yet there is perhaps an assumption on the part of judges, not unlike that of Dorothy and the Munchkins, or of the fans of *CSI*, that the sorts of evidence forensic experts provide, first to the Crown and then to the court, are more objective and scientific than their discipline can deliver, particularly in regard to infant deaths.

In this chapter, I argue that forensic scientific expertise enjoys a unique privilege in relation to the courts and the broader public. This privilege is linked to the rise in the "science of the criminal" developed throughout the 19th century (Garland, 1992, 1997). This special authority of science provides forensic experts with the opportunity to mobilize particular ideas about culpability which

---

1 This is an abridged and revised version of a paper that appeared in the *Canadian Journal of Criminology and Criminal Justice*.

have come into play in recent wrongful accusations of and convictions for murder in Ontario, especially some involving working-class mothers and caregivers.

WRONGFUL PROSECUTION AND CONVICTION IN CASES INVOLVING BABIES

William Mullins-Johnson was recently released on bail after being incarcerated for twelve and a half years following his conviction for the rape and murder of his 4-year-old niece. His murder conviction rested partly on the expert testimony of forensic pathologist Dr. Charles Smith (Rusk, 2005, p. A17). Smith provided evidence that the 4-year-old victim has been raped and murdered. But Dr. Michael Pollanen, Ontario's chief forensic pathologist who later reviewed the findings, concluded otherwise. According to *The Globe and Mail:*

> Valin was not raped before she died. The enlarged anus that Dr. Smith and two other doctors cited as evidence of abuse was a natural occurrence that resulted from the relaxing of muscles after death, . . . and the genital bruising taken as evidence of abuse, as well as the bruising on the neck that led the doctors to conclude she was strangled or smothered, were the result of blood pooling in those areas after death. (Friesen, 2005, p. A14)

Throughout his years in prison, Mullins-Johnson maintained his innocence, and his case eventually came to the attention of the Association in Defence of the Wrongfully Convicted (AIDWYC). When it was discovered that Smith had mishandled 12-year-old tissue samples (later found in an envelope on his desk) the Hospital for Sick Children commenced a review of his work. Mullins-Johnson was released after more than a decade in prison because Smith's conclusions in a number of other cases came under scrutiny when defence counsel, judges, expert witness and criminologists drew attention to his zealous suspicion of working-class single mothers and caregivers.

Louise Reynolds spent three and a half years in pretrial detention pending her trial for the second-degree murder of her 7-year-old daughter in 1997. The murder charge laid against Reynolds stemmed largely from the interpretation of forensic evidence provided to the Crown by Smith. Smith submitted that Reynolds had stabbed her daughter 82 times with a pair of scissors (Makin, 2005a, p. A5) and that she had done so because she was angry at her daughter for having head lice. It was not until 2001 that the murder charge was dropped following the submission of a forensic interpretation at odds with that provided by Smith and his colleague, Dr. Wood. Dr. John Ferris, an Australian forensic pathologist hired by Reynolds's defence lawyers, corroborated Reynolds's statement that the little girl had been attacked by a friend's pit bull (Shephard, 2001, p. A10).[2] Dr. David Chaisson reached a similar conclusion after exhuming the child's body to conduct another autopsy. Furthermore, Dr. Steven Symes, an expert in tool marks on human bones, concluded that all the marks were from dog bites except for six or seven that had been made by a sharp knife or scalpel and a few that were possible scrape marks from a knife. No weapon was ever found at Reynolds's home. In the face of mounting contradictory evidence, Smith

---

2   The expert was also involved in the infamous Australian case involving the death of Azaria Chamberlain at Ayers Rock, Australia, in 1980. Her mother, Lindy Chamberlain, was accused of her murder on the basis of a coroner's inquest. Chamberlain claimed that her 9-week-old baby had been snatched and eaten by a dingo in the 1980s.

altered his conclusion and conceded that the marks could have been dog bites (Canadian Press Newswire, 2001).

While Reynolds was in prison, Children's Aid put her youngest daughter, Kaitlyn, up for adoption. Because the child was only 3 years old at the time of the adoption, she did not remember her mother 3 years later when the charges were dropped.

In 2001, Reynolds filed a seven-million-dollar lawsuit against the provincial authorities for being wrongly accused of killing her daughter (Appleby, 2001, p. A5). In November 2005, the AIDWC demanded a review of all of Smith's cases that had resulted in convictions and that Ontario Attorney General Michael Bryant call a public inquiry into the Smith affair (Rusk, 2005, p. A17). In a highly unusual move on the part of the Ontario courts, Reynolds was recently given permission to sue Smith personally for his allegations against her.

Similarly, Brenda Waudby was charged by police in 1997 for killing her daughter, Jenna, on the basis of Smith's forensic evidence. At the time of the wrongful accusation, Brenda Waudby was a single mother who had had problems with cocaine addiction. The Toronto police infiltrated the Narcotics Anonymous group attended by Waudby posing as a friend in order to gather evidence to charge her with the murder of her daughter. It was later discovered that Smith had hidden a pubic hair that he found on Jenna Waudby's body in his shirt pocket and later in his desk drawer. It is significant to note that it was only once this deceit was discovered that the coroner's office announced a review of Smith's autopsy findings, which were used as evidence of culpability by the Crown. The teenaged babysitter Waudby had hired later confessed to killing Jenna.

This shocking pattern of behaviour among police, the Office of the Chief Coroner for Ontario and Charles Smith in particular had begun many years before. In 1991, Ontario provincial court judge Patrick Dunn had criticized Smith in his commentary from the bench in a case involving a Timmins, Ontario, girl who was a grade 6 student accused of shaking a baby to death (O'Hara, 2001). Jim Cairns, deputy chief coroner at the time, concluded that the judge did not understand the medical evidence despite the fact that Cairns himself had no forensic training.

A similar pattern of events unfolded in Sudbury, Ontario, when the Ontario chief coroner's office empowered Smith to review the death of Lianne Gagnon's 11-month-old son, Nicolas. Smith exhumed the dead child's body while his own 11-year-old son watched and later concluded on the basis of his autopsy that the baby died from a head injury despite the fact that the police investigation 1 year earlier had ruled out foul play. When the Crown did not lay charges, Smith approached Children's Aid in Sudbury and told them he was certain that Lianne Gagnon (now Lianne Thibault and pregnant with her second child) had killed Nicolas. As a result, Children's Aid workers sought wardship of the unborn child and had Thibault's name placed on a list of known child abusers. After she gave birth to her daughter, Nicole, Thibault was not allowed to be alone with her newborn baby (O'Hara, 2001). Her father, Maurice Gagnon, then began a legal battle that cost him well over $100,000 to prevent his daughter from being charged with murder and to clear her of the allegations made by Smith and the Office of the Chief Coroner for Ontario (O'Hara, 2001).

The William Mullins-Johnson, Louise Reynolds, Brenda Waudby and Lianne Thibault cases of wrongful prosecution and conviction were among at least 44 child death cases that had been sent to Smith for examination by the Ontario chief coroner's office and which became the subject of a public inquiry in Ontario headed by Stephen T. Goudge (for more information on the "Goudge Inquiry," see www.goudgeinquiry.com). In each case, the allegations were based on faulty conclusions derived from forensic evidence provided by Smith, who was empowered to investigate these cases by the Ontario chief coroner's office under the direction of Jim Cairns.

WHAT CAN WE LEARN FROM THESE CASES?

The cases provide the opportunity to examine the effects of clashing epistemological and conceptual frameworks. The material presented in this paper considers what are perhaps unique cases of what one judge described as "tunnel vision" on the part of a forensic expert (Makin, 2005a, p. A5), but one which reflects the broader problems linked to expert medical testimony in these cases. They involved the acceptance of conclusions arrived at by one of Canada's leading forensic-medical experts. Smith was the director of the Ontario Paediatric Forensic Pathology unit at the Hospital for Sick Children in Toronto, and he was empowered by the coroner's office to give testimony in criminal cases involving the deaths of infants. Given its position as both a medical and a legal expert, the Office of the Chief Coroner for Ontario was able to generate authoritative claims on the basis of forensic science alone. Through this activity, a coroner may focus intense humanitarian concern on a social issue such as child abuse homicide. However, when coroners give evidence at trial, they provide the courts with an interpretation of medical evidence and assist in the process of the administration of justice. Acting in this capacity, coroners provide a particular kind of "opinion evidence" because they possess a special kind of expertise that can assist the judge. The forensic expert witness is empowered to "assist" the trier of fact because he or she "possesses special knowledge and experience going beyond that of the trier of fact" (Paciocco & Stuesser, 2005, p. 181). Because reliability is an important factor in assessing the benefit of expert evidence, scientific evidence tends to meet the criteria for admissibility more easily and to be more highly valued by courts than other forms of opinion expert evidence.[3] What is particularly important here is that once the evidence is heard and accepted by a judge, it becomes a legal fact. Once it is a legal fact, it becomes practically unassailable.

LOOKING BEYOND THE AUTOPSY

When forensic experts arrive at a cause of death, it must be understood that they do so with special attention to extramedical and circumstantial evidence. In cases of the "sudden unexplained death" of babies, forensic experts will intentionally look beyond the biological markers on the body (such as petechial hemorrhage) to the social and economic familial circumstances within which the babies were raised.[4] Since the early 1980s (and perhaps even earlier) forensic science instruction manuals (texts) training pathologists on unexplained infant deaths instructs the student to look well beyond their medical autopsy results

---

3   The test for admissibility of expert opinion evidence was established by the Supreme Court of Canada in *R v. Mohan* [1994] 2 SCR 9. Expert opinion evidence does not have to be "scientific" in order to be of benefit to the judge—the criteria spelled out by the court focus on questions such as the capacity of the expert to explain matters that might be outside the knowledge or experience of the trier of fact, the reliability of the expert's evidence, the expert's ability to demonstrate that he or she possesses relevant expertise and the absence of other exclusionary rules.

4   According to Statistics Canada (2002), SIDS is the leading cause of postneonatal death in Canada. In 1999, 144 deaths, or 26% of all postneonatal deaths, were caused by SIDS.

to the social and familial circumstances of the victims and their parents by incorporating a thorough crime scene investigation and reconstruction into their final decisions as to cause of death (Kirschner, 1997, pp. 248–295). The professional literature provides these instructions precisely because autopsy results on otherwise healthy infants are usually completely negative (Li, Fowler, Liu, Ripple, Lambros & Smialek, 2005), making the determination of whether asphyxia from a compromised airway is the cause of death very, very difficult. This is what leads to the sudden infant death syndrome (SIDS), or sudden unexpected death syndrome (SUDS) and now sudden unexpected death at infancy (SUDI) finding at autopsy which frustrates the forensic advocate looking to offer police evidence of a homicide. Forensic pathologists are instructed, therefore, to look "beyond" the autopsy, yet they are not trained in criminology, social work or sociology. In my view, the work of the forensic expert is to provide medical evidence as to cause of death based on their medical training. Finally, the forensic science practice of incorporating extramedical factors, coupled with the professional advocacy role adopted by the coroner, is surely intensified when the victims are the babies of single working-class mothers (see Chen, 2003; Kramar, 2005).

SPEAKING FOR THE DEAD

Coroners see themselves as death-cause experts for public safety. In that regard, they see themselves as advocates for the victim and protectors of the public. This is best illustrated by the motto of the coroner: "We speak for the dead to protect the living." Coroners' understanding of themselves as experts on death risks in the service of the "living" public is also expressed in the mission statement of the Ontario office:

> The office of the chief coroner for Ontario serves the living through high quality death investigations and inquests to ensure that no death will be overlooked, concealed or ignored. The findings are used to generate recommendations to help improve public safety and prevent deaths in similar circumstances. (Ontario, 2004)

The Ontario Centre for Forensic Science, which offers specialized forensic analysis and conducts autopsies for the chief coroner's office of Ontario, describes its own mandate as "science for justice" (Ontario, 2004). It is because coroners view themselves as advocates for the dead in the service of the living that they are often led to actively campaign *as interested medical experts* for social and political change through policy recommendations and in criminal courts of law. In fact, the *Coroners Act* mandates the coroner to "bring the findings and recommendations of coroners' juries to the attention of appropriate persons, agencies and ministries of government."[5] Therefore, when there is an infant death and the coroner believes there are suspicious circumstances, the office of the coroner cooperates with a variety of professionals, including social workers, police, doctors and lawyers to mount a seamless prosecution. The full resources of the state are mobilized to achieve a conviction for murder, with the key suspects being mothers. A review of the cases handled by the chief coroner's office of Ontario reveals that there is little doubt that a key feature in the successful articulation of the wrongful accusations is the preexisting suspicion within the broader community that mothers especially are the culprits when infants and children die (Kramar, 2005).

---

5 *Coroners Act,* R.S.O. 1990, c. C.37, s. 4 (1).

By claiming to have discovered, through forensic science, the proximate cause of death of babies and children, the coroner directed police attention toward the parents and care-givers of the babies and children they deemed to have been the victims of unmistakable foul play (Kramar, 2005). The death investigators at the Ontario chief coroner's office were concerned that unexplained causes of death (SIDS, SUDS or SUDI) were masking inten-tional homicides by mothers allowing them to "get away with" murder. In that context, many, if not all, cases of child death came to be understood as the outcome of sustained child abuse murder because the coroner was able to redirect the professional discourse through the use of forensic medical knowledge in the form of the autopsy. Once stereotyp-ical ideas about parental brutality are transformed into medico-legal discourse, they acquire the legitimate authority which grounds wrongful accusations and convictions for infant and child murder (see also Naughton, 2005). They were able to achieve this authority and articulate the position in courts of law despite there being no requirement that deputy chief and chief coroners have any formal forensic science training.

MEDICAL EXPERTISE AND WRONGFUL CONVICTION IN ENGLAND

These Canadian cases are not isolated events that involve medical experts providing tes-timony in courts. The Canadian cases mirror similar events in England, where expert medical testimony provided by paediatrician and self-described child abuse expert Sir Professor Roy Meadow resulted in the wrongful convictions. Three women in particular whose babies died unexpectedly from sudden unexplained infant death, Angela Cannings, Sally Clark and Trupti Patel, were later cleared. In all three cases in Britain, cot death (as it was then called) was the cause of the infants' deaths. These cases reveal a similar pattern of suspicion directed at women in which preexisting prejudice toward women is mobilized through science. Clark was given two life sentences for the murder of her two sons in November 1999 after Meadow testified that the odds of two innocent infant deaths occurring in a family were akin to "winning the lottery," and the chance of two babies dying of cot death within an affluent family was "one in 73 million" (McCarthy, 2005, p. 14).

A paediatrician by training, Meadow established himself as an expert in child abuse when he published an article in *The Lancet* in 1977 describing a condition in women known as "Munchausen syndrome by proxy." This is a form of abuse in which mothers induce illness in their children in order to gain attention for themselves,[6] which has been described as a phoney diagnostic category (Allison & Roberts, 1998). Again, this led certain medical and legal authorities to believe that the babies may have been murdered because of the widespread belief, beginning in the mid-1980s when the child abuse detec-tion movement was at its height, that categories such as SIDS mask intentional homicide. In part, the Munchausen phenomenon is linked to SIDS because of an article published in the 1960s that argued that SIDS was a medical condition passed on by the parents to children. That research was based on the supposed SIDS deaths of the children of Waneta Hoyt in the state of New York. She was subsequently discovered to have killed four biological children and was "diagnosed" as suffering from the newly minted medical

---

6   Meadow, R. (1977, August 13). Munchausen syndrome by proxy: The hinterland of child abuse. *The Lancet, 2*(8033). 343–345.

condition of Munchausen syndrome by proxy.[7] The discovery discredited the legitimacy of unexplained infant death despite the fact that Hoyt is the sole woman to have been accused and convicted for murder after doctors inaccurately concluded that her children died of unexplained causes.

Conclusion

Each of the wrongful prosecutions and convictions is partly a product of clashing epistemological assumptions informing legal and medical-scientific discourses and practitioners about the role of expert forensic medical evidence. Forensic science provides the opportunity for the deployment of extramedical theories about mothers in pseudoscientific terms, but this often goes unnoticed and unchallenged by judges and counsel. More than this, forensic scientific experts often rely on their prejudices to construction conclusions as to cause of death, particularly when they are unable to determine the exact cause of death from the medical evidence. In the Canadian cases, Lianne Thibault, Louise Reynolds, Brenda Waudby and William Mullins-Johnson and others were subject to intensive investigation and prosecution by the authorities on the basis of existing suspicion toward mothers and caregivers buttressed by false autopsy evidence provided by one forensic pathologist who was considered by the Office of the Chief Coroner for Ontario to be the leading expert in paediatric forensics. When the forensic science practice of incorporating extramedical and circumstantial assumptions into their scientific cause of death determinations is injected into a criminal court of law engaged in evidentiary fact finding, the result may be the unlawful conviction of innocent parents and caregivers, who are primarily women, because some forensic experts have been seen to be acting in their role as advocate for the victim—speaking for the dead—rather than a disinterested scientific expert.

References

Allison, D. B., & Roberts, M. S. (1998). Disordered mother or disordered diagnosis? Munchausen by proxy syndrome. London: The Analytic Press.

Appleby, T. (2001, February 9). Woman sues Kingston police. *The Globe and Mail*, Toronto edition, p. A5.

Caffey, J. (1946). Multiple fractures in the long bones of infants suffering from chronic subdural hematoma. *American Journal of Radiology, 56,* 163–173.

Canadian Press Newswire. (2001, February 25). Police defend investigation into child's death despite dropped charges. *Canadian Business and Current Affairs*.

Chen, X. (2003). Constituting dangerous parents through the spectre of child death: A critique of child protection restructuring in Ontario. In D. Brock (Ed.), *Making normal: Social regulation in Canada*. Toronto: Thomson Nelson.

Firstman R., & Talan, J. (1997). *The death of innocents: A true story of murder, medicine and high-stakes science.* New York: Bantam Books.

Foucault, M. (1991). Governmentality. In Gordon Burchell, Colin Gordon, & Paul Miller (Eds.), *The Foucault effect: Studies in governmentality*. Chicago: University of Chicago Press.

---

7   See Firstman and Talan (1997) in which the case of Waneta Hoyt is chronicled to show that the deaths of her five children from sudden infant death syndrome were actually missed murders perpetrated by Hoyt, who was later diagnosed with Munchausen syndrome by proxy.

Friesen, J. (2005, September 14). I prayed for this every night. *The Globe and Mail*, Prairie edition, pp. A1, A14.

Garland, D. (1992). Criminological knowledge and its relation to power: Foucault's genealogy and criminology. *British Journal of Criminology, 32*(4), 403–422.

Garland, D. (1997). Governmentality and the problem of crime: Foucault, criminology, sociology. *Theoretical Criminology*, 1(2), 173–214.

Gordon, C. (1991). Governmental rationality: An introduction. In Gordon Burchell, Colin Gordon & Paul Miller (Eds.), *The Foucault effect: Studies in governmentality*. Chicago: University of Chicago Press.

Greenland, C. (1987). *Preventing CAN deaths: An international study of deaths due to child abuse and neglect*. London: Tavistock.

Janakiram, P., & Gupta, A. (2003). Forensic pathology: Unraveling the mysteries of death. *McMaster University Medical Journal, 1*(1), 55–56.

Johnson-McGrath, J. (1995). Speaking for the dead: Forensic pathologists and criminal justice in the United States. *Science, Technology, & Human Values, 20*(4), 438–459.

Kirschner, R. H. (1997). The pathology of child abuse. In M. E. Helfer, R. S. Kempe, & R. D. Krugman (Eds.), *The battered child* (5th ed.). Chicago: University of Chicago Press.

Kramar, K. J. (2005). *Unwilling mothers, unwanted babies: Infanticide in Canada*. Vancouver: UBC Press.

Laqueur, T. W. (1989). Bodies, details, and the humanitarian narrative. In Linda Hunt (Ed.), *The new cultural history*. Berkeley, CA: University of California Press.

Li, L., Fowler, D., Lu, L., Ripple, M. G. Lambros, Z., & Smialek, J. E. (2005). Investigation of sudden infant deaths in the state of Maryland (1990–2000). *Forensic Science International, 148*, 85–92.

Makin, K. (2005a, April 22). MD's troubles case cloud over 25 child-death cases. *The Globe and Mail*, Prairie edition, pp. A1 and A5.

Makin, K. (2005b, April 23). Review infant autopsies, criminologist urges. *The Globe and Mail*, Prairie edition, p. A11.

Marshall, D. T. (1991). *Canadian law of inquests*. (2nd ed.). Toronto: Carswell.

Marland, H. (2002). Getting away with murder? Puerperal insanity, infanticide and the defence plea. In Mark Jackson (Ed.), *Infanticide: Historical perspectives on child murder and concealment 1550–2000*. Burlington, VT: Ashgate.

Manitoba. Minister of Justice. (2000). *The role of the chief medical examiner's office*. Retrieved from http://www.gov.mb.ca/justice/about/chief.html

McCarthy, M. (2005, July 14). Meadow failed in his duty as expert witness, GMC rules. *The Independent*, p. 14.

Naughton, M. (2005). 'Evidence-based policy' and the government of the criminal justice system - Only if the evidence fits! *Critical Social Policy, 25*(1), 47–69.

O'Hara, J. (2001, May 14). Dead wrong. *Maclean's, 114*(20), 54–59.

Ontario. Ministry of Community Safety and Correctional Service, Office of the Chief Coroner. (2004). *Office of the chief coroner*. Toronto: Queen's Printer for Ontario.

Paciocco, D. M., & Stuesser, L. (2005). *The law of evidence*. (4th ed.). Toronto: Irwin Law.

Rusk, J. (2005, November 2). Child pathologist's work under review: Experts to examine 44 homicide and criminally suspicious cases handled by former Ontario doctor. *The Globe and Mail*, Prairie edition, p. A17.

Shephard, M. (2001, January 26). Dog may have killed 7-year-old, experts say; murder charge dropped against Kingston mom. *The Cambridge Reporter*, p. A10.

Statistics Canada. (2002). *Mortality—summary list of causes 1999*. Ottawa: Health Statistics Division, catalogue no. 84F0Z09XPE.

U.S. Department of Health and Human Services, Centers for Disease Control (2001). *An unsystematic system: Coroners vs. medical examiners*. Washington, DC: Centers for Disease Control.

U.S. Department of Health and Human Services, National Institutes of Health, National Library of Medicine. (2006). *Visible proofs: Forensic views of the body*. Retrieved from http://www.nlm.nih.gov/exhibition/visibleproofs/

Valverde, M. (2003). Law's dream of a common knowledge. Princeton, NJ: Princeton University Press.

Walter, T. (2005). Mediator deathwork. *Death Studies, 29,* 383–412.

Cases

R v. Mohan [1994] 2 SCR 9

CHAPTER 14

Talking Trash with the Supreme Court of Canada:

The Reasonable Expectation of Privacy under the *Charter*

Richard Jochelson, University of Winnipeg

INTRODUCTION

You are reading scholarship written by a legal scholar. Let us make no mistake that the author of this piece (me!) is writing about the formal legal apparati of the state. In this chapter, I am not concerned with the Foucauldian notions of "power through the capillaries" (Litowitz, 1997, p. 74; Foucault, 1980, p. 102). Rather, the work you are about to read is power rendered from a main artery of regulation—the Supreme Court of Canada. Further, you will find me referring to technologies of power in the most literal sense—for what could be, at first blush, a more "rational, practical and regulatory technology" (Valverde, Levi, Shearing, Condon, & O'Malley, 1999) than the legal tests of the Supreme Court of Canada itself.

In this chapter we find ourselves squarely within the neoliberal apparatus—in the lion's den— gnawing at the bones of contention that are at stake in the guise of neoliberal values in neoliberal institutions. That being said, these bones of contention remain profoundly important, if nothing else, because the decisions rendered from the Supreme Court of Canada have final and precedential impact on all of Canada and in the context of criminal justice have the potential to impact upon whatever liberty interests the system claims that a criminal defendant possesses.

With these admissions in place, let us zone in on our topic—trash! The mundane and often unhygienic bag of refuse you leave at your curb has recently become of interest to the Supreme Court of Canada, and its recent adjudication over the issue of trash has profound implications for the liberal construction of privacy in the millennial era. Whether or not one believes that privacy is a value in a neoliberal state ought not distract us from the continued encroachments that the high court allows law enforcement in the wake of Court's approach to trash—most recently in the *R. v. Patrick* (2009) case.

The *Patrick* case is a capstone on a recent canon of Supreme Court cases since 2004 that have revisited the threshold issue for determining whether or not an accused should be protected from unreasonable searches and seizures at the hands of law enforcement—a protection under section 8 of the *Canadian Charter of Rights and Freedoms*. This threshold issue is governed by the seemingly simple question of whether an accused is entitled to a reasonable expectation of privacy. If no expectation of privacy exists, police may embark upon relatively unconstrained searches.

In the forthcoming pages we will explore how the Court's approach to this threshold issue of privacy has changed over the past 5 years. This will in turn allow us to consider how the judicial constitutional philosophy toward police powers may have also subsequently changed. These changes will allow us to conclude that the open textured nature of legal tests, such as the one for a reasonable expectation of privacy, allows for power interests to inhabit those open spaces, and potentially allows for law enforcement values to achieve more prominence in judicial reasoning. The judicial apparatus has developed "technology" (i.e., legal tests) for devolving further discretion to law enforcement—liberal and critical scholars alike ought to be interested.

REVIEWING SOME BASICS

In Chapter 2, Professor Young exposed us to the basics of *Charter*-era search and seizure protections. You learned that the *Charter* is part of the *Constitution* of Canada—the supreme law—and that its guarantee is to ensure that all legislation and governmental action meet its requirements. Yet when it comes to search and seizure, the *Charter* provides minimal textual guidelines. There is little clarity in the original constitutional text (the search and seizure must be "reasonable" under section 8 of the *Charter*), and the constitutional history is such that an original intent of its drafters is difficult to surmise (Stribopoulos, 2005, p. 15; Marin, 2005). For instance, Jean Chrétien, in the drafting process of section 8, explained that the determination of a breach of section 8 of the *Charter* will "have to meet the tests of being reasonable and not being arbitrary"—hardly definitive (Stribopoulos, 2005, p. 15). Others argue that since the French version of section 8 uses the terms "abusif" (abusive) rather than "déraisonnable" (unreasonable), the Court should protect citizens from "abuses of state power" rather than providing an accused with a positive zone of liberty (Genest, 2007, para. 201; Dawe, 1993, p. 61).

The Supreme Court was left then, to give content to the legislative vacuum through its interpretive processes. The Supreme Court's original position on search and seizure after the passing of the *Charter* seemed simple enough. An individual entitled to a reasonable expectation of privacy would be protected against unreasonable searches by police—police would need reasonable grounds and prior authorization, in the form of a search warrant before they could conduct a search (*Hunter v. Southam* 1984, paras. 29, 43). This clarity, though, would soon fade. What seemed like a bright line quickly receded and the Court outlined a "contextual" test for determining whether an accused was even entitled to a reasonable expectation of privacy (Stuart, 1999; Stuart, 1998; Stribopoulos, 1999; Schwartz, 1998).

For instance, in *R. v. Edwards* (1996) the Court outlined a complicated test of context for whether an accused was entitled to a reasonable expectation of privacy.[1] The test was one that involved assessing the totality of the circumstances, including:

  (i)   presence at the time of the search;

  (ii) possession or control of the property or place searched;

  (iii) ownership of the property or place;

  (iv) historical use of the property or item;

  (v)   the ability to regulate access, including the right to admit or exclude others from the place;

  (vi) the existence of a subjective expectation of privacy; and

  (vii) the objective reasonableness of the expectation. (Edwards, para 45)

In *Edwards,* the Court denied an accused a privacy interest in his girlfriend's apartment, a place where he had been storing drugs. Since the accused had no privacy interest in his girlfriend's apartment, police were able to search for the drugs with little constraint and use those drugs as evidence in the criminal trial.

---

1   The issue of reasonable expectation of privacy was also pivotal in *R. v. Colarusso,* [1994] 1 S.C.R. 20 (where blood samples held by a coroner and released to police, nonetheless required Hunter-esque privacy protections), *R. v. Plant,* [1993] 3 S.C.R. 281 [*Plant*] (where computerized electrical consumption records did not trigger the privacy rights of the accused), and *R. v. Wong,* [1990] 3 S.C.R. 36 (where privacy rights of an accused conducting illegal activities in a hotel were affirmed), but *Edwards* represented the Court's first opportunity to delineate a cogent privacy test.

Many critiques of the *Edwards* criteria seemed to focus on factors i–iv, principally because those factors seemed to indicate a discursive turn toward privileging property rights at the expense of personal rights—a strategy that is the linchpin of the American approach to search and seizure (Mackinnon, 2007). However, subsequent cases seemed to suggest a Court that was most concerned with the subjective and objective existence of a reasonable expectation of privacy—this was indicative of a Court willing to adjudicate privacy guarantees in context.

For instance, in *R. v. M.(M. R.)* (1998), where the Court was scrutinizing the searches by public school officials of students, the Court emphasized the factors of subjectivity and objectivity of the expectation of privacy as paramount. These contextual factors allowed the Court to find that a midway point between an absolute privacy guarantee (replete with reasonable and probable grounds and a warrant) and an absent privacy guarantee (with no constitutional protections) could exist. Thus, in the school context, a diminished expectation of privacy existed which could allow school officials to conduct searches without a warrant on the basis of a reasonable suspicion standard (paras. 50, 58). Similar decisions were rendered in the context of Customs Canada searches (*R. v. Monney*, 1999).[2]

2004 AND BEYOND

The move to contextualism achieved a tipping point in *R. v. Tessling* (2004) where the Court analyzed whether the use, over flight, of Forward Looking Infrared (FLIR) cameras, which identified heat waves rising from an accused's home (thus suggesting a drug operation), was a search which violated the accused's privacy rights. Had the court viewed the home as the most sacrosanct of searchable areas, the case would have proven difficult for the Crown. However, the Court was able to reconstruct the way we ought to conceive of privacy in Canada (Pomerance, 2005).

Indeed, in reorienting the reasonable expectation of privacy test toward subjective and objectively held assessments of privacy, the Court went to great lengths to differentiate the property-based American privacy approach. The Court noted that the expectation of privacy may have once been rooted in old common law notions of proprietary interests but that new values had emerged. While "much of the law . . . betray[ed] its early roots in the law of trespass" it was now the case that "as the state's technical capacity for peeking and snooping increased," the "protected sphere of privacy" should be "refined and developed" (*Tessling*, 2004, para. 16). The Court determined that the search in question in this case, through the use of FLIR, was better described as informational in nature: The search in question was "more accurately characterized as an external search for information *about* the home*" rather than being characterized as a search of the home (para. 27). The Court characterized the FLIR search as a search for information only and thus no reasonable expectation of privacy in the heat waves existed; indeed, such searches, according to the Court, were generally less intrusive than searches of the home or person. The Court did,

---

2   Certainly, middle ground protections are now well entrenched, due principally to the ancillary powers test for police powers applied in the cases of *Dedman v. The Queen*, [1985] 2 S.C.R. 2, *R. v. Godoy*, [1999] 1 S.C.R. 311 [*Godoy*], *R. v. Mann*, 2004 SCC 52, [2004] 3 S.C.R. 59. *R. v. Clayton*, 2007 SCC 32 and more generally as searches incident to motor vehicle detention—see *R. v. Ladouceur*, [1990] 1 S.C.R. 1257, *R. v. Hufsky*, [1988] 1 S.C.R. 621; and *R. v. Mellenthin*, [1992] 3 S.C.R. 615. For more on this point see Jochelson, 2008.

however, allow that when searches for information touched on the "biographical core" of an individual (i.e., where very personal information was revealed), more robust privacy protections might be at play (para. 63).[3]

Thus two themes emerged in the Court's jurisprudence, culminating in *Tessling*. First, privacy protections could be more dilute and result in protections that did away with the warrant requirement, requiring only reasonable suspicion. Second, the test for reasonable expectation of privacy was beginning to emphasize progressively more objective assessments that depended on context—for instance, was the search merely informational, and how intrusive was the information revealed by the search? These trends continued through the "sniffer dog" cases, where the Court allowed for the possibilities of sniffer dog searches of baggage without a warrant on a reasonable suspicion standard in schools and in bus stations (*R. v. Kang-Brown, R. v. A.M.*, 2008; Jochelson, 2009).

This move toward contextualism in the construction of privacy protections has more recently been articulated in the *Patrick* case. The facts of *Patrick* were relatively simple. The accused was suspected of operating an ecstasy lab in his home in Calgary. On several occasions, the police reached over the accused's property line to obtain access to the accused's garbage which was at the rear of his property, abutting the rear alleyway. Based on the evidence contained in the garbage, the police obtained a warrant to search the accused's house, which resulted in seizures of more key evidence. Ultimately, the accused was convicted of controlled substances violations, and later he launched an unsuccessful appeal at the Court of Appeal of Alberta. The majority of the Supreme Court concluded that the accused had no subsisting privacy interests in the garbage, and therefore than no section 8 violation of the *Charter* could have occurred (Jochelson, 2009).

In making its decision, the majority of the Court endorsed the use of the *Tessling* indicia in order to analyse the existence of a reasonable expectation of privacy:

1. What was the nature or subject matter of the evidence gathered by the police?

2. Did the appellant have a direct interest in the contents?

3. Did the appellant have a subjective expectation of privacy in the informational content of the garbage?

4. If so, was the expectation objectively reasonable? In this respect, regard must be had to:

   a. the place where the alleged "search" occurred; in particular, did the police trespass on the appellant's property and, if so, what is the impact of such a finding on the privacy analysis?

   b. whether the informational content of the subject matter was in public view;

   c. whether the informational content of the subject matter had been abandoned;

   d. whether such information was already in the hands of third parties; if so, was it subject to an obligation of confidentiality?

   e. whether the police technique was intrusive in relation to the privacy interest;

   f. whether the use of this evidence gathering technique was itself objectively unreasonable;

   g. whether the informational content exposed any intimate details of the appellant's lifestyle, or information of a biographic nature. (*Patrick*, 2009, para. 27)

---

3 For a comprehensive discussion of the paradigmatic shift that *Tessling* represented for technologically advanced investigation techniques I strongly recommend reading the special edition of the *Canadian Journal of Criminology and Criminal Justice,* vol. 50, no. 3 in 2008—see references for details.

At first blush, it is clear that the Court has adopted a framework that is not only multi-variable but which directs the bulk of the analysis toward the constitution of objective criteria of privacy. The message that the Court sends is that privacy is constituted less by what individuals expect than by what a reasonable observer would expect (on the basis of criteria a–g listed above). If there were any doubt as to the Court's privileging of the privacy guarantee to serve the objective inquiry, it can be resolved by the Court's turn in nomenclature. The Court suggests that garbage is not just waste but is a "bag of information" that reveals "what is going on in our homes" (*Patrick*, 2009, para. 30). Here the Court has reconstituted the idea of garbage—garbage is given legal status not by its proprietary connection to its owner, nor by its location on the lot of an accused, but on the basis of what that item tells us about a person. The garbage is constituted as a conduit to observing an individual's behaviour rather than as an emanation from a person or a person's property. This shift to informational construction allows the Court to assert that it is undertaking a decidedly non-American approach to search and seizure law, while at the same time increasing the law enforcement discretion of a searching officer—this provides a moment where the Court can deny the inherent capitalism of ownership under such an approach; ironically, at the same time a neoliberal effect is achieved in the form of increased latitude for law enforcement searches of garbage because garbage is informational, not proprietary, in nature.

The linchpin of the majority's decision turns on the issue of "abandonment" and the notion that a truly abandoned privacy right obfuscates any tenable objectively held reasonable expectation of privacy. The majority's bright line between the existence of the expectation and its abandonment seems to be when the garbage is "placed at or within reach of the lot line" (*Patrick*, 2009, para. 62). If the garbage is placed "on a porch or in a garage or within the immediate vicinity of the dwelling" then a privacy interest may well persist—but when garbage approaches the lot line, the expectation of privacy is abandoned (paras. 62–63). The Court notes that the act of bringing garbage to the lot line is evidence of an accused "acting in a manner inconsistent with the reasonable assertion of a continuing privacy interest" (para. 64). In other words, it is contextual factor to be weighed in the analytical analysis of the objective existence of a reasonably held expectation of privacy. The *Patrick* analysis erodes the privacy right as part of the objective assessment of privacy, and therefore from a territorial perspective, further shrinks the zone of privacy around one's home. The Court uses the following revealing paragraph to justify its conclusion on abandonment:

> Abandonment occurred when the appellant placed his garbage bags for collection in the open container at the back of his property adjacent to the lot line. He had done everything required of him to commit his rubbish to the municipal collection system. The bags were unprotected and within easy reach of anyone walking by in a public alleyway, including street people, bottle pickers, urban foragers, nosey neighbours and mischievous children, not to mention dogs and assorted wildlife, as well as the garbage collectors and the police. (*Patrick*, 2009, para. 55)

Here, the Court seems to be admitting that the way we conceive of our privacy rights has more to do with urban and community disorder rather than any personal or territorial stake we have in an item. It does not require a litany of analytic contortions to imagine that those who live in urban areas, in more impoverished areas or without a home at all, are increasingly likely to have abandoned their privacy rights under such reasoning in comparison to those who live in suburban or gated settings.

It is quite clear that the *Patrick* case is a capstone in the postmillennial adjudication of privacy rights in the context of criminal investigations. What may be more surprising to the initiated reader is how pliable legal doctrines and guarantees can be. Students are schooled on the guarantees of the *Charter*. We believe in such values as equality, freedom of speech and religion, and the protection from unreasonable incursions into our liberty interests. We are taught that the *Charter* is a promise to all citizens, that it is a governmental signature on a moral and social contract of governance with citizenry.

More recently though comparative constitutional scholars have begun positing that even written promises of constitutional documents may be labile. Perhaps the guarantees of our Constitution are veiled promises that have a certain amount of "give." Some have referred to this idea as "thin constitutionalism"—a Constitution is made up of fundamental precepts such as equal citizenship, the content of which is admittedly contested (Tushnet, 1999, at 11–14; Cohn & Kremnitzer, 2005, p. 352). For instance, the section 8 right to be free from unreasonable search and seizure contains within itself a core constitutional value—the idea that a zone of privacy exists for Canadian citizens (Jochelson, 2009, pp. 187–188). Thin constitutionalism suggests that while the promise of the privacy guarantee persists, its operational construction on the ground may change from era to era and in different social contexts.

The contextualism of the reasonable expectation of privacy threshold question allows for this pliability by being able to absorb technological innovations of policing. The Court has relatively recently indicated that courts must act expediently to allow the police the latitude they require to act efficiently: "[A]s criminals become more sophisticated and devise new ways to cover their tracks, the police constantly upgrade their own techniques and equipment . . . it is not necessary for the police to keep returning to Parliament for authority to make use of tools deployed in full public view like sniffer dogs" (*Kang-Brown,* 2008, at para. 54). While originally the Court spoke of striking a balance between individual liberty and collective welfare (*Hunter,* 1984, para. 43), the Court's vision since *Tessling* (and the interrogation of FLIR technology) suggests a Court that is mediating toward a crime control interest: "[S]ocial and economic life creates competing demands. The community wants privacy but it also insists on protection. Safety, security and the suppression of crime are legitimate countervailing concerns" (*Tessling,* 2004, para. 12; Jochelson, 2009, pp. 186, 187).

In *Patrick*, the majority also seemed acutely concerned about the efficacy of law enforcement policy—"the police practice of looking through garbage has in the past been an important source of probative evidence for the courts in the search for truth" (*Patrick,* 2009, para. 21). Here, the Court clearly aligns itself with concerns for the investigatory tactics of police. This Court is interested in law enforcement efficiency (Jochelson, 2009, pp. 186, 187).

The reasonable expectation of privacy analysis acts as a threshold for a citizen to access the thin value of privacy. Without access to the value, s.8 can provide the citizen with no protection. I have argued that the threshold question has shifted in content since *Tessling*. Undoubtedly, the Court has iterated an approach that is contextual in nature, providing greater emphasis on objective determination of privacy. The Court has given voice to the doctrine of abandonment in a way that is more likely to disadvantage certain citizens in the context of police investigations—urban residents, those who live in impoverished neighbourhoods and those who are homeless. Last, the Court has created a test which allows a greater voice for law enforcement efficacy in the determination of whether a privacy right can be objectively held by an accused. We can debate whether these shifts are useful for a post-9/11 society. We could vigorously defend either position as saleable given our political predilections. However, we simply cannot deny that the ground has shifted (Jochelson, 2009, p. 188).

The promise of privacy in the *Charter* through the guarantee to be free from unreasonable search and seizure continues to be in flux. Its content continues to be a moving target that is given skeletal outline by a Supreme Court "test" that relies increasingly on objective assessments—assessments that can be informed more and more by law enforcement agendas, especially when the Court itself is sensitive to the evolving technologies of law enforcement. Admittedly, the flexibility of the test also means that a differently constituted Court in a differently constituted era might reach different conclusions on the content of our privacy rights. That is the privilege of technologies such as the reasonable expectation of privacy test—its elastic contextualism provides infinite analyses by which a Court could empower police to discipline us. In this way, the privacy guarantee is no different than any other governmental guarantee in late modernity, and the sweeping reach of the Court is no more insidious than the reach of the auditor or technologies of self-governance—with the proviso that tamer privacy protections increase one's probability for the deprivation of physical liberty through incarceration. Perhaps then, keeping our eye upon what the Supreme Court places in the trash might be prudent after all.

Conclusion

In this chapter, we have explored the threshold issue in achieving access to the section 8 guarantee to be free from unreasonable search and seizure under the *Charter*. Search and seizure law remains a complicated area. Yet before an accused can claim section 8 protection, he or she must first have a reasonable expectation of privacy in something. We have seen how complicated this calculus has become even in the context of something as simple as trash. If we increasingly disambiguate privacy from property to the point where any object can be re-characterized as a type of information, do we compromise liberty? Is territorial or proprietary liberty a bright line worth defending in late-modern Canada? Should we care that trash (through the doctrine of abandonment) might functionally be communal property that is accessible to anyone, and does this shift further marginalize those who have less power, capital or access to justice? That is the neoliberal conundrum—the move toward rationality tempered by risk avoidance further disempowers the disempowered, while we are told that the technologies that govern us (e.g., the right to privacy) are really liberatory. Regardless of whether you think these are interesting questions or whether you believe that the *Charter* is a gold standard of liberty, I urge you to at least consider that critical interrogation of our fundamental values remains important even as we have passed the silver anniversary of the *Charter*. Despite the technological innovations of police surveillance, the analytical treasures of simple trash are still profoundly interesting.

References

Adams, C., & Piñero, V. B. (2008). Addendum: A brief note on privacy from a technological perspective. *Canadian Journal of Criminology and Criminal Justice, 50*(3), 389–398.

Bailey, J. (2008). Framed by section 8: Constitutional protection of privacy in Canada. *Canadian Journal of Criminology and Criminal Justice, 50*(3), 279–306.

Dawe, J. (1993). Standing to challenge searches and seizures under the Charter: The lessons of the American experience and their application to Canadian law. *University of Toronto Faculty Law Review, 52*, 39.

Denning, B. P. (2008). In defense of a thin Second Amendment: Culture, the Constitution, and the gun control debate. *Albany Government Law Review, 1*, 102.

Foucault, M. (1980). Two lectures. In *Power/Knowledge: Selected interviews and other writings, 1972–77* (Colin Gordon et al., Trans. and Colin Gordon, Ed.). New York: Pantheon.

Genest, A. (2007). Privacy as construed during the *Tessling* era: Revisiting the "totality of circumstances test," standing and third party rights. *Revue juridique Thémis, 41*, 337–397.

Jochelson, R. (2008). Crossing the Rubicon: Of sniffer dogs, justifications, and preemptive deference. *Review of Constitutional Studies, 13*(2), 209–240.

Jochelson, R. (2009). Trashcans and constitutional custodians: The liminal spaces of privacy in the wake of *Patrick*. *Saskatchewan Law Review, 72*, 165–199.

Kerr, I., Binnie, M., & Aok, C. (2008). Tessling on my brain: The future of lie detection and brain privacy in the criminal justice system. *Canadian Journal of Criminology and Criminal Justice, 50*(3), 367–387.

Litowitz, D. E. (1997). *Postmodern philosophy and the law*. Lawrence, KS: University Press of Kansas.

MacKinnon, W. (2007). Tessling, Brown and A.M.: Towards a principled approach to section 8. *Alberta Law Review, 45*, 79–116.

Marin, J. R. (2005). *R. v. Mann:* Further down the slippery slope. *Alberta Law Review, 42*, 1123.

Pomerance, R. M. (2005). Shedding light on the nature of heat: Defining privacy in the wake of *R. v. Tessling. Criminal Reports, 23*, 229.

Schwartz, D. (1998). Front and rear door exceptions to the right to be secure from unreasonable search and seizure. *Criminal Reports, 10*, 100.

Stribopoulos, J. (2005). In search of dialogue: The Supreme Court, police powers and the *Charter*. *Queen's Law Journal, 31*, 1–74.

Stribopoulos, J. (1999). Reasonable expectation of privacy and "Open Fields": Taking the "American Risk" analysis head on. *Criminal Reports, 25*, 351–361.

Steeves V., & Piñero, V. B. (2008). Privacy and police powers: Situating the reasonable expectation of privacy test. *Canadian Journal of Criminology and Criminal Justice, 50*(3), 263–269.

Stuart, D. (1998). Eight plus twenty-four two equals zero. *Criminal Reports 13*, 50.

Stuart, D. (1999). The unfortunate dilution of section 8 protection: Some teeth remain. *Queen's Law Journal, 25*, 65–94.

Tushnet, M. (1999). *Taking the Constitution away from the courts*. Princeton, NJ: Princeton University Press.

Valverde, M., Levi, R., Shearing, C., Condon, M., & O'Malley, P. (1999). *Democracy in governance: A socio-legal framework*. Ottawa: Law Commission of Canada.

Cases

Dedman v. The Queen, [1985] 2 S.C.R. 2.

Hunter v. Southam [1984] 2 S.C.R. 145.

R. v. A.M., 2008 SCC 19.

R. v. Clayton, 2007 SCC 32.

R. v. Colarusso, [1994] 1 S.C.R. 20.

R. v. Godoy, [1999] 1 S.C.R. 311.

R. v. Hufsky, [1988] 1 S.C.R. 621.

R. v. Kang-Brown [2008] SCC 18.

R. v. Ladouceur, [1990] 1 S.C.R. 1257.

R. v. M. (M.R.) [1998] 3 S.C.R. 393.

R. v. Mann, [2004] SCC 52, [2004] 3 S.C.R. 59.

R. v. Monney [1999] 1 S.C.R. 652.

R. v. Mellenthin, [1992] 3 S.C.R. 615.

R. v. Patrick [2009] SCC 17.

R. v. Patrick, [2005] ABPC 242, 388 A.R. 203.

R. v. Patrick, [2007] ABCA 308, 417 A.R. 276.

R. v. Plant, [1993] 3 S.C.R. 281.

R. v. Tessling [2004] SCC 67.

R. v. Wong, [1990] 3 S.C.R. 36.

Statutes

Canadian Charter of Rights and Freedoms, Part I of the *Constitution Act, 1982*, being Schedule B to the *Canada Act 1982* (U.K.), 1982, c. 11.

Index

A

Abbate, G., 183
Abell, J., 4–6
Abelson, E. S., 129
Aboriginal people
  Canada
    British and French colony, 170
    colonial legacy, 166
    conversion to Christianity, 167
    criminal justice systems, 166
    culture of deprivation, 169
    governments treatment of, 166
    overrepresentation, Canada's criminal justice
      system, 166–167
  contemporary periods, overincarceration, 161
  overincarceration, 163
Academic criminology
  in Canada, 8
  crime control policy, 8
  in Italy, 7
Adler, F., 126
Administrative criminology, 7
Affirmative defences
  necessity and duress
    actus reus and *mens rea*, 27
  self-defence
    negligence cases, 26
    R. v. Lavallee, 26–27
    R. v. McConnell, 27
    Section 34 of *Criminal Code,* 25
Agonzio, B., 164
Alain, M., 211
Alcoholics Anonymous programs, 194
Allison, D. B., 228
American prison system, 164–165
American sociological positivism
  in 1895–1920, 100
  mid-century
    decriminalization, 108
    deviance amplification, 108
    labelling acts and deviant, 107
    social reaction, 107
    victimless crimes, 108
Anderson, B., 52
Anglo-American jurisdictions, 58
Anonymization, 183
Anti-Chinese laws, 6
Appleby, T., 225
Appleton, C., 59, 73

Arar commission, Canada, 216
Arneil, B., 168
Australia's Children's Protection
    Act of 1872, 61
Ayling, J., 212–213
Ayres, I., 215

B

Backhouse, C., 6, 167
Bala, N., 58–60, 62–68, 70–73
Balfour, G., 140
"Band-Aid" approaches, 194
Baranek, P., 210
Barnhorst, R., 67, 69–70, 73
Battered woman syndrome (BWS)
  legal excuse, 136
  woman's self-defence, 135
Bayley, D., 208–209
Bazemore, G., 59, 72–73
Beccaria, C., 81
Benton, T., 149
Bernard, T., 8
Best, J., 49–50, 108
Bhaskar, R., 150
Bittle, S., 5
Blackburn, S., 208
Blaikie, N., 149, 156
Blair, I., 213
Blue drain phenomenon, 215
Bonnycastle, K., 135
Bosk, C. L., 49
Bourdieu, P., 214
Bowker, G. C., 48, 52
Braithwaite, J., 207
Brenda Waudby case, 225
Britain, New left criminology in
  correctionalism, 111
  labelling framework, 110–111
  left realism, defined, 111
  Marxist-based analysis, 110
  social construction of social problems, 111
Brown, M., 169, 178
Brzozowski, J-A., 71
Bullen, J., 58, 61, 63
Burbidge, S., 216
Burnett, J., 208
Burnett, R., 59, 73
Burris, S., 211
Butts, J. A., 58–59, 63, 69

Buzawa, E., 193
BWS. *See* Battered woman syndrome (BWS)

C
Calverley, D., 66, 71
Camhi, L., 129
Campbell, K., 60, 63, 66, 68–69, 73
Canada
 criminal justice system
  Aboriginal peoples, 166
 criminal law, 17
 criminal, statistics and governance, 33
  assorted informational traces, 35
  children and youth, survey of, 34
  financial situation, 34
  historical emergence, 34
  market-based statistical scrutiny, 36
  personal experience, 34
  politicians and advertisers, 35
  public opinion, 35
  "rate of mental illness", 35
  statistics deal, 34
  surveillance society, 34
 provincial women's prisons, 181
 youth, criminal justice system
  1908 Juvenile Delinquents Act, 57
  1984 Young Offenders Act, 57
Canadian Advisory Council on Status of Women
  (CACSW), 195
Canadian Centre for Justice Statistics (CCJS), 36
Canadian Charter of Rights and Freedoms, 64
The Canadian Charter of Rights and Freedoms, 27
 and police, 28
 and prosecution of criminal cases, 29
  Criminal Code, 30
  R. v. Butler, 30
  RIDE programs, 29
  Section 9, 29
Carriere, K., 181–182
Carrigan, D. O., 58, 60–61, 63, 66
Cavender, G., 58, 64
Cayley, D., 7
CCJS. *See* Canadian Centre for Justice Statistics
  (CCJS)
CCTV camera, 177
"Certificate of Death", 223
Cesaroni, C., 66, 71
Chakrabarty, D., 166
Chambliss, W., 109
Chan, J., 210
Charter-era, 234
The Charter of Rights and Freedoms,
  25, 27
 Section 1, 28
Chen, X., 227
Chicago school, sociological criminology

concentric ring model, 101
 racial group conflicts, 101
 social disorganization, 101
Children's Aid Societies (CAS), 61
Christian moralism and scientific theories, 81
Chunn, D. E., 58, 62–63, 67
Civil wrongs, 16
Clapaud, A., 213
Cohen, S., 111
Colonialism, 159
Comack, E., 110, 122, 133, 136, 140–141
Comaroff, J., 170
Common law, 17
Condon, M., 176
Constitution Act of 1982, 18
Controlled Drugs and Substances Act, 17–18
Cooke, D., 71–72
Cope, S., 207
Cornes, R., 216
Coroners Act, 227
Correctionalism, 7
Correctional Service Canada (CSC), 141, 166
Court of Appeal of Alberta, 236
Cowie, J., 125–126, 132
Craib, I., 149, 153–154
Crawford, A., 58–60, 73, 178, 208, 213–214, 216
Creating Choices report, 180
Crenshaw, K., 200
Crime
 behaviours and *Criminal Code*
  prohibited and sanctioned, 17
 concept of, 4
 dark figure, 41
 defined, 4
 definitions from
  Criminal Code in 1892, 5
  English Draft Code of 1879, 5
  Indian Act in 1884, 5
 discourse, 10
  legal responses, 11
  moral regulation, 11
  power/knowledge, 11
  sexuality and, 11
  surveillance in penal governance, 10
 dramas on, 8
 drunk driving, 4
 funnel, 41
 historical/political context, 5
 level of harm, 4
 norm violations, 4
 offences, 16
  actus reus and *mens rea,* 19
  defined, 17
  physical act, 19
  R. v. Latimer, 20
  unintentional harms, 20

and punishment, 5
representations of, 8–9
responsibility, 18
psychology and psychiatry, 19
sexual practices, 5
social pressures, 4
television dramas, 10
types, 8
and unwanted behaviour, 4
Crime and deviance studying
cautions about crime statistics
cumulative effect, 39
death determinations cause, 40–41
gang incident, 39–40
limitations, 38
medical examiners, 40
reporting crime, 39
social reality and documentary reality, 39
"street-level enumerators", 39
victimization, 38
official crime data, 36–38
Crime of Week
advertisements, 181
aim, 181
clearance rate, 182
corporate crime, 182
discourse, 182
private insurance industry, 183
Crime scene investigation (CSI), 223
Crime stoppers (CS)
anonymity
anonymization, 183
risk management, 183–184
tipsters' fear, 183
Canadian, 181
launche, 181
moral categorization and tipsters
"good citizen", 184–185
localization, advanced liberalism, 185
"narc", "rat" and "snitch" identities, 184
partnerships, 185
promotions and partnerships
Crime of Week advertisements, 181–182
crime types, 182
private insurance industry, 183
sponsors, 182
rewards, risk and tipsters
monetary, 184
"risk to caller" and "repeat caller", 184
Criminal Code
amendment, 22
"hybrid" offences, 18
and sexual assault, 22
Criminal law, 4
nature of, 11
and punishment frameworks, 5

Criminal Law Amendment Act, 1968–69, 4
Criminology
branches of
administrative, 7
scientific, 7
crimes and criminal justice responses, 146
criminal law categories, 145
defined, 7
induction, deduction and retroduction
classical sociological theory, 156–157
definition, 154
descriptive theories, 153
justification logics, 155
levels of crime, 157
positivism and conventionalism, 156
positivist criminologist, 154
practice of social theory, 153–154
rational choice theory, 155
relative poverty of community, 155
retroductive inference, 155–156
systematic conceptualizing, 154
metatheory
crime and criminal justice, 146–147
criminal justice categorizations and
responses, 151
in criminology and sociology, 147–148
epistemological and ontological positions, 148
Gramsci's entreaty, 153
identify specific conditions, 146
interrelated elements, 147
large-scale structural attributes, 151
metatheoretical assumptions, 147
nature of social reality, 148
object of investigation, 148
positivist and conventionalist, 149–150
realism's ontologically, 151
social reality, 152
technical philosophical language, 150
positivist and conventionalist metatheory
presence and absence of factors, 145–146
sexual activities, 146
social ordering, 145
Crown attorneys, 18
Cruikshank, B., 178–179
Cullen, F. T., 58, 180
Culpability, negligence and standard, 20–22
Cunningham, W., 207
Currie, D., 196
Curtis, B., 154, 185
Customs and Excise Act, 18

D
Danermark, B., 146
Dauvergne, M., 66, 71, 73
Davis, A., 121, 164
Dawe, J., 234

Dean, M., 173–174, 176–177
Death, forensic science and wrongful convictions
　autopsy
　　asphyxia infants, 227
　　babies, sudden unexplained death, 226–227
　　beyond, 227
　　extramedical and circumstantial evidence, 226
　Coroners, 227
　CSI, 223
　and medical expertise, England
　　Canadian cases, 228
　　cot death, 228
　　Munchausen phenomenon, SIDS,
　　　228–229
　　"Munchausen syndrome by proxy", 228
　Ontario Centre for Forensic Science, 227
　parental brutality and medico-legal discourse, 228
　police attention, baby parents and caregivers, 228
　and prosecution, babies case
　　Brenda Waudby, murder, 225
　　faulty conclusions, 225–226
　　Lianne Thibault, murder, 225
　　Louise Reynolds, murder, 224–225
　　Ontario Paediatric Forensic Pathology,
　　　Smith, 226
　　"opinion evidence", 226
　　rape and murder, William Mullins-Johnson, 224
　"science of the criminal", 223–224
Decorte, T., 216
Deflem, M., 211
Delanty, G., 149
Delegation, governing security
　in Australian states and France, 213
　in Japan, 213
　revenues, 212
　in United States and Canada, 212–213
Demonological approach, crime as sin
　antisocial personality disorder, 81
　spiritualism characteristics during Middle
　　Ages, 80
　transgression, 80
Denov, M. S., 58–60, 66, 68
Des Rosiers, N., 5
De Waard, J., 207
Discipline and Punish, 10, 174
Doob, A. N., 59, 66, 68, 70–71, 73, 127, 167
Downes, D., 104, 121, 123, 126–127, 131
Doyle, A., 183, 210
Driving, fatal injury associated with, 5
Drug trade and street prostitution, 4
DThomas, W. I., 121–123, 126
Dumm, T., 165–166
Dupont, B., 205–217
Dupont, D., 12
Duress defence, 27
Durkheim, É., 99, 102, 156–157

E
Economic fraud, 9
Eisler, L., 71
Emsley, C., 207
Engels, F., 96
England's Protection Act of 1889, 61
Erickson, B., 216
Ericson, R. V., 34, 39, 182–183, 210–211, 214
Erikson, K., 8
Espeland, W., 215
Estrada, F., 59
Eugenics, defined, 86

F
Farrington, D. P., 59, 72
Federal system of government
　in Canada
　　police force, 18
　　public safety and, 18
Feeley, M., 160
Feminist activism and violence against women
　mandatory charging and prosecution
　　jurisdictions, 197
　　LCCFV, 196
　　police mandates, 197
　　RCMP, 196
　　Victims' Bill of Rights, 197
　　victims of abuse, 198
　　zero tolerance approaches, 197–199
　societal and criminal justice responses
　　corporal punishment of women, husbands, 193
　　domestic aggression, televisions comedies, 193
　　domestic violence, 192
　　male, alcohol abuse, 192–193
　　National Commission on Causes and Prevention
　　　of Violence survey, 193
　　police culture, 193
　　private family affair, 193
　state and praxis
　　consciousness-raising and public education, 194
　　police and courts, allies, 195
　theorizations, domestic violence
　　alcohol abuse prevention programs, 194
　　male, 194
　　mandatory charging and prosecution, 195
Feminist contributions, criminology
　criminal law and justice policy, 119
　deviance
　　biological conditions, 128
　　infanticide, 129
　　kleptomania diagnosis, 129
　　medicalization, 127
　　psychiatric and psychological ideas, 127
　　sadism, masochism and lesbianism, 128
　　sexual independence, 128
　　socioeconomic responsibility, 130

emancipation hypothesis, 127–128
feminine sexuality, 129
liberal democratic ideals, 119
passive female criminal, 121–122
patriarchy, 130
punishment practices, treatment
   Aboriginal women, 141
   physical and sexual abuse, 140–141
   prison population and rehabilitation, 140
second-and third-wave, 119
sexism
   within criminological theory, 119–120
   in early theories, 120–123
   in post-World War II theories, 123–127
sexist assumptions, 118–119
women in prison
   inhumane and unconstitutional treatment, 141
   reform and guiding principles, 142
   solitary confinement wing, 141
   women-centred programs, 142
women offenders, 118
women's sexuality
   contraception and abortion, 137
   obscenity, harms-based interpretation, 138–140
   pornography's challenge, 138
women victims, male violence
   battered woman syndrome, 135–136
   rape, 131–132
   spousal assault, 132–135
Ferrero, G., 121–123, 125, 128
Fillieule, O., 212
Financial Transactions and Reports Analysis Centre
   of Canada (FINTRAC), 212
Finlay, J., 71–72
Finnane, M., 207
Fleming, J., 206
Forcese, D., 210
Foucauldian social theory, 19
Foucault effect, 173
Foucault, M., 10–12, 19, 24, 82–83, 88, 94, 112, 164,
   173–174, 176–178, 186
Fowler, D., 227
Francis, D., 52, 169
Fraser, N., 186
Frauley, J., 145–157
French sociological positivism
   anomie and normlessness, 98
   causes of crime, 112
   collective conscience, 98
   correctionalism, 112
   forms of punishment, 112–13
   function
      adaptation (innovation), 99
      boundary-setting, 99
      group solidarity, 99
      tension-reduction, 99
   genealogy, 112
   mechanical solidarity, 98
   neo-Marxist theories, 113
   restitutive punishments, 98
   scientific discourses, 112
   social solidarity, 97–98
   sociological criminology, 97
   systems of regulation, 112
Freud, S., 121

G
Gabor, T., 46
Gaebler, T., 206–207
Gaetz, S., 67, 71
Gall, F. J., 83
Gambetta, D., 209
Gandy, O., 35
Gannon, M., 37, 43, 71
Ganon, M., 44
Gans, J., 213
Garland, D., 7–8, 10–12, 58–59, 63, 68, 72, 120,
   160–162, 175, 178, 185, 223
Gavigan, S. A. M., 67
General Social Survey (GSS), 43
Genest, A., 234
German sociological positivism
   capitalism, 96
   communist system, 96
   criminal justice system, 97
   Feudalism to capitalism, 95
   ideology by Marx, 97
   modes of production, 96
   revolutionary transformation, 96
   social relations, 96
Giever, D. M., 59
Gilbert, K. E., 180
Gilbert, N., 50
Giles, C., 58–59, 66–68
Gilling, D., 59, 69, 72
Gill, M., 210
Goldberg, D. T., 52, 161–162, 164, 168
Goudge Inquiry, 225
Governance, defined, 174
Governing security
   actors and levels
      authorization function, 208
      illegal, 209
      instrumental function, 208
      interinstitutional governance, 210–211
      international/transnational security
         governance, 211
      matrix, 208–209
      media, 210
      microgovernance, 210
      participation, governance processes, 210
      police unions, 210

Governing security (*continued*)
  policing activities, 209
  "security governance", 209
  Sicilian and Russian mafias, 209
 citizens, 205
 definition, 206
 effectiveness and accountability
  Arar commission, Canada, 216
  "blue drain" phenomenon, 215–216
  club goods, 216
  crime statistics, fluctuation, 215
  district policing partnership, 216
  Patten Commission, Northern Ireland, 216
  pluralization, 215
  redeployment, sources and function, 216–217
 exchanges, globalization, 205
 "governance of security" definition, 205
 private, 205
 public police, 205
 relational typology
  actors, 214–215
  gifts, police organizations, 214
  interaction categories, 212
  private security companies, 211–212
  responsibility delegation, 212–213
  sale, 213–214
  swaps, 214
  third-party policing, 212
  urban, 215
 state, market and networks
  features, 208
  hybridization process, 208
  Keynesian welfare state model, 207
  Osborne and Gaebler's nautical metaphor, 207
  private security, 207
  "unholy Trinity", 206
Governmental criminology, 7
Governmentality
 concepts
  abstract things, 177
  programs, 176
  rationalities, 176
  technologies, 176
 criticisms
  discourse and discursive realm, 185
  governmentality-informed criminology and
   scholarship, 186
  programs, 185–186
  totalizing claims, 186
 CS
  anonymity, 183–184
  Canadian, 181
  moral categorization and tipsters, 184–185
  promotions and partnerships, 181–183
  rewards, risk and tipsters, 184
 description, 173

 features and concepts
  criminal behaviour, crime rates and, 174
  criminological knowledge, 175
  language, 175
  real/reality, 174–175
  theories, 175–176
 governance, defined, 174
 liberalism, advanced
  expertise, population, 178
  freedom, 177
  localization and responsibilization, 178
  pastoralism, 178–180
  rule, 178
  social, 177
 "On Governmentality"
  population and mundane governance, 174
  rules, 16th and 17th centuries, 173–174
  sovereignty/sovereign power, 174
 prison and empowerment
  Canadian provincial women's prisons, 181
  community, 180
  Creating Choices report, 180
  enhanced security cells, 180–181
  individual freedom, liberalism, 180
  prison for women (P4W), 179
  responsibilization strategy, 180
  strategies, 179
  TFFSW, 179
"Governmentality" concept, 11–12
Grabe, M. E., 125
Grabosky, P., 209, 212–214
Groneman, C., 128
GSS. *See* General Social Survey (GSS)

H
Hacking, I., 52, 86
Haggerty, K., 211, 214
Haggerty, K. D., 33–53
Hanna, C., 198
Hannah-Moffat, K., 58–59, 72, 141–142,
  179–181, 186
Harris, P., 67–69, 71–73
Hartnagel, T. F., 58–60, 63, 66–69
Hartnett, S., 210
Havemann, P., 58, 63, 71
Heathenism, 5
Hedonism
  academic theories, 81
  British utilitarianism, 81
  Enlightenment positivism, 81
  graduated system of punishment, 82
  modern criminal justice systems, 82
  pleasure–pain principle, 82
Highway Traffic Act, 16
Hilgartner, S., 49
Hillian, D., 59, 63, 66–67, 69, 72

Hilton, N. Z., 193, 196
Hogeveen, B. R., 58–59, 63, 66–69, 72
Hood, R., 162
Huey, L., 214
Hughes, G., 69, 72
Hunt, A., 84, 86, 88, 177
Hurst, L., 71

I
Identity and statistics
    relationship between, 50
        identity, 52–53
        norms, 51–52
Immigrant and refugee women, domestic
            violence policy
    feminist activism and violence against
        mandatory charging and prosecution policies,
            196–198
        societal and criminal justice responses, 192–193
        state and praxis, 194–195
        theorizations, 194
    Hadley inquests, 191
    immigration status
        mandatory arrest, 199
        residence, 199
    isolation
        community networks, 200
        mandatory arrest, 200
    linguistic and financial dependence
        employment difficulties, 201
        mandatory charging, 200–201
    mandatory charging and prosecution,
        191–192, 201
    mandatory criminal justice, 202
    May–Iles inquest, 191
    police, distrust and fear
        mandatory charging, 199
        racism and xenophobia, 199–200
    zero tolerance approaches, 192, 202
Indian Act of Canada
    Aboriginal women and men, 6
Integrated National Security Enforcement
        Teams, 210
Interinstitutional governance
    air transport, 211
    insurance companies, 211
    intelligence agencies, 211
    small-to medium-sized police organizations,
        210–211
International/transnational security governance
    institutional actors, 211

J
Jackson, M., 58–59, 66–68
Jaffe, P. G., 63, 196
Jenkins, R., 52

Jobard, F., 212
Jochelson, R., 232–239
Johnson, K., 133, 135
Johnson, S., 71
Johnston, L., 210, 216
Joint Terrorism Task Forces, 210
Jurik, N. C., 59, 72
Juristat, 36
Justice system
    Crown attorneys, 18
    Crown offices, 18
Juvenile Delinquents Act
    in 1907
        community-based supervision, 63
        Criminal Code, 62
        parental abuse and neglect act, 62
        trials, 62
    Canadian child savers
        Apprehended children, 61
        Australia's Children's Protection
            Act of 1872, 61
        child protection agencies, 61
        Children's Aid Societies (CAS),
            61–62
        England's Protection Act of 1889, 61
        George Brown, *Toronto Globe* reporter, 60
        Juvenile Delinquents Act in 1907,
            61–62
        legislative actions, 60–61
        Ontario passed 888 Act, 61
        Superintendent of Neglected and Dependent
            Children, 61
        Toronto Children's Aid Society, 61
        Young Offenders Act in 1984, 63–65
        youth reformatory, 60–61

K
Kalifa, D., 207
Kalnuta-Crumpton, A., 162
Kandrack, M. A., 135
Kappeler, V., 211
Keat, R., 149
Kellough, G., 162
Kempa, M., 216
Kerr, D., 185
Kesby, M., 178
Keynesian welfare state model
    decline of, 207
    implementation, 207
Kinsman, G. W., 140
Kirschner, R. H., 226
Klein, D., 121–123
Knight, G., 58, 67
Kramar, K., 3–12, 117–142, 223–229
Kraska, P., 211
Kuykendall, J., 207

L

Lambros, Z., 227
Landau, T., 198
LaPrairie, C., 167
Lavater, J. K., 83
Laycock, G., 212
Layder, D., 15, 152
Lear, M., 125
Leeder, J., 215
Leishman, F., 207
Lemieux, F., 210
Leonard, L., 59
Levi, R., 176
Levitt, S., 215
Lianne Thibault case, 225
Liberal welfarism, 177
Lichtblau, E., 211
Lichtenstein, A., 165–166
Li, G., 66, 72
Li, L., 227
Lippert, R., 173–187
Lister, S., 208, 213–214
Loader, I., 210, 213
Lojack car-tracking system, 215
Lombroso, C., 7, 84, 121–122
London Coordinating Committee on Family Violence
   (LCCFV), 196
Lopez, J., 153
Louise Reynolds case, 224–225
Lundman, R. J., 65
Lyon, D., 34

M

Mackinnon, W., 235
MacLeod, L., 193–195, 198, 200
MADD. *See* Mothers Against Drunk
   Driving (MADD)
Maguire, M., 36
Makin, K., 224, 226
Mann, R. M., 57–73
Marin, J. R., 234
Market-based statistical scrutiny, 36
Marquis, G., 207
Marsden, R., 156
Marshall, D. T., 168–169
Martel, J., 181
Martin, D. L., 200–202
Marx, K., 96–97
Matthews, R., 59, 69
Maurutto, P., 58–59, 72
Mauss, M., 214
Mawani, R., 5, 159–170
Mawby, R., 210
Mays, G. L., 59
Mazerolle, L., 212
McCarthy, M., 228

McConville, M., 210
McKay, H., 102
McLaughlin, E., 207
McLean-Candis, A., 18/3
Mears, D. P., 58–59, 63, 69
Meehan, A. J., 39
Mehta, U. S., 166, 168
Melchers, R., 71
Melossi, D., 8
Menjívar, C., 200
Mental disorder
   Criminal Code, 23
   criminal responsibility, 23
   defence, 23
   Foucaultian theorists, 24
   law and psychiatry, 24
   physical consequences, 23
Merton, R., 102–104, 107
Messerschmidt, J. W., 102, 106, 108–109
Metatheory
   crime and criminal justice, 146–147
   criminal justice categorizations and
      responses, 151
   in criminology and sociology, 147–148
   epistemological and ontological positions, 148
   Gramsci's entreaty, 153
   identify specific conditions, 146
   interrelated elements, 147
   large-scale structural attributes, 151
   metatheoretical assumptions, 147
   nature of social reality, 148
   object of investigation, 148
   positivist and conventionalist, 149–150
   realism's ontologically, 151
   social reality, 152
   technical philosophical language, 150
Microgovernance
   communities, 210
   Zwelethemba model, 210
Miethe, T. D., 36
Mihorean, K., 44
Miller, J., 162
Miller, P., 175–178
Mill, J. S., 168–169
Moak, S. C., 58–60
Modified objective standard, 26
Moon, M. M., 58–59
Moral regulation, 11
Morn, F., 207, 210
Morris, P., 125
Morrow, M., 195
Morton, J. H., 129
Mosher, C. J., 36, 193, 199–202
Mothers Against Drunk Driving (MADD), 4
Munchausen phenomenon, 228–229
Muncie, J., 58–60, 66, 73

Murji, K., 207
Murphy, C., 207, 210, 213–214

N
Naming and shaming approach, 212
Narcotics possession, 20
National Commission on Causes and Prevention of
      Violence, 193
Naughton, M., 228
Negligence and standard of culpability, 20–22
Neoliberal penalty, 161
Neo-Marxism
   capitalism, 109–110
   crimes of accommodation, 109
   crimes of domination, 109
   criminalization and social control, 109
   ideological nature of law, 110
   instrumental analyses, 110
Newburn, T., 58–60, 63, 65, 69, 73, 81, 208
New left criminology in Britain
   correctionalism, 111
   labelling framework, 110–111
   left realism, defined, 111
   Marxist-based analysis, 110
   social construction of social problems, 111

O
O'Connor, D., 208, 216
O'Hara, J., 225
O'Malley, P., 11, 57–60, 173–174, 176, 178, 184
"On Governmentality", 173
Ontario Paediatric Forensic Pathology, 226
Orcutt, J. D., 50
Orientalism, 159
Osborne and Gaebler's nautical metaphor, 207
Osborne, D., 206–207
Osborne, T., 35

P
Paciocco, D. M., 226
Palmer, D., 178
Park, G., 173–187
Parnaby, P., 67
Pathological approach, criminality
   biological explanations, 80
   bio-psychological theories, 80
      classical liberal discourses, 87–88
      neurochemical determinism, 87
      psychocentrism, 88
      self-defence, 87
   Canadian criminal justice policies, 79
   criminal by nature, 79
   and genetics
      eugenics, 86
      heritability of criminal conduct, 86
      moral insanity, 86
   as hedonism
      academic theories, 81
      British utilitarianism, 81
      Enlightenment positivism, 81
      graduated system of punishment, 82
      modern criminal justice systems, 82
      pleasure–pain principle, 82
   inventing normal
   personal weakness, 86
   positivism
      and criminology, 79
   and psychology
      control theory, 89
      deterministic individualism, 89
      feminists and critical thinkers, 89
      human scientific knowledge, 87
      internal factors, 86–87
   root of criminal activity, 80
   as sickness
      anti-social personality disorder, 84
      atavism, 85
      facial features and character, 83
      natural laws, 83
      phrenology and physiognomy, 84
      physical factors, 85
      positivism, 82–83
      spiritual characterology, 84
      standards of normality, 85
   as sin
      criminal conduct causes, 80–81
      demonological approach, 80
      moral insanity, 81
      statistical data on social characteristics, 85
Pawson, R., 157
Paymar, M., 192, 200
Pearce, F., 12, 156
Penal welfarism, 161
Pence, E., 192, 200
Pérez, E., 213, 216
Pfohl, S. J., 80
Phillips, D. M., 36
Politics and statistics
   battle for public attention, 49
   considerations, 48
   data presentations/manipulations, 49
   dynamics of statistics, 48–49
   elderly people abused, 50
   misrepresentation, 47
   operational definition, 48
   public problem, 49
   public relations dilemma, 48
   statistical agencies, 47–48
   "statistical governance", 48
Pollak, O., 121, 123–124, 132
Pomerance, R. M., 235
"Populist punitiveness", 8

Postcolonialism and criminology
  colonial administrators, 159
  colonial knowledges and Aboriginal crime
    Aboriginal people, 166
    Canada's liberal democracy, 168
    clash of civilizations, 166
    cultural difference and colonial legacy, 167–168
    culture of deprivation, 169
    empire and colonial racism, 168
    illiberality, 169
    imperialism, 168
    indigenous customs and spirituality, 167
    liberalism, 169
    liberty, 168
    religious and healing practices, 166–167
  critique possibilities
    Aboriginal crime, 170
    societies in Africa, 170
  culture of control
    Aboriginal peoples, 161
    African-Americans overincarceration, United
      States, 160–161
    antiracist multiculturalism, 161
    neoliberal penalty, 161
    overimprisonment, racialized minority, 161
    penal modernity, 161
    penal welfarism, 161
    race and colonialism, 161
    race and punishment, post–civil rights
      period, 161
    racialized minorities, United States, Canada,
      South Africa, 160
    slavery and residential segregation, European
      colonialism, 161–162
    Western crime control, 160
  fingerprinting, 159
  objectives, 159
  race and incarceration
    African-Americans, United States, 163–165
    American prison system, 164–165
    American-style ghettos, 165
    arrest, prosecution and, 162
    colonial knowledges, 166
    critical sociology, Marxism, 163
    culture of violence literature, 163
    Enlightenment narratives, 165
    Enlightenment rationality, 165
    European and non-European immigrants, 165
    lynching, African-Americans, 165–166
    Marxist literature, 164
    overincarceration, 162
    penal system, 164
    prison–industrial complex, 164
    racial differences, 162–163
    racial minority, overincarceration, 163
Pratt, J., 58, 69, 72–73

Prison for women (P4W), 179
Prison industrial complex, 7
Procedural law, 17
Procedural matters
  Criminal Code
    criminal responsibility within, 24
  power of Crown, 24
  section 16 defence, 25
  and Supreme Court of Canada, 25
  "type of person", 24

R
Race and crime statistics, 42–43
Radzinowicz, L., 8
Rafter, N., 84, 86
Ransley, J., 212
Raynor, P., 58–59, 63, 65, 72
RCMP. *See* Royal Canadian Mounted Police
    (RCMP)
Reagan regime, 161
Regulatory offences, 16
Reid, S. A., 58–60, 65–66, 73
Reiss, A., 213
Rhodes, R. W. A., 206, 208
Richardson, R., 165
Rigakos, G., 135, 209, 214
Rimke, H., 79–90
Ripple, M. G., 227
Risen, J., 211
Roach, K., 167
Roberg, R., 207
Roberts, J., 42, 59–60, 62, 64–66, 68–71, 73, 228
Rock, P., 105, 121, 123, 126–127, 131
Rose, N., 11, 35, 86, 174–178, 207
Rosen, P., 63, 65–66
Ross, T., 166
Royal Canadian Mounted Police (RCMP), 18, 196
Rubin, J., 167
Ruddell, R., 59
Rush, C., 215
Rusk, J., 224–225

S
Said, E. W., 166, 170
Salcido, O., 200
Sales, governing security
  Canadian police organizations, 213
  commercial exchanges, 213
  risk, public service, 213–214
  United Kingdom, 213
  United States, 213
Sanders, T., 207–208
Sandler, T., 216
Sarbanes-Oxley Act of 2002, 212
Sauvêtre, N., 210
Sayer, A., 150, 154

Schehr, R. C., 58
Schissel, B., 71
Schwartz, D., 234
Sealy, D., 159–170
Section 8 of *Canadian Charter of Rights and
   Freedoms,* 233
Seidman, R. B., 109
Self-defence
   negligence cases, 26
   R. v. Lavallee, 26–27
   R. v. McConnell, 27
   Section 34 of *Criminal Code,* 25
Self-report studies and victimization
   among sociodemographic groups, 44
   household
      break and enter, 43
      motor vehicle/parts theft, 43
      reasons for not reporting, 45
      theft of household property, 43
      vandalism, 43
   official crime statistics, 44
   theft of personal property, 43
   victimization incidents reported, 44
   violent, 43
Sellin, T., 42
Shaffer, M., 135
Shaw, C., 102
Shaw, M., 142
Shearing, C., 176, 185, 208–210, 215
Sheehy, E. A., 4–6
Shephard, M., 224
Shepherd, D., 210
Shin, M. Y., 200
Shirwadkar, S., 200
Simon, J., 175, 178
Simon, R., 126
Singh, R., 191–202
Skogan, W., 210
Slater, E., 125
Smart, C., 121–127, 202
Smialek, J. E., 227
Smith, D., 39
Smith, E., 200–201
Snider, L., 9, 133
Sniffer dog cases, 236
Snipes, J., 8
Social harm, 9
Social liberalism
   description, 177
   objectives of, 177
Social strain and anomie
   class structures in USA, 104
   crime and delinquency, 102
   individualistic explanations, 103
   Mertonian framework, 104
   socially desired goals, 103

Sociological criminology, Chicago school
   concentric ring model, 101
   racial group conflicts, 101
   social disorganization, 101
Sociological theories
   and positivism
      conceptual frameworks, 94
      criminal justice system, 94
      criminological thinking, 95
      individualistic variant, 93
      justice and harmony, 94
      rights and freedoms, 94
      techniques of natural sciences, 93–94
   zone of transition
      consensus model, 101
      working-class and manufacturing district, 101
Sovereign power, 174
Sparks, P., 7–8, 10
Spohn, C. C., 125
Sprott, J. B., 59, 66, 68, 70–71, 73, 127
Starie, P., 207
Star, S. L., 48, 52
Stenning, P., 207, 215–216
Stenson, K., 58–59, 178, 185–186
Stoler, A. L., 162
Strauss, M., 193
Stribopoulos, J., 234
Stuart, D., 234
Stuesser, L., 226
Sundt, J. L., 58
Supreme Court of Canada, trash
   2004 and beyond
      abandonment, 237
      American privacy approach,
         property-based, 235
      Charter, 238–239
      expectation of privacy, 236, 238–239
      forward looking infrared (FLIR) camera
         search, 235–236
      garbage, 237
      non-American approach, 237
      Patrick case, privacy protections, 236, 238
      privacy protections, 236
      R. v. Tessling, 235
      "sniffer dog" cases, 236
      Tessling indicia use, 236
   basics, review
      Charter-era, 234
      R. v. Edwards (1996), privacy,
         234–235
      in *R. v. M.(M. R.)* (1998), 235
      section 8, 234
Swaps, governing security
   characterization, 214
   exchanges, 214
   Toronto and Vancouver police, 214

T

Tanner, J., 58, 60, 62–66, 71, 162

Tant, A. P., 48

Task Force on Federally Sentenced Women
(TFFSW), 141, 179
Creating Choices report, 179–180
responsibilization, 179
women-centred correctional model, 179

Taylor-Butts, A., 71

Taylor, K. A., 86

Taylor, T., 110, 207

TFFSW. *See* Task Force on Federally Sentenced
Women (TFFSW)

Thatcher regime, 161

Thomas, J., 71

Thomas, W. I., 121–123, 126

Tilly, C., 208

Timmermans, S., 40

Titley, B. E., 5

Tonry, M., 162

Toronto Children's Aid Society, 61

Trager, K. D., 125

"Treaty Indians", 6

Trépanier, J., 58, 60–61, 63, 65–66, 68, 70

Trials in criminal matters, 16

Turner, J. B., 50

Turow, J., 35

Turpel M. E., 168

Tushnet, M., 238

U

UCR. *See* Uniform Crime Reports (UCR)

Unholy Trinity, 206

Uniform Crime Reports (UCR), 36

Urry, J., 149

V

Valier, C., 101, 111, 117

Valverde, M., 11, 85, 118, 174–176

Van Laethem, W., 216

Van Outrive, L., 216

Varese, F., 209

Victimization and self-report studies
among sociodemographic groups, 44
cursory examination of data, 46
household
break and enter, 43
motor vehicle/parts theft, 43
reasons for not reporting, 45
theft of household property, 43
vandalism, 43
lifestyle patterns, 46
official crime statistics, 44
risk of, 46
state-sponsored, 46
surveys and, 47

theft of personal property, 43
traumatized, 46
victimization incidents reported, 44
violent, 43

Vold, G., 8

Volkov, V., 209

Volunteer-run shelters, 194

W

Wachholz, S., 199–200

Wacquant, L., 161, 164–165

Wait, P., 211

Waldram, J. B., 166–167, 169

Walker, N., 205, 210

Wallace, L. H., 58–60

Wallace, M., 36

Walton, P., 80, 111

Wanless, M., 198

Wasserman, D., 86

Weir, L., 154, 185

Welfare liberalism, 177

Welsh, B. C., 59, 72

White-collar crime
criminal and anti-criminal patterns, 106
criminal behaviour, 105
social distribution, 106
sociological theory of crime, 104
violation of law, 105

White Women's Labour Law, 6

Wickham, G., 177

Williams, J., 174, 178, 186, 215

Wilson, D., 165

Women's criminality, sexism
criminological theory
criminal justice system, 120
doubly deviant, 120
female offenders, 119–120
medicalization of women's deviance, 120
prejudices and preoccupations, 119
in early theories
emancipation hypothesis, 122–123
passive female criminal, 121–122
post-World War II theories
chivalry hypothesis, 124
contemporary degeneracy theory, 125–126
conventional sexual politics, 124
emancipation hypothesis, 126–127
female crime, 123–124
prostitution, 123
stereotypes of women, 124

Women's sexuality, criminal law regulation
contraception and abortion
hospital-based therapeutic abortion
committee, 137
reproductive freedom, 137
social conditions, 125

obscenity
Canadian *Criminal Code,* 138
Criminal Code, 138–139
free and democratic society, 139
freedom of expression, 138
moral regulation, 140
undue exploitation of sex, 139
pornography's challenge
Charter of Rights and Freedoms, 138
sexualization of violence, 138
types, 139
prostitution, 137
second-wave feminist, 136
Women victims, male violence
battered woman syndrome
abusive relationship, 135–136
feminist criminologists, 136
gender bias in selfdefence, 135
potential limitations, 136
testimony of premenstrual syndrome, 135
rape
mistaken belief, 132
sexual relations, 131–132
twin myths, 131
spousal assault
Aboriginal women, 134
domestic violence, 132–133
feminist criminologists, 133–134
Ratushny's recommendations, 134
self-report victimization surveys, 133
zero tolerance policy, 133
Woodiwiss, A., 156
Wood, J., 210
Wortley, S., 162
Wright, J. P., 58

Y
Young, D., 15–30
Young, J., 80, 111
Young Offenders Act in 1984
alternative measures
Canada gained international notoriety for, 66
community-based programs, 66
innovative restorative justice, 66
Juvenile Delinquents Act-era diversion
programs, 66
provincial-territorial policy, 66
Quebec, 65–66
and children, extension of due process rights, 64
contradictory provisions
Canadian Bill of Rights, 64
Canadian Charter of Rights and Freedoms, 64
custodial and noncustodial dispositions, 64

Declaration of Principle Act, 64–65
radical non-intervention, 65
Young Offenders Act, 65
law and order, 63
managing discontent
Chrétien government's Youth Justice Renewal
Initiative, 67
federal and provincial-territorial
governments, 66
Progressive Conservative government, 67
Quebec politicians and, 66
Young Offenders Act, 67
Youth Criminal Justice Act, 67–70
Progressive Conservative politicians, 63–64
vocal and arguably, 63
Youth Criminal Justice Act, 58, 82
Chrétien government Youth Justice Renewal
Initiative, 67
Liberal government, 67
Mike Harris Ontario government, 68
outcomes, 70–72
philosophy and provisions, 68–70
preventative partnerships, 57
Youth justice in global context
Anglo-American jurisdictions, 58
Children's rights, discourse of, 58
Constitution, 60
international rights instrument, 59
Juvenile Delinquents Act, 60
Canadian child savers, 60–65
phase, 58–59
penal incarceration-sanctions, 58
political agency, 59
prevention programs, 59
punishment and deterrence, downplaying, 58
rediscoveries, 59
restorative/quasi restorative community justice, 59
supervise and rehabilitate, 58
treatment and rehabilitation, 59
Young Offenders Act in 1984
alternative measures, 66
and children, extension of due process rights, 64
contradictory provisions, 64–65
law and order, 63
managing discontent, 67–72
Progressive Conservative politicians,
63–64
vocal and arguably, 63

Z
Zero tolerance approach, 191–192, 202
Zuker, M. A, 58–60, 65–66, 73
Zwelethemba model, 210